THE PLANETS

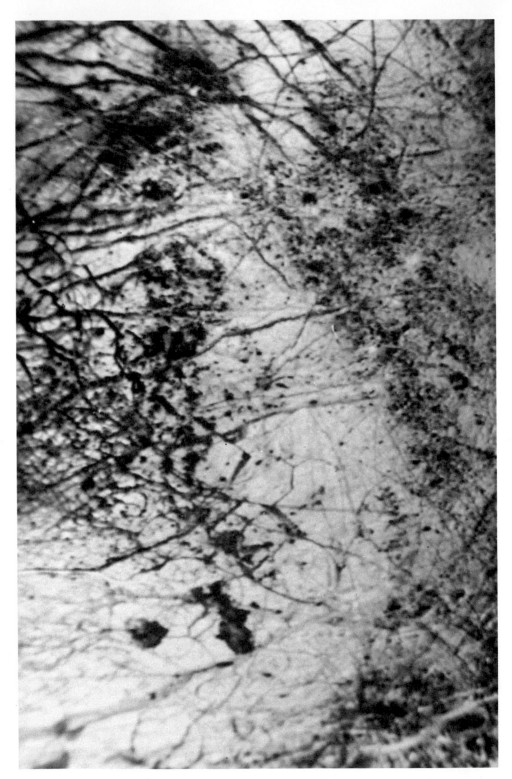

Enhanced Voyager view of the cracks in the icy surface of one of Jupiter's moons, Europa (Computer processed images by A. McEuen and L. Soderblom, U.S.G.S.)

THE PLANETS

Byron Preiss, Editor

Dr. Andrew Fraknoi, Scientific Consultant

BANTAM BOOKS
TORONTO · NEW YORK · LONDON · SYDNEY · AUCKLAND

In memory of my grandparents,
Isadore and Sarah Krasnor.

THE PLANETS

A Bantam Book/December 1985

Special thanks to Lou Aronica,
Senior Editor and Publishing Director
of the Spectra Line,
for his care and support.

Book design by Leslie Miller.

Associate Editor: Ruth Ashby.

Library of Congress Cataloging-in-Publication Data

The Planets.

1. Life on other planets—Fiction.   2. Science fiction, American.
3. Planets—Addresses, essays, lectures.   4. Solar system—Addresses,
essays, lectures.   I. Preiss, Byron.
PS648.L53P57   1985   813′.0876′08   85-47649
ISBN 0-553-05109-1

Published simultaneously in the United States and Canada

PRINTED IN THE UNITED STATES OF AMERICA

WAK   0 9 8 7 6 5 4 3 2 1

CONTENTS

DIVERSITY

Byron Preiss

MINE IS THE LAST generation for which the exploration of the solar system was a dream, not a reality. In the fifties our illusions were many, our reverie of space flight fired by science fiction and the prospect of alien life. It was a time when the gulf between science and science fiction was still great, when America no sooner thought of putting a man on the Moon than a woman in the White House. How far we have come.

I remember the dawn of space flight. In our house, every major launch meant a holiday from school, and to this day I am grateful to NASA for having the wisdom to schedule the majority of the Mercury flights between Monday and Friday from September to June. I watched those early countdowns with my grandfather. He had emigrated to America from Russia before the turn of the century, and he had made a successful career as a builder and architect using nothing more than his pride, heritage and intelligence. I can still recall the fascination with which he watched those early forays out of Earth's atmosphere. The giant booster rockets were some sort of grand affirmation of humanity's will to succeed against all odds, something my grandfather himself had done. We knew only the public personae of the Glenns, the Shepards and the Carpenters in those days, but we recognized them as heroes in the best sense of the word. Their deeds inspired faith in the potential of mankind and directed me and thousands of other kids to the world of the imagination, to the stories of authors such as Ray Bradbury, Arthur C. Clarke, Isaac Asimov and the colorful cinema-on-paper of comic books. Here we found our secret hopes realized: voyages to far-off planets, superpowered humans and super-talented extraterrestrials. Science fiction was not as popular then as it is now, nor was it deemed respectable by mainstream critics. I doubt that my grandfather ever read a single science fiction story, but as one who had been present for the birth and adolescence of the modern age, the invention of automobiles and rockets, the pogroms of Russia and Germany, I don't think he would have been quick to dismiss science fiction's cogent visions of utopia or dystopia. Science fiction was, after all, the literature born of the wild twentieth century, the century of science, the century of technology, the century of progress!

My world changed greatly after my grandfather died. The social and political upheavals of the sixties and the scandal of Watergate in the seventies would have roused strong sentiment in him I am sure, but I think the child in him would have greeted with wonder the continued success of America's program in space as we left our footprint on the lunar surface, gazed through electronic eyes at Mars and flew by satellite past the astonishing worlds of Jupiter and Saturn. How ironic it is that, as we gain a fuller sense of the nearly incomprehensible diversity of the natural world, post-industrial society is mired in the loss of individuality, a diminished sense of culpability, and self-destructive behavior. As science opens new realms, we seem to be endangering our own values and surroundings. In our quest for material wealth, humanity has embarked on a truly tragic assault upon the environment. Few greater examples of this exist than the decimation by man of the world's rain forests. In a drive for more lumber, more cattle and more industrial wealth, millions upon millions of acres of tropical rain forest, which replenish a critical amount of the world's oxygen, are vanishing. Over half the Earth's plant, insect and animal species live in less than two percent of these rain forests' total area. The secrets seeded in the genetic codes of those diverse life forms are just beginning to be fully understood by us. For example, over two-thirds of the plants with known anticancerous properties come from the world's rain forests. Experiments in every field of medicine are dependent on the myriad species of the world for breakthroughs. When diversity is diminished, when extinction occurs, it is forever, and it is diversity which unites the physical world of man, the Earth, the planets and the stars.

At the limits of our current astronomical knowledge we perceive space as a huge black expanse, dimly lit by superclusters of galaxies billions of light years from Earth. Within each supercluster, we can discern diverse clusters of galaxies, some with thousands of members. Responsive to the gravitational pull of one of these clusters, the Virgo Cluster, is an outlying galaxy called the Milky Way. Spanning hundreds of thousands of light years, this flat swirling disk of stars has in its spiral our own Sun, a star orbiting the Milky Way once every 200 million years.

In orbits that stretch up to over 11 billion kilometers from Earth, the outer planetary bodies rotate around our Sun: Jupiter, Saturn, Uranus, Neptune, Pluto and their moons, ranging from the iceball of Europa to the crater-scarred Mimas. In closer proximity to the Sun, we encounter our own planet Earth, orbiting with the inner planets and their moons: Mars, Venus, Mercury, all worlds of different colors, textures and sizes. It is a solar system of stunning extremes, of fiery satellites and frozen terrain, of gas giants and barren moons, of rings and valleys, and in at least one tiny corner, of life.

Distinguished by the gift of life, the planet Earth holds wonders that repeat on an ever-diminishing scale the cosmic splendor beyond it. Imagine a world in which sound is a constantly shifting mosaic of environmental change and communication, and in which the pitches, tones and rhythms vary with the spectrum of life. Imagine a world where color is a factor of survival, where every conceivable niche is occupied by a variety of fascinating forms. Imagine a world where water is abundant, teeming with intelligent life. Imagine life so overwhelming in its diversity that species exist in nearly every habitat and climate. Imagine a world where the most advanced species, man, is so successful that he can reproduce in unchecked numbers and in rich cultural diversity across all real and imaginary borders. In Nigeria alone, population by the year 2035 is estimated to exceed that of the entire continent of Africa today, and in each and every Nigerian there is an entire universe invisible to the naked eye, a body filled with diverse living organisms—blood corpuscles resembling a distant moon; millions of cells, each with a nucleus controlling its functions. Within every person on this planet are 100 times more cells than there are stars in the Milky Way galaxy, and within each cell can be found the ladders of life: DNA molecules, common to all humanity, but in a different combination for each individual.

Millions upon millions of DNA molecules, themselves made up of millions upon millions of carbon and hydrogen atoms, themselves made up of even smaller atomic particles, are all present in billions of human beings all existing on one planet in one solar system in one galaxy in one cluster of galaxies in one group of galaxies in God's miracle of diversity, the universe.

As I sit writing this today, there are probably fewer stars visible in the sky than when my grandfather and I sat outdoors two decades ago. Pollution has taken its toll, as has the ambient light from the city. When viewed from the sky however, the lights of New York most resemble the stars themselves. Yet it is the stars which these city lights deny us. Such is the paradox of progress. In the stunning discoveries we have made about the invisible world of space and the microscopic world inside us all, we are becoming blind to the visible world around us. Balancing the two is a challenge facing mankind. For if we are sending out a signal from our collective subconscious through the starry lights of the city, if we are truly reaching for the stars, then we must protect that aspiration by protecting the diversity of that with which we have been blessed here on Earth.

I would like to think that there will come a time when first contact with another intelligent civilization is made, and that communication will depend on a tiny insect in Amazonia, whose humming sound resembles not so much a housefly as a cosmic chord, common to all life, diverse and wondrous, on another planet, and that the insect will be alive to greet these extraterrestrial visitors in a glorious symphony of verdant tropical rain forest, itself a microcosm within a microcosm, nestled peacefully in a tiny corner of one galaxy that is home to our planet.

Which brings us to the purpose of this book. It was our hope to explore the diversity of the solar system in a way that suggests the possibilities it holds for humanity. To accomplish this task, it seemed important to deal with both the present reality of the planets and their possible futures. To my knowledge, there has never been a meeting ground in print for the scientists and dreamers whose collective work has influenced my generation, and this task presented a compelling reason for such a meeting ground to be established.

Astronomy and science fiction share a love for the unknown and the best

9

talents in both fields have influenced mankind's expectations of the future. In my mind, it is no coincidence that the man who conceived of the communications satellite was also a science fiction author, Arthur C. Clarke. Nor is it surprising to me that the authors of some of the best science fiction being written today are scientists, such as Dr. Gregory Benford. With the age of space colonization ahead of us and the threat of star wars hanging over us, it has become all the more urgent to take an optimistic, exhilirating and panoramic tour of our solar system, not only as it exists now but as it may become, in the hope that lessons learned about Earth's environment will be applied to the planets. Who better to conduct this tour than men and women who have devoted their professional lives to space, real and imagined?

To this end, we have assembled, under the guidance of Andrew Fraknoi, Executive Officer of the Astronomical Society of the Pacific, some of the finest astronomers and scientists in America. Many have been intimately involved in NASA programs past and present, and are considered the leading experts in their fields of study. Enhancing their work are full color photographs from NASA, the Jet Propulsion Laboratory and others, selected (under the influence of Fraknoi and Morrison) for their scientific importance and beauty.

Finding appropriate science fiction authors to write about the futures of specific planets was a rare opportunity. Effort was made to select individuals with different areas of interest, so that the relationships between the planets and such fields as science, politics and the arts could be explored. Each author was asked to speculate about the planets and their moons as accurately as possible, allowing for poetic license on the part of Ray Bradbury, without whose delicate concept of Mars this book and literature in general would be sadly deficient, and Philip José Farmer, whose participation implies that a sense of humor should be part of man's exploration of space. Robert Silverberg was the first to contribute to this book, and as a writer of science fiction and science was asked to do both the speculation and the essay about frigid Pluto.

Science fiction and imaginative literature have had a long relationship with illustration. Modern science fiction has profited from the efforts of some of the finest visionary artists alive, including production designers Robert McCall and Ralph McQuarrie, whose work on *2001* and *Star Wars* respectively have had a profound influence of what we think the future will look like. I am privileged to present the diverse and talented group of artists in this book.

Special mention must be made of the roles of Andrew Fraknoi and Ruth Ashby. Mr. Fraknoi reviewed all the scientific writing to ensure its fidelity to existing research and worked closely with us and the scientists involved. Ms. Ashby, Associate Editor, carefully coordinated over thirty contributors to the book and reviewed drafts of all the manuscripts. Both have been instrumental in shaping the extraordinary material herein into a cohesive book.

There are many explorations to come, but this time you will be the planetary traveler. Welcome to *The Planets!*

THE SOLAR SYSTEM: AN INTRODUCTION

Andrew Fraknoi

In the last few decades, within the time of one generation, we have learned more about the planets than in all the centuries that went before. We have made the first on-site measurements, taken the first close-up photos, sent our first messengers into the vastness of space. It has been an almost unprecedented era of exploration, revealing the planets and satellites in our solar system not just as shimmering disks or pinpoints of light, but as *worlds*—vast domains even more alien and more beautiful than we had imagined. Each world has suddenly become an individual place, with its own history, unique geography, and even local weather conditions.

And what discoveries we have made!

On the Martian surface, there rises a volcano so large that its base would more than cover the entire state of Nebraska.

On Venus, clouds of sulfuric acid droplets obscure the Sun, while temperatures on the surface hover at 450 degrees Celsius, hotter than a self-cleaning oven.

In Jupiter's upper atmosphere, an anticyclone so large that three Earths could fit side by side within it has raged unabated for at least three centuries.

Around Saturn, an enormously complex ring system is stretched so wide it would fill most of the space between Earth and the Moon.

And each of the outer planets turns out to have a family of satellites at least as interesting and varied as the planets themselves.

All in all, there are more than forty individual worlds in our solar system, each of them different, each of them fascinating, and each of them awaiting our further exploration.

Today, when television and jet aircraft have made even the more remote parts of our globe seem familiar, the planets and satellites in the solar system are humankind's newest frontier. Our first tantalizing glimpses of these bodies, through large telescopes and visiting robot spacecraft, challenge our imagination and wanderlust as powerfully as the American West or Earth's poles did in the past.

The solar system is an immense frontier, by any human measure. Formed from the same cloud of gas and dust that spawned our Sun, the planets, moons, and asteroids are mostly concentrated in a huge, flat pancake of space around the Sun. The orbit of the outermost known planet, Pluto, spans eleven billion kilometers of space. If the enormous globe of our Sun were reduced to the size of a basketball, Pluto would be a tiny grain of sand more than a kilometer from the ball!

Although our firm knowledge of the system ends with Pluto, there is some evidence that a distant cloud of icy pieces stretches out perhaps halfway to the next star. It is probably from this remote reservoir that the objects we call comets enter the known solar system and fall toward the Sun, shedding tails of gas and dust along their paths.

While astronomers are still debating the details, a consensus has emerged about the general outlines of the solar system's origins some five billion years ago. Drawing on our observations of how other star systems form today, we surmise that the process began with a large cloud of gas and dust that began to contract. (There is some evidence that the explosion of an older star not too far away may have played a significant role in starting this contraction.)

Since our protoplanetary cloud was spinning, its contraction caused its rotation to quicken, just as a skater can twirl faster if she pulls her arms in more tightly. The faster the cloud spun, the more flattened its outer portions became. Eventually, the huge ball of material at the center contracted to become the Sun, while the material further out became a flat, disk-shaped expanse of chunks of various sizes that coagulated to make the planets and satellites that are the topic of this book.

The details of the formation process are complicated and not completely understood, but we believe the building blocks of the larger bodies were chunks of intermediate size within that disk that we have called *planetesimals*. In a 100-million-year epoch of unimaginable violence, collisions between the planetesimals, which ranged in size from dust particles to mountains, led to the formation of the larger worlds we have today. While weather and water have erased almost all traces of these collisions on Earth, on airless worlds like our Moon, Mercury, and some of the outer satellites, giant impact craters bear

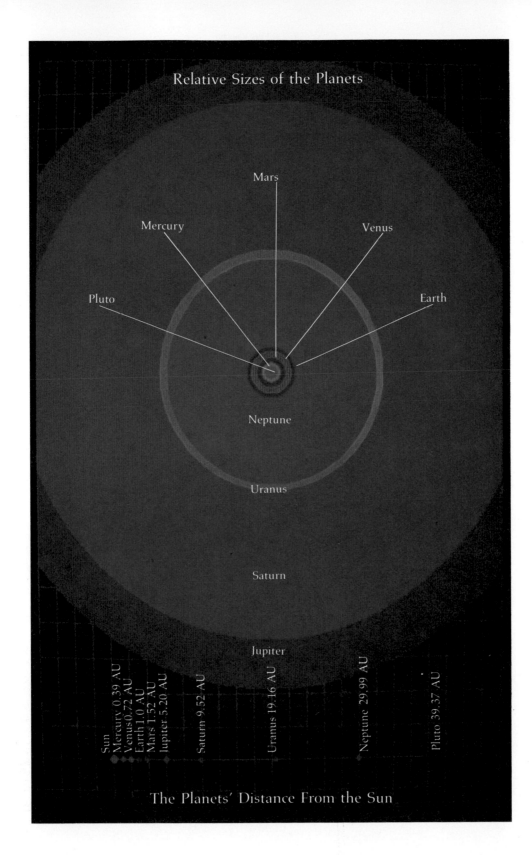

Relative Sizes of the Planets

Mars

Mercury

Venus

Pluto

Earth

Neptune

Uranus

Saturn

Jupiter

Sun
Mercury 0.39 AU
Venus 0.72 AU
Earth 1.0 AU
Mars 1.52 AU
Jupiter 5.20 AU
Saturn 9.52 AU
Uranus 19.16 AU
Neptune 29.99 AU
Pluto 39.37 AU

The Planets' Distance From the Sun

silent witness to the chaotic period during which our solar system gathered itself together.

The comets, too, may have formed in this way in cooler regions of the solar system, but for reasons we have not yet fully understood, they did not become incorporated into the planets and other bodies closer to the Sun. Their antisocial behavior is a great boon for astronomers, however. Since they spend most of their time in the deep-freeze of interstellar space, they have not participated in the many changes that befall the bodies nearer the Sun. They are, therefore, excellent "fossils" that may tell us much about the earliest history of our system.

Astronomers divide the planets into two broad groups—(1) the solid terrestrial planets that resemble our own Earth and (2) the "gas giants," or Jovian-type planets, in the outer solar system. When the planets and the Sun were first forming some 4.5 billion years ago, temperatures near the center of our system were extremely hot. The lighter elements, which evaporated easily, were driven by heat and the intense solar wind of that era to the outer regions of the solar system. Thus the inner planets have a much higher proportion of rocky solid material than do the outer planets, which retain many of the lighter materials that also characterize the Sun and other stars.

However, one thing we have learned from the last few decades of planetary exploration is that simple divisions and pat generalizations about the solar system rarely do justice to its complexity. As on Earth, nature in the solar system has seemed to revel in diversity. No two worlds are exactly alike. In their atmospheres, on their surfaces, in their deep cores, the planets and moons maintain their individuality.

Even among satellites of the same planet, the differences can be striking. Jupiter's moon Io is so richly covered with the residue of its volcanic vents, spewing sulfur compounds in vast geysers, that it resembles nothing so much as rotting pizza. Yet the very next moon outward in the Jupiter system, Europa, has a smooth, icy surface that reminds the casual viewer of cracked eggshells.

Rings have been found surrounding at least three planets—and, again, the ring systems are more different than alike. Jupiter's single ring, Saturn's huge, intricate ring system, and Uranus's narrow hoops each have their own story to tell us about the way rings form and sustain themselves.

In fact, as you will see throughout this book, each planet and satellite has at least a few special characteristics that fascinate and perplex us and a few special sights that will be required viewing for future tourists.

Seen from within, our solar system appears very large in extent and complicated in detail. But seen in the context of our entire galaxy of stars, it is not a particularly significant place. The Sun and its retinue of planets are just one of more than 200 billion star systems composing the great spiral we call the Milky Way. We are located on what appears to be a minor local spur extending from one of the spiral's arms, a spur that is more than halfway out from the galactic center. Recent evidence suggests that the Milky Way galaxy may be significantly larger than we once thought, but even using conservative estimates of the galaxy's size we find that light, traveling at about 960 million kilometers per hour, would take at least 100,000 years to cross the Milky Way. And human ships, unable at present to manage even a tiny fraction of that speed, would take epochs to cross any significant part of that great expanse.

Right now there are four spacecraft—named Pioneer and Voyager—on their ways out of the solar system. Having completed their missions of interplanetary exploration, three of the probes are quietly leaving the realm of the planets under their own momentum. The fourth, Voyager 2, is set to rendezvous with Uranus in 1986 and if all goes well, with Neptune in 1989. Eventually, all four will be coasting through the vastness of interstellar space for millennia—indeed, it will most likely be *millions* of years before they come near another body of significant size. Even if one of the craft were directed at the closest other star— and none is—it would take more than a hundred thousand years to get there, powerful testimony to the gulfs that separate star systems in the galaxy.

These great distances explain why it is so difficult to see planets that may exist outside our solar system. Planets are much dimmer than stars, shining for the most part by reflecting the light of their parent sun. If the most powerful telescope on Earth could be transported to even the nearest star and if astronomers could then look back in the direction of our Sun, they would not be able to see the Earth or the other planets.

What if, despite the great emptiness out there, a Pioneer or Voyager craft does encounter someone or something intelligent one day? America has placed humanity's calling card on each probe: The Pioneers carry a plaque inscribed with a message that pictures our species and tries to describe our location in space and time. The Voyagers have a video record on board, together with its own stylus, featuring the sights and sounds of Earth. They are, in some sense, our "messages in a bottle" to the universe, announcing our arrival on the cosmic scene.

Some scientists have pointed out that the most likely readers of the messages will be future humans, whose faster craft may someday overtake the capsules and bring them back to Earth as museum pieces. Nevertheless, the messages, like the science-fiction stories in this book, turn our imaginations to the future and challenge us to think about what will happen in either event.

Right now, then, ours is the only example we have of a planetary system anywhere in the universe. Many of our theories of how new stars form predict that planetary systems should be relatively common, but finding such systems is far trickier than predicting their existence.

A decade or so ago, there was a flurry of excitement when astronomers thought they had detected planetary "wiggles" in the long-term motions of a few nearby stars. To see what this wiggle might mean, imagine a star moving through space accompanied by a single large planet. We can see the star, but the planet, shining only by reflected starlight, is too faint to be visible to us. When the planet is to the left of the star, its gravity pulls the star ever so slightly to the left. Then, as the years pass, the planet moves to the right side of the star and tugs its parent to that side. If we follow the star's path over the decades, we will see it shift, or wiggle, a bit to the left, a bit to the right, a bit to the left again, and so forth, and this wiggle in its motion reveals the influence of its planetary companion, which would have otherwise remained an undetected phantom to even our most advanced equipment.

Unfortunately, it now appears that the first "wiggle observations," which were extremely difficult to carry out in practice, were flawed and have to be repeated with better equipment. The new work is under way but will take many years to complete. An excellent place from which to carry out such long-term measurements with great accuracy would be the stable platform provided by a large orbiting space station, and astronomers at NASA and the University of Arizona have recently proposed building a telescope to put on the first American space station for just that purpose.

More recently, a new satellite observatory called IRAS—designed to search not for cosmic light but for heat rays—revealed that several nearby stars seem to be surrounded by swarms of solid particles that could range in size from dust grains to mountains and that are spread around their parent stars for a considerable distance. Some astronomers interpret this evidence to mean that we have found an asteroid or comet belt around these stars. (If there are planets in these systems, by the way, the IRAS instruments would not have revealed them.)

Just a few months before this book went to press, two teams of astronomers found the first confirmed example of a so-called brown dwarf, a stellar companion that is thought to be halfway between a planet and a star. More substantial than the planets we know, but still too small for nuclear reactions to have begun within them, brown dwarfs had been predicted by astronomers using some of the same ideas that lead us to believe that planets are common elsewhere. Some astronomers feel that their existence strengthens the case for the existence of smaller, planet-sized chunks of matter in the universe.

Since no one has seen a family of planets other than our own, everything we know about planets and smaller bodies comes from the observations of the system that gave us birth. And while we search eagerly for other examples, you will see throughout this book that we still have plenty to learn and understand about our "home base."

After more than a decade of regular spacecraft voyages to the planets, the pace of planetary exploration has begun to slow in the 1980s. In the U.S., budget problems and other Earthbound concerns have sharply reduced the funding available for planetary missions. In response, NASA convened a special Solar System Exploration Committee, now chaired by Dr. David Morrison, who contributed the Saturn chapter of this book. The committee has been able to make some ingenious proposals for more limited future missions at reduced cost, some of which have now been incorporated into NASA's long-range plans. These include using standardized designs for spacecraft to be used in exploring several different planets. Still, the overall result of our hesitation has been that the US planetary exploration program will be operating at a significantly scaled-back level for at least a decade.

What have we gained from the extraterrestrial voyages of discovery (and the telescopic observations) whose results are described in this book? We have seen our Earth as a unique world, very different from its neighbors. We have explored alien environments so hostile that no Earthlings could survive them unprotected. Some of these other worlds can tell us about dangers that may lie ahead for our own planet, especially if we do not gain better control of our waste products, our population, and our penchant for war.

But most importantly, the missions have begun humankind's long climb out of the cosmic "crib"—and our emergence into the larger universe that lies beyond the Earth. How will we respond to the call of the solar system? How will we comport ourselves as we continue the initial steps of exploration? And how far can we reach with our voyages? These are questions that future generations will probably greet as some of the greatest challenges of their time.

WRITING OF TWO SORTS

Isaac Asimov

WHY WRITE ABOUT SCIENCE? What does it accomplish?

To begin with, people who write about science do what they do because it pleases them. It may give them pleasure to explain what has been learned about the universe. By making the effort to organize the information for the general reader, they may sharpen and clarify their own thinking. And, of course, (let's not forget the mundane) they may make a little money out of it.

In addition to these purely personal reasons for writing about science, there are also what we might call social reasons.

First, through the wise use of scientific knowledge humanity has a chance to solve the otherwise overwhelming problems that face it. How do we increase our supply of materials and energy and prevent waste and pollution? How do we make life more comfortable and secure? How do we ameliorate the ravages of disease and old age? If these problems can't be solved by science, they can't be solved at all. On the other hand, the unwise use of scientific knowledge may destroy us all through nuclear warfare, pollution, desertification, uncontrolled population increase, and so on.

If the world is to learn how to use science wisely and to shun the unwise, as many people as possible must learn about science—not, perhaps, enough to become scientists themselves, but at least enough to have a chance to come to sensible decisions and to exert the force of public opinion on their leaders in the direction of sense.

A fine example of this is the agreement to ban the atmospheric testing of nuclear explosions in 1963. The governments involved were not keen on this, being driven by mutual fear and hatred in the direction of suicide. It was an aroused world opinion that forced sanity upon them very much against their wills.

Second, science has reached the stage where it needs far more investment than the scientists themselves can supply. Even private industry may fall short

where the greatest projects are concerned. No source remains but governments—that is, the public purse. If the public is expected to pay, it would be best if they understood what they were paying for.

Third, for science to advance, there must be a continuing supply of bright young men and women who are willing to devote their lives to scientific advance. The supply can best be increased in both quantity and quality if the general public continues to be well informed as to the nature and content of science.

For all these reasons, the science writer performs a useful, even a vital, function.

But where in all this does the science fiction writer come in? Let us compare the two.

Science writers, if they do it well, both inform and entertain, but the task of informing is primary. They must, under no circumstances, misinform. If they do, their work is worthless and even harmful—all the more worthless and harmful if it is entertaining and attracts readers.

Science fiction writers must also inform and entertain, but here it is entertainment that is primary. If they do not entertain they will not be read—if, in fact, they are published in the first place. Naturally, good science fiction writers try not to misinform, but if, for one reason or another, they are in error, it is not necessarily fatal. Jules Verne could have his heroes reach the Moon by being fired out of a cannon, and H. G. Wells could do it by means of antigravity, but in neither case does the impossibility spoil the story.

What, then, is the importance of science fiction writing that is, to some extent at least, independent of accuracy?

First, it is the very essence of science fiction that the story is set against a social background different from our own, a background that differs (not invariably, but almost always) in two ways: it is set in the future and exhibits a level of science and technology that is to some degree more advanced than our own.

Such stories, accurate in detail or not, probable in forecasting the future or not, serve to accustom their readers to the idea of change—to the *inevitability* of change—as time goes on. Furthermore, readers are taught to expect change primarily through scientific and technologic advance. Think of the changes in human society brought about by the development of agriculture or the invention of printing. In contemporary times, think what has happened through the invention of the automobile, the jet plane, the television set, or the computer.

Change has always been with us, but the *rate* of change is what really counts. That rate has increased steadily in the course of human history, and beginning about 1800, it became rapid enough to make change visible in the course of a single lifetime. (It was soon after 1800 that science fiction began to be written). The rate of change has further increased until it is now a whirl-wind that is whipping us all into the unforeseen.

If we are to control our own destinies, we dare not ignore the inevitability of change, or fight it blindly as something that is annoying and undesirable. We must accept it and attempt to channel it in what seems to us to be a desirable direction. It helps if we are acquainted with science fiction and have therefore learned to treat change as something familiar. Science fiction readers, in other words, are relatively immune to future shock.

Second, even if science fiction does not inform very accurately, good and gripping science fiction may *inspire*. H. G. Wells' science fiction novels, written at the turn of the century, caught hold of the imagination of innumerable youngsters. Robert Goddard had his eyes first turned to the heavens by his reading of H. G. Wells, and it was Goddard who fired off the first liquid-fueled rockets. Indeed, all the early pioneers in rocket research in the 1920s and 1930s were inspired by their reading of Wells or of science fiction writers who were themselves inspired by Wells. We might then say that it was Wells who drove us on to the Moon, though he himself never did even the most trifling work in the field of rocketry.

Another example (which I am forced to make in defiance of my well-known modesty) is that of the robot stories I wrote in the 1940s. They were put together in a book *I, Robot* in 1950 and served to inspire a number of young people, who found themselves intrigued by the notion of robots as I saw them. Whereas earlier science fiction writers pictured robots as symbolic embodiments of human intellectual arrogance, or as literary examples of the oppressed of society, I saw them as simple machines with built-in safeguards (the Three Laws of Robotics).

The result is that a surprising percentage of those who went on to study and develop the field of robotics (a word, incidentally, which I coined in 1942) were inspired by these robot stories of mine. (I like to think that all of them were, but I don't quite dare make that blanket assertion.) Consequently, even though I myself have never done any work in robotics at all, I am widely looked upon as a kind of grandfather of the field.

Well, then, here in this book we have gathered together articles by scientists *and* by science fiction writers—by masters in each field. What's more, we have chosen the same subject for all. The scientists discuss each planet in turn as it is known to us through the work of modern astronomers with their rockets and probes. The science fiction writers discuss each planet in turn as their imagination tells them it will be some time in the future, when human beings have had their chance to explore, modify, and transform it.

You, the reader, will be both informed and inspired. You can have the pleasure of directly comparing the two sorts of writing, and to come to your own conclusions concerning them.

SPACE FLIGHT: IMAGINATION AND REALITY

Arthur C. Clarke

THE EXPLORATION OF SPACE was anticipated for centuries before the reality met the dream. It is not only interesting but also valuable to look back on some of those old ideas and speculations, to see what we can learn from their successes as well as their failures. For much that has occurred since the space age opened in 1957 was foreseen with remarkable accuracy; yet there were also some stunning surprises. So it will be in the future.

It is somewhat ironic that the first truly *scientific* space voyage involved supernatural forces. This was the *Somnium* (1634) written by no less a man than Kepler—to whom astronautics owes as much as to Newton himself. The discoverer of the laws governing the motion of planets—and hence of spaceships—was both a scientist and a mystic; his background may be judged by the fact that his own mother barely escaped execution for sorcery.

In the *Somnium*, Kepler employed demons to carry his hero to the Moon, and made the significant remark that as the voyage progressed it would no longer be necessary to use any force for propulsion. His description of the Moon, based on the knowledge revealed by the newly invented telescope, was also as scientifically accurate as was possible at the time—though like many later writers, he assumed the existence of water, air, and life.

As is well known, demons are often unreliable servants, though perhaps not as unreliable as some of the early rockets. Other writers have used mysterious mental forces to carry their heroes to other worlds—often at speeds far exceeding the miserable velocity of light. Olaf Stapledon used such a device in his magnificent *Starmaker* (1937), as did C. S. Lewis in *Perelandra* (1944; also known as *Voyage to Venus*). Descending slightly in the literary scale, Edgar Rice Burroughs used the power of the mind to transport his muscular hero, John Carter, to the planet Mars—or Barsoom, as its inhabitants call it.

His example had a great influence on Carl Sagan, who has written "I can remember spending many an hour in my boyhood, arms resolutely outstretched in an empty field, imploring what I believed to be Mars to transport me there. It never worked." From what we now know of conditions on Mars, it was very lucky for Carl that it didn't. . . .

Some early writers who did not approve of trafficking with supernatural powers—transactions in which, however carefully one read the contract, there always seemed to be some unsuspected penalty clause—used natural agencies to convey their heroes away from Earth. This was the case with the ancestor of all space travel stories, the *Vera Historia* (True History) written by Lucian of Samosata in A.D. 160. In this misleadingly entitled tale, a ship sailing in the dangerous and unexplored region beyond the Pillars of Hercules was caught up in a whirlwind and deposited on the Moon. It is true that the Bay of Biscay has a bad reputation, but this must have been an unusually rough passage.

About a millenium and a half later, the great Jules Verne improved on this slightly with his *Hector Servadac* (1877), an unlikely tale in which a comet grazes Earth, scoops up two Frenchmen, and takes them on a trip around the solar system. As they explore the comet they encounter bits of Earth that it had acquired during the collision—some of them still inhabited. A fragment of the Rock of Gibraltar is discovered, occupied by two Englishmen playing chess and, according to Verne, quite unaware of their predicament. I doubt this: it seems much more likely that they were perfectly well aware of the fact that they were aboard a comet but had come to a crucial point in their game and, with typically English *sang-froid*, refused to be distracted by such trivialities.

Perhaps the most ingenious use of natural forces was that employed by Cyrano de Bergerac in his classics, *A Voyage to the Moon* (1656) and *A Voyage to the Sun* (1662). In the first of his several interplanetary voyages, the motive power was provided by vials of dew strapped round his waist—for Cyrano very logically argued that as the sun sucked up the dew in the morning, it would carry him with it. . . .

So much for magic. Now for machines.

With the development of the scientific method in the seventeenth and eighteenth centuries, and a fuller understanding of what space travel *really* implied, authors went to greater lengths to give their stories some plausibility, and the first primitive spaceships began to appear in literature. The discovery of explosives and the invention of artillery showed that there was one way of escaping from Earth; thus, the "space gun" arrived on the scene.

The most famous version, of course, is that in Jules Verne's *From the Earth to the Moon* (1865), but it was not the first. That dubious honor goes to an obscure Irish writer, Murtagh McDermot, who as early as 1728 wrote *A Trip to the Moon.* Amazingly, he used a space gun *to come home*, after persuading the Selenites to dig a great hole containing 7,000 barrels of gunpowder. He placed himself in the middle of ten concentric wooden vessels, "to lessen the shock," and provided himself with wings so that he could glide down to Earth when he arrived.

How did he get to the Moon in the first place? By rocket! Altogether, a remarkable effort for two and a half centuries ago. McDermot was certainly much more farsighted than many of his successors.

Nearer our own time, it is difficult to say how seriously Verne took his mammoth cannon, because so much of the story is facetiously written, usually at the expense of the Americans. But he went to a great deal of trouble with his astronomical facts and figures; the *Columbiad* was a 300-meter vertical barrel sunk in the Florida soil—not far from Cape Canaveral!—and packed with 200 tons of gun cotton. The projectile itself was made of the newly discovered wonder-metal, aluminum.

Ignoring the slight impossibility of the passengers—or, indeed, the vehicle—surviving the concussion, Verne's projectile must be considered as the first scientifically conceived spacecraft. It had shock absorbers, air-conditioning, padded walls with windows set in them, and similar arrangements which we now accept as commonplace in any well-ordered spaceship.

The last—I hope—space gun was that devised by H. G. Wells for his film *Things to Come* (1936). It was visually spectacular, but of course scientific nonsense, and we members of the three-year-old British Interplanetary Society were quite upset. We wrote Wells a "more in sorrow than in anger" letter, and received a kind but unrepentant answer.

Because guns are so obviously impractical, there have been many attempts to devise alternative, and less violent, means of escaping from Earth. The American writer Edward E. Hale, author of *The Brick Moon* (1870)—the very first suggestion ever made for an artificial satellite—proposed giant flywheels that could be brought up to speed over a long period of time. At the appropriate moment the payload would be dropped on the rim and flicked into orbit. I need hardly say that *this* suggestion is even more absurd than a space gun—as Hale undoubtedly knew, since he was writing with his tongue firmly in his cheek.

If you could make a gun long enough, of course, the initial shock might be reduced to acceptable figures; hence the concept of the launching track. The earliest version of this I have been able to discover is in a story called *The Moon Conquerors* (1930) by a German author, R. H. Romans. In this, a series of giant magnets was used to shoot a spaceship to the Moon, and many later authors have developed the same idea.

But the Earth-based launching track has some fundamental flaws. It would have to be at least 1,000 kilometers long, if human passengers were to survive the acceleration, so the cost would be astronomical. It could only do part of the job, though admittedly the most difficult part—the escape from Earth. The spacecraft would still require a self-contained propulsion system for the landing and return. And as a last fatal defect, any object given the escape velocity of 11.2 kilometers a second near the surface of Earth would burn up like a meteor in the dense lower atmosphere.

The only way an Earth-based launcher could operate is if it were built in the form of a slowly ascending ramp the whole width of equatorial Africa or South America, starting from sea level and climbing to a height of, say, 20 kilometers. I do not know if anyone has ever had the temerity to suggest this, so I cheerfully do so now.

More than thirty years ago ("Electromagnetic Launching as a Major Contribution to Space-Flight," *J.B.I.S.* Vol. 9, No. 6, November 1950) I pointed out that the ideal place for a launcher is the Moon; the low gravity and absence of atmosphere make it the perfect location. Such a launcher could be used for countless purposes, since it could economically project material—and even fragile human passengers—to almost any point in the solar system. This concept, rechristened the "mass launcher," is the basis of the schemes for space colonization recently popularized by Dr. Gerald O'Neill in *The High Frontier* (1976).

But you can't build a lunar launcher until you've escaped from Earth, so it was of no use in the pioneering days. Before the possibilities of the rocket were realized, many writers of space travel stories sought an answer in forces that could overcome gravity. The most famous development of this idea is in H. G. Wells's *The First Men in the Moon* (1901)—still the greatest of all interplanetary stories, despite its inevitable dating.

Wells's "Cavorite" was a substance which blocked gravity, just as a sheet of metal blocks light. You had only to coat a sphere with it, and you would fly away from Earth. You could steer simply by removing the section of Cavorite facing the body you wished to approach, so that its attraction could act upon you. So much more civilized than those noisy and dangerous rockets!

Is such a thing even theoretically possible? As far as Cavorite is concerned, the answer is a resounding no, as can be very easily proved by a simple "thought experiment."

Imagine a large flywheel, mounted vertically, with a sheet of Cavorite placed beneath one side. By definition, that side would be weightless, while the other half would have normal weight. Thus there would be a continual unbalance, so the wheel would revolve more and more rapidly. It could be a permanent source of energy—a perpetual-motion machine, defying the most fundamental law of physics. QED.

Amusingly enough, Jules Verne pointed this out to the young Wells in no uncertain terms. "I make use of physics. He invents. I go to the moon in a cannon-ball . . . he constructs a metal which does away with the law of gravitation. . . . *Très joli*—but show me this metal. Let him produce it." Perhaps this justified criticism induced Wells, a third of a century later, to take his retrograde step of using the space gun in *Things to Come;* but I rather doubt it. Wells was too great an artist to let himself be unduly restricted by mere facts.

Though a *passive* gravity shield of the type imagined by Wells (and many other writers, before and since) is impossible, the laws of physics do not rule out some interesting alternatives. There is no fundamental objection to a substance which is repelled, instead of being attracted, by gravity, just as similar electric charges repel each other. We are hardly likely to discover such a material on Earth, since if it ever occurred naturally it would long ago have shot off into space. But if we could manufacture such an interesting substance, then in principle it could be used to lift a spaceship—though we would have to jettison it to come home or to land on another planet. The technique of travel with a gravity-repellent material would be rather like old-style hydrogen ballooning. The gas can take you up, but you have to get rid of it when you want to come down again.

Nor is there any objection to an antigravity device *which is driven by some appropriate source of energy*, so that it does not produce something for nothing. I suppose the innumerable "space drives" of science fiction, some of which I have occasionally used myself, come under this heading. They may not defy the law of the conservation of energy, but it is hard to see how they can avoid a conflict with something equally fundamental, Newton's third law; for every action there is an equal and opposite reaction. *All* motion, without exception, depends upon this law. Even a spaceship must have something to push against; in the case of a rocket, of course, that something is its ejected propellent mass.

During the mid-1950s—just after the announcement of the Vanguard Earth Satellite Program, which may or may not have been a coincidence—there was a rash of reports from the United States about "electrogravitics." The Princeton Institute for Advanced Studies, Convair, the Glen Martin Company, among others, were involved; Martin actually placed advertisements to recruit scientists "interested in gravity." The whole thing rapidly fizzled out; one cynic told me that it was "much ado about nothing, started by a bunch of engineers who didn't know enough physics." That certainly seems to have been the case. Electrogravitics, like exobiology, remains a science without a single specimen for study. . . .

Yet, the subject is not closed, and probably never will be. A few years ago one of the United Kingdom's best-known engineers, Eric Laithwaite, Professor of Heavy Electrical Engineering at Imperial College, London, startled everyone by claiming that a system of two spinning gyroscopes could produce an out-of-balance force; in other words, mechanically produced antigravity.

Interestingly enough, exactly the same conclusion was once reached by *each* of the great pioneers of astronautics—Tsiolkovsky, Goddard, Oberth. As very young men, they all thought that some arrangement of spinning weights could produce a lift, but very quickly discovered a fallacy in their reasoning. Oberth has complained that some inventor approaches him once a month, on the average, with variants of this idea. But Professor Laithwaite is no crackpot inventor, and proposes to conduct a crucial experiment on *his* system in the weightless environment of the space shuttle. I wish him luck.

If we ever do invent a "space drive," however, it will surely depend upon some new fundamental discovery in subatomic physics, or the structure of space time. Until then, we are stuck with rockets—chemical, electric, or nuclear.

There is, it is true, one other known alternative, but that is of very limited application. I refer to "solar sailing."

The fact that sunlight produces a tiny, but measurable, pressure when it falls upon a surface has already been used to control the orientation of satellites. Since even a minute force can produce large effects if it operates over a sufficiently long time, small reflecting panels can be used to make a satellite turn around its axis and point in any desired direction. If these panels were large enough—and by large, I mean kilometers on a side—they could produce major orbital changes.

Hence the delightful fantasy—and perhaps one day it may be more than that—of "solar yachts" furling gigantic, gossamer-thin sails as they race from world to world. Solar sailing would be the most spectacular sport ever developed; but it will not be a very exciting one, because even the simplest maneuver would take hours or days. And as it is a technology which can only be used in the zero-gravity vacuum of deep space, the use of the Sun's radiation pressure for propulsion still depends on the rocket for its initial stages.

Though it was mentioned in passing from time to time—for example by the ingenious Cyrano de Bergerac—the rocket did not enter the literature of space travel until surprisingly late. Its first serious appearance may have been in Verne's sequel *Round the Moon* (1870), where it was used to change the orbit of the projectile. Verne—unlike *The The New York Times,* in a notorious editorial about Goddard's folly, half a century later—clearly understood that rockets could provide thrust in a vacuum. It is a pity he did not consider them adequate for the whole job; his impossible gun may have set back the conquest of space by years, though hardly by decades.

Popular attention began to focus on rockets from 1925 onward with the appearance of serious technical literature and the rise of small experimental groups in Germany, the U.S.S.R., and elsewhere. For a long time, fact and fiction were inextricably entangled; many of the pioneers were writers and used their pens to spread the news that space travel need no longer be fantasy. It is hard to believe that this pioneering era is only half a century ago, and that a mere forty years after the flight of the first liquid-fueled rocket in 1926, men were preparing to go to the Moon.

The "spaceflight revolution," as Williams Sims Bainbridge called it in his book of that name, was one of the swiftest and most remarkable in human history. Most technological developments arise naturally when some social need is matched by a corresponding invention; the steam engine, the telephone, and the automobile are obvious examples. But, to be perfectly honest, no one really *needed* spaceships in the mid-twentieth century, and a lot of people still rather wish they'd go away. Sooner or later, of course, space transportation would have evolved, probably out of high-altitude aviation, but things didn't happen that way. As Bainbridge points out, the imagination and determination of a mere handful of men—of whom the Russian Korolev and the German Von Braun were by far the most important—opened up the space frontier decades ahead of any historically plausible scenario.

The full implications of this will not be known for centuries, but let me leave this analogy for you to meditate upon. In 1492, Christopher Columbus did something much more important than merely discovering America—which

after all had been known to quite at few people for at least 20,000 years. He opened up the road between the Old World and the New.

Yet some Renaissance Korolev or Von Braun *could* have made that happen fifty—a hundred years—earlier than it actually did; the Vikings almost succeeded. One day we may be very glad that we got to the Moon in 1969, instead of, well 2001 . . . or even 2051.

And to those who think that the landing on the Moon was merely a technological *tour de force* of little ultimate importance in human affairs, I offer another lesson from history. One of the early explorers of Australia reported proudly to his Mission Control, back in Whitehall: "I have now mapped this continent so thoroughly *that no one need ever go there again.*" You may laugh, but as far as space is concerned, there are equally short-sighted people around today.

Among them I would include all those distinguished scientists who keep telling us that the exploration of space can best be carried out by robots. Well, Europe could have waited 500 years and sent remote-controlled cameras to survey America. Of course, this is a ridiculous analogy—but then the whole debate is ridiculous. Robots are essential as pioneers, and there are environments which only they can penetrate. But there are also missions where it is far more effective—and even cheaper—to have men in the loop, if only to deal with unexpected emergencies. (Remember the Skylab salvage operation and Apollo 13.)

However, cost effectiveness is not the only criterion. Like all his fellow primates, Man is an inquisitive animal, and seldom stops to calculate the number of bits per buck. He wants to go and see things for himself. And what he has discovered he never abandons, except temporarily—as in the case of the South Pole between 1912 and 1957, and the Moon between 1972 and 19—??

The science fiction writers and the pioneers of astronautics have imagined human settlements on all the worlds of the solar system—even in space itself. They have dreamed that we will extend our commerce beyond the atmosphere, into the final frontier (to coin a phrase). And if anyone thinks that this idea is fantastic, let I remind him that half a century ago a single man in the Atlantic sky was headline news. How many thousands are up there at this very moment, dozing through the in-flight movie?

The analogy may be false; perhaps there is nothing in space to attract more than the occasional scientific mission or asteroid mining consortium. And even if the solar system is full of opportunity, it may be argued that the enormous cost of escaping from Earth will always place a severe limit on our ability to exploit extraterrestrial resources. Our great airports are already bad enough; even if we could afford it, do we really want a space shuttle taking off from somewhere on Earth every few minutes and—almost as bad—booming back into the atmosphere?

Well, there is an alternative, and it's not antigravity, which may be impossible even in theory. It's the space elevator, or orbital tower, conceived in 1960 by the Russian engineer Yuri Artsutanov, and since reinvented at least five times.

For those of you who are not familiar with this at-first-sight preposterous idea, let me summarize briefly. It follows from the concept of stationary satellites, which everyone now takes for granted. Clearly, if a satellite can remain poised forever above the same spot on the equator, then in principle it should be possible to lower a cable from orbit to Earth, performing an Indian rope trick 36,000 kilometers high.

And if we can do that, we can go further. We can build an elevator system to send payloads into space without rockets, purely by electrical energy. This would totally transform the economics of spaceflight—as you will appreciate when I tell you that the cost, *in energy*, of carrying a man to the Moon is less than ten dollars.

The engineering problems are, of course, enormous, but extensive studies have found no fundamental flaw in the concept, which is now the basis of a rapidly expanding literature, to which I refer those who would like more details. Much ingenuity has now been applied to extending Artsutanov's basic idea, and it appears—surprisingly—that "skyhooks" or "Jacob's ladders" can be built to virtually any altitude, from any spot on Earth, though at the cost of rather appalling mechanical complexities.

Whether these daring concepts will ever be realized in practice, only the future will tell. But the imagination of the engineers has now opened up wholly new vistas in space, and also presented us with a beautiful paradox. On the small scale, space travel will always be extremely expensive. Yet if—and it's a big if—it can ever be justified on a really massive scale, it could be one of the cheapest forms of transportation ever devised. As in the case of the familiar terrestrial elevator, a space elevator would require very little energy to run, because the traffic moving downward would lift that on the way up. Of course, the capital cost would be enormous; but a well-designed space elevator could last for centuries and would be an even better long-term investment than that other expensive but highly profitable tourist attraction, the Great Pyramid.

Perhaps you may consider that the space elevator puts too much of a strain on the imagination—but without imagination, nothing is ever achieved, as the history of astronautics amply proves. Yet it is possible to have too much of a good thing; uncontrolled imagination can be an even bigger menace than short-sighted conservatism because it can lead to much greater disasters.

I would like to conclude with two dreadful, or at least tragicomic, examples of this. One is past history; the other remains a continuing nuisance.

For almost two generations, the planet Mars was central in all discussions of extraterrestrial life, largely owing to the influence of one man, the American astronomer Percival Lowell. His dramatic claim to have discovered a network of apparently artificial "canals" covering the face of the planet generated millions of words of controversy, as well as some of the most enjoyable science fiction ever written—Burroughs, Weinbaum, Bradbury, to name the best-known.

We now know, thanks to the Mariner and Viking space probes, that the Martian canals are a total illusion, created in the mind's eye from the infinity of detail that can be glimpsed on the planet during the rare moments when it can be seen clearly. Yet Lowell—and many other astronomers!—drew them consistently for decades. How could this happen? The explanation, I suspect, runs something like this:

Lowell was so determined to find intelligence on Mars that he created what he was looking for, as we have all done at some time or another. His drawings of Mars became more and more artificial, until eventually they looked like maps of the world's airlines. As an artist can do, he created a style, which was copied by others who were infected by his enthusiasm. More skeptical astronomers saw merely the natural patterns of light and shade, which we now know represent the real Mars. The canals were a, shall we say, *infectious hallucination*, but to Lowell they were perfectly real.

His wealth and prestige—not to mention his considerable literary gifts—enabled him to sustain the illusion. When his very able assistant A. E. Douglass eventually became skeptical—*dis*illusioned—and decided that the canals lay in the eye of the observer, what did Lowell do? He fired him—I am sure with genuine reluctance.

When Lowell died, so did the canals, though slowly. It took the Mariners and Vikings to inflict the final coup de grace.

On a much larger scale, I am now convinced that something like this is responsible for the few UFO sightings that do not have trivial explanations. Let me devote a couple of minutes to the two cases that provided my own moments of truth and that closed the subject as far as I am concerned—at least until some fundamentally new evidence comes along, which hasn't happened for twenty years. . . .

In one famous incident, many eyewitnesses saw the classic spaceship, complete with lighted windows, flying a few thousand meters overhead. Some of them thought it had landed not far away. They weren't lying; they had indeed seen something unusual—and we know exactly what it was, without a shadow of doubt.

It was not a spaceship a few kilometers up; it was a reentering satellite at fifty times that altitude, burning up spectacularly in a trail of fire halfway across the sky. But the people who were expecting to see a spaceship saw one. It was the Lowell Effect again.

There are so many hundreds of similar—and even more fantastic—misinterpretations, described ad nauseam in the literature, that I no longer waste any time on reports of strange things seen in the sky, even by competent observers. I've been fooled too often myself: one of my own half-dozen UFOs took weeks to identify. So my philosophy now is very simple and based on that extremely rare commodity, common sense. Here is Clarke's Rule for dealing with a UFO: even if it comes from Proxima Centauri, if it doesn't stop, there's nothing you can prove one way or the other. So take pity on suffering humanity: *forget* it. Nothing will be lost. When there really *is* a landing, the fact will be established, without a shadow of doubt, within half an hour. We won't still be waving our arms, thirty years later.

Then what about the hundreds of "close encounters," sometimes —though not always—reported by apparently sane and honest people?

Yes, it's the Lowell Effect again, in considerably more virulent form. My first glimpse of this obvious truth came when I was sent a book giving an account of a UFO kidnapping, full of drawings showing the spaceship and its occupants. I recognized the ship instantly; I'd known it for thirty years. And so has every American who's spent much time watching the Late, Late Show. Now, it is possible that a superior space-faring civilization *may* base its designs on 1950 Hollywood movies, but frankly I doubt it. Yet I don't doubt the honesty of the person who drew the sketches; they were no more faked than Lowell's maps of Mars. But they were also no *less* faked.

What clinched the matter, as far as I'm concerned, is the very recent discovery that some people can hallucinate so perfectly that even the electrical patterns in their brains agree with their visions. What this does to our concepts of reality I'm not quite sure. I hope I'm not hallucinating you or, even worse, that you're not hallucinating *me*.

I'm sorry about this rather long digression, but UFOs are such an obstacle to serious discussions of life in space that perhaps you'll forgive me. After all, I am trying to distinguish between imagination and reality.

So I would like to end by repeating, virtually unchanged, some words I addressed to the British Interplanetary Society in 1950—seven years before the explosive dawn of the space age. After surveying the writings of the past, I posed this question: What will happen to tales of interplanetary adventure when space travel actually begins? Will they become extinct, as some foolish critics indeed predicted the morning after Sputnik 1!

This is what I said, thirty-two years ago.

When space travel is achieved, the frontier will merely shift outward, and I think we can rely on the ingenuity of the authors to always keep a few jumps ahead of history. And how much more material they will have on which to base their tales! It should never be forgotten that without some foundation of reality, science fiction would be impossible and that therefore exact knowledge is the friend, not the enemy, of imagination and fantasy. It was only possible to write stories about the Martians when science had discovered that a certain moving point of light was a world. By the time that science has proved or disproved the existence of Martians, it will have provided hundreds of other interesting and less accessible worlds for the authors to get busy with.

So perhaps the interplanetary story will never lose its appeal, even if a time should come when all the cosmos has been explored and there are no more universes to beckon men outward across infinity. If our descendants in that age are remotely human, and still indulge in art and science and similar nursery games, I think that they will not altogether abandon the theme of interplanetary flight—though their approach to it will be very different from ours.

To us, the interplanetary story provides a glimpse of the wonders whose dawn we shall see, but of whose full glory we can only guess. To them, on the other hand, it will be something achieved, a thing completed and done countless eons ago. They may sometimes look back, perhaps a little wistfully, to the splendid, dangerous ages when the frontiers were being driven outward across space, when no one knew what marvel or what terror the next returning ship might bring, when, for good or evil, the barriers set between the peoples of the universe were irrevocably breached. With all things achieved, all knowledge safely harvested, what more, indeed, will there be for them to do as the lights of the last stars sink slowly toward evening, but to go back into history and relive again the great adventures of their remote and legendary past?

Yet we have the better bargain, for all these things still lie ahead of us.

EARTH

ESSAY BY
Ursula B. Marvin

SPECULATION BY
Harry Harrison

EARTH: THE WATER PLANET

Ursula B. Marvin

Water, water, everywhere . . .
SAMUEL COLERIDGE

THUS QUOTH THE ANCIENT MARINER, and so it seems to us as we look around our world. If we were to hover in a spacecraft and watch Earth rotate beneath us, the single most striking feature to meet our eye would be the vast expanse of ocean water girdling the globe. Each ocean and sea has its own individual name, but, linking together through broad passages and narrow straits, they encircle every continent and island with a line of restless surf. Salty ocean waters make up 97 percent of all the waters of Earth, and they cover 70 percent of its surface, leaving less than one-third of it dry land.

As we well know, however, the dry lands are not really dry. Many of us live where misty droplets moisten the grasses on summer mornings and feathery crystals of hoar frost or snow do so in winter. We are never far from rushing streams or broad rivers, and we seek out lakes and ponds on our holidays. In the highest mountain ranges we can hear water trickling through minute cracks and crevices and watch it carving intricate networks of gullies and canyons that feed great watercourses on the flatlands below. And everywhere, even in the driest deserts, where rain never falls and streams never flow, waters saturate the ground, at shallow levels or deep. Here and there groundwaters seep to the surface in springs; in rare instances they erupt in powerful geysers. In many places they lie so deep they must be pumped to the surface to irrigate farmlands or supply cities. We ourselves are made mostly of water, as are most living things, and we must drink it every day in order to keep on living.

The water we drink, however, must be fresh. If we drink from the ocean, the dissolved salts will poison us. We are, therefore, entirely dependent on the hydrologic cycle, a global system in which large volumes of salt-free water evaporate from the oceans, condense in clouds, and fall on the land as rain or snow. Rivers of fresh water complete the cycle when they enter the sea. To us, fresh water seems so abundant that it may come as a surprise to learn that

36

all the rivers, streams, and lakes combined contain less than 1 percent of the world's nonoceanic waters. Groundwaters account for a little more than 22 percent, but by far the greater portion, fully 77 percent, of the fresh waters of the world are locked up in ice.

Ice, which lasts the year around, covers Earth's polar regions and occurs as glaciers in high mountain ranges. At the North Pole, sea ice, from which the salts have been frozen out, forms a dense pack on the Arctic Ocean. Extending southward from the Arctic Circle, all of the large island of Greenland, except its ragged coastlines fringed with glacier-carved fjords, is covered by an ice sheet 1,725,000 square kilometers in area and up to 3,200 meters thick. At the South Pole a huge dome of ice covers all but a few mountain peaks and dry valleys on the continent of Antarctica. This immense ice sheet, 12 million square kilometers in area and 4,800 meters in maximum thickness, stores 24 million cubic kilometers of fresh water—75 percent of the world's supply. We believe that the ice sheet began to form 20 million years ago and achieved its maximum extent and thickness about 18,000 years ago at the climax of the last glacial period.

The Antarctic ice sheet is constantly in motion, constantly renewing itself. From the high interior plateau, the ice creeps slowly down the flanks of the dome—more or less northward in all directions—at average rates of 1 to 10 meters per year. When it reaches the coast the ice pushes seaward in thick marginal shelves or calves off as icebergs. A few centimeters of fresh snow falling on the interior each year maintain the system in approximate balance. The 2,500-meter mean elevation of the ice plateau makes Antarctica the highest of continents. A hemispheric wind pattern, in which warm air rises in the tropics and flows southward where it cools, loses its moisture, and courses down the steep slopes of the ice sheet, makes Antarctica the driest and windiest continent. Antarctica is also the coldest of continents, with a record low temperature of $-88°C$. The ice in the remote interior has been crystallized and recrystallized until it is as sterile as triply distilled water; the ice sheet is the largest source of pure water in the world.

On first thought, it may seem regrettable that this great reservoir is situated literally at the end of Earth, where it cannot easily be tapped for use in potentially fertile temperate and tropical deserts. But facts of history and geography have made the continued presence of the Antarctic ice sheet essential to us. If a global warming were to melt that ice sheet away, sea level would rise 60 meters. If all the world's glacial ice were to melt, sea level would rise an additional 10 meters. Sea level has risen and lowered dramatically many times in the past, but since the last great northern and southern continental ice sheets began melting backward 11,000 years ago, civilization has sprung up and populations have concentrated on shorelines around the world.

Today, a sea level rise of 70 meters would flood every coastal city and fishing village, cover thousands of islands, and spread salt water over low-lying areas of every continent. In fact, 15 percent of our present land area would be lost to the oceans. Most of Florida, for example, would disappear beneath the waves, as would New York and London, and only their steep, spectacular hills would mark the sites of Rio de Janeiro and Hong Kong. We are fortunate indeed that great volumes of water remain locked in cold storage in the polar regions. Yet, are we living in a postglacial period or an interglacial one? Can we expect a future advance or a further retreat of polar ice sheets? We have no clear answers to these questions, but specialists of many kinds are monitoring the condition of the ice sheets and keeping track of any alterations in the Sun's radiation or in the oceans or atmosphere that could signal future changes. To reverse a trend might well lie beyond our capabilities, but early recognition of one could be all-important in helping humanity to cope with significant changes in global climate or sea level.

THE PLANETARY OASIS

To us, water appears to be a universal element. In fact it is exceedingly rare. We could voyage all the way across the solar system from the surface of the Sun to the orbit of Pluto, a distance of some 6 billion kilometers, without ever finding a single puddle of liquid water except on Earth. Lying close to the Sun in the full glare of solar radiation, the scarred face of Mercury could not hold water for an instant. Traces of water vapor have been detected in the thick, hot atmosphere of Venus, but that H_2O links with sulfurous gases to form droplets of concentrated sulfuric acid, or with chlorine or fluorine to form hydrochloric and hydrofluoric acids—an acid rain indeed, if these droplets ever survive the heavy atmospheric pressure of Venus and fall to the surface.

The bone-dry character of our nearest neighbor, the Moon, was one of the great surprises of the Apollo missions. Although nobody expected to find lunar rivers or lakes, some scientists believed that temporary streams of water once eroded valleys on the Moon, and many more expected to find a layer of Arctic-style permafrost in the detritus that blankets the Moon. Of water or ice there was not a trace. Not only is the Moon devoid of moisture today, but no sign of water, nor even of hydroxyl ions (OH), was found in lavas that crystallized more than 3 billion years ago. The Moon was waterless from the beginning;

as a result the lunar rocks are as fresh and glistening as the day they formed, showing no sign of turning to rust or clay.

In the cold, rarefied atmosphere of Mars, we could find small traces of water vapor, and water ice and dry ice (frozen CO_2) make up the thin Martian polar ice caps, but these bear no comparison in magnitude with those of Earth. Deep canyons on Mars look as though they were carved by rushing streams, but no sign of water appears on the dusty surface of that planet today. Some scientists believe that Mars may be experiencing an ice age, and that all the running and standing waters have sunk into the ground, turning it gelid with permafrost. We cannot test this hypothesis without making more exploratory voyages to Mars. Meanwhile, the red deserts of Mars hold out no promise for a thirsty space voyager in search of a drink of water.

The low densities of the giant planets, and of some of their satellites, in the reaches of the solar system beyond Mars indicate that they consist largely of ice, and some of them may have liquid water beneath their frozen crusts. Ice also binds together the nuclei of comets, which occasionally pass Earth on long journeys around the Sun from their place of ultimate origin halfway to the nearest star. From our quick survey, we conclude that the solar system is a forbidding place, where every planetary body but our own is either scorching or frigid (or alternately both) and bone-dry or swathed in noxious gases. We inhabit the single oasis in a vast solar system. For warmth and water and a congenial climate we must return to Earth. The welcoming vision of a gleaming blue globe, veiled with wispy clouds, will remind us of one more feature unique to Earth—our limpid atmosphere.

THE ATMOSPHERE

Automatically breathing air in and out of our lungs every moment of the day and night, we take the atmosphere for granted, although we cannot see it, feel it, taste it, or smell it unless it is perfumed or polluted. Our very life depends upon it, however, as we are oxygen-breathing creatures, and of all the planetary atmospheres in the solar system, only that of Earth contains an abundance of free oxygen (O_2).

Earth, as seen from space, emits a soft blue glow unlike that of any other planet. Pictures taken by astronauts show a thin band of vivid blue rimming the horizon, then quickly giving way to the blackness of space. The blue light results from the way the gases and dust of our atmosphere scatter sunlight. The scattering also provides us with the suffused lights of dawn and twilight and the brilliant colors of sunsets and afterglows. Without its atmosphere Earth would reflect sunlight unaltered, as the Moon does, and the brilliant days would alternate with the blackest of nights.

Our familiar atmosphere—the domain of wind and weather and flying birds and the changes of the seasons; the medium that transmits the vibrations of music and voices and other sound waves; the air that is rich in nitrogen, oxygen, water vapor, and carbon dioxide—extends to an altitude of only about 12 kilometers above Earth's surface. Above that lies the stratosphere, 35 kilometers thick, which includes a layer rich in ozone (O_3). The ozone layer serves the indispensible function of shielding Earth's surface from the full intensity of ultraviolet and cosmic radiation. Higher still are several more layers, each with its own composition and temperature, until the atmosphere gradually gives way to the vacuum of space at an altitude of about 500 kilometers.

The atmosphere shields us not only from radiation but from a daily bombardment by billions of dust grains that hurtle across Earth's path at cosmic velocities of up to 42 kilometers per second. Air friction slows down these miniprojectiles and burns most of them to ash before they penetrate below an altitude of about 60 kilometers. These are the "shooting stars" that we all can see on every clear night. Incoming meteorites plunge to deeper levels, where the ever-thickening atmosphere envelops them with incandescent gases and strips away layer after layer of thin surface melt, leaving trails of fiery droplets. These are the great fireballs that only a few of us ever see in a lifetime. At altitudes of 10 to 20 kilometers above Earth, most meteorites either explode into showers of small fragments or simply burn out and plummet to Earth at the velocity of free-fall. We estimate that one or two meteorites strike Earth each day. Most of them drop into the oceans, and most of those falling on land do little damage beyond puncturing small holes in the soil.

On rare occasions, however, a huge body hurtles at cosmic velocity all the way through the atmosphere, plunges into Earth, and explodes—vaporizing itself, excavating a crater, melting and shock-metamorphosing the target rock, and blanketing the countryside with ejecta, all in a matter of seconds. Earth's surface still bears the scars of at least two hundred such encounters, the oldest of which occurred 1.9 billion years ago and the most recent only forty years ago. But Earth's record of meteorite impacts is scant indeed compared with that of our airless Moon, whose unshielded face preserves the evidence of more than 4 billion years of direct hits. The face of Mercury is much the same. Half of Mars is heavily cratered—the half lacking young volcanics—and the moons of Mars are so pockmarked and misshapen that they look like the remains of asteroids captured from the adjacent belt where collisions are routine and many a body has been reduced to rubble. Meteorite impact is a universal process which has marked all the bodies of the inner solar system and those whose surfaces are visible to us in the outer solar system. Of all planetary bodies, however, Earth, with its deep shield of atmosphere and its global oceans, its perennial cycles of weathering, erosion, and sedimentation, and its internal dynamism that continually alters its surface features, has been the most effective, by far, in buffering and healing the effects of this cosmic bombardment.

SOURCES OF WATER AND THE ATMOSPHERE

Where do the waters of the oceans and the gases of the atmosphere come from? The two are so closely linked they must have originated from the same source. Most geologists believe that the water and atmosphere arose from inside Earth, expelled through multitudes of hot springs and volcanic vents, which began to erupt soon after the planet first formed. Scientists picture the force of gravity first pulling together the fragments of rock and metal that coalesced to form Earth; as the planet was heated by the energy of the infalling material and by its radioactive elements, the heavy metallic components fell to the center and formed a core surrounded by a mantle of silicate rocks. Along with molten lavas, the hot, wet silicates emitted steam, carbon dioxide, nitrogen, hydrogen, and sulfurous gases, most of which were too heavy to escape the pull of gravity. As soon as the surface cooled sufficiently, the first pools of water appeared.

How quickly did a great ocean form? Geologists have disputed whether the process we call the "outgassing" of the mantle occurred all at once and created a global ocean early in Earth's history (the big-burp hypothesis), or in a series of individual events (the many-burp hypothesis), or continuously, from the beginning to the present. It seems probable that a large ocean formed early, and then, as the rate of outgassing declined, a global recycling system began to operate by which waters locked in sediments were expelled back into the oceans when those sediments were heated and metamorphosed. Much of the water of today's oceans has been recycled, but not quite all. Within recent years, waters bearing a chemical signature indicating an origin directly from the mantle have been found emanating from certain submarine volcanoes. Thus, small but constant increments of what we call "juvenile" waters are added to the world's supply.

It is difficult to decipher the planet's early history by looking at Earth itself, because the oldest patches of crustal rocks yet discovered are granitic gneisses that formed 3.8 billion years ago at Isua (a name meaning "the furthest you can go") in southwest Greenland. Inasmuch as Earth originated 4.6 billion years ago, a gap of 800 million years occurs between that event and the emplacement of the first permanent pieces of the crust. For clues to that missing interval we can look at our nearest neighbor, the Moon, which formed when Earth did but quickly cooled and acquired a rigid crust. The face of the Moon preserves clear evidence of a massive bombardment by great basin-forming meteorites between about 4.2 and 3.9 billion years ago. If the Moon was thus targeted, so was Earth, but the projectiles striking this warm, dynamic planet evidently destroyed every vestige of preexisting crust.

The Isua rocks mentioned above postdated the great bombardment, but rather then being igneous rocks newly erupted 3.8 billion years ago, they are sediments that were metamorphosed at that time. These sediments bespeak the existence of even older crustal rocks, which had been weathered and eroded and their detritus carried away by running waters and deposited in an ocean basin—large or small. Oceans, therefore, existed at least as early as 3.9 to 4 billion years ago, as did areas of continental crust, however small and patchy. The atmosphere also existed very early, but not an atmosphere that would be recognizable to us today. Earth's early atmosphere contained no oxygen, which is a product of one more feature that sets this planet apart from all others: that self-replicating entity we call life.

LIFE

Life originated on Earth at some unknown moment billions of years ago when short chains of amino acids linked together to form longer chains and these, in turn, linked with long chains of nucleic acids, and the combination was catalyzed to produce a self-reproducing chemical system. The preexisting amino acids, nucleic acids, and numerous other compounds of carbon, nitrogen, hydrogen, and oxygen, which we call "organic" molecules, were formed earlier by inorganic processes. (The common usage that equates "organic" with "living" matter reflects a problem in semantics left over from the nineteenth century.)

We know that such molecules can be formed by inorganic processes because chemists have repeatedly produced them in the laboratory by passing electric discharges through vacuum jars filled with ammonia, carbon dioxide, carbon monoxide, methane, and water vapor—the very gases that made up Earth's earliest atmosphere. We conclude that a large array of organic materials could have originated in that atmosphere from the effects of lightning bolts or ultraviolet radiation. The production of such molecules, however, is by no means unique to Earth. Traces of amino acids, fatty acids, and about twenty other organic molecules have been identified in certain carbon-rich meteorites that are 4.6 billion years old. Comet spectra reveal the presence of hydrocarbon compounds in those icy bodies, and radio astronomers have detected a number of organic compounds, including formaldehyde, in clouds in interstellar space. Most, if not all, of these organic materials occur in living matter, but they are a far cry from constituting life itself. None of the artificial or meteoritic hydrocarbons show the optical activities that are characteristic of organic molecules of biologic origin.

The complex series of linkages and catalytic reactions that led from organic molecules to living cells was, so far as we *know,* unique to Earth. Once the first self-replicating system was formed, it immediately began exchanging components with its surrounding media in ways that would alter the chemistry of Earth's waters, air, and soils irreversibly. We do not know exactly when this occurred, but, in sedimentary rocks of western Australia, we have positively identified fossilized structures created by algae that lived 3.5 billion years ago. Clearly, life was burgeoning on Earth within the first billion years after the planet's formation. The ancient gneisses at Isua in Greenland, 300 million years older than the Australian rocks, contain bands of graphite with hydrocarbon molecules. We cannot be certain, however, whether those molecules represent the remains of fossilized living matter or are simply the inorganic species discussed above.

The earliest forms of life were *prokaryotes:* single-celled organisms without nuclei that reproduced asexually by splitting in two. These prokaryotes diversified into innumerable types and spread over the world. While the presence of oxygen would have threatened them with instant combustion, they thrived in the atmosphere of early Earth. However, two processes began to operate that would eventually enrich the atmosphere with free oxygen: without the barrier of the ozone layer, ultraviolet radiation from the Sun was able to dissociate water vapor into gaseous hydrogen and oxygen, and rafts of single-celled blue-green bacteria (commonly called algae), floating in shallow pools, could utilize solar energy to break down carbon dioxide and water to release oxygen. This process, which we call photosynthesis, is still carried on by all chlorophyll-bearing green plants, which supply us with fresh oxygen daily while gaining their own nourishment partly from the carbon dioxide we expel in breathing. When it was first released in the air or water, oxygen proved to be a highly reactive substance that quickly recombined with hydrogen, or carbon, or other elements. For a long period, between about 3.3 and 2 billion years ago, oxygen linked with iron and silicon and precipitated massive deposits of hematite and jasper, which, today, are the chief source of the world's iron ores. Then conditions changed, oxygen began to build up in the atmosphere, and some living organisms developed means of using oxygen in their metabolic processes.

For nearly 2 billion years prokaryotes were the only form of life on Earth. They still exist today and, as bacteria, share Earth with us. At some time between 1.3 and 2 billion years ago, however, something momentous took place: cells evolved that were ten times larger and vastly more complex than any that had existed previously. The new paired chromosomes cells were called *eukaryotes*, which have nuclei and paired chromosomes and reproduce sexually. Eukaryotes make up all multicellular plants and animals, including ourselves.

Developments among single-celled organisms are difficult to trace because, being soft-bodied, they left a patchy fossil record. After more than 3 billion years of life on Earth, however, organisms with hard parts evolved, and, 650 million years ago, the shales and limestones of the world began to preserve the teeming marine fauna of the Cambrian Period. From that time to the present, the stratigraphic record displays the marvelous multiplicity of forms assumed by living things. Many species have exploded upon the scene and become extinct. We have increasingly good evidence that some of the more wholesale extinctions may have been caused by the aftereffects of hypervelocity impacts by comets or asteroids, which sent huge volumes of dust or water vapor into the stratosphere, temporarily altering the balance of heat and light. But whenever some species disappear, others replace them, keeping quick with life every ecological niche on the planet. The dinosaurs vanished; mammals inherited the Earth. We cannot say for certain that single-celled organisms have never existed on other planets, but we can say that nothing approaching the fecund history of life on Earth has happened anywhere else in the solar system.

THE DYNAMIC EARTH

While most of the processes that drive the winds and recycle the waters and nourish life at the surface of Earth derive their energy from the Sun, the planet itself runs on heat energy from the deep interior. Earth is a dynamic body where volcanoes, erupting somewhere every year, bear witness to the high temperatures of the lower crust and upper mantle and earthquakes continually remind us of the instability of the solid rock beneath our feet. On every side we see evidence of forces that have repeatedly deformed the crust. Great folded mountain ranges rim the Pacific basin and loop across Eurasia from China to Spain, reflecting immense compressional forces. The deep rift valleys of East Africa, and the broken ranges of the American Great Basin, signify powerful tensional stress. Above all, the configuration of Earth's seven ragged continents, rising out of the oceans, suggests large-scale dislocations of a type we have learned to decipher only within the past three decades.

The very existence of continents, standing high amid the floors of the oceans, sets Earth apart from all the other planets. Let us go back into space once more to get a better look at Earth's major crustal features—only this time let us figuratively drain away the waters and sediments and gaze directly at the floors of the great oceans. That is a valid thing to do because during and after World

War II we developed an array of sounding and profiling devices that, for the first time, allowed us to map the topography of oceanic bedrock. We have also measured the seismic and magnetic properties of the ocean floors and recovered samples from deep drill holes that have allowed us to determine, by careful measurements of radioactive materials and their products the dates when the ocean floors formed.

These studies have yielded many surprises. Since the beginning of this century we have known of the existence of a steep north-south submarine ridge bisecting the Atlantic Ocean, but not until the 1960s did we learn that all oceans have ridges, which link together to form a world-encircling feature 65,000 kilometers long. Fresh lavas, accompanied by shallow-focus earthquakes, erupt along the ridge crests. The rocks on opposite flanks of the ridge crests bear symmetrical patterns of subparallel stripes that record a long series of reversals of Earth's magnetic field. Perhaps most surprising of all was the discovery that the ocean floors are young! All of the ocean floors consist of dark-colored basaltic lavas that erupted less than 200 million years ago!

Rising steeply out of the ocean floors are a few irregularly shaped continents, most of them clustered in the northern hemisphere opposite the vast Pacific basin. Even if it were possible to smooth out all the folds and overthrust faults

Gemini 5 photo of Youthful Mountains in the Karakoram Range between Kashmir and China. (NASA)

of present and past mountain ranges, there would not be nearly enough continental rock to cover the whole Earth. Indeed, continents have apparently always been individual patches of land that grew up around ancient "nuclei," where eruptions of relatively low-density, silica-rich lavas built islands, and the processes of erosion, deposition, and metamorphism first began. The continents consist of light-colored granitic rock that differs from that of the ocean floors in density, chemical composition, and age. In contrast to the youthful ocean floors, the continents include rocks of all ages from the early Precambrian gneisses of Greenland, 3.8 billion years old, to lavas that were erupted this morning.

From our vantage point in space we may be struck with the impression that some of the continents—perhaps all of them—could be fitted together like pieces in a jigsaw puzzle. If so, pieces of the crust must have split apart and moved horizontally for long distances. Is such motion possible? Earlier in this century, when the idea of moving continents was first seriously proposed, it met with powerful opposition from a majority of geologists, who pointed to compelling evidence that Earth's crust is too strong and rigid for continents to slip sideways from one place to another. Earthquakes, propagated at depths of hundreds of kilometers seemed to indicate that rocks are brittle to those depths; mountains stand high for millions of years without slowly spreading out under the pull of gravity; and no forces were known to be powerful enough to push or pull continents horizontally. In the late 1960s, however, new information and new

The effects of running water on the Earth: The Alps near Chamonix (Photo by David Morrison)

insights into the nature of Earth led to the theory of plate tectonics, which showed us how to reconcile the visual evidence for crustal motion with the geophysical evidence for crustal strength.

Briefly, that theory says that Earth's crust is broken into large individual plates, each one about 100 kilometers thick, which move slowly about in response to heat gradients in a weak, semimolten layer of underlying mantle. Each plate has a leading margin, a trailing margin, and two side margins, which shear past adjacent plates. The oceanic ridge crests are open sutures where plates separate and move apart down the flanks in opposite directions, while fresh basalt, magnetized in the direction of Earth's field at the time of cooling, is added to their trailing edges. Where oncoming oceanic plates collide, one of them bends beneath the other and slips downward into the mantle, where it is reassimilated by a process called *subduction*. Deep trenches mark subduction zones in the ocean floor, and deep-focus earthquakes signal the progress of the plunging plate. We now know that these earthquakes, which were formerly taken as evidence for rigidity of the entire crust to depths of 700 kilometers, are limited to subduction zones. The continual creation of new ocean floor at the ridges and the destruction of old floor at the trenches endows the ocean floors with their eternal youth.

Continents ride piggyback on the oceanic plates. Continental rock is too buoyant to be subducted, so, once emplaced, it remains continental. The continents have slowly grown in area as oceanic sediments, riding the downgoing slabs, have remelted, erupted to the surface in andesitic volcanoes, and adhered to continental margins. Continents may not be destroyed, but they may be split apart if a new pattern of motion of the hot mantle material creates a spreading zone beneath them. As a first sign of this, long rift valleys will form and then widen into new oceans; finally pieces of a continent will be rafted apart. That happened 180 million years ago to a supercontinent we call Pangaea, which broke into pieces that moved in all directions. The continents we live on today are bits of that planetary jigsaw puzzle.

Wherever plate motions cause continents to collide, the margins compress into great folds and faults like those we see in the Alps and Himalayas. Along the sides of the moving plates, great megashears slice through the crust, marking continents and ocean floors with offset fault lines hundreds or thousands of kilometers long.

Don't all planets—or at least all the terrestrial planets—have highlands and lowlands, and don't they all display a long record of tectonic activity? In fact they do not, and, on those showing any evidence of volcanism or structural changes, the tectonic style is very different from that of Earth. No other planets have crusts made of two totally different types of rock. The lava plains of the Moon fill basins in the highlands crust, which continues under their floors and covers the entire body. The Moon appears to have been a tectonically dead body for the past 2 to 3 billion years. Mercury shows evidence of minor contraction during cooling, and Mars of minor expansion. We could search in vain for a single folded mountain range like those that festoon Earth anywhere else in the solar system, and equally in vain for a system of moving plates.

POSTSCRIPT

Thinking over Earth's special attributes—water, free oxygen, life, and tectonic dynamism—we realize that each one depends on the planet's size and geographical position in the solar system. Earth is large enough to have remained hot and to exert a gravitational force strong enough to bind water and air to its surface. This planet is neither too close to the Sun, nor too far away; its surface temperature remains within the range of 60°C to 90°C. Living organisms were able to arise in this environment and are critically dependent on it for survival. A few degrees of temperature fluctuation either up or down could irreversibly alter the delicate balance that maintains life. For us, Earth is indeed the right body in the right place at the right time. It is the different planet. Vive la difference!

A typical view of the Earth's surface (Photo by David Morrison)

AFTER THE STORM

Harry Harrison

THE TIDE WAS ON THE WAY OUT, leaving a strip of hard sand that felt good to jog upon. The sun, just clear of the horizon, was already hot on my face. Last night's storm had finally blown itself out, although the long Atlantic rollers were still crashing onto the beach with its memory. It was going to be hot, but the sand was still cool under my bare toes as I jogged along easily, the last surge of the surf breaking around my ankles. I was very much at peace with the world: this was a good time of day.

There was something that caught my eye ahead, dark against the white foam. Driftwood, very good, it would make a lovely fire in the winter. It was a long plank with something draped over it. As I splashed toward it I felt a chill down my bare back, a sudden fear.

It was a body, a man's body.

I did not want to look too closely at this waterlogged corpse. I hesitated and stopped, with the water surging about my legs, unsure of what I should do. Phone the police? But if I did that it might wash out to sea again while I was away. I had to pull it in—but did not want to go near it. A wave surged up and over the body and strands of seaweed tangled in the long hair. The head lifted and dropped back.

He was still alive.

But cold as death. I felt the chill when I seized his hands and dragged him, a dead weight, through the shallow water to the beach. Dropped him face down, his forearm under his mouth and nose to keep them out of the sand, then leaned hard on his back. And again—until he coughed and gasped, emptying his stomach of sea water. He groaned when I rolled him onto his back and his eyelids moved and opened. His eyes were a transparent pale blue and they had trouble focusing.

"You are all right," I said. "Ashore and safe."

He frowned at my words, and I wondered if he could understand me. "Do you speak English?"

"I do. . . ." He coughed, then rubbed his lips. "Could you tell me the name of this place?"

"Manhasset, north shore of Long Island."

"One of the states of the United States, is it?"

"You're Irish?"

"Aye. And a devil of a long way from home."

He struggled to his feet, swaying, and would have fallen again if I hadn't caught him.

"Lean on me," I said. "The house isn't far. We'll get some dry clothes on you, something warm to drink."

When we reached the patio he dropped onto the bench with a sigh. "I could do with that cup of tea now," he said.

"No tea—what about coffee?"

"Good man, that'll do me fine."

"Cream and sugar?" I asked as I punched in the order on the keyboard on the wall. He nodded and his eyebrows rose as I took the steaming cup from the dispenser. He sipped it gingerly, then drank deep. He drained the cup before he spoke again.

"That's a miraculous yoke you have there. Could you do it again?"

I wondered just where he was from that he had never seen an ordinary dispenser before. I dropped his cup into the recycler and passed him a full one.

"From Ireland," he said, answering my unspoken question. "Five weeks out of Arklow when the storm caught us. Had a load of cured hides for the Canadians. Gone now, with the rest of the crew, God rest their souls. The name is Byrne, Cormac Byrne, sir."

"Bil Cohn-Greavy. Would you like to get out of those wet clothes?"

"Fine now, Mr. Greavy, just sitting in the sun here. . . ."

"Cohn-Greavy. Matronym, patronym. Been the law now for what? . . . at least a hundred years. I suppose on your side of the ocean you just use your father's name?"

"We do, we do. Things change that slowly in Ireland. But you say that it's the law of the land that you must use both your mother and your father's family name?"

I nodded and wondered how it was that an ordinary sailor understood a bit of Latin. "The feminist block pushed it through Congress in the 2030s when Mary Wheeler became president. Look, I have to make a phone call. Just sit here and rest. Back in a moment."

It's a responsibility that cannot be avoided. If you own shore property you are sworn in as an auxiliary Coast Guard. Anything that comes ashore had to be reported. I even had a gun to warn off anyone who tried to land. Immigration is very illegal in the United States. I imagined that this included shipwrecked sailors.

"Coast Guard emergency," I said and the screen lit up at once. The gray-haired duty chief looked up from my ID, which would be automatically displayed.

"Report, Cohn-Greavy."

"I have a man here, washed ashore from a wreck, sir. Foreign national."

"Right. Detain him. Patrol's on the way."

It was my duty, of course. There were sound reasons for this country's immigration policy. The glass door opened as I approached, and I could hear a familiar voice. I called out.

"Is that you, Kriket?"

"None other."

She had come along the shore, for her legs were sandy, the seat of her bikini bottom as well. Like most girls she went topless in the summer, and her breasts were as tan as the rest of her. As beautiful as her mother. Then I noticed that Byrne was standing, facing out to sea, the back of his neck burning red. I was puzzled for a moment—then had to smile.

"Kriket, this is Mr. Byrne from Ireland." He nodded quickly, still not facing her, and I waved her inside. "If you have a moment there is something I want to show you."

She looked at me, puzzled, as I waited until the door had closed before I spoke again. "I have a feeling that our guest is not used to naked girls."

"Dads, what on earth do you mean? I'm dressed. . . ."

"Not on top. Be a jagster and pull on one of my shirts. I'll bet you billions to bytes that girls don't flaunt their bare topsides where he comes from."

"How revoltingly ancient." But she was going toward the bedroom when she said it. As I went back to the patio a big white copter was just setting down on the shore. The Irishman was gaping at it as though he had never seen one before. Perhaps he hadn't. This was indeed his day for surprises. A Coast Guard captain and two Shore Patrolmen dropped down and walked briskly to the house. The captain stopped in front of Byrne while the others stood ready, hands resting on their revolvers. He frowned up at the Irishman—who was a head taller—and spoke brusquely.

"I want your name, place of birth, age, name of your vessel, last port of call, port of registry, the reason you have illegally entered our country. . . ."

"Shipwrecked, your honor, shipwrecked," he said in a gentle voice. With an edge to it that might have been laughter. Not really enough for insult, though the captain's scowl deepened as he punched the answers into his hand terminal.

"Remain here," he said when all of the questions had been answered, then turned to me. "I would like to use your phone. Would you show me where it is?"

Everything he had entered into his cellular terminal was already in the base computer, so there was no need for my phone. He was silent until we were inside.

"We have reason to suspect that this is more than a simple case of shipwreck. It has therefore been decided that instead of taking the suspect into custody he will remain here with you where he can be observed. . . ."

"I'm sorry, that is just not possible. I have my work."

Even as I spoke he was stabbing at his hand terminal. Behind me my printer pinged and a sheet dropped into the hopper.

"Yeoman Cohn-Greavy, you have just been recalled to active status in the Coast Guard. You will follow your orders, you will not ask questions, you are now subject to the Official Secrets Act of 2085 and will be courtmartialed if you speak of this matter to anyone." He took up the sheet of paper and handed it to me. "Here is a copy of your orders. The suspect will remain here. All of the pickups in this house have been activated and all conversations are to be recorded. You will have no conversations away from the house. If the suspect leaves the vicinity of this house you will instantly inform us. Do you understand these orders?"

"Aye, aye, sir."

He ignored the sarcasm in my tone, turned and stamped out, waving me after him. I kept my anger down—I had no other choice—and followed meekly after. He ordered the SPs into the copter, then faced the Irishman.

"Although immigration is restricted, there are regulations concerning shipwreck. Until a decision has been reached in your case, you will remain here with Mr. Cohn-Greavy. Since public funds are not available for your welfare, he has volunteered to look after you for the time being. That is all."

Byrne watched the copter leave before he turned to me. "You are a kind man, Mr. Cohn-Greavy. . . ."

"The name is Bil." I wanted no thanks for hospitality I had been ordered to extend.

"You have my thanks, Bil. And Cormac is my Christian name."

The door slid open and Kriket emerged, wearing one of my shirts with the tails knotted at her waist. "I heard the copter. What's happening?"

"Coast Guard patrol. They must have seen me dragging Cormac ashore." The first of many lies; I did not like it. "He'll be staying with me."

"Wonderful. A new beast will liven up the neighborhood."

Cormac flushed at her words and pushed at his sodden clothing. "I beg your pardon. I'm sure I look the beast. . . ."

He blushed harder when she laughed. "Silly man. It's just an expression. A beast is a man, any man. I could call Dads a beast and he wouldn't mind. Are you married, Cormac?"

"I am."

"Good. I like married men. Makes the chase more exciting and sexy. I'm divorced. Twice."

"You'll excuse us, Kriket," I broke in. "I'm going to show Cormac the shower and get him some dry clothes. Then we'll have breakfast out here before it gets too hot."

"Fair-diddly," she agreed. "I'll read the paper—and don't be too long or I'll suspect buggery."

Cormac's skin was now as red as a tomato. I had the feeling that the social customs he was used to did not include the casualness of my daughter's speech. Young people today said things that would have been shocking to my generation. I led the way to the bath, then went to get him some clothes.

"Bil," he called after me. "Could I ask a favor? This shower-bath here—it doesn't have any knobs."

I tried not to smile even though I wasn't sure what knobs on a shower were.

"To turn it on just tell it to. . . . Wait, I'll do it." I poked my head into the shower enclosure. "Thirty-five degrees, soap, on." It burst into steaming life. "After you've lathered just say 'rinse,' then say 'off' when you are through. I'll put some clothes on the bed."

I was on my second cup of coffee when he reappeared. I had laid out a selection and he had, predictably perhaps, chosen dark trousers and a long-sleeved dark shirt.

"What's to feet?" Kriket asked, her fingers poised over the keyboard.

"Translation: What would you like to eat?" I said.

"Whatever's on the fire, thank you, I'm that famished."

"I'll take care of it," Kriket said, touching the keys. I was intrigued and wanted to hear more about this place named Ireland. A fire in the kitchen! I had a vision of it crackling away in the middle of the floor, smoke curling all along the ceiling.

His plate appeared heaped with scrambled eggs, pork chops, fried potatoes, rice, and noodles. Kriket's idea of a joke. But it backfired for he tucked in and looked able to demolish the lot.

"Tell me about Ireland," Kriket said. He smiled and washed down a heroic mouthful with coffee before he spoke.

"What's to say, miss? It's the same place it has always been."

"That's what I mean. All this is strange to you. I saw you bugging your eyes at the copter. Never seen one before?"

"In God's truth, no, though certainly I've read about the creatures and seen their likeness in the books. Nor have I ever seen a fine meal like this appear steaming from a hole in the wall, or ever talked before to a shower. You live in a land of miracles, you do."

"And yourself?"

He laid his fork down and slowly sipped his coffee before he answered.

"I suppose you would think our life primitive, compared to yours, that is. But we're comfortable, well fed, and as happy as anyone is happy in this mortal sphere. The Emerald Isle has always been an underpopulated and agricultural place. When the oil ran out we never had the trouble old England had. None of the riots and shootings. We had it a bit hard at first, of course. People leaving the cities, back to the country when the electricity was turned off and the motorcars stopped running. But peat makes a good fire, and cutting it keeps you warm. A donkey cart will take you most places you want to go, there are trains twice a week now to Dublin and Cork. Fish in the ocean, cattle and sheep in the meadow, it's not a bad life, you know."

"Sounds lovely and primitive, like being back in the Stone Age living in a cave and all that."

"Don't be insulting, Kriket."

"Dads, I'm not! Did I insult you, Cormac?"

"No insult given, none taken."

"See, Dads? Now what was that you said about England? Isn't that part of Ireland?" She was never very strong on geography.

"Not exactly—though the English have thought so from time to time. It's another island, just next to ours. Very industrialized they used to be, right up to the end of the twentieth century. That ended when the oil ran out and the economy collapsed completely. Been well on its way for years, right up to the Second Civil War. North against the south they say, really the rich against the poor. The UNO refused to intervene the way they did in North Ireland, sending in the Swedish troops when the Brits pulled out early one rainy morning. Now Britain is pretty much like Ireland, except for the ruins of the cities of course. Mostly agricultural, though manufacturing still goes on in the Midlands. After all, they did win the war. You're the lucky ones here. The Quick Wars never crossed the Atlantic. Though you did have your troubles. At least that's what the history books say."

"Communist propaganda," Kriket said in firm tones, the way one corrects a child. "We know all about that. Jealousy on their part with the world falling apart and America staying strong and secure."

"I'm sorry. But I am of the opinion that your books have it wrong," he said, all too blandly. "We were always taught that the States sealed their borders tight. An armed wall. . . ."

"We had no choice. It was the only thing possible to protect us against the starving Third Worlders."

"Didn't you add slightly to those Third Worlders?"

This was treacherous ground—and every word of it being recorded. There was nothing I could say, but I hoped he would show more discretion.

"That's nonsense, criminal nonsense! I majored in history and I know. Of course there were some illegal immigrants and they had to be ejected."

"What about the inner city deportations? The Detroit and Harlem trans-shipments?"

Kriket was angry now, her words sharp. "I don't know what kind of communist propaganda they feed you on your little cow-shit-covered island but—"

"Kriket, Cormac is our guest. And the events he mentioned did happen." I had to watch my words now or I would be in trouble myself. "Well before you were born I taught history at Harvard. Of course, that was before it was computerized and closed. You'll find all of the Congressional investigations on the record. Those were hard times, hungry times, and there were excesses. General Schultz, you will remember, died in jail for his part in the Harlem shipments. There were excesses and they were punished. Justice was not only done but seen to be done." That for the record and now to get back on safer ground. "Ireland has one of the oldest and best-known universities in the world, Trinity College. Is it still open?"

"TCD? Who would dare close it? I went to Bellfield myself, one year studying law. Then the brother went down with the Flying Cloud and the money ran out and I went back to the shipyard then to sea like the others. But you said closed, Harvard closed? I can't believe it—in Ireland we've heard of Harvard. Was it a fire or like disaster?"

I smiled at that and shook my head. "Not really closed, Cormac, I said, computerized. Here, I'll show you." I went into the house and accessed my files, took the black disc from the hopper, and returned. Handed it to Cormac. "You've got it there," I said.

He turned it over and over in his hands, rubbed the gold terminals with his fingers, then looked up. "Sure and I'm afraid I don't understand."

"Mass storage. When computer memories went to a molecular level it wasn't long before they could store ten to the sixteenth bytes on a wafer that size. A significant figure."

He shook his head, puzzled.

"The memory capacity of the human brain," Kriket said smugly. "That wafer holds infinitely more than that."

"It contains Harvard University," I said. "All the libraries, the professors, lecturers, lectures, and laboratories. Everyone goes to university now—everyone who can afford the twenty-five dollars that a university costs. I'm in there,

I'm proud to say. All of my best lectures and tutorials. I'm even there in an RS on the early nineteenth-century slave trade. That's what I did my doctorate on."

"An RS?"

"Response Simulation. All the responses are cross-indexed by key words and relationships, and the answers are speaker-simulated. Put simply, it means you sit and talk with me on the screen, and I answer all your questions. In great detail."

"Holy Mother . . ." he said, staring wide-eyed at Harvard University. Then passed it back quickly as though it were burning his fingers.

"What was it you said about boat building?" Kriket asked, politics thankfully forgotten for the moment.

"I worked at it, there in the yard in Arklow. Prime oak forest all around the Wicklow hills. Build fine boats, they do."

"Do you mean *wooden* ships?" she asked, laughing. Cormac was a hard man to anger; he nodded and smiled in return. "Really? It's like something out of prehistory. Dads, can I use your terminal for a moment?"

"Help yourself. Do you remember the access code?"

"Have you forgotten? I stole it when I was fifteen and ran up all those frightening bills. Be right back."

"Excuse me for asking," Cormac said, his eyes never moving as she walked by in front of him, all brown flesh and female. A strange reaction, any American male would have watched her, a visual compliment "With the university closed, where do you teach now?"

"I don't. Retraining for new skills is a requirement these days. You do it two, three times in a lifetime as jobs are eliminated and new ones take their place. Right now I'm a metal dealer."

I caught him looking about and he stopped, embarrassed. "A good business. You keep it behind the house?"

He was even more embarrassed when I laughed: I couldn't help myself. I had a vision of myself cruising the roads in a broken-down truck heaped high with junk.

"I do all my work at the terminal. Wrote my own programs. I keep track of every importer, smelter, and breaker in the country. My computer accesses theirs at local closing time every day and copies their inventory. I know to the gram where every rare metal is at any time. Manufacturers phone in requests, and I arrange for shipments, bill them, and pass on payment minus my commission. I have everything so automated it could almost run itself. Most businesses work that way. It makes life easier."

"You couldn't do that in Ireland. We have only two phones in Arklow and one is at the Guardai barracks. But still—you can't build ships or farm by phone."

"Yes you can. Our farms are fully automated so that less than two percent of the population are farmers. As to ships—here, I'll show you."

I turned on the daylight screen, punched the library menu, then found a shipbuilding film. Cormac gaped at the automated assembly—not a man in sight—as the great plates were moved into place and welded together.

"Not quite the way we build them," he finally said. Kriket came out of the house at this moment and heard him.

"How well do you know your boat business?" she asked.

"Well enough. Built enough of them."

"I hope so, because I just got you a contract. I work on programming for the network. I checked the archives and we have nothing on hand-building a wooden craft. We'll supply tools and wood, pay an advance and commission against points on residuals. . . ."

"Kriket—I haven't the slightest idea what you are talking about."

I interrupted before she could speak again.

"You're being offered a job, Cormac. If you build a small boat from scratch, they'll make a film of it and pay you a lot of money. What do you think?"

"I think that it is madness—and I'll do it! Then I can pay you back, Bil, for your hospitality, which is greater than that of your government's. Do they really not have funds to feed a shipwrecked mariner?"

"This is a cash-and-carry economy. You pay for what you get. And now you can pay, so there is no problem."

Not for him, but for me and those listening ears. There was enough about economics on the tapes for one day.

Kriket's network did not waste time. Next day a skyhook dropped a prefab studio behind the house, fully equipped to Cormac's specifications. The automated cameras, controlled from the studio, tracked him as he tightened the first piece of wood into the vice.

"She's going to be klinker-built, mast forward, a ten-footer," Cormac explained into the mike that hovered above his head.

"What is a footer?" the director asked, his voice coming over the speaker in the ceiling.

"Not footer, feet. Ten feet in length she'll be."

"How many feet in a meter?"

The pager in my watch buzzed and I went to the nearest phone. The screen was dark, which meant something very official, since only the government can legally blank a screen.

"This phone is not secure. Go to one inside the house," the voice ordered. I went to my study, closed the door, and activated the phone there. The speaker was heavyset and grim, as official as his voice.

"I am Gregory, your case officer. I have been through yesterday's tapes, and the suspect is very subversive."

"Really? I thought everything he said was a matter of public record."

"It is not. Subversive statements were made about England. This evening you will lead the conversation to other European states. In particular Bohemia, Napoli, and Georgia. Do you understand?"

"Do I understand that I am now an unpaid police informer?"

He looked at me in cold silence, and I had the feeling that I had gone too far.

"No," he finally said. "You are not unpaid. You are on active duty with the Coast Guard and will receive your salary in addition to your normal income. Will you do this—or will I make a permanent record of your remark about a police informer?"

I knew I was getting a second chance. The permanent record was already made, but attention would not be drawn to it if I cooperated.

"You will have to excuse me. I spoke hastily, without thinking. I will, of course, cooperate with the authorities."

The screen went dark. I saw that there were four orders waiting for me; I punched them up, happy to work and take my mind off the affair at hand.

Kriket became a more frequent visitor in the next weeks, until she was there for dinner nearly every night. Not from any newfound filial responsibility, I was sure. She could never resist a man who offered a real challenge, and Cormac was challenge enough for anyone. The summer was turning into a long, hot one, and they swam every afternoon now when he had finished work. I watched this, had a call from Gregory every day, brought up topics at the dinner table that I had no interest in—and generally began to get very irritated at myself. I put off the moment as long as I could, until I noticed that Kriket was again swimming topless. It was time to act. I changed into swimming trunks as well.

"Hello you two," I said, striding through the bubbling surf toward them. "A scorcher. Mind if I join you for a swim?"

Cormac stepped away from her a bit when I appeared.

"You hate swimming, Dads," she said, looking puzzled.

"Not on a day like this. And I bet I can still outswim you. Out to the buoy and back, what do you say?"

I touched my finger to my lips as I took the pager bracelet off my wrist. Then reached out and unclasped Kriket's necklace with the pendant dolphin that disguised her pager. I held them below the surface of the water and swished them around before I spoke.

"Most people don't realize that these things are two-way. I want this conversation to be private."

"Dads, you're being paranoid. . . ."

"Quite the contrary. Everything said in the house is being recorded by security. They think that Cormac is some kind of spy. I might have kept my silence except for the fact that I don't want you hurt."

I didn't think that he could do it, but Cormac managed to blush under his new tan. Kriket laughed.

"How sweet and medieval, Dads. But I can take care of myself."

"I hope so—although two divorces in three years is not much of a track record. Normally I would say it is your life and leave you to it. But Cormac is a foreign national, illegally in this country, suspected of a major crime."

"I don't believe a word of it! Cormac, sweet beast, tell Dads that he's brain-drained, that you're no spy."

"Your father is right, Kriket. According to your laws I'm here illegally, and they'll put me away as soon as it suits their fancy. I'm for a swim."

He dived in and splashed away. I noticed that he hadn't denied the spy charges. "Think about it," I said, then handed her back her necklace and plunged in as well.

The first of the autumn storms blew the heat away in September. We were watching them film the last of the series with a live interviewer. Thunder was rumbling outside, but the filter circuits would grab the sound and nullify it.

"An ancient craft, nay verily, 'tis an art that is still practiced by aboriginals at the far ends of the world," the interviewer said. "But you have seen the incredibly ancient done right before your eyes, and I know that you, like me, have thrilled to see these lost skills exhumed from the darkness of history at last and displayed for all to see. That's it, cut and end."

"You're finished, then?" Cormac asked.

"In the can and we pull the set tomorrow."

"You do know that you were talking diabolical rubbish?"

"Of course. And you're being paid for it, Charley, don't forget that. With the average mental age of TV viewers hovering around twelve and a half, no one is going to lose money playing to that audience."

"And the boat?"

"Property of the network, Charley, read your contract. It goes with the rest tomorrow."

Cormac rested his hand on the smooth wood, rubbing it lightly. "Treat her well. You'll enjoy sailing in her."

"Going to sell her for money, Charley. Plenty of offers."

"Well, then," Cormac turned his back on the boat, already forgetting her. "If it suits your pleasure, Bil, I would greatly enjoy some of your bourbon, which, while not Irish whiskey, will do until the next bottle of Jamie comes along."

The rain was still lashing down and we ran the few meters to the house.

Kriket went off to dry her hair, and I poured two large drinks.

"Here's to you," he said, raising his. "May the road rise up before you and may you be in heaven a year before the devil knows you're gone."

"Are you saying good-bye?"

"I am. A wee man with bandy legs and a vile disposition, name of Gregory, talked to me today. Asked a lot of political questions—even more than you have. He's coming for me in a few minutes, but I wanted to say good-bye first."

"So quickly? And about those questions, I'm sorry. I simply did as I was asked."

"A man can do no more. I appreciate your hospitality—and would have done the same myself. I have had the money I earned transferred to your account. I can't use it where I'm going."

"That's not fair—"

"It is, and I'll have it no other way."

He raised his head and I heard it too, the sound of a copter almost drowned out by the rain. He stood.

"I would like to go now, before your daughter returns. Say good-bye for me. She's a fine girl. I'll just get my raincoat. I'm not to take anything else."

Then he was gone, and I felt there were things I should have said that would now remain unsaid. The patio door opened and Gregory came in, dripping onto the carpet. His legs were too short for his body, bowed as well. He was far more impressive on the phone.

"I've come for Byrne."

"He told me. He's getting his coat. Isn't this all rather sudden?"

"No. Just in time. We finally pressured the English police. Sent them Byrne's prints from one of your glasses. He's not what he seems."

"He seems to be a sailor, a fisherman, and a boatwright, or whatever they are called."

"Perhaps." His smile was humorless. "He is also a colonel in the Irish Army."

"So I'm a yeoman in the Coast Guard. Is either a crime?"

"I am not here to talk to you. Get him."

"I dislike being ordered about in my own home."

I weakened my protest by doing as he bid. The door to the bath was open, and Kriket was still drying her hair. "Be with you in a moment," she called out over the hum of the machine. I went to Cormac's room and looked in. Closed the door and returned to the living room. Sat and sipped some of my drink before I spoke.

"He's not there."

"Where is he?"

"How should I know?"

His chair went over as he rushed from the room. "In quite a hurry, isn't he?" Kriket said as she came in. "Can I have a drink?"

"Bourbon on the rocks, of course."

I reached out and touched her hair; it was still damp.

"Cormac is gone," I said as I poured the drink.

"So I heard. But he can't get far."

She smiled as she said this and made a very rude signal in the direction of the door. Then sipped demurely as Gregory came back in, streaming water and anger.

"He's gone—and his goddamn ship is gone too. You knew about this."

"Everything said here is being recorded, Gregory," I said, cold anger in my voice. "So watch your accusations, or I'll have you in court. I have co-operated with you every millimeter of the way. My daughter and I were right here when Cormac left. If there is any blame—why, you will just have to blame yourself."

"I'll get him!"

"I doubt it. The sea brought him—and now it will take him away. To report all the government secrets that he learned here." I could not help smiling.

"Are you laughing at me?"

"Yes. You and your kind. This is a free country, and I would like to see it freer. We survived the crises of the twentieth century that wreaked destruction on the rest of the world. But we paid—are still paying—a very high price for this. It is time now that we opened our borders again and rejoined the rest of mankind."

"I know what Cormac was doing here," Kriket said suddenly, and we both turned to look at her. "He was a spy all right. A spy from Europe come to look us over. And I know his reasons, too. He wants to see if we are acceptable to the rest of the human race."

Gregory snorted in disgust and stamped out. For myself—I wasn't so sure. Perhaps Kriket was right.

Moon

ESSAY BY
G. Jeffrey Taylor

SPECULATION BY
William K. Hartmann

EARTH'S MOON: DOORWAY TO THE SOLAR SYSTEM

G. Jeffrey Taylor

ONLY TWELVE PERSONS have visited the Moon so far. Those dozen Earthlings report that our planet's closest neighbor is extraordinarily unlike the blue, oxygen-rich, nurturing planet on which we live. Nevertheless, the Moon—that amazing object that decorates the sky at night; the bright, usually crescent-shaped ornament that inspires lovers, poets, and scientists; that lovely, huge rock in orbit around Earth—clutches to its cratered breast some of the secrets of planet formation and early planetary history.

THE LUNAR LANDSCAPE

The lucky dozen have described a world that is bleak yet awesome, lifeless but filled with adventure. The surface is more barren than the Sahara or the endless ice fields of Antarctica. There are no maples that blaze red in autumn, no crocuses that signal spring's arrival, no grassy meadows to lay in, no streams to wade in. Everywhere you look you see a gray or charcoal surface that lightens to beige near the horizon and is livened here and there by splotches of white surrounding a young crater, like the carnation in a funeral director's lapel. The ground is covered with dust formed by tiny meteorites that have ripped into the defenseless lunar surface and chiseled rocks for billions of years. The dust gets all over your space suit and tools, lunar explorers report, and when you close the hatch of your spaceship and remove your helmet, you notice that moon dirt smells like gunpowder. Some rocks lie strewn in the dirt, like boulders poking up through powdery snow. The rocks are relative newcomers to the Moon's surface, either dislodged by a moonquake or gravity and sent tumbling down a mountainside or delivered a mere few hundred million years ago when a meteorite excavated a crater.

A lifetime of earthly perceptions do not prepare us for lunar hikes. Distances are hard to estimate because no familiar objects dot the landscape. We are as lost as people from the rain forests when they wander onto a plain for the first time. The horizon is only a mile away. Shadows are much darker, and their borders crisper, than on Earth, a consequence of the lack of air on the Moon, so they must be crossed with caution, lest an unseen hazard send you tumbling to the dusty ground. But you would fall in slow motion, the Moon's modest gravity tugging only one-sixth as strongly as Earth's. Thus you might trip on an unseen rock, fall slowly, and bound up again, like falling on a trampoline.

The Moon's landscape may be drab, dusty, dry, and devoid of life, but it is far from a boring, featureless plain. Mountains rise abruptly from lowlands. Craters and steep-walled valleys gash both mountains and plains. Most mountains are the outer margins of enormous craters formed billions of years ago when bodies the size of Rhode Island hit the Moon and violently excavated large, circular basins. Smaller craters are everywhere. Some are too small to see, others are many miles across. Most have been eroded slowly over hundreds of millions of years, as smaller impacts smoothed the original contours, causing even the flattest areas to be undulating plains. Lunar explorers visited several young craters roughly a mile across but dared not go too close to the edge. Young craters (less than 100 million years old) are steep, deep holes—a crater 1 kilometer across is 200 meters deep—surrounded by rugged boulder fields, resembling talus slopes above timberline in the Rockies.

"Why study Moon rocks?" friends ask me. "Are you still finding things out from those rocks after all this time?" Of course we are still discovering more about the Moon, still exploring it without going back for more rocks— yet. A certain kind of truth is tied up in those rocks, carefully encoded by nature to challenge us. And like most truths in life, it takes hard work to uncover it, years of painstaking work, of grueling analysis, contemplative thought, patience with wrong roads taken. The Moon is the most accessible body in the solar system, except the one we live on. We have actual pieces of it, not only pictures of one sort or another. Knowing the Moon helps us know the other planets and how they formed and evolved. To determine what happened early in Earth's history we must study the Moon because the first 700 million years of our planet's history has been destroyed by vigorous geologic activity. The record of events during this crucial period is preserved on the Moon. So a group of us earthbound scientists continue to analyze and think, driven by a passionate desire to know all about the Moon. It peers down at us each night, dominating the mostly dark sky, demanding that we study it, know it, and figure out how it got there.

WHAT THE MOON IS MADE OF

The Moon's overall composition is similar to Earth's in many ways. It most resembles Earth's mantle, that region of Earth between its metallic iron core and the thin crust on which we walk, run, drive, and water our lawns, and from which we extract raw materials to feed our factories. The most profound likeness between Earth and Moon is in the relative abundance of oxygen *isotopes*. (Different isotopes of an element contain the same number of protons in their atomic nuclei but have different numbers of neutrons.) Meteorite studies seem to indicate that the three isotopes of oxygen provide a chemical code that is characteristic of the region of the solar system in which a body was made. Earth and Moon have nearly identical proportions of the three oxygen isotopes, indicating an important kinship. They probably formed in the same region of the solar system.

Although the Moon's composition is similar to Earth's in many ways, there are a few important differences. The most startling is the absence of water or organic chemicals on the Moon. The Moon is dry and lifeless. It also contains smaller amounts of elements that evaporate easily, such as sodium. Finally, the Moon's iron core is only a small percentage of its mass. This is a sharp contrast to Earth, which has a large metallic core. Consequently, Earth has a much larger iron content.

There are two distinct terrains on the Moon. The *highlands* are lighter in color, older, and more rugged than the *maria*, which are darker, younger, and smoother. The highlands are rugged because the lunar crust was bombarded by millions of meteoroids early in its history. These blasted out huge craters, some the size of Texas. The maria formed when lavas flowed across the lunar surface after most of the intense bombardment had ended. The maria still have craters, but far fewer than the highlands.

Rocks of the highlands bear the scars of the fierce bombardment the Moon suffered. Most of them, called *breccias*, are composed of broken fragments of other rocks. Many of the rock fragments inside breccias are themselves breccias, and sometimes inside those fragments are still more breccias. The rocks are as complex and intricate as an Escher lithograph. They show the effects of repeated impacts and attest to the important role impacts played early in planetary history.

Although a few new minerals have been discovered in lunar samples, most are the same old friends that reside in Earth rocks. Highland rocks are rich in a white mineral called feldspar, a silicate compound containing calcium and aluminum. Some rocks are composed almost entirely of feldspar. Others contain less feldspar and more olivine and pyroxene, both of which are silicates of iron and magnesium. Still other highland rocks contain considerable amounts of

Too Beautiful to Have Happened by Accident.

potassium (K), rare earth elements (REE), and phosphorus (P). This chemical trait led a group of scientists at the Johnson Space Center in Houston to nickname these rocks "KREEP."

It took years of research to divide lunar highland rocks into these three broad categories (and into subcategories too complicted and jargon-riddled to go into here). The main stumbling block was, and still is, that so many of the rocks are breccias. The original rock types have been forcibly mixed with one another so intimately that it requires heroic efforts to unravel the mixture. Fortunately, some rocks survived the bombardment and exist as rock fragments inside breccias. Some are smaller than a marble, others the size of a fist. Lunar scientists call these nuggets of the early lunar crust "pristine rocks." And even these have not totally escaped the intense bombardment. Most are cracked and crushed, their original textures (acquired when they crystallized from molten rock called *magma*) obscured by supersonic shock waves generated by huge impacts. A few have survived with their textures intact, and some lunar scientists refer informally to such samples as "virginal."

Scientists can determine the ages of rocks by measuring the abundances of certain radioactive elements and the elements to which they decay. For example, an isotope of potassium decays to one of argon. Most rocks from the highlands have had their radioactive clocks reset by the heat associated with giant impacts. Their ages cluster around 3.9 and 4 billion years, which tells us that the bombardment dwindled at that time. Some of the pristine rocks, the hardy survivors of the blitzkrieg, have ages as old as the Moon itself, 4.6 billion years.

The rocks of the lunar maria are different from those of the highlands. The dark, relatively smooth maria are covered by volcanic lava flows that crystallized to form basalts. Called *mare basalts,* these solidified lavas contain much more olivine and pyroxene (the iron-magnesium silicates) and less feldspar than highland rocks. In addition, the basalts also contain substantial amounts of the mineral ilmenite, an oxide of iron and titanium.

Mare basalts formed inside the Moon when parts of the lunar interior heated up to temperatures sufficient to cause melting. The molten material, or magma, rose toward the surface because it was less dense than its solid surroundings. At the surface, red-hot lava oozed from long cracks in the surface and flowed hundreds of miles, dribbling into low areas. Few volcanoes of the type found in the northwestern United States or Hawaii formed on the Moon because the lunar lavas were more fluid than those on Earth. Ages of lunar samples indicate that most of the volcanic activity on the maria occurred between 3 and 4 billion years ago.

A layer of loose, dusty material covers the Moon in both mare and highland areas. This is the dusty material that soiled the astronauts' space suits. Called the lunar *regolith,* this layer of dust and rock fragments averages only 4.5 to

9 meters thick. It was produced when meteorites ranging in size from those smaller than a red corpuscle to those about the size of a soft-drink vending machine hit the Moon at 16 kilometers per second. For the past 3 to 4 billion years these cosmic bullets have broken rocks and minerals, melted dust and welded it together, added fresh material from time to time, and mixed up the resulting pile of debris. It is an extremely slow process: an astronaut's footprint will last millions of years. Nevertheless, even a slow process can make progress when it operates for billions of years.

THE ORIGIN OF THE MOON

Like archaeologists reconstructing life in ancient Mesopotamia, lunar scientists have reconstructed the Moon's history. This intellectual feat required its own kind of archaeological dig. Some scientists made thousands of analyses of Moon rocks. Others stared at thousands of photographs of the Moon's face. Using computers, another group repeatedly manipulated chemical data obtained from Apollo spacecraft as they orbited the Moon. Geophysicists unraveled the complex seismograms recorded by three moonquake detectors set up by astronauts. Most importantly, the scientists used their imaginations and geological savvy to piece together the Moon's origin and evolution.

The first and perhaps most fundamentally important event is the formation of the Moon. This is the hardest one to figure out, and no significant progress was made until 1984, when a new theory for the Moon's origin blossomed. The three classic hypotheses for the Moon's origin—fission from the Earth, capture by it, and formation with it as a double-planet system—all have distressing flaws.

The notion that Earth's gravity could pull in a fully formed body as large as the Moon has never really caught hold. It is theoretically possible, but the circumstances (mostly concerning the orbits of Earth and Moon around the Sun) are so unusual that the chances of it actually happening are minuscule. A close encounter that did not result in a collision with Earth would fling the Moon into a different orbit around the Sun, and it would probably never meet up with Earth again. Also, if the captured Moon had formed elsewhere in the solar system, as most versions of the capture theory presume, the Moon would have different proportions of oxygen isotopes. A variation of the capture idea proposes that numerous solid bodies, ranging from a few kilometers to hundreds of kilometers in diameter, passed near enough to Earth for gravitational forces to rip off their outer parts, providing the raw materials for the Moon. However, recent calculations show that solid bodies are too strong to lose more than a few percent of their masses when passing close to Earth.

The fission theory, in which the Moon spins off from a rapidly rotating molten Earth, has had a much more distinguished history and still has its dedicated supporters. Its main problem is that in order to spin off the glob of material from which the Moon arose, the primitive Earth would have to be spinning once every 2.5 hours (in contrast to once every twenty-four hours now). Nobody can imagine a way to get Earth to spin that fast. In fact, it is difficult to figure out why Earth is spinning as fast as it is.

The double-planet theory depicts the Moon forming with the Earth. The raw materials for the Moon came from a ring of debris in orbit around Earth. As Earth grew, so did the ring and the fledgling Moon in it. The double-planet idea has fervent proponents and cannot be ruled out yet. However, it has trouble explaining Earth's rotation rate and why the material forming the Moon stayed in orbit around the young Earth, rather than falling into it. (These problems with the rate at which Earth is spinning actually also involve the Moon's orbit around Earth. All this rotating and revolving is expressed as *angular momentum*, a physical property of any system having circular motions.)

The flaws in the classic theories prompted scientists to think about other possibilities. This search has led to a new and dramatic story of the Moon's birth: Earth formed by accreting smaller bodies to it, attracting with its gravity miniplanets the way spilled maple syrup attracts ants. These bodies, called *planetesimals*, were up to a few hundred miles across and had formed from still smaller ones. Near the end of Earth's formation, the new theory goes, while it was still molten but after its large metallic core had formed, the accreting planetesimals had grown to substantial sizes. One or two of them were at least as large as the planet Mars. They had diameters about half of Earth's and masses about 10 percent of Earth's. One of these large leftovers smashed into our fledgling future home at an oblique angle. This cataclysm vaporized and melted great quantities of both Earth and the impactor and deposited some of the hot debris into orbit around Earth. The primitive Moon formed from this material. What a violent beginning for such a beautiful pair of planetary bodies!

The big-impact theory seems to overcome the problems that plagued the disgarded theories. The oblique angle of the impact imparts plenty of rotation to the Earth and the debris delivered into orbit, thus accounting for the total amount of spin, or angular momentum, possessed by the Earth and Moon. The theory explains the large difference in iron content between the two bodies by having the impact take place after the metallic cores in Earth and the impactor had formed. Consequently, the Moon formed from the mantles of Earth and the impactor. Because the large impacting body formed in Earth's neighborhood, the theory also accounts for the identical oxygen isotopic compositions of Earth and the Moon. Finally, calculations that simulate planet formation indicate that the existence of a few bodies as large as the one postulated is not surprising. The monumental impact, therefore, is not only plausible; it may be unavoidable.

LUNAR HISTORY

Regardless of precisely how the Moon formed, studies of lunar samples and of the Moon's surface from orbiting spacecraft demonstrate that when the Moon formed 4.6 billion years ago, it was substantially, perhaps entirely, molten. Lunar scientists call this huge body of molten rock the lunar *magma ocean*. As the Moon cooled, the magma began to solidify. Heavier minerals, such as olivine and pyroxene, sank and tended to concentrate toward the Moon's center. Feldspar, being lighter (less dense), floated and accumulated to form the feldspar-rich highland crust. The concept of the magma ocean was formulated, in fact, as a way of explaining why there is so much feldspar in the highlands. In this scenario, the magma ocean solidified about 4.4 billion years ago.

From 4.4 to about 4 billion years ago, new magmas formed by remelting of the Moon's interior. These magmas forced their way into the solid crust and formed the highland rocks that contain less feldspar than do the older, feldspar-rich ones. Near the end of this period, KREEP rocks formed, again by melting inside the Moon. The KREEP magmas seem to have erupted as lava flowed on the lunar surface. At the same time all this melting was taking place, huge meteorites, probably stragglers from the time when the planets formed, bombarded the Moon. They formed one immense crater on top of another, melting, mixing, and demolishing the original rock formations, reducing the outer few miles of the Moon to a rubble pile. The bombardment lasted until 3.9 billion years ago, when the impact rate decreased drastically.

Beginning around 4 billion years ago the inside of the Moon began to melt again. The areas that melted this time must have been different from those that melted to form highland rocks, because mare basalts began to erupt in large quantities. The heat for the melting came from the decay of radioactive elements such as uranium and thorium. Blazing rivers of lava flowed across the stark, cratered lunar landscape and filled the enormous, circular scars left by the great bombardment. The formerly red-hot lavas are now the dark areas on the Moon.

Mare basalts stopped erupting around 3 billion years ago. The Moon's geological engine stalled, its fuel—heat—apparently exhausted. Not much has happened since then on its bleak surface, except for small impacts reworking the dusty regolith and occasional potent impacts forming craters up to tens of miles across. And, of course, except for several recent visits by curious people and their incredible flying machines.

QUESTIONS AND PROBLEMS

Although the Moon's story as related above is probably correct in general, it lacks detail. We know the basic design of the dress, but we do not know much about the fabric from which it is made or the buttons and bows that decorate it. We do not yet know, for example, the full range of rock types that exist in either the maria or the highlands. New types are discovered each year by examining rocks collected during the Apollo missions to the Moon and the unmanned Russian Luna missions, which snatched an important few ounces of Moon dirt and brought them back to us. Furthermore, telescopic observations of the Moon from Earth provide chemical information that demonstrates that we have directly sampled less than half of the types of mare basalts. Each new rock type is a piece of the jigsaw puzzle; we need more pieces.

The Moon was substantially molten when it formed, but we do not know precisely how extensive the melting was. Was the Moon totally molten? Or molten only in the outer few hundred kilometers? In either case, we must also learn much more about the physics and chemistry of gigantic bodies of magma. We have to understand what happens inside them as they cool and crystallize. Besides additional studies of lunar samples, this requires laboratory experiments, computer calculations, and studies of the largest magma bodies in Earth's crust.

The Moon is asymmetric. Almost all the maria are on the side of the Moon that faces Earth; the KREEP rocks are concentrated on the western half of the Earth side. (The Moon keeps the same hemisphere toward us because Earth's gravity has reached out and grabbed the Moon, locking its rotation.) How did these asymmetries form? Does the crust vary laterally or vertically in composition? Or are the asymmetries surface expressions of compositional variations deep within the Moon? Did the enormous impacts 4 billion years ago produce some of the differences? Or did the large impacts blur even more pronounced, primordial differences? Answering these questions requires continued studies of Moon rocks.

The big-impact theory of the Moon's origin has captivated planetary scientists, but what we do *not* know about the hypothetical event could fill a large crater. Our knowledge of the processes that operate during large impacts has increased dramatically during the past several years. This new level of understanding is due partly to research into the effects of large impacts on life on Earth and partly to the availability of inexpensive yet large and fast computers. Nevertheless, great uncertainties exist about the hypothetical Moon-making impact. How much of the material lifted into orbit around Earth came from the primitive Earth, and how much came from the impacting body? How much of the material was vaporized rather than merely melted? What kinds of chemical processes operated in the hot cloud around Earth? What elements would be lost or gained? The list goes on and on.

Senator Schmitt Samples Subsurface Soil.

THE LUNAR CURATORIAL LABORATORY

American space travelers brought back about (381 kilograms) of rock and dirt from the Moon. Can we still learn from the same rocks after more than 15 years of intense study? Without a doubt!

Most of the treasure is stored at the Lunar Curatorial Laboratory at the Johnson Space Center in Houston, Texas. What a dull name for such a wonderful place! It's more like Mecca or St. Peter's. Those of us who work on Moon rocks receive (usually via registered mail) small fragments for analysis. Sometimes the pieces are smaller than a chocolate chip. But in Houston football-sized chunks of the Moon flaunt their beauty.

The Curatorial Lab is the cleanest place I have ever been. The air is filtered to remove Earthly dust, which might contaminate the lunar samples. The samples are stored in cabinets made of stainless steel and glass, with black rubber gloves protruding like arms beckoning you to reach in and touch a piece of the heavens. Dry nitrogen gas flows through the cabinets, protecting the samples from Earth's oxygen-rich and wet atmosphere. Workers in the lab wear nylon suits, hats, boots, and gloves, affectionately known as "bunny suits."

Except for being as clean as the lunar surface is dusty, the Curatorial Lab has much in common with the Moon. Shades of gray abound: stainless steel, black gloves, speckled gray linoleum tiles on the floor, gray walls, and off-white ceilings. The bunny suits provide splotches of white and serve as our space suits. Perhaps it sounds like a drab, dull, and sterile place, but it isn't at all. It is the ideal showcase for Moon rocks. Lunar samples, like the surface they were collected on, are shades of gray to black, livened with white. The neutral colors let the laboratory stand aside so all your attention is focused on the main attractions.

Working in the Curatorial Lab is always exciting. Not only do you get to see pieces of another world, but you get to heft them. Turn them over. I am still amazed that we actually built spaceships that traveled all the way to the Moon and returned with boxes of rock. That alone is exciting, but I am also filled with a sense of adventure. The spirit of exploration. I look down at a rock, see gray, black, and white areas intermingled in baffling ways. Even after looking at numerous rocks in the lab I am as thrilled as when I saw the Mona Lisa for the first (and only) time. Like her subtle smile, the rocks hide secrets.

Examining and extracting samples from a lunar breccia is surprisingly time-consuming. A slab sawn from one of them is typically half an inch thick and contains hundreds of individual chunks of rocks and minerals. It takes hours to describe the largest quarter of them and to map their locations on photographs. While mapping and describing, we choose likely candidates to extract from the rock. I concentrate on rock fragments that have a good chance of

Alan Bean, Apollo 12 astronaut, taking a sample from the unmanned Surveyor III spacecraft, which had landed two and a half years earlier. The Apollo 12 Lunar Module stands in the background, 600 feet away. Just as Bean and his companion Pete Conrad return to a previous landing site, Earthlings will eventually return to the Moon. But this time they will establish a permanently staffed base.

being pristine—survivors of the cataclysm. Most turn out not to be pristine, and the few that do are usually the smallest, no doubt in accordance with Murphy's Law of Lunar Rock Studies.

Chiseling the samples free from the host rock requires skill and patience. The rock must be photographed before and after each chip breaks off. The careful documentation ensures maximum scientific use of each rock. The chipping and photography are done by skilled laboratory technicians; we klutzes from the outside are not permitted to demolish lunar rocks.

After the samples are described, chosen, chiseled, and photographed, they are sent to several investigators for detailed study. It takes a year or two until the results are available. You've got to be patient in this business.

The 381-kilogram treasure from the Moon will continue to be useful to scientists trying to unravel the Moon's history. In the long run, however, we must return to the Moon and explore it thoroughly. The first step will be to hurtle an unstaffed spacecraft into an orbit around the Moon's poles. The instruments on board will peer down at the Moon with special eyes that will perceive the chemical composition of the entire lunar surface; with other eyes that will determine mineral abundances; with still others that will see the surface as we do. Other instruments will sense the Moon's magnetic and gravity fields. All this is essential before we return in person. Astonishing as it seems, the planet Mars has been mapped and photographed more thoroughly than the Moon.

Important scientific experiments will be done when people once again cross 400,000 kilometers of space to land on the Moon. We must set up instruments such as moonquake detectors to monitor the Moon's vital signs and to deduce its chemical and mineralogical nature at depth. When we return geologists will be able to search for layers of rock that escaped the bombardment—for whole cliffs of pristine rock. This will help us understand the relationship that highland rock types have to each other and to the magma ocean. We will be able to sample all types of mare basalts to help us understand how lunar volcanism changed through time. We will be able to write the Moon's biography in the detail that the fascinating body deserves.

When we return to the Moon this time, I think it will be to stay. Earthlings, hopefully from many nations, will establish a permanently staffed lunar base. The inhabitants will explore the Moon, mine and process its raw materials for use in space, build astronomical observatories, and conduct experiments in physics, chemistry, and biology. Humanity will have taken the first bold move to inhabit the heavens.

HANDPRINTS ON THE MOON

William K. Hartmann

THREE DAYS AFTER OUR ARRIVAL at the Imbrium Base we were rolling across the gray plains of the Moon. Our vehicle—our beetle, as we called it—was brilliant blue-enameled metal and clear plexiglass. I visualized it gleaming in the sun among the dark rocks, crawling with its head down, its antennae up. With its spidery wheels and high carriage, it looked like some sort of Victorian snowmobile. Home away from home away from home. It purred along quietly, kicking up little splashes of dust occasionally as we made a turn. The side windows gave us excellent visibility.

Now that Jack and I had arrived on the Moon, now that we were confronted with the actual lunar desert on the other side of the window, the place seemed curiously disconnected from our training back on Earth—disconnected from the paperwork, from the hustling back and forth between Jack's graduate student cubicle in the Arizona Astronomy Department and my similar digs in Geology. The patient, gray landscape outside seemed anticlimatic to the chaotic prelude that brought us here—the excitement of our bureau-delayed acceptance into the lunar graduate research program, the rush of our orientation trip to rain-swept Washington, D.C., the dash to Kennedy Launch Center.

Jack Constantine made a surreal epic of the story, especially Washington. With each retelling, he made the lecture by—who was it? some undersecretary of state—sound more unreal. Jack mimicked the poor man with a strained, East Coast accent: " 'Make a mark for America,' the guy told us. 'Show the world that even on the Moon our system is more productive than the Soviet system practiced at the Lenin Lab.' This guy was pleasant; he was earnest; he had spent his whole life jockeying for position. His position. America's position."

The building where we convened in Washington impressed Jack. "This auditorium was not just indoors—it was *way* indoors! No windows. I mean, can you imagine those guys trying to run the *world* from rooms with no windows? Even in Imbrium Base we've got some windows, for Crisssake!"

To me, the Washington lecture had sounded okay, Earthside. But now that the real Moon slid by outside, the speech seemed an echo from . . . history. An alien history. The Moon seemed to set its own priorities. The Moon was a place away from jockeying. A place to work.

Jack was getting itchy. He rapped on the window. "Riding in this thing is like going on a damn Gray Line tour."

I pictured us as more like GIs in the back of a big truck, moving to the front lines in one of those old war movies. We were following an old road. It looked like one of those old desert trails in the Southwest's reopened Wilderness Areas. But gray instead of tan. With boulders instead of bushes.

Inside the beetle we had been told to keep our suits on, but we had our helmets and gloves off. There were ten of us, besides the driver and mechanic. I struggled to forget my metal collar ring and tried to relax, to watch, to dream of a history older than could be found in any landscape of Earth. Outside, the sunlight had a peculiar edge. My first long ride across the Moon. I didn't care if I looked like a tourist, gawking out the window.

On the Moon, you don't have to follow the trail; you can drive anywhere across the rolling plain. But there were no tracks wandering off at random. When we asked the driver about it, he said the trail was smoother and faster; the rocks were pressed into the dust. But the unspoken reason slowly dawned on us: Each beetle and each human moving on the Moon left tracks that would still scar the surface in ten million years. The scattered rocks around us had lain still and silent, sunrise and sunset, like monuments, since Copernicus Crater had been blasted into existence. That craggy boulder, sitting out there like a duck: it had been sitting there since the first trilobites wriggled blindly in the dark Cambrian slime under (miracle of miracles in the solar system) *meters of liquid water*! The trilobites had been four hundred thousand kilometers away, in the sky. These silent rocks had watched Earth all those years—witnessed it all. It was sacrilegious to wander off the trail unnecessarily—like smashing in a bus through a museum of crystal.

(My daydream went on as the beetle jostled along. I imagined kids here some day, racing around in their lunar dune buggies, ravaging pristine, million-year-old crater rims, just for the fun of seeing their own trails of destruction: the way they had destroyed the original simulated lunar crater field in a volcanic playa near Flagstaff, where the first Apollo astronauts had trained. . . .)

The trail curved on, detouring around ten-meter craters, bending around an occasional hundred-meter crater, deflecting rarely around the plateaulike rims of thousand-meter craters. Their interiors, invisible from our vantage point beyond their outer walls, tantalized us. The absence of tracks showed

that many had never been visited. Did one of these bowls hold some secret we we missing?

Most small craters, passing just outside the window, were soft and shallow, sandblasted by aeons of meteoritic bombardment. Occasional pits were fresher: stratified lava layers jutted out of the slip-slide gravel of their walls. Fields of boulders were scattered around them, blown out during their explosive births. Impatiently, I fingered the large-format digicam in my lap. In addition to my thesis work on the substructure of the giant-impact basins, I had my own private dream of amassing the best collection of photos of lunar surface structures. Aesthetic but geologically informed—what I perceived as a rare combination. I couldn't wait to get out, find the perfect vantage points that had been missed by earlier workers in their haste to get their samples, to emplace their own special instrument.

Jack Constantine was still excited—puzzled—about why we should get out on the surface so soon after arriving. Usually there was a longer breaking-in period for greenhorns. ". . . so I go in to see the chief about my missing screens. I tell him about this great work I'm doing on the beacon. Not too much, see? Just enough to keep him interested. And I tell him I'm hung up if the screens don't come through."

Jack was telling me this as if we had a conspiracy. He glanced up occasionally at Dr. Irwin, the base director. Irwin sat in the front, reading a journal and conversing with the driver.

"What'd Irwin say?" (If they had been planning a run out to Copernicus today, I thought, why *shouldn't* we get to ride along?)

"Irwin sits there, twinkling his eyes. So I start giving him hell about my scanning screens being bumped by some sort of classified shipments. How you and I went down to the shipping room and they wouldn't tell us why my stuff was bumped."

"Classified? Who *said* classified?"

"Classified . . . secret . . . I don't know. If they won't tell you, it means it's a secret, doesn't it? I got the impression some big shipment of something had displaced my screens, and he wouldn't tell me about it?"

"Who? I mean, who can make secret shipments to the Moon? There's not supposed to be any military involvement out here. It doesn't make sense."

"Well, anyway, I told him. I mean, it's just dumb to send me all the way up here without my screens. The chief just sits back and finally says—he was talking about both of us—'You two guys are intelligent fellows. I'm glad you're here. I want you to understand some things about how this base is run. What they didn't prepare you for are the conflicting pressures I have to try to balance. I have to optimize science, right? And . . .' He just kind of trailed off. Then he says there's a trip on to Copernicus, and that we should come. He says, 'I want you to reserve judgment on what you see, and then we'll talk, after we get back.' "

Later that same day, the chief had ferreted me out, in the labyrinths of the Imbrium Base. He gave me the same pep talk. At the end, he said "Reserve judgment." And then he added, "We've never had anybody come up here who ended up disagreeing with how we operate."

The trail was rising through the hills of the outer rim of Copernicus. Copernicus . . . incredible pit too big to be called a pit . . . the site of a vast, silent explosion. I fingered the digicam in my lap, rehearsing to myself that I would be on the lookout for the special scenes—the key spots that revealed in some clean detail the superhuman processes that had been at work. The explosion nine hundred million years ago on this spot happened when some errant interplanetary mountain fell onto the moon. The crater, blasted out of lava plains, yawns ninety kilometers across. Like a time-lapse flower, it opened in minutes, throwing pulverized rocks and house-sized boulders hundreds of kilometers across the lavas. Today, white streamers, jets of powder and rubble and glass, radiate across the dark plain—the complex pattern of debris. This bright fingerprint is visible to the naked eye from Earth—a bright splotch near the center of the lunar disk.

As we chugged along, now crossing rises and hollows like a boat on the sea, I could remember summer evenings when the moon was high at dusk and I was a boy. We would visit my grandfather in Illinois—he had his own backyard. I would bring my three-foot, homemade, cardboard-and-aluminum telescope. Free of high-school cares for a season, I would spend the long evenings among the fireflies, looking at the Moon. There, shimmering and wavering in the eyepiece, was Copernicus magnified two hundred times, a craggy pit coming into the sun. Morning in Copernicus. The floor was partly shaded by the eastern wall. The west wall was a brilliant arc, glaring in the full light of the rising sun. I could see the rugged slumps and terraces of the walls, sloping down to the circular floor. The floor was broken by the cluster of peaks in the center. Outside the rim, the outer ramparts rose gently like a blister in the dark gray lava plain. Then the mosquitoes would bite and it was time to put the telescope away.

Now we were climbing the hummocky slopes of the blister. Copernicus is so big that you could not look out the front window and say, "Ah, there it is." Instead, the landscape turned more difficult, and the road began twisting more, around peculiar asymmetric pits and dunelike hills. There was a general rise, and the view ahead seemed dominated by an irregular, but not precipitous, range of hills. We were approaching the rim.

81

Finally, high among the hills in a place that looked undistinguished, the beetle halted.

"Time to suit up," Irwin told us. Four of the others—two women and two men—were a team of geologists who had a sampling program. They were first out onto the surface, rushing and bouncing among the boulders that sprouted like bushes. They brandished their gleaming rock hammers and were soon chipping away—silent blows—at carefully selected boulders. These rocks seemed unremarkable from our distance, but were obviously fascinating to them. Putting on our helmets, we tuned to their frequency. In the midst of the sounds of muffled hammer blows and suit rustle, one of the men said, "God, its good to be outside again hitting rocks."

"Typical geologists," Jack muttered as he clamped his helmet.

Irwin scurried past us to the back of the beetle, where he looked at some instruments—perfunctorily, I thought. He returned to Jack and me. "There are a couple things to see here before we get down to business."

After we clambered outside, leaving the driver and mechanic inside, there was a short walk. In spite of the suits we felt light, bouncy, bubbly. Low gravity and high spirits. The trick to lunar walking is to learn to *feel* the ground. With the reduced weight and the lunar dust, you don't have the normal pressure on your heels and balls of your feet, and you get the sensation you are out of balance or tipping over. You bounce till you get used to it. The Newcomers Polka, they called it.

I picked up an apple-sized rock chunk, which I turned over and over as we trudged up the trail. The suits were designed with membranelike fingerpads that gave a good tactile sense: the rock had an abrasive quality. Individual crystals protrude from surfaces that had been literally torn from parent rock during the Copernicus explosion.

The ridge we were climbing looked no different from others we had crossed in the beetle. But overlapping footprints, a churned nimbus of dust darker than the undisturbed surroundings, revealed a trail that many others had taken. As our eye level reached the ridgetop, we knew something was different. There was nothing beyond this ridge but an enormously distant flat horizon. Another step forward revealed the drop to the floor of Copernicus. The hillside dropped away to a steep talus slope, beyond which were more ridges, terraces, canyons, stepping down and down, thousands of meters.

Some scenes, like the ocean surface from a descending aircraft, give no clue to scale. Those patterns—are they swells a hundred meters wide and a hundred meters apart, or waves ten meters wide and ten meters apart, or ripples a meter wide, a meter apart? Boulders, ridges, pits, fissures lightly blanketed with lunar dust. Near ones looked like far ones, big ones, the same shape as little ones.

At first it looked like a view across chaotic badlands. Inky shadows and bright cliffs. Impossible to photograph. Yet slowly it began to cohere. A sweep of the horizon revealed an astonishing unity to the whole scene. That wall on the distant horizon was a continuation of the hill we were standing on. To the left or right, it swept around in a continuous arc—a perfect circle. In the digicam, I could zoom to wide angle and frame the curving arc as a single dark shape emphasized by the shadows on the wall.

The floor was a flat circle in the center, just as I had seen from an Illinois backyard . . . up there. I glanced up. The blue-and-white marble was still there. Were there still boys or girls in backyards looking at Copernicus through homemade telescopes? I fought off an impulse to wave.

The floor was more pocked than I expected. Nearly on the horizon (my mental map, learned in Illinois, told me it was the crater's center) rose the rugged cluster of central peaks. I zoomed for a telephoto view of Mt. Pieters, the summit peak, broken by rugged, upthrust rock masses. The rugged profiles contrasted with the softly rounded forms of most lunar mountains. The inside of Copernicus has not yet been sandblasted by four billion years of meteorites.

Irwin over the suit radio: "What do you think?"

Jack: "I'm not going to open my mouth. Anything I'd say would sound like everything everybody's already said, from Armstrong on. I promised myself I'd never say all those things again."

Lamely, I said it was amazing. The kind of statement you spend the rest of the day improving.

Jack picked up a rock that had been lying in its spot a million years. He turned it over once and spun it out like a bullet over the rim, over the talus. It spun in the sunlight and hardly dropped at all, vanishing instead into the distance in front of us.

Someone's voice came on. "They're here."

We walked back from the rim to the beetle and found that it had been joined by another beetle. Like an American car next to a European car, they had been designed for the same function, but they were different. The second beetle had a hammer and sickle painted on the front.

In the gray hills of the Copernicus rim, our two parties stood facing each other. In the background Russian teams worked in groups of five, stringing cable and examining the larger boulders. A group banging on a rock with glittering hammers could have been members of our party, except for the unfamiliar shape of their helmet visors. I nudged Jack and pointed. "Damn geologists," he said on our frequency.

The chief held up four fingers and clicked his radio to their band. We did the same.

"Late as usual," Irwin boomed out. It was funny how he shouted, as if calling across the street. (He always shouted over the phone link to Earth, too.)

One of the Russians in a space suit with a green helmet waved. "You got a head start." Russian accent. Irwin chuckled as if sharing a private joke.

When we got close to them, the chief waved us over. He took Jack and me by the arm. "Jack, Kevin, I want you to meet Dr. Krinov, director of the Lenin Lab."

I couldn't see him inside the sunscreen visor, but we clasped gloves awkwardly.

It was a bizarre scene. Here was Gregory Krinov, who, in the early nineties, had synthesized the first objects identified as living cells. I remember being taken to some revivalist meeting by an aunt, when I was about ten. This preacher from Tennessee or somewhere said God would look the other way if Krinov, the antichrist, were murdered.

Suddenly I realized that the strangeness of the scene was not in the inhuman contortions of billion-year-old, airless rock, but in the human, political atmosphere enveloping us. The Moon had no real atmosphere, only a political ether; the strangeness lay in it. Meeting the Russians unexpectedly at Copernicus made no sense. It could not be by chance. Crews from Imbrium and Lenin would not turn up in this (godforsaken?—no, it was the realm of the gods) place at the same time. It had to be planned. But such a meeting ran against all policy—at least any policy I ever heard about back home.

Jack remained hidden and silent in his suit. At the time, I felt only confusion. It is hard to explain the strangeness of that first meeting with the Russians. My generation had been raised in the atmosphere of the America's Right movement in the nineties. In the face of spreading inertia-crushed socialist states, the failure of American-style consumption-oriented governments, the ideology-bogged decline of the old Soviet leadership, the movement's name had come to signify not only that America had been correct all along (even if no one else listened), but that (with its unique monopoly on understanding) America had the right to follow her own course, self-sufficient, pursuing space resources, regardless of the rest of the world. We had shut ourselves off.

I had never expected to witness any dealings with the crew of the Russian base. The Russians on the Moon had been presented to us as industrial spies. Everyone smirked when they set up their base a few years after ours went in, in '96. "Oh yeah," they said, "they're just trying to keep tabs on us to see if we learn anything. Just like down here." We were, I suppose, like the generation that was surprised when the shirt-sleeved tractor drivers of Russia put up Earth's first artificial satellite. Even when I got my grant to go to the Paris conference on lunar geology, I got stern advice from State Department officials who told us not to mix with the Russians, Chinese, French—a whole long list of delegates.

It had been that way since the Security Act of 1994.

Yet here was Krinov, talking and bantering. He was not so bad. He had a sense of humor, strained perhaps, and masking a tendency to dodge certain questions. It was a trait I later came to associate with most of them.

Dr. Irwin explained that I was working on problems of geologic substructure under the giant lunar impact basins, and Jack, on astronomy. "It's time for them to broaden their educations," the chief chuckled. "I wanted them to meet you and your associates." ("Reserve judgment," I could hear him thinking at us.)

As if on cue, Krinov called one of the space-suited Russians. "Valentina, take these young gentlemen and show them the cave."

As we left, I saw Irwin handing Krinov a bulky envelope.

Valentina Levin, she was. My first impression was of one more puffy suit, with a yellow helmet.

She led us away from the two beetles and the cluster of figures. We marched downslope, along the wheelprints to a point where footprints led off to the east. We curved between low, rounded hills, pocked here and there with pits and loose rubble. The rocks had abrasive, broken surfaces, remarkably free of the dust that blanketed the older rocks on the Imbrium plain. Occasionally I caught the flash of a crystal or irridescent gleam of glass on a rock surface. Above us, upslope to the left, the rim of Copernicus loomed, disguised once more as another gray ridge.

I watched Valentina's peculiar stride—the graceful ballet of a lunar veteran— and imagined (tried to imagine?) that the movements of her woman's body were different from those of the men around the beetles. Or was it a difference in construction in the Russian suits? "Your Dr. Irwin," she said, "he used to know Krinov back on Earth." She made it sound like an explanation when no question had been asked. "They used to get together and enjoy arguments at all those conferences after we brought back the prebiota samples from Mars."

Suddenly we emerged between two hillocks to stand on a low ridge above a strange, pondlike plain. It was, in fact, a frozen pond—a pond of lava, looking strangely smooth and out of place among the rambling hills and slopes of Copernicus's outer rim. It was a few hundred meters across. Its surface bore faint lines and concentric waves—the original lava textures, layered by a thin blanket of pulverized debris.

"It's a lava pond," I told Jack. "During the impact, volumes of rock were melted. These little lava ponds form in the hollows in the rim structure. One of the current problems is to figure out the mechanics of emplacement—how the lava actually got there. All the big craters have them."

"But this one is special," Valentina said cheerily. She took an enormous leap off the ridge, landing slowly and gracefully on the flat lava surface.

More cautiously, we followed her. Around the edges of the pond, ridges were pushed up and frozen where the lava had lapped against the surrounding slopes and solidified. Frozen waves. Valentina struck out directly across the pond. It was easier to traverse than most of the Moon. There were no loose rocks, little dust to kick up. Soon we were bouncing lightheartedly like kids in a meadow.

"Wait till you see the other end, where the lava came out." I liked the softness in her voice. Each word was like a feather, with soft edges. Less accent than I would have expected. Like most Europeans, she had learned our language well. Personification of the evil we had been conditioned to dread, she suddenly represented merely a foreign life, full of experiences I could never guess at— about which I would like to hear. The kind of lady that Uncle (not mother) had warned me about.

At the far end of the pond, the hills on either side rose in a peculiar bluff. The flow seemed to rise and thicken, with a furrow running up the middle. The smooth lava ended in a pile of rubble, where a part of the bluff seemed to have collapsed, exposing a gaping hole in a sloping surface. The hole was twice the height of a man.

Above the mouth of the cave, on the slope, was an array of solar panels from which cables led into the black cavity.

"Careful." Valentina hopped and bounced her way across the larger rock slabs in the jumble. I framed a picture of the cave mouth, waiting till she clambered into view. She paused on a rock, I snapped, and then she disappeared into the darkness. "Come on!" She couldn't allow us to stand still for a minute.

We picked our way across the rocks.

"I don't understand . . ." Jack was saying, very matter-of-factly.

"You've never seen a lava tube?" Valentina teased him. The teasing came in the way she used her voice. Was it hard or natural to learn to do that in another language? She had mastered it.

"No."

Valentina and I explained it to him. "If you have a big lava flow, it gets sluggish as it starts to solidify. It starts to form a solid crust all around the surface, because the surface is coolest."

"Inside," I added, "it hasn't had time to cool yet. It's insulated by the outer crust. So the flow is still molten inside."

"If a rupture occurs on the outer crust, the inner molten lava flows out and leaves a tunnel behind."

We had all stepped into the tube. As we turned toward the dark interior, Valentina instinctively pushed up the solar visor on her helmet, reminding

Jack and me to do the same. Diffuse light from the landscape outside illuminated the mouth of the cave. Through confused reflections on Valentina's faceplate I could begin to glimpse her face. A hint of Oriental features. Dark eyes. Dark hair, long but pulled back; soft light on high cheekbones with smooth facial planes. She looked intently at me for a moment with dark, open curiosity. From her manner it seemed apparent that she had spent time with many Americans, yet there seemed to be attitude . . . as if she had been waiting for us. Expecting something?

"The walls of lava tubes are often smooth and cylindrical," she concluded, "because of the thermal contours when the lava cools."

I stroked the walls with my fingertips. They were smooth, a gentle curve, unlike the roughness of the rocks outside. I had a vision of some lunar craftsman, finishing the wall with steel wool. Suddenly I was struck by a recollection that H.G. Wells's selenites—the menacing lunar creatures of his story, *The First Men in the Moon*—lived out of sight in lunar caves and tunnels. The place suddenly seemed more spooky.

Jack stroked the curved wall of the tunnel. "What kind of work do you do in here?"

"Come on." Valentina broke out a light and led us back into the darkness, where the tunnel ran for perhaps twenty meters, curving to the right.

The walk back into the tube sent me into another reverie. On a field trip to study basaltic lava emplacement, we had been in Hawaii. On a day off, I had been able to spend an afternoon at a beach on the northwest shore. Our whole party had been there, but Ann and I (dear Ann; I wished she were here instead of back on Earth) had waded out at one end of the beach, around a stubby headland of black lava crags, gleaming from the wet spray of the waves. We had been surprised to find a little inlet, a ten-meter bit of white sand leading into a rounded cave mouth, high enough to walk into. It was a small lava tube, exposed as the waves battered the end of an old flow that had reached the sea. We were hardly the first to discover it, as footprints testified, but it was a mysterious spot. Laughter ceased for a moment as we walked back into its cool darkness, among black monoliths that protruded from the soft sand. We imagined the thousand couples, dotted through twenty centuries of Hawaiian history, who had lain here, looking out through the black-arched entrance to the brilliant blue sky, luminous turquoise water, and glaring white surf of Earth. Reacting less to lust than to simple fellowship in the face of beauty, we held each other before wading back through the waves. . . .

In the darkness of the Moon, in the playing glow of Valentina's light, our way was suddenly blocked by a wall. It appeared to be a wall of thin foil, sealed around the edges of the lava cave. A sealed doorway marked its center. A glass panel exposed only inky blackness on the other side.

Valentina touched a switch and dim light illuminated the rest of the cave, on the other side of the wall. Through the glass we could see the cave narrowing and descending another twenty meters, with the end blocked by a rockfall of loose, jagged boulders. They looked strange without the mantle of dust that softened most rocks on the lunar surface. In the midst of the chamber some instruments sat on the rock floor. They were fed by the cables that ran into the chamber from the solar panels outside.

"The wall is a vapor barrier," Valentina explained. "We have detectors looking for native lunar gases. The wall slows the loss of any vapors coming into the chamber; it gives us a two-hundred-and-fifty-times increase in collection efficiency, according to the calculations."

"What are you talking about?" Jack was agitated. "There're no gases on the Moon. There're no volatiles."

"Of course not, if you're talking crude levels of accuracy—a part per billion. But at some level, the Moon must be emitting gas. Radioactive byproducts, maybe volatiles trapped during accretion. And what about the Copernicus impactor? We're sitting right on top of one of the youngest, freshest craters. If it was caused by the impact of a comet, what happened to the gases released by the comet's ice when it vaporized on impact?"

I chimed in. "Don't forget the radon emissions at Aristarchus."

A smile from Valentina. "Exactly. What better place to look than in a lava tube shielded from solar gases and exterior contamination. A lava tube sitting right on Copernicus, connected to deep fractures. We've got collectors here that have been integrating for a year. Of course, Krinov wants to find comet organics."

Jack was becoming a believer. "Any results yet?"

Valentina's demeanor changed. The enthusiasm in her voice became a flatness. "We haven't analyzed all the results yet."

"But, I mean, Jeez, you've been collecting data for a year!"

"We have to complete the analysis." Flat voice. She turned away from the window.

The Russian curtain had descended. Not a curtain of iron, now, but of gauze. A veil. "We haven't analyzed all the data yet" was the Russian euphemism for, "I'm not allowed to tell you."

Jack started sputtering again. In all the briefings we'd received, hadn't he learned anything about the Russians? I elbowed him as Valentina turned away.

She switched gears deftly. "I'm a biochemist. I'm working with Krinov. His dream is to find organic compounds in primitive lunar material. It's nonsense, of course, but our dialectic is that organic chemistry—perhaps even life itself—should have arisen in many places. If we could find evidence of biosynthesis in lunar material, or in material that hit the Moon, it would help put an end to your ridiculous American theory of a special creation of life unique to the Earth."

A hint of the teasing was returning to her voice. Jack had not caught the hint.

"Now wait a minute. That's no *American* theory. Just because some . . ."

"It was your president who said . . ."

"Don't saddle us with that. He doesn't speak for scientists."

She broke into laughter. "You're so intense. Anyway, that isn't why I brought you here." She set the light on the floor, shining on the ceiling. "Look around. Do you notice anything?"

The light was dim on our side of the foil barrier—a cold, faint glow from the mouth of the tube around the bend, the warm glow of the flashlight off the dark roof, a little light spilling out of the window. Slowly our eyes adapted to the darkness.

Jack was turning one way, then another. Then he stopped. "Oh, my God," he said.

Finally I began to see them. Along the smooth panel of one black lava wall were sixty, a hundred, handprints—black silhouettes with fingers outstretched, outlined in white smudges. It was a scene from the Neolithic caves in France and Spain.

"It was Alexie Pushkov's idea. He's my friend. It's the signature of every human being who's been on the Moon since we started the lab. It's what our ancestors did to assert their humanity . . . when they became concious of themselves starting a new world. We're starting a new world. . . ."

The hands stretched, row on row. It was eerie. I began to feel a tide of pleasure rising after the initial wave of surprise.

"Who?. . . How do you know who's who?"

"There's a record book. One kept here and a copy back in the lab. All the identifications and signatures are recorded."

"I've never heard of this. . . ." Jack's voice was suddenly sullen; the world had kept a secret from him.

"We don't tell them back home. This wall has everyone: Soviets, Americans, French, Indians, English. If we publicized this little joint venture back home, someone might get angry and shut us down. It's our little ceremonial secret, just for those who've put in their time on the Moon. Some day people will be able to come and see this. Some day they'll *want* to—but not now." She picked up a can. "Here." She took my hand, bulky glove and all, and put it on the wall. "Hold still." White mist appeared and disappeared.

"Hey, what about my glove?" I didn't like the idea of my suit fittings gummed up with some kind of paint.

"Well, brush it off before it sticks, silly." The white material flaked off my glove. The white aureole around my black handprint seemed to settle into the wall.

"Very nice, if I do say so." Valentina studied her work.

Jack was chuckling when she enshrined him in the gallery while I signed a book in large script by the dim light. Finally, we stood quietly for a moment. We had performed our mystic rite in the back of the cave. Now we had become conscious. Now we were ready to set out into our own new world to begin the hunt for . . . facts? Ourselves? What is the lunar equivalent of the woolly mammoth?

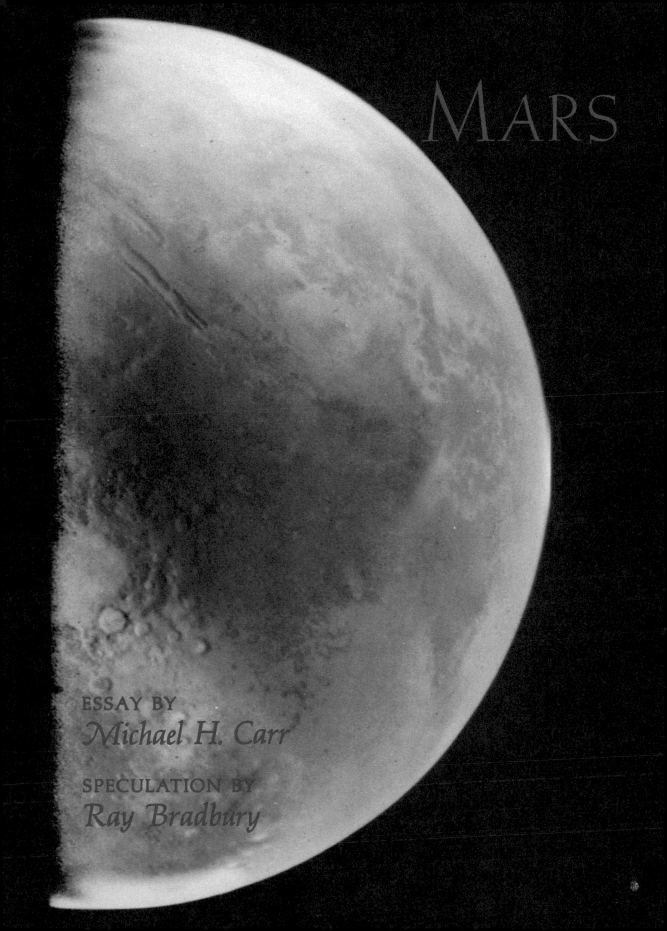

MARS

ESSAY BY
Michael H. Carr

SPECULATION BY
Ray Bradbury

MARS: THE RED PLANET

Michael H. Carr

EXPLORING MARS

ON JULY 20, 1976, the seventh anniversary of Neil Armstrong's historic first walk on the Moon, the Viking 1 lander slowly descended through the Martian atmosphere and settled onto the surface of Chryse Planitia, Mars. The weather there was clear with light breezes from the southwest and occasional gusts up to 50 kilometers per hour. The temperature was −55°C. The expected high was −30°C and the expected low −85°C. The view from the lander was reminiscent of some of the desert landscape of the southwestern United States. Most of the surface was strewn with rocks, all draped with red dust, and in the middle distance were numerous reddish dunes. There was no sign of life. Thus began the most recent episode in our continuing exploration of Mars.

The fourth planet out from the Sun, Mars, has long been an object of fascination for scientists and dreamers alike. Its red color makes it readily identifiable in the night sky. To the ancients the color evoked images of blood and fire, so Mars came to symbolize the carnage and destruction of war. But since the invention of the telescope at the beginning of the seventeenth century, the main fascination of Mars has stemmed from the prospect that life might exist there. For almost three centuries Mars was perceived as Earth-like. Its dark markings were interpreted as oceans, its ice caps were seen to advance and recede with the seasons, and bright spots that came and went were interpreted as clouds. There seemed little reason to doubt that Mars would be hospitable to life, and many prominent eighteenth- and nineteenth-century scientists speculated on what Martians would look like and how we might communicate with them.

A major change in our view of the planet occurred in 1877, when Mars passed by Earth at the unusually close distance of 55 million kilometers. Astronomers everywhere took advantage of this viewing opportunity to observe

Mars at the telescope. During this year the U.S. astronomer Asaph Hall discovered two moons around Mars, which were subsequently named Phobos and Deimos. But it was the observation of the Italian astronomer Schiaparelli that caused the greatest excitement. He thought he saw, during periods of unusually good visibility, a network of linear markings which he termed *canali*, meaning "grooves" or "channels." These "canals" rapidly became the planet's most renowned feature, and they were portrayed on almost every map of Mars published between 1877 and 1970. As astronomers everywhere strained to see the elusive canals, some began to draw elaborate maps which showed oases and lakes where the canals met and deserts in the intervening areas. Canals were also observed in the dark areas, "proving" that these were not oceans as previously thought.

The idea that the canals were built by intelligent beings was vigorously advocated by a Bostonian businessman named Percival Lowell, who, on hearing of the canals, abandoned his business pursuits and devoted the rest of his life to achieving a better understanding of Mars and its canals. He suggested that the canals had been built in response to the progressive drying out of the planet, and that the canals' function was to transport water from the wet poles to the dry equatorial deserts. He speculated further that such an elaborate system could be built and maintained only under an orderly and intelligent society in which war had been forever outlawed.

While only a few scientists held views as extreme as Lowell's, during the first half of this century many believed that Mars had linear markings, and that some form of life probably existed there. These beliefs were shattered in 1965 when Mariner 4, the first spacecraft to visit the planet, sent back to Earth several close-up pictures. Although blurred and indistinct, the pictures revealed a seemingly lifeless, ancient surface that looked much like that of the Moon. There was no sign of the canals. We now think that they existed only in the eyes and imaginations of observers who were straining to view features at the limits of their telescopes.

In 1969, two further missions seemed to confirm the disappointing news that Mars looked more like the Moon than the world envisaged by Percival Lowell. However, Mars continued to deceive us, for when yet another spacecraft, Mariner 9, started to systematically photograph the surface in 1971, it revealed a very un-Moon-like planet, a geologic wonderland with huge volcanoes, deep canyons, enormous dry river beds, and vast dune fields. In turned out that the previous spacecraft had all provided a misleading view by passing over only the most Moon-like parts of the planet. The Mariner 9 results were timely, since by then plans were well underway to land a spacecraft on the planet and look for life.

These plans were brought to fruition with the landing of two Viking space-craft on the planet in 1976. While the landers analyzed materials at the surface and made numerous measurements of surface temperatures, pressures, wind speeds, and so forth, two orbiters photographed the planet from above. The landers also performed the first rigorous tests for living organisms on the red planet. Although these proved negative, the tests do not exclude the possibility that life existed on Mars during some earlier epoch. The increase in our knowledge of Mars during the 1970s was so enormous that today, even though we may not know exactly how the planet evolved to its present state, we have an excellent idea of the nature of the Martian surface and current climatic conditions.

While there are currently no firm plans for manned missions to Mars, we will almost inevitably visit other planets, and Mars will almost certainly be the first, since it is relatively easy to get to, and the most hospitable. Unmanned orbital missions are currently planned for the early 1990s by both the United States and the Soviet Union. Their main intent is to determine the chemical and mineralogical variability of the surface, to monitor meteorological changes, and to get closer looks at the two moons of Mars, Phobos and Deimos. These missions will probably be followed several years later by unmanned vehicles that can roam across the surface, collect samples, and return them to Earth. Meanwhile both the United States and the Soviet Union are developing capabilities that will provide a foundation for manned interplanetary travel. Permanent manned space stations presently being planned for Earth orbit will provide bases for assembly of the complex, bulky spacecraft needed for manned flights beyond the Earth-Moon system. Experience is being gained on the physiological effects of extended space flights, and the unmanned missions to Mars in the 1990s will provide additional engineering information that is needed for sustaining people on the surface. Of special interest, of course, is the availability of water. Thus the necessary first steps toward manned exploration of Mars are already being taken, and its achievement would be a spectacular inauguration for the new millenium that starts with the year 2000.

MARS AND EARTH COMPARED

With a diameter of 6,786 kilometers, Mars is intermediate in size between the Earth (12,756 kilometers) and the Moon (3,476 kilometers). The Martian year is 687 Earth days, almost twice as long as the Earth's, but the Martian day is 24 hours, 40 minutes, almost the same as Earth's. The axis about which Mars spins is tilted 25 degrees so Mars has seasons for the same reason that Earth does: for close to half the year the northern hemisphere is tilted toward the

Sun, and for the other half of the year the southern hemisphere faces the Sun.

The atmosphere on Mars is composed mostly of carbon dioxide, with small amounts of nitrogen and argon and almost no oxygen. It is also very thin, the surface pressure being less than one-hundredth that on Earth. The thin atmosphere and the greater distance of Mars from the Sun cause surface temperatures to be much colder and to have a wider daily range than on Earth. During summer in the middle latitudes, the temperature of the surface may reach 15°C at noon, but at night falls to −80°C, close to the lowest temperatures ever recorded on the surface of Earth. In winter at high latitudes temperatures drop to a chillling −125°C. At this temperature carbon dioxide in the atmosphere starts to freeze out, and the surface becomes covered with dry ice. Thus the polar caps that form in winter and dissipate in the summer are composed of carbon dioxide ice, not water ice as on Earth, although there are small water ice caps right at the poles, under the seasonal caps. So much carbon dioxide freezes out of the atmosphere at midwinter in the south that the air pressure drops by one-third. Another consequence of the tenuous state of the atmosphere and its composition is that the atmosphere absorbs little of the Sun's ultraviolet radiation. Protection from ultraviolet radiation is crucial for life, since the ultraviolet rays tend to destroy the complex organic molecules that comprise living things. On Earth protection is provided largely by a high-altitude ozone layer, which is absent on Mars.

Under these conditions liquid water is unstable everywhere on the surface. If water were brought to the surface, it would rapidly freeze. At low latitudes even water ice is unstable and will slowly evaporate into the atmosphere. Thus, although abundant water ice may be present in and on the ground at high latitudes, materials near the surface at low latitudes are probably devoid of both ice and liquid water. This is puzzling because, as we shall see, the surface shows abundant evidence of having been eroded by running water. It seems that climatic conditions have been considerably different in the past.

One dramatic feature of the current Martian weather patterns is the annual recurrence of gigantic dust storms. During most of the year wind speeds near the surface range from 10 to 15 kilometers per hour. However, during spring and summer in the southern hemisphere winds may gust to 150 to 300 kilometers per hour, raising dust into the atmosphere and creating local dust storms. Once or twice a year the local storms may grow to envelop large regions and possibly the entire planet, thereby obscuring the surface from view for several months. So large are the dust storms that they were identified from telescopic observations long before spacecraft visited the planet.

As a result of these conditions a visitor would find the surface of Mars harsh and inhospitable, providing little more protection to human life than the surface of the Moon. People could walk around only with suits that insulated them from the wide temperature fluctuations, protected them from the ultra-violet radiation and the wind-blown dust, and provided them with oxygen to breathe. However, water, one of the most important necessities for human survival, may be abundant as near-surface ice, particularly at high latitudes.

TAKING A TOUR

A flight across the Martian surface would immediately reveal enormous differences from Earth. Most striking, of course, would be the lack of oceans and vegetation. But one would also be impressed by the numerous impact craters on Mars. Over large areas, craters tens to hundreds of kilometers across stand shoulder to shoulder. These are the areas resembling the Moon that the early Mariner spacecraft photographed. The presence of the craters, each formed by the impact of a large meteorite, is a clear indication that Mars is geologically far less active than Earth. Impact craters have formed at about the same rate on Earth as on Mars, but here on Earth the craters rapidly fill or are eroded away, largely as a result of water action. On Mars infilling and erosion are extremely slow, so slow that many of the large craters have survived from around 4 billion years ago—an epoch near the beginning of the solar system when impacts were much more common than at present.

Although these ancient, heavily cratered areas superficially resemble the lunar highlands, closer examination shows distinctive differences. First, we notice occasional branching valleys that look somewhat like terrestrial river valleys. Although they appear to have formed by running water, the erosion could not have lasted very long, for the ancient landscape is still preserved and large areas are completely unaffected. We will discuss these mysterious channels further in a moment, but we should say right away that they are far too small to be the *canali* that Schiaparelli and Lowell thought they saw.

Second, we notice that the craters look different from those on the Moon. Particularly striking is the appearance of the material that was thrown out of the craters by the impacts. It appears to have had a mudlike consistency and to have flowed across the surface after it fell back to the ground following ejection. The excavated material appears to have contained significant amounts of water, suggesting that abundant water is present at depths below the surface, even though the surface itself is very dry.

Not all the surface consists of large craters. Almost half of the planet is covered with plains on which craters larger than 20 miles across are quite rare. But even these plains have many impact craters that are 2 kilometers across or smaller. We believe the plains formed after the period of heavy meteorite bombardment that ended around 4 billion years ago, but most are still probably over 1 billion years old. Most of the plains are volcanic, for in many places one can see the lobate outlines of huge lava flows, as on the lunar maria. The flows are much larger than those we see on the flanks of volcanoes on Earth and must have formed by eruptions involving enormous volumes of lava. We can tell that the flows formed at different times because they have different numbers of superimposed impact craters.

We know what some of these plains look like on the ground from the Viking lander pictures. They are strewn with blocks of volcanic rock that have been thrown out of nearby impact craters. A reddish-brown dust is draped thickly over the blocks and piled in the lee of boulders. Occasional dunelike hills are comprised of partly cemented dust. The surface bears little resemblance to a terrestrial lava flow. The cumulative effect of hundreds of millions of years of meteorite impacts and dust storms has so modified the surface that the original volcanic features have been destroyed. If we dug through the loose dust we would find, at a shallow depth, a hardpan, or caliche, in which the soil has been cemented by various salts such as sodium chloride and calcium carbonate. The salts have been left behind following upward migration of small amounts of saline water to the surface and subsequent evaporation of the water.

GIANT VOLCANOES

While these vast lava plains may represent the bulk of the volcanic materials erupted onto the planet's surface, the most spectacular results of volcanism are the huge volcanoes. Most lie in a region called Tharsis, centered on the equator at a longitude of around 100 degrees W. In many respects the Tharsis volcanoes resemble those that make up the islands of Hawaii, which form by relatively quiet eruptions of fluid lava rather than by explosive eruptions of ash as at Mount Saint Helens. Like their Hawaiian counterparts, the Martian volcanoes have gently sloping flanks covered with lava flows and a roughly circular crater at their summits. The main difference between the Martian and Hawaiian volcanoes is the enormous size of those on Mars. The largest, Olympus Mons, is 550 kilometers across, and its 90-kilometer diameter summit crater is at an elevation 27,000 meters above the surrounding plains. Thus the volcano is over two and a half times as high as Mount Everest. For comparison, Moana Loa, the largest volcano on Earth is 120 kilometers across and its 2.5-kilometer diameter summit crater is 9,000 meters above the ocean floor.

Olympus Mons is surrounded by steep, outward-facing cliffs that are over 5,000 meters high in places. Numerous lava flows are draped over the cliffs. Apparently, when flows reached the cliffs after traveling down the gentle upper flanks of the volcano, they cascaded over the cliffs, dropping many thousands of feet in gigantic firefalls. Beyond the cliff there is a depression mostly filled with lava that has spilled over the cliffs. The depression is caused by warping of the planet's crust as a result of the tremendous weight of the volcano. The immense size of Olympus Mons and other Martian volcanoes is a result, in part, of the stability of the Martian crust. The Earth's crust is mobile. Differential movement of different sections of the crust creates much of Earth's surface relief, such as the ocean deeps and the linear mountain chains like the Andes and the Himalayas. Because of the constant movement terrestrial volcanoes are short-lived. Old volcanoes become extinct and new ones form on time scales measured in hundreds of thousands of years. In contrast the Mars crust is very stable and volcanoes continue to erupt for hundreds of millions of years, thereby growing to immense sizes. Olympus Mons and some of the other large Martian volcanoes may still be active. Eruptions are probably widely spaced in time, occurring only every few thousand years, but each eruption is probably very large, judging from the size of the flows on the flanks.

FAULTS AND CANYONS

The volcanic region of Tharsis is at the center of a bulge on the Martian surface about 4,000 kilometers across and 8,000 meters high in the middle. Around the bulge, and affecting about one-third of the planet's surface, is an array of faults, pointing away from the bulge and visible as cliffs hundreds of kilometers long and several hundred kilometers high. The faults are almost parallel to one another and, in many places, closely packed to form numerous narrow, steep-sided, linear valleys. To traverse such an area one would have to repeatedly climb a cliff out of a valley, cross the intervening plateau, then climb down a cliff into the adjacent valley. The valleys are, of course, not water-worn, like most terrestrial valleys, but formed by movement along the radial faults. Each movement would be accompanied by a quake that would be felt over large areas of the planet.

The most spectacular result of this faulting is a series of enormous interconnected canyons that stretch for 4,000 kilometers eastward from the center of the bulge in Tharsis. At their western end the canyons have a random orientation and form a labyrinth of intersecting valleys called Noctis Labyrinthus, after Nox, the goddess of night. Farther east the different canyons all extend roughly east-west, radial to the bulge. Many individual canyons are over a hundred kilometers across and over 3,000 meters deep. In the central section three parallel canyons merge to form a depression almost 700 kilometers across and over 8,000 meters deep. This section is so deep that it could contain Mount

(Top) Mars as seen from the Viking 2 Lander (Bottom) Olympus Mons, the largest Martian volcano (NASA)

Everest, and the atmospheric pressure in the deepest parts is two and a half times that on the rim.

Most of the canyon's relief is the result of faulting. Movement along faults radial to Tharsis has formed the steep canyon walls and resulted in down-dropping of the canyon floors. The steep walls have subsequently been eroded, possibly with the aid of groundwater seepage, to form gullies and side canyons, some as large as the Grand Canyon in Arizona. In other places the walls have collapsed in giant landslides, some over 80 kilometers across. Collapse must have been instantaneous, for one can see how the landslides have ridden up and over obstacles in their path. The landsliding was likely triggered by quakes along the faults that form the canyon walls, and aided by the presence of water-saturated materials behind the walls. Movement along faults may also have caused release of groundwater into the canyons, for in many places there are sequences of layered sediments that appear to be water-deposited. Indeed, the canyons may have contained lakes at times in the past. If climatic conditions were similar to the present, the lakes would have rapidly frozen over, but they could have survived for long periods, especially if fed by the seepage of ground-water. Thus, here in the canyons we have additional evidence to support the hint we already had from impact craters that there is abundant groundwater at depths below the Martian surface.

DRY RIVER VALLEYS

To the east the canyons merge into what has been called "chaotic terrain." In these areas the ground has seemingly collapsed over hundreds of square miles to form a surface of jostled blocks at a lower elevation than the surroundings. Emerging from the chaotic terrain are several large channels that extend north-ward for over 1,000 kilometers. In places the channels are over 150 kilometers across and contain numerous teardrop-shaped islands. Geologists have puzzled over the origin of these channels since they were discovered in 1972. Originally there was considerable resistance to accepting the idea that they were formed by water erosion because the Martian surface is so dry, but now most geologists believe that the valleys were formed by floods of water. They differ from most terrestrial valleys in that they emerge full-size from the chaotic terrain, have no tributaries, and maintain their size downstream.

In fact, the channels more closely resemble large terrestrial flood features than typical river valleys. One of the largest floods known on Earth is one that crossed the eastern half of the state of Washington 10,000 to 20,000 years ago. The flood is thought to have resulted from rapid emptying of a lake that covered much of western Montana. The lake was dammed by ice, and the flood followed when the ice dam collapsed. The released water swept over eastern Washington, eroding deep channels, scouring wide swaths of ground, and carving teardrop-shaped islands like those on Mars. Discharges of about one hundred times that of the Amazon River persisted for several days. The resemblance between the large Martian channels and the eastern Washington flood is so close that few geologists doubt that both were formed in a similar manner. One difference is that the Martian floods were larger, possibly having discharges over one thousand times that of the Amazon.

How, then, could such enormous amounts of water be suddenly released, and why do so many of the channels start in collapsed ground? A strong possibility is that the floods were caused by rapid release of groundwater. We have seen that the surface of Mars is extremely cold. Temperatures at the equator are such that the ground is permanently frozen to depths of about a mile. At higher latitudes this permafrost zone is even thicker. The zone acts as a seal, trapping groundwater beneath. The water below the permafrost may be under great pressure, so if the permafrost seal were somehow disrupted, as by a large impact or by faulting, then water would be forced rapidly to the surface. Calculations indicate that under certain circumstances, particularly where there is considerable surface relief, water could be erupted rapidly enough to carve the enormous features that we see. Water would be brought to the surface so rapidly that the deep water-bearing layer itself would disintegrate and its rocky materials carried along with the flood. A void would thus be left below the permafrost and the ground would collapse to form the chaotic terrain that we see. Once released, the water would surge across the surface, creating a wave hundreds of feet high, carrying boulders the size of houses, and cutting the large channels in days or even hours. The floods can be traced northward for hundreds of miles from the vicinity of the canyons near the equator to the low-lying plains between latitudes 30°N and 40°N. Here the floodwater presumably pooled and froze, possibly to form permanent ice sheets, now covered with younger lavas or wind-blown dust and sand.

The floods could form under present climatic conditions. Indeed, the mechanism just described requires that climatic conditions be similar to those at present. Different climatic conditions may, however, be required to form the small branching valleys that are common in the old, heavily cratered highlands. These appear to have formed not by floods but by slow erosion of running water, like most terrestrial valleys. The water may have been derived by slow seepage from the ground or by precipitation from the atmosphere. In either case, conditions would have had to be considerably warmer than at present. Most of the branching valleys are in the oldest parts of the planet's surface. They may, therefore, indicate that the climate early in the planet's history was quite different from the present.

WHERE IS THE MARTIAN WATER?

One puzzling aspect of water on Mars is where it all is now. As we have discussed, some may be buried as ice beneath the surface of the northern plains. We know definitely that there is water ice at the poles. In summer, when most of the carbon dioxide ice has dissipated, a small water ice cap is exposed. This rests on a thick sequence of layered deposits that are believed to be composed of dust and water ice. The deposits can be seen extending out from each pole to the 80 degree latitude circle. They are at least 3,000 meters thick, and the layering, which is visible down to a scale of a few tens of meters, is believed to be caused by variations in the proportions of the two components. Cut into the layers are valleys that spiral out from the pole to give each pole a characteristic summer swirl texture.

The deposits have aroused considerable interest because the layering may preserve a record of variations in climate in the recent geologic past. The Mars rotation axis is inclined 25 degrees to the Sun, but the inclination changes between 15 degrees and 35 degrees on a time scale of 1 million years. On Earth, we believe that just a few degrees change in inclination caused the ice ages. The effects of the larger inclination changes on Mars are thus likely to be substantial. They have probably caused the atmospheric pressure to change by at least a factor of 10 and affected global winds, the incidence of dust storms, and the stability of water ice. Any of these factors could have caused the layering in the polar sediments. However, the climatic changes that result from the inclination variations are unlikely to have been so dramatic that liquid water became stable anywhere on the surface.

The edge of the polar layered deposits is marked by an outward-facing cliff. If we stood in summer on the cliff at the edge of the northern layered deposits near one of the spiral valleys and looked toward the pole, we would see a white rolling plain, covered with snow and ice—a scene resembling Antarctica. Looking across one of the spiral valleys toward the sunlit, south-facing slope we would see several hundred meters of layered sediments, each layer made visible by its own characteristic shade of reddish brown. The shaded north-facing slope would be covered with ice. If we looked south from the cliff edge, the scene would be entirely different. The northern layered deposits are almost completely surrounded by a vast field of dunes, so dunes would extend as far as we could see. The dunes are mostly closely spaced, parallel ridges a few hundred meters across, but in places the ridges break up into individual dunes with crescent outlines. Many of the dunes may still retain frost in shady areas.

While the dune field around the north pole is one of the most obvious results of wind action, we also see the effects of wind elsewhere. Small dune fields occur almost everywhere, but they are especially common inside craters at high southern latitudes. In some places the ground has been scoured by the wind into long curvilinear grooves. In other places, the near surface materials have been partly stripped away to form irregularly shaped hollows. Nevertheless, it is surprising, in view of the repetitive violence of the global dust storms, that we do not see more evidence of wind action. The wind appears to have mostly affected loosely consolidated materials. Hard, coherent rocks have barely been changed despite exposure to millions of dust storms throughout the planet's history. However, ever-present reminders of the action of the wind are the red dust draped over everything and the pale pinkish tinge of the atmosphere caused by the entrained dust.

Thus we see that in many ways Mars resembles Earth. It has an atmosphere, it is volcanically active, and it has a surface that has been modified by wind and water. Despite these similarities, differences between the two planets remain profound. One reason for the differences is their contrasting geologic framework. The Mars crust is stable and not divided into moving plates like Earth's. Thus Mars lacks linear mountain chains, and because of the stable crust its volcanoes and canyons have grown to immense sizes. A second reason for differences with Earth are climatic conditions which greatly hinder the flow of water across the Martian surface. On Earth, water affects everything, tending to reduce areas of high relief and fill low areas with sediments. While there has been some water erosion on Mars, it has had a negligible effect on reducing relief. The result is an active planet with enormous heights and depths on which a wide variety of geologic features are preserved on a grand scale and in almost pristine condition.

Viking 2 photo showing carbon dioxide frost over some of the surface rocks on Mars (NASA image; courtesy of Astronomical Society of the Pacific)

THE LOVE AFFAIR

Ray Bradbury

A MARTIAN CHRONICLES STORY

ALL MORNING LONG the scent was in the clear air, of cut grain or green grass or flowers, Sio didn't know which, he couldn't tell. He would walk down the hill from his secret cave and turn about and raise his fine head and strain his eyes to see, and the breeze blew steadily, raising the tide of sweet odor about him. It was like a spring in autumn. He looked for the dark flowers that clustered under the hard rocks, probing up, but found none. He searched for a sign of grass, that swift tide that rolled over Mars for a brief week each spring, but the land was bone and pebble and the color of blood.

Sio returned to his cave, frowning. He watched the sky and saw the rockets of the Earthmen blaze down, far away, near the newly building towns. Sometimes, at night, he crept in a quiet, swimming silence down the canals by boat, lodged the boat in a hidden place, and then swam, with quiet hands and limbs, to the edge of the fresh towns, and there peered out at the hammering, nailing, painting men, at the men shouting late into the night at their labor of constructing a strange thing upon this planet. He would listen to their odd language and try to understand, and watch the rockets gather up great plumes of beautiful fire and go booming into the stars; an incredible people. And then, alive and undiseased, alone, Sio would return to his cave. Sometimes he walked many miles through the mountains to find others of his own hiding race, a few men, fewer women, to talk to, but now he had a habit of solitude, and lived alone, thinking on the destiny that had finally killed his people. He did not blame the Earthmen; it had been an accidental thing, the disease that had burned his father and mother in their sleep, and burned the fathers and mothers of great multitudes of sons.

He sniffed the air again. That strange aroma. That sweet, drifting scent of compounded flowers and green moss.

"What is it?" He narrowed his golden eyes in four directions.

He was tall and a boy still, though eighteen summers had lengthened the muscles in his arms, and his legs were long from seasons of swimming in the canals and daring to run, take cover, run again, take swift cover, over the blazing dead sea bottoms or going on the long patrols with silver cages to bring back assassin-flowers and fire-lizards to feed them. It seemed that his life had been full of swimming and marching, the things young men do to take their energies and passions, until they are married and a woman soon does what mountains and rivers once did. He had carried the passion for distance and walking later into young manhood than most, and while many another man had been drifting off down the dying canals in a slim boat with a woman like a bas-relief across his body, Sio had continued leaping and sporting, much of the time by himself, often speaking alone to himself. The worry of his parents, he had been, and the despair of women who had watched his shadow lengthening handsomely from the hour of his fourteenth birthday, and nodded to each other, watching the calendar for another year and just *another* year to pass . . .

But since the invasion and the Disease, he had slowed to stillness. His universe was sunken away by death. The sawed and hammered and freshly painted towns were carriers of disease. The weight of so much dying rested heavily on his dreams. Often he woke weeping and put his hands out on the night air. But his parents were gone and it was time, past time, for one special friend, one touching, one love.

The wind was circling and spreading the bright odor. Sio took a deeper breath and felt his flesh warm.

And then there was a sound. It was like a small orchestra playing. The music came up through the narrow stone valley to his cave.

A puff of smoke idled into the sky about a half mile away. Below, by the ancient canal, stood a small house that the men of Earth had built for an archaeological crew, a year ago. It had been abandoned and Sio had crept down to peer into the empty rooms several times, not entering, for he was afraid of the black disease that might touch him.

The music was coming from that house.

"An entire orchestra in that small house?" he wondered, and ran silently down the valley in the early afternoon light.

The house looked empty, despite the music which poured out the open windows. Sio scrambled from rock to rock, taking half an hour to lie within thirty yards of the frightful, dinning house. He lay on his stomach, keeping close to the canal. If anything happened, he could leap into the water and let the current rush him swiftly back into the hills.

The music rose, crashed over the rocks, hummed in the hot air, quivered in his bones. Dust shook from the quaking roof of the house. Paint fell in a soft snowstorm from the peeling wood.

Sio leapt up and dropped back. He could see no orchestra within. Only flowery curtains. The front door stood wide.

The music stopped and started again. The same tune was repeated ten times. And the odor that had lured him down from his stone retreat was thick here, like a clear water moving about his perspiring face.

At last, in a burst of running, he reached the window, looked in.

Upon a low table, a brown machine glistened. In the machine, a silver needle pressed a spinning black disc. The orchestra thundered! Sio stared at the strange device.

The music paused. In that interval of hissing quiet, he heard footsteps. Running, he plunged into the canal.

Falling down under the cool water, he lay at the bottom, holding his breath, waiting. Had it been a trap? Had they lured him down to capture and kill him?

A minute ticked by, bubbles escaped his nostrils. He stirred and rose slowly toward the glassy wet world above.

He was swimming and looking up through the cool green current when he saw her.

Her face was like a white stone above him.

He did not move, nor stir for a moment, but he saw her. He held his breath. He let the current slide him slowly, slowly away, and she was very beautiful, she was from Earth, she had come in a rocket that scorched the land and baked the air, and she was as white as a stone.

The canal water carried him among the hills. He climbed out, dripping.

"She was beautiful," he thought. He sat on the canal rim, gasping. His chest was constricted. The blood burned in his face. He looked at his hands. Was the black disease in him? Had looking at her contaminated him?

I should have gone up, he thought, as she bent down, and clasped my hands to her neck. She killed us, she killed us. He saw her white throat, her white shoulders. What a peculiar color, he thought. But, no, he thought, she did not kill us. It was the disease. In so much whiteness, can darkness stay?

"Did she see me?" He stood up, drying in the sun. He put his hand to his chest, his brown, slender hand. He felt his heart beating rapidly. "Oh," he said. "I saw *her*!"

He walked back to the cave, not slowly, not swiftly. The music still crashed from the house below, like a festival all to itself.

Without speaking, he began, certainly and accurately, to pack his belongings. He threw pieces of phosphorous chalk, food, and several books into a cloth, and tied them up firmly. He saw that his hands shook. He turned his fingers over, his eyes wide. He stood up hurriedly, the small packet under one arm, and walked out of the cave and started up the canyon, away from the music and the strong perfume.

He did not look back.

The sun was going down the sky now. He felt his shadow move away behind to stay where he should have stayed. It was not good, leaving the cave where he had often lived as a child. In that cave he had found for himself a dozen hobbies, developed a hundred tastes. He had hollowed a kiln in the rock and baked himself fresh cakes each day, of a marvelous texture and variety. He had raised grain for food in a little mountain field. He had made himself clear, sparkling wines. He had created musical instruments, flutes of silver and thorn-metal, and small harps. He had written songs. He had built small chairs and woven the fabric of his clothing. And he had painted pictures on the cave walls in crimson and cobalt phosphorous, pictures that glowed through the long nights, pictures of great intricacy and beauty. And he had often read a book of poems that he had written when he was fifteen and which, proudly, but calmly, his parents had read aloud to a select few. It had been a good existence, the cave, his small arts.

As the sun was setting, he reached the top of the mountain pass. The music was gone. Then scent was gone. He sighed and sat to rest a moment before going on over the mountains. He shut his eyes.

A white face came down through green water.

He put his fingers to his shut eyes, feeling.

White arms gestured through currents of rushing tide.

He started up, seized his packet of keepsakes, and was about to hurry off, when the wind shifted.

Faintly, faintly, there was the music. The insane, metallic blaring, music, miles away.

Faintly, the last fragrance of perfume found its way among the rocks.

As the moons were rising, Sio turned and found his way back to the cave.

The cave was cold and alien. He built a fire and ate a small dinner of bread and wild berries from the moss-rocks. So soon, after he had left it, the cave had grown cold and hard. His own breathing sounded strangely off the walls.

He extinguished the fire and lay down to sleep. But now there was a dim shaft of light touching the cave wall. He knew that this light had traveled half a mile up from the windows of the house by the canal. He shut his eyes but the light was there. It was either the light or the music or the smell of flowers. He found himself looking or listening or breathing for any one of the incredible three.

At midnight he stood outside his cave.

Like a bright toy, the house lights were yellow in the valley. In one of the windows, it seemed he saw a figure dancing.

"I must go down and kill her," he said. "*That* is why I came back to the cave. To kill, to bury her."

When he was half asleep, he heard a lost voice say, "You are a great liar." He did not open his eyes.

She lived alone. On the second day, he saw her walking in the foothills. On the third day, she was swimming, swimming for hours, in the canal. On the fourth day and the fifth day, Sio came down nearer and nearer to the house, until, at sunset at the sixth day, with dark closing in, he stood outside the window of the house and watched the woman living there.

She sat at a table upon which stood twenty tiny brass tubes of red color. She slapped a white, cool-looking cream on her face, making a mask. She wiped it on tissues which she threw in a basket. She tested one tube of color, pressing in on her wide lips, clamping her lips together, wiping it, adding another color, wiping *it* off, testing a third, a fifth, a ninth color, touching her cheeks with red, also, tweezing her brows with a silver pincers. Rolling her hair up in incomprehensible devices, she buffed her fingernails while she sang a sweet strange alien song, a song in her own language, a song that must have been very beautiful. She hummed it, tapping her high heels on the hardwood floor. She sang it walking about the room, clothed only in her white body, or lying on the bed in her white flesh, her head down, the yellow hair flaming back to the floor, while she held a fire cylinder to her red red lips, sucking, eyes closed, to let long slow chutes of smoke slip out her pinched nostrils and lazy mouth into great ghost forms on the air. Sio trembled. The ghosts. The strange ghosts from her mouth. So casually. So easily. Without looking at them, she created them.

Her feet, when she arose, exploded on the hardwood floor. Again she sang. She whirled about. She sang to the ceiling. She snapped her fingers. She put her hands out, like birds, flying, and danced alone, her heels cracking the floor, around, around.

The alien song. He wished he could understand. He wished that he had the ability that some of his own people often had, to project the mind, to read, to know, to interpret, instantly; foreign tongues, foreign thoughts. He tried. But there was nothing. She went on singing the beautiful, unknown song, none of which he could understand:

"Ain't Misbehavin', I'm savin' my love for you . . . "

He grew faint, watching her Earth body, her Earth beauty, so totally different, something from so many millions of miles away. His hands were moist, his eyelids jerked unpleasantly.

A bell rang.

There she was, picking up a strange black instrument, the function of which was not unlike a similar device of Sio's people.

"Hello, Janice? God, it's good to hear from you!"

109

Sio smiled. She was talking to a distant town. Her voice was thrilling to hear. But what were the words?

"God, Janice, what a hell-out-of-the-way place you sent me to. I know, honey, a vacation. But, it's sixty miles from Nowhere. All I do is play cards and swim in the damned canal."

The black machine buzzed in reply.

"I can't stand it here, Janice. I know, I know. The churches. It's a damn shame they ever came up here. Everything was going so nice. What *I* want to know is when do we open up again?"

Lovely, thought Sio. Gracious. Incredible. He stood in the night beyond her open window, looking at her amazing face and body. And what were they talking about? Art, literature, music, yes, music, for she sang, she sang all of the time. An odd music, but one could not expect to understand the music of another world. Or the customs or the language or the literature. One must judge by instinct alone. The old ideas must be set aside. It was to be admitted that her beauty was not like Martian beauty, the soft slim brown beauty of the dying race. His mother had had golden eyes and slender hips. But here, this one, singing alone in the desert, she was of larger stuffs, large breasts, large hips, and the legs, yes, of white fire, and the peculiar custom of walking about without clothes, with only those strange knocking slippers on the feet. But all women of Earth did that, yes? He nodded. You must understand. The women of that far world, naked, yellow-haired, large-bodied, loud-heeled, he could see them. And the magic with the mouth and nostrils. The ghosts, the souls issuing from the lips in smoky patterns. Certainly a magical creature of fire and imagination. She shaped bodies in the air, with her brilliant mind. What else but a mind of clarity and clear genius could drink the gray-cherryred fire, and plume out architectural perfections of intricate and fine beauty from her nostrils. The genius! An artist! A creator! How was it done, how many years might one study to do this? How did one apply one's time? His head whirled with her presence. He felt he must cry out to her, "Teach me!" But he was afraid. He felt like a child. He saw the forms, the lines, the smoke swirl into infinity. She was here, in the wilderness, to be alone, to create her fantasies in absolute security, unwatched. One did not bother creators, writers, painters. One stood back and kept one's thoughts silent.

What a people! he thought. Are all of the women of that fiery green world like this? Are they fiery ghosts and music? Do they walk blazingly naked in their loud houses?

"I must watch this," he said, half aloud. "I must study." He felt his hands curl. He wanted to touch. He wanted her to sing for him, to construct the artistic fragments in the air for him, to teach him, to tell him about that far gone world and its books and its fine music . . .

"God, Janice, but how soon? What about the other girls? What about the other towns?"

The telephone burred like an insect.

"All of them closed down? On the whole damn planet? There must be *one* place! If you don't find a place for me soon, I'll. . . !"

Everything was strange about. It was like seeing a woman for the first time. The way she held her head back, the way she moved her red-fingernailed hands, all new and different. She crossed her white legs, leaning forward, her elbow on a bare knee, summoning and exhaling spirits, talking, squinting at the window where he, yes, he stood in shadow, she looked right through him, oh, if she knew, what would she do?

"Who, me, afraid of living out here alone?"

She laughed, Sio laughed in cadence, in the moonlit darkness. Oh the beauty of her alien laughter, her head thrown back, the mystic clouds jetting and shaping from her nostrils.

He had to turn away from the window, gasping.

"Yeah! Sure!"

What fine rare words of living, music, poetry was she speaking now?

"Well, Janice, who's afraid of any Martian? How many are left, a dozen, two dozen. Line 'em up, bring 'em on, right? Right!"

Her laughter followed as he stumbled blindly around the corner of her house, his feet thrashing a litter of bottles. Eyes shut, he saw the print of her phosphorous skin, the phantoms leaping from her mouth in sorceries and evocations of cloud, rain and wind. Oh, to translate! Oh, gods, to *know*. Listen! What's that word, and that, and, yes then, that!? Did she call out after him. No. Was that his name?

At the cave he ate but was not hungry.

He sat in the mouth of the cave for an hour, as the moons rose and hurtled across the cold sky and he saw his breath on the air, like the spirits, the fiery silences that breathed about her face, and she was talking, talking, he heard or did not hear her voice moving up the hill, among the rocks, and he could smell her breath, that breath of smoking promise, of warm words heated in her mouth.

And at last he thought, I will go down and speak to her very quietly, and speak to her every night until she understands what I say and I know her words and she then comes with me back into the hills where we will be content. I will tell her of my people and my being alone and how I have watched her and listened to her for so many nights . . .

But . . . *she is Death.*

He shivered. The thought, the words would not go away.

How could he have forgotten?

He need only touch her hand, her cheek, and he would wither in a few hours, a week at the latest. He would change color and fall in folds of ink and turn to ash, black fragments of leaf that would break and fly away in the wind.

One touch and . . . Death.

But a further thought came. She lives alone, away from the others of her race. She must like her own thoughts, to be so much apart. Are we not the same, then? And, because she is separate from the towns, perhaps the Death is not in her. . . ? Yes! Perhaps!

How fine to be with her for a day, a week, a month, to swim with her in the canals, to walk in the hills and have her sing that strange song and he, in turn, would touch the old harp books and let them sing back to her! Wouldn't that be worth anything, everything? A man died when he was alone, did he not? So, consider the yellow lights in the house below. A month of real understanding and being and living with beauty and a maker of ghosts, the souls that came from the mouth, wouldn't it be a chance worth taking? And if death came . . . how fine and original it would be!

He stood up. He moved. He lit a candle in a niche of the cave where the images of his parents trembled in the light. Outside, the dark flowers waited for the dawn when they would quiver and open and she would be here to see them and tend them and walk with him in the hills. The moons were gone now. He had to fix his special sight to see the way.

He listened. Below in the night, the music played. Below in the dark, her voice spoke wonders across time. Below in the shadows, her white flesh burned, and the ghosts danced about her head.

He moved swiftly now.

At precisely ninety-forty-five that night, she heard the soft tapping at her front door.

JUPITER

ESSAY BY
Joseph Veverka

SPECULATION BY
Gregory Benford

JUPITER'S WORLD: A COLOSSAL REALM

Joseph Veverka

IN LATE 1988 after a voyage of more than two years NASA's Project Galileo Probe will penetrate the clouds of Jupiter and become the first spacecraft ever to investigate directly the atmosphere of a giant planet. Atmospheric friction will rapidly slow the probe down from its initial entry speed of over 1,500 kilometers an hour, releasing so much heat that about one-half of the probe's mass (consisting of heat shields) will vaporize away, producing a spectacular fireball.

Having survived its fiery entry, the probe will descend deeper and deeper into Jupiter's atmosphere, making precise measurements of conditions below the planet's outermost clouds. Unlike Earth, Jupiter does not have a solid surface. As the probe descends deeper and deeper, it will encounter higher and higher pressures and temperatures; some 30 minutes after entry, the probe's signals will finally be silenced, but those 30 minutes of data should profoundly improve our understanding of our solar system's largest planet.

As inhabitants of a tiny planet we find it difficult to appreciate how colossal Jupiter actually is. Saying that its diameter is almost twelve times that of Earth, or that its mass exceeds that of our planet by more than 300 times, may be impressive statistics, but they are difficult for most of us to comprehend. To state it more dramatically, it would take more than 1,000 Earths to make up the volume of Jupiter, and that if we lumped all the other known planets (including Earth) together, we would make up no more than about one-third of Jupiter's bulk.

Named appropriately after the most powerful god of the Roman pantheon, Jupiter's gravitational influence pervades the solar system. The planet's pull is known to alter drastically the orbits of passing comets and has been postulated to be responsible for the existence of the asteroid belt: the idea is that Jupiter's powerful presence prevented the buildup of a single large planet between its orbit and that of Mars. For thousands of years, astrologers have endowed it with strange influences on human destiny; more recently, but no less fancifully, it was invoked as the indirect cause of devastating earthquakes in southern California, and presumably elsewhere on Earth.

While the Galileo probe will be the first to penetrate Jupiter's multilayered clouds, it will not be the first spacecraft to explore Jupiter's neighborhood. Four American spacecraft, two Pioneers and two Voyagers, flew by the planet during the 1970s. Pioneer 10 in 1973 and Pioneer 11 in 1974 mapped out the planet's intense magnetic field and provided detailed measurements of its gravity field. These precise gravity measurements proved beyond serious doubt that Jupiter is a vast fluid planet, with no solid surface anywhere below its clouds. In 1979, Voyager 1 and 2 provided a wealth of new data about the planet and its retinue of satellites. Color movies vividly documented the complex cloud motions in Jupiter's brightly colored atmosphere. Many spectacular discoveries were made: the planet has a ring; one of its satellites is volcanically active; lightning is common in the planet's atmosphere. Yet, in terms of detailed knowledge about the planet itself, the Voyager results did not yield all the answers. What lies below the topmost layer of visible clouds? What produces the striking colors of these clouds? These are only two examples of fundamental questions left unaddressed by Voyager—questions which Galileo is specifically designed to answer.

JUPITER: A VERY DIFFERENT PLANET

Jupiter is very different from Earth, not merely in size but also in terms of other important physical attributes. In fact, in our solar system the asteroid belt defines a convenient demarcation line between the inner planets (like Earth) and the outer planets (like Jupiter). The inner planets tend to be small rocky bodies. With the exception of Mercury, they have atmospheres that are rich in either oxygen or oxygen compounds. They have few, if any, satellites and no rings. Pluto aside, planets beyond the asteroid belt are much larger and made of stuff quite different from that of the closer planets. Like the Sun, Jupiter and Saturn consist predominantly of the simplest elements, hydrogen and helium. Uranus and Neptune have somewhat larger proportions of ice-forming materials, such as water, methane, and ammonia, in addition to hydrogen and helium. Planets like Jupiter and Saturn almost certainly do not have solid surfaces. Most outer planets have an abundance of satellites, and at least three of the four have rings.

Since the deep interior of Jupiter cannot be explored directly, the inside of the planet is a scientific puzzle. An essential first clue in solving the puzzle is the planet's low mean density: an average cubic centimeter of Jupiter has a mass of only 1.3 grams, or about four times less than the material making up our Earth. Clearly, Jupiter is made of much lighter stuff. Precise calculations show that one can reproduce the size, mass, and density of the planet by using a chemical mix of elements identical with that of the Sun: by mass almost 75 percent hydrogen, 25 percent helium, and less than 1 percent of all the remaining elements. Both Jupiter and the Sun are believed to have much the same composition as the nebula out of which our solar system condensed about 4.6 billion years ago. (Small planets like Earth were always gravitationally too weak to hold on to very light gases such as hydrogen and helium effectively.)

It may sound paradoxical to say that Jupiter and the Sun have identical chemical compositions, given that one is a planet and the other a star. The difference is one of size. Consider the collapse of a cloud of hydrogen and helium under the influence of gravity. As the collapse proceeds, energy is released, and the gases heat up until enough pressure is produced inside the body to balance gravity and stop the collapse. Whether our object becomes a planet or a star depends on the temperature reached deep inside at the end of the collapse stage. In turn, this temperature depends critically on the total mass that has collapsed: the more mass, the more energy released during the collapse, the higher the temperature reached. If the temperature reached is high enough for nuclear reactions to begin (specifically for hydrogen to fuse into helium when atoms collide), the body can tap an efficient source of energy and a star is born.

If the maximum temperature reached after collapse falls short of the critical limit, the body is a star that failed. Never able to generate internal energy through nuclear reactions, it is doomed to slowly lose the heat that was stored within it upon collapse, with no hope of replenishing it in any significant way. This is what happened to Jupiter. Jupiter is simply too small to have become a star—but not by much. Calculations show that had its initial mass been greater by only a factor of 10, it would have become a very faint red star.

Even though Jupiter did not have the mass to make it as a star, there is still significant heat leaking out of the planet today, heat that was stored deep in the interior when the planet formed 4.6 billion years ago. A simple way of understanding the source of this heat is to realize that it would take a lot of work—or energy—to take a massive planet like Jupiter apart piece by piece. Since a large input of energy would be needed to break Jupiter apart into individual, widely separated atoms, a lot of energy must have been released when the reverse process occurred during the formation of the solar system. Some of this energy was radiated away at the time, but some of it remained trapped in the deep interior and has been leaking out slowly ever since. Measurements suggest that right now Jupiter is losing about as much heat from its interior as it receives from the Sun. Owing to this heat loss, Jupiter is still cooling very, very slowly, and as it does its radius contracts very gradually.

There are no direct ways of probing the deep interior of the planet, but calculations suggest that the temperature increases with depth at an average rate of about a third of a degree every kilometer. Since the cloud tops are near 125°K, temperatures of about 20,000°K are attained near the center. These considerations, and clues derived from precise measurements of the gravity field and shape of the planet, strongly indicate that the planet is fluid throughout. We believe that approximately the outer one-quarter of the planet (by radius) consists of a shell of hydrogen in molecular form (with helium and other atoms mixed into it). The visible clouds form the outermost layers of this "atmospheric" shell. Some 17,000 kilometers below the visible clouds the pressure is about 3 million times higher than that at Earth's surface. This is the critical pressure at which molecular hydrogen turns into "metallic" hydrogen. For our purposes the transition may be viewed rather simply. As the pressure increases, the atoms and molecules are pressed closer and closer together: at some point electrons are no longer associated with individual atoms, but are free to wander throughout the material as they do in a metal.

One important consequence of such a change is that the electrical conductivity of the substance goes up dramatically. It is believed that motions in this fluid conductive layer give rise to currents, which produce Jupiter's intense magnetic field. This field, which at the surface is more than twenty times as powerful as that of Earth, controls a vast sea of energetic charged particles (mostly electrons and protons), analogous to Earth's Van Allen radiation belts. The charged particles in Jupiter's vicinity have a strong influence on the surfaces of some inner satellites and on the particles that make up Jupiter's ring. An indication of the extensive influence of Jupiter's magnetic field is that the Voyager spacecraft found that its effects at times extend out to the next planet, Saturn, a distance of over 600 million kilometers.

At the very heart of Jupiter may be a concentration of heavier atoms. The size and state of this "rocky core" is uncertain, but it is unlikely to be solid. Thus, the largest planet of our solar system is fluid throughout its bulk. Estimates of the pressure at the very center are an astounding 100 million bars— 1 million times more than at the surface of Earth, and over 25 times more than the pressure at the center of Earth.

JUPITER'S ATMOSPHERE

It is important to realize that our speculations about the interior of Jupiter are based on inference, rather than direct observation. When we look at Jupiter from the outside, what we see is a vividly colored planet, its clouds arranged in alternate bands of bluish-white "zones" and orange-red "belts." The immediate impression is that of a very dynamically active atmosphere. Winds as high as 200 kilometers per hour have been measured. An old suggestion is that the zones may be regions of updraft, while the belts correspond to downdrafts.

An important question concerning Jupiter's atmosphere is whether the circulation is shallow and driven primarily by solar energy (as are the winds in the atmosphere of Earth) or deep-seated and controlled significantly by the planet's internal heat. In the latter case, it is conceivable that if the Sun's power were suddenly turned off, the meteorology of Jupiter would be little affected. While Voyager movies document in detail very complex patterns of wind motion near the planet's cloud tops, there is little direct information on how deeply into the atmosphere these motions reach.

We also do not understand some of the large oval cloud patterns that are so conspicuous on Jupiter. The largest, the Great Red Spot, has existed for at least three centuries. Voyager images and detailed photographs from Earth show that the Great Red Spot—a feature some 40,000 kilometers long into which three Earths could fit side by side—whirls around in a counterclockwise direction once every six days. This spot and the smaller ovals have been likened to large, whirling storm systems on Earth. A particular puzzle is why the largest, the Great Red Spot, is red, whereas the smaller ones (which typically last for decades) are whitish like the zones. In fact, we know very little about what determines the colors of any of Jupiter's clouds.

While the spectroscopic techniques that we use to study Jupiter from the outside are very sensitive for detecting the gaseous constituents of the atmosphere, they are not very effective for determining the composition of the cloud particles. From spectroscopy we know that in addition to hydrogen and helium, the atmosphere near the visible clouds contains ammonia, methane, more complex hydrocarbons such as ethane, traces of water vapor, and unusual gases such as phosphene (a compound of hydrogen and phosphorus). But most of our ideas about the composition of the clouds come from indirect arguments, such as those worked out by the American cosmochemist John Lewis. His calculations suggest that the existence of at least three cloud layers is likely. The uppermost layer is almost certainly a cirruslike haze of ammonia crystals, thickest in the bluish-white zones and very thin or absent in the belts. Theoretically, the next layer should consist of ammonium hydrosulfate, a colorless substance that by itself cannot account for the reddish color of the belts. Various suggestions have been made that the reddish color seen in the belts is due to a reaction product—something that forms from the ammonium hydrosulfate, perhaps as a result of lightning in Jupiter's clouds. It has been proposed variously that the reddish colors seen in the belts are due to sulfur, or sulfur compounds, or nitrogen compounds, or even organic compounds. Voyager images show a whole range of colors in Jupiter's clouds: light blues, pale yellows, vivid reds, deep browns, and so on. It is likely that more than one *chromophore*, or coloring material, is involved, but at present we cannot conclusively identify a single one. It has even been suggested that some of the very red colors—such as those in the Great Red Spot—are due to red phosphorus, a breakdown product of the gas phosphene.

A major goal for the Galileo probe will be to explore the nature of the outermost clouds and determine what lies below them. The probe can measure the temperature, pressure, and composition of gases; it can also determine various properties of the cloud layers through which it descends. It is expected that the probe will first penetrate the layer of ammonia clouds somewhere near a pressure of 0.5 bars and a temperature of 125°K. (One bar is the atmospheric pressure at the surface of the Earth.) Some 60 kilometers lower, it should encounter the hypothesized ammonium hydrosulfate cloud layer and perhaps solve the mystery of the reddish chromophores in Jupiter's clouds. Deeper still, the probe should run into a layer of water clouds. Evidence of water clouds has been obtained spectroscopically by peering through occasional breaks in the upper cloud layers; their presence is also indicated by model calculations. It will take the Galileo probe some 30 minutes to reach this level. By the time that the probe has reached well within the water cloud layer at some 100 kilometers below the visible cloud tops, it should be recording pressures of about 10 bars and temperatures of 300°K. Soon after, the probe's weak signals will no longer reach the orbiter and the probe's mission will be over. It will continue to sink deeper into Jupiter's atmosphere until it is crushed by high pressures or eventually vaporized by high temperature. Certainly, it will never reach a solid surface.

After the probe's brief but spectacular descent we should know precisely the vertical structure of the cloud layers in Jupiter's atmosphere and the composition of the different clouds. We should thereby have solved the vexing problem of what it is that colors the clouds of the giant planet. True, the probe's measurements will be made only at a single point, but they should suffice to indicate whether our basic ideas about the planet's clouds are correct.

JUPITER'S RETINUE

Appropriately for the Sun's largest planet, Jupiter has the most massive satellite system, and one which includes the largest moon in the Sun's family. Ganymede, with its radius of 2,630 kilometers (about 1.5 times bigger than our Moon), is larger than the two smallest planets, Pluto and Mercury. Right now we know of sixteen satellites of Jupiter, the smallest being only tens of kilometers wide and therefore extremely difficult to observe at Jupiter's distance from Earth. Four of these small bodies have been discovered within the past decade, and almost certainly more exist.

Of Jupiter's four large satellites—called the Galilean satellites after one of their discoverers—Ganymede is the largest and Europa, with a radius of 1,570 kilometers (0.9 times the size of our Moon), is the smallest. For a long time we have known that these four bodies have average densities that increase with increasing distance from Jupiter. Thus, the material that the four satellites are made of must differ. The two inner ones, Io and Europa, have densities comparable to that of our Moon and must, therefore, be predominantly rocky bodies like our own satellite. The outer two, Ganymede and Callisto, have densities below 2 grams per centimeter, indicating that by bulk they are about half water ice and half rock. This trend in composition—rocky bodies close in and more volatile objects farther out—is reminiscent of our solar system. There is a standard explanation for this planetary pattern: Close to the forming Sun temperatures were too hot for ices to condense and only rocky bodies formed; farther out where temperatures were cooler, the condensing bodies incorporated both rock and ice. So it appears to be with the Galilean satellites in the vicinity of forming Jupiter. Calculations show that early on, Jupiter was considerably hotter than it is today and that its heat had a profound effect on what materials could condense in its neighborhood. Temperatures were too hot at the distances at which Io and Europa formed for these bodies to accumulate much ice, contrary to the situation for more remote Ganymede and Callisto.

CALLISTO

Today on Callisto we see an ancient, very heavily cratered, icy surface. Like Europa and Ganymede, Callisto does not have an atmosphere. There is clear evidence that some of the giant impact scars—for example, the "bullseye" feature called Valhalla—were formed at a very distant epoch, when part of the icy crust may have been molten, or at least somewhat soft. The heat responsible was derived either from radioactive material in the rocky component of Callisto or from the gravitational energy released during the satellite's formation. In either case, the heat waned after a billion years or so. Today Callisto has a rigid crust of cold ice, a crust cratered by the impacts of stray meteoroids.

Callisto's heavily cratered surface is a constant reminder that the number of impacting objects hitting the Galilean satellites has been significant throughout the period of existence of the solar system. Therefore, unless strong internal geologic activity occurred on the other three Galilean satellites, we must expect

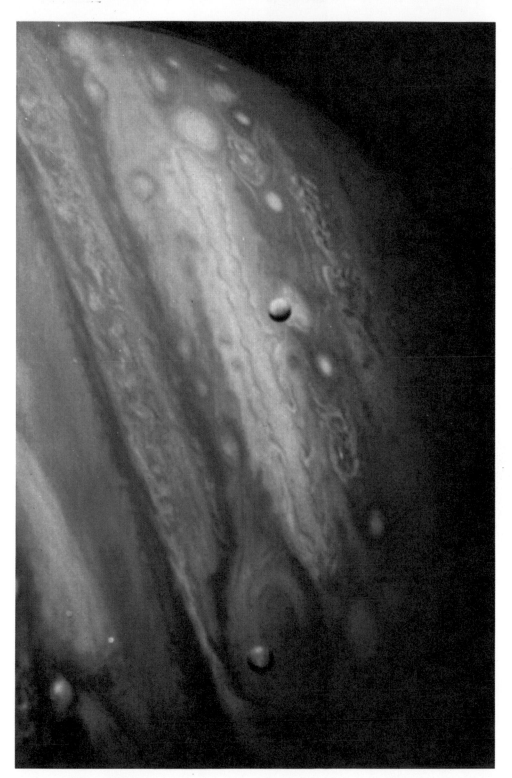

Voyager 1 view of Jupiter with Io (left) and Europa (NASA Photo; courtesy of Astronomical Society of the Pacific)

that they, like Callisto, should have heavily cratered, ancient surfaces. The fact that they do not is an immediate sign that these bodies have had much more eventful histories.

GANYMEDE

About half of the surface of Ganymede is covered with an ancient, heavily cratered terrain reminiscent of Callisto. But the terrain is broken apart by swaths of a younger, less-cratered surface, which in many places is characterized by a striking grooved texture. It is believed that at the time of Ganymede's formation there was a gradual warming of the satellite's interior, which resulted in the separation of most of the rocky material into a core and the icy material into an outer mantle. The process may have peaked 4 billion years ago. Such a colossal rearrangement within a large ice-and-rock satellite should lead to a slight increase in volume; this increase would cause the crust to crack and could culminate in the formation of the grooved terrain.

It is interesting to ask why the other icy satellite, Callisto, escaped a similar process. Being a little smaller and lighter than Ganymede, Callisto does not have quite as much rocky material. Since radioactive elements are concentrated in rocks, perhaps Callisto never heated up enough to fully differentiate and expand enough to crack its crust.

EUROPA

Europa is very different from both Ganymede and Callisto. Spectroscopy shows that its surface consists of relatively clean, bright water ice; yet Europa's high mean density implies that the icy crust cannot be very thick. Most of Europa must be rock, but since we don't know how dense the rock on the inside really is, it is impossible to calculate accurately the thickness of the icy mantle. Probably it is not more than 100 kilometers deep; perhaps much less.

Europa's surface is remarkable in that it is very flat and virtually devoid of craters. It is crisscrossed by a bizarre pattern of linear "bands"; some of these extend for more than 1,000 kilometers. Some appear to be ridges, but most look like fractures in a thin solid crust overlying a more fluid layer below. Several fracturing mechanisms have been suggested, including tidal pulling by Jupiter, cracking by impacts, and fracturing from internal forces of expansion. At present it is difficult to choose among these possibilities; to some extent they may all be responsible. Undeniably, tne pattern bears some resemblance (except in scale) to leads and pressure ridges that develop in ice floes on Earth's polar oceans. The suggestion has been made that Europa is a satellite covered by a global ocean of liquid water whose top is frozen owing to the low temperatures that prevail at Europa's distance from the Sun. It is certainly true that Europa's surface is very young: no more than 100 million years, and perhaps much less. (Fewer than half a dozen craters have been identified in the Voyager images!)

The model outlined above implies that Europa heated up internally and differentiated almost completely: even though Europa is smaller than Ganymede, its rocky component is larger. Once differentiated, the satellite might have cooled down rapidly; however, calculations suggest that tidal heating by Jupiter may have kept part of the icy mantle of Europa molten to this very day—a process that we see on Io.

IO

Io is a rocky body the size and density of our Moon, but there the similarity ends. Io's surface is a clash of colors, most likely owing to deposits of sulfur and sulfur compounds. Far from being scarred by impact craters like our Moon, Io is dotted with active volcanoes! Unlike our Moon, which has been geologically dead for more than 3 billion years, Io is geologically alive today. What is the source of energy that drives this activity, and why is Io so different from our own Moon?

The mechanism that keeps Io so hot today is energy from tides caused by the proximity of Jupiter—an idea suggested shortly before Voyager 1 first discovered erupting volcanoes on Io in March 1979. It is not difficult to believe that a massive planet like Jupiter should produce strong tides on a nearby satellite. Tides have the tendency to distort the satellite's outline slightly into a football shape, with one of the long ends pointing in the general direction of the planet. Since tides depend very strongly on distance, the amount of the distortion depends on how far the satellite is from Jupiter. If the satellite's orbit were perfectly circular, the satellite's distance from Jupiter would not change and the amount of distortion would remain constant throughout an orbit. But real orbits are never exactly circular; in general, as Kepler showed almost 300 years ago, they are ellipses. Therefore, there is a time during each orbit when Io is closest to Jupiter; it is then that tides are most intense and the satellite's distortion greatest. Half an orbital period later, Io will be at its farthest point from Jupiter. Here tides will be smallest and distortion least. Thus, as Io orbits Jupiter, its diameter is being constantly distorted, back and forth, into more or less elongated football shapes. It has been estimated that the average distortion of Io's diameter (3,630 kilometers) could be as large as

15 kilometers. Variation in extension at a point on the equator could reach some 100 meters during one orbit.

Because of friction, Io's constant flexing creates heat inside the satellite—try bending an old spoon back and forth many times and feel how much it will heat up! It is this heat that keeps the inside of Io intensely hot and the whole satellite vigorously active volcanically. Since Europa is farther away from Jupiter, tidal heating of this satellite is considerably less intense, but may be sufficient to keep part of the icy mantle molten today. Ganymede and Callisto are far enough from Jupiter that tidal energy has never played a significant role in their heat budgets.

There is no reason to believe that the intense tidal heating of Io is a recent phenomenon; therefore, almost certainly Io has been thoroughly cooked on the inside. It is to be expected that most lighter volatile materials (including water, nitrogen, and carbon dioxide) would have been boiled out of the interior long ago and escaped from the satellite's weak gravity. We would expect that after more than 4 billion years of outgassing only the heaviest volatile materials remain. Based on cosmic abundances of elements, we would predict sulfur and sulfur dioxide to be the major volatile compounds left on such a well-cooked satellite. We know from the Voyager data that sulfur dioxide is being vented by the volcanoes, that it forms a very thin temporary atmosphere, and that it freezes out into bright white patches of sulfur dioxide frost on the surface. The more brightly colored areas on Io's surface—pale yellows, oranges, reds, and browns—are widely believed to be sulfur, in part because rapidly cooled molten sulfur can form different *allotropes,* or forms, which display a similar range of tints. Supporting this identification is the fact that many volcanic calderas on Io have the very dark brown, almost black, colors characteristic of rapidly cooled boiling sulfur. Unfortunately, the precise identification of the materials that make up the colored areas on Io is hampered by the limited information obtained by Voyager. On the basis of the Voyager data alone it is difficult to be sure that these are sulfur, rather than sulfur compounds. This issue will be resolved in 1988 when the Galileo orbiter begins its two-year tour of the Galilean satellite system with a very close flyby of Io. Among other instruments on board will be a very sensitive camera and a newly developed infrared mapping spectrometer; together these two instruments should tell us more precisely what makes up individual regions on Io.

While sulfur and sulfur compounds may be the patina that colors Io's surface, the crust must also contain rocky materials. In some Voyager images we see what may be basaltic lava flows. There are also high mountains and steep cliffs; sulfur and sulfur dioxide are not strong enough to support such rugged topography.

The high mountains also indicate that Io's crust must be fairly solid (at

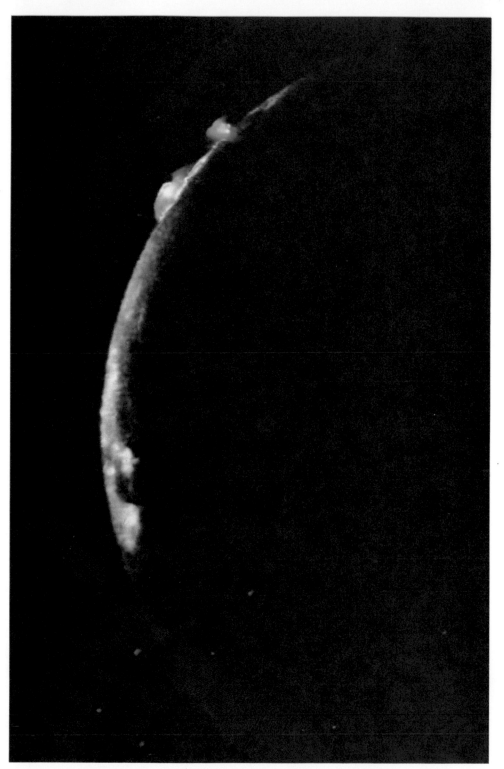
Voyager 2 view of a crescent Io showing two volcanic plumes. (NASA)

least in certain areas), even though the intensity of tidal heating must mean that the satellite is molten at a relatively shallow depth, perhaps as little as 10 to 20 kilometers below the surface. We know that the tidal heating is concentrated in the outer layers of the satellite, so it is conceivable that the deep interior is very hot, but solid. One way to find out would be to place seismometers on Io's surface, as was done on our own Moon during the Apollo missions. It is unlikely that such an elaborate experiment will be carried out in the foreseeable future, so we must rely on less precise, more indirect methods such as the Galileo probe.

The general consensus among planetary scientists is that there really are volcanoes on Io, but that they differ from those on Earth in that the driving volatile is not water (or steam) but either molten sulfur or sulfur dioxide. Exotic explanations for the extraordinary height of the plumes—up to 300 kilometers—are not necessary. As the American geologist S. Kieffer has stressed, even something as puny as Old Faithful (a geyser, not a volcano), which throws up hot water and steam to a height of 30 meters on Earth, could shoot material to a spectacular height of 38 kilometers on Io, given the satellite's lower gravity and almost total lack of an atmosphere.

Now that Voyager has called attention to the existence of active volcanoes on Io, astronomers have learned to identify the "heat signatures" of volcanic eruptions in infrared observations made from Earth. Owing to Io's vast distance from us, we cannot hope to obtain "pictures" in this way, but from infrared data we can determine that an eruption is taking place and even crudely estimate its location. For example, William Sinton, an astronomer at the University of Hawaii, observed a new volcanic eruption in the interval between the Voyager 1 encounter (March 1979) and Voyager 2's visit (July 1979). Approximately in the region suggested by Sinton's observations a new caldera (volcanic opening) was found in Voyager 2 images that had not been there four months earlier. This is only one small piece of evidence that suggests that Io's surface is changing at an astoundingly rapid rate. Indeed, there is some chance that in the pictures taken by Galileo in 1988, certain parts of Io may not look much like they did a decade earlier when Voyager flew by.

What is the fate of the gases and small particles that Io's volcanoes throw up? Some of this material falls out or condenses onto the surface, thus producing some of the patches of white and colored materials and eventually obliterating small impact craters and smoothing out small-scale topography. But some of the gases must escape, since Io's gravity is relatively weak (like that of our Moon, only one-sixth that of Earth). A more important factor is that Io lives in the depths of Jupiter's magnetosphere, a region characterized by intense magnetic fields and high fluxes of electrons and protons. One likely result is that these particles hit Io's surface or at least impinge on the thin atmosphere and the tops of the volcanic plumes. Such an interaction will transfer enough energy to an atom to enable it to escape Io's pull.

While such material can escape from Io, it will usually not have enough energy to leave Jupiter. The result is that often it will end up following an orbit around Jupiter, closely similar to that of Io. In 1973 astronomers noticed that Io's orbit is enshrouded by a torus of glowing sodium atoms—atoms that seem to have been "sputtered" off Io. While "sputtering" can remove neutral atoms from Io, the process of removing charged atoms (ions) and, indeed, small, electrically charged particles of "dust" (for example, little bits of sulfur from the tops of plumes) is even more dramatic. Any charged particle near the top of Io's thin atmosphere will be swept up by Jupiter's magnetic field, which swings by Io at a speed of over 50 kilometers per second. (While Io orbits around Jupiter once in 42 hours, Jupiter's magnetic field, tied to the rotation of the planet, swings by with a period of 10 hours.) The material thus swept up diffuses throughout the magnetosphere, but should be concentrated in the plane of Jupiter's magnetic equator at about Io's distance from the planet. Indeed, both Earth-based and spacecraft observations have mapped out the extent of this torus, which to no one's surprise (now that we know what Io's volcanoes puff out) consists of sulfur and oxygen ions.

OTHER SATELLITES

Before Voyager it was believed that there was only one small satellite, Amalthea, inside Io's orbit and that the planet had no ring. Voyager not only discovered a faint ring, but two tiny satellites—25 and 40 kilometers across—embedded in the ring's outer fringe. Possibly much of the material in the ring—known to consist of small dark particles—has been chipped off these small satellites by collisions with meteoroids. Voyager discovered a third small satellite (about 80 kilometers wide) between the orbits of Io and Amalthea. The latter, the largest of the inner satellites, was discovered by the American astronomer E. E. Barnard back in 1892, no small feat of visual acuity given how difficult it is to pick out Amalthea in Jupiter's bright glare. From Voyager images we know that Amalthea is a very irregular body, with dimensions approximately 270 by 165 by 150 kilometers. Its surface is heavily cratered and has an extremely low albedo (almost black) and very red color. In part, the deep red color may be due to contamination by sulfur from Io.

Aside from the four large Galilean satellites and the four small inner satellites, Jupiter's family includes eight other tiny satellites that orbit the planet in very extended paths. With the exception of Himalia, which is almost the size of Amalthea (perhaps 170 kilometers across), all of these bodies are less than 100 kilometers across. All seem to be made of some very dark, probably carbonaceous material. While it is likely that they, or their parent bodies, were captured early in Jupiter's history, the details of such a capture are unclear.

Unfortunately, when the Galileo spacecraft explores the Jupiter system at the end of this decade, it will not come close to any of the outer satellites. Yet, indirectly, it will provide important new information about what these small bodies are like. NASA has announced that on its way to Jupiter, the Galileo spacecraft will fly close to one of the larger small planets in the asteroid belt, asteroid 29, Amphitrite. The flyby will occur in December 1986, some six months after launch. While the composition of Amphitrite is different from that of the outer satellites of Jupiter, the asteroid's size (diameter about 200 kilometers) is comparable to that of Himalia. Thus, what Galileo sees on the surface of Amphitrite in 1986 may be a good clue to what some future explorers will find when they set foot on the dark, cold surface of Himalia sometime in the twenty-first century.

Voyager 2 view of the large Ganymede showing the hemisphere that faces away from Jupiter (NASA)

THE FUTURE OF THE JOVIAN SYSTEM

Gregory Benford

Father of all! in every age,
In every clime ador'd,
By saint, by savage, and by sage,
Jehovah, Jove, or Lord!
—ALEXANDER POPE

HOW THE SOLAR SYTEM WAS WON

T HEY SAID, OF COURSE, that it was impossible. They always do.

Even after the human race had moved into the near-Earth orbits, scattering their spindly factories and cylinder-cities and rock-hopping entrepreneurs, the human race was dominated by nay-saying stay-at-homes. Sure, they said, space worked. Slinging airtight homes into orbit at about one astronomical unit's distance from the Sun was—in retrospect—an obvious step. After all, there was a convenient moon nearby to provide mass and resources. But Earth, they said, was a benign neighborhood. You could resupply most outposts within a few days. Except for the occasional solar storm, when winds of high energy particles lashed out, the radiation levels were low. There was plenty of sunshine to focus with mirrors, capture in great sheets of conversion wafers, and turn into bountiful, high-quality energy.

But Jupiter? Why go *there*? Scientific teams had already touched down on the big moons and dipped into the thick atmosphere. By counting craters and taking core samples, they deduced what they could about how the solar system evolved. After that brief era of quick-payoff visits, nobody had gone back. One big reason, everyone was quick to point out, was the death rate in those expeditions: half never saw Earth again, except as a distant blue-white dot.

Scientists don't tame new worlds; pioneers do. And except for the bands of religious or political refugee-fanatics, pioneers don't do it for nothing. To understand why mankind undertook the most dangerous development project

129

in its history (so far), you have to ask the eternal question: Who stood to make a buck out of it?

By the year 2124 humans had already begun to spread out of the near-Earth zone. The bait was the asteroids—big tumbling lodes of metal and rock, rich in heavy elements. These flying mountains could be steered slowly from their looping orbits and brought into near-Earth rendezvous. The Delta V wasn't all that large.

There, smelters melted them down and fed the factories steady streams of precious raw materials: manganese, platinum, cadmium, chromium, molybdenum, tellerium, vanadium, tungsten, and all the rare metals. Earth was running out of these, or else was unwilling to pollute its biosphere to scratch the last fraction out of the crust. Processing metals is messy and dangerous. The space factories could throw their waste into the solar wind, letting the gentle push of protons blow it out to the stars.

Early in the space-manufacturing venture, people realized that it was cheaper in energy to tug small asteroids in from the orbits between Mars and Jupiter than to lift them with mighty rocket engines from Earth. Asteroid prospecting became the gold rush of the late twenty-first century. Corporations grubstaked loners who went out in pressurized tin cans, sniffing with their spectrometers at the myriad chunks. Most of them were duds, but a rich lode of vanadium, say, could make a haggard, antisocial rockrat into a wealthy man. Living in zero-gravity craft wasn't particularly healthy, of course. You had to scramble if a solar storm blew in and crouch behind an asteroid for shelter. Most rockhoppers disdained the heavy shielding that would ward off cosmic rays, figuring that their stay would be short and lucky, so the radiation damage wouldn't be fatal. Many lost that bet. One thing they could not do without, though, was food and air. That proved to be the pivot-point that drove humanity still farther out.

Life runs on the simplest chemicals. A closed artificial biosphere is basically a series of smouldering fires: hydrogen burns (that is, combines with oxygen) to give water; carbon burns into carbon dioxide, which plants eat; nitrogen combines in the soil so the plants can make proteins, enabling humans to be smart enough to arrange all this artificially.

The colonies that swam in near-Earth orbits had run into this problem early. They needed a steady flow of organic matter and liquids to keep their biospheres balanced. Supply from Earth was expensive. A better solution was to search out the few asteroids which had significant carbonaceous chondrites—rock rich in light elements: hydrogen, oxygen, carbon, nitrogen. There were surprisingly few. Most were pushed painfully back to Earth orbit and gobbled up by the colonies. By the time the rock-hoppers needed light elements, the asteroid belt had been picked clean. Besides, bare rock is unforgiving stuff.

Getting blood from a stone was possible in the energy-rich cylinder-cities. The loose, thinly spread coalition of prospectors couldn't pay the stiff bills needed for a big-style conversion plant.

From Ceres, the largest asteroid, Jupiter looms like a candy-striped beacon, far larger than Earth. The rockrats lived in the broad band between two and three astronomical units out from the sun—they were used to a wan, diminished sunshine and had already been tutored in the awful cold. For them it was no great leap to Jove, hanging there 5.2 times farther from the Sun than Earth.

They went for the liquids. Three of the big moons—Europa, Ganymede, and Callisto—were immense iceballs. True, they circled endlessly the most massive planet of all, three hundred and eighteen times the mass of Earth. That put them deep down in a gravitational well. Still, it was far cheaper to send a robot ship coasting out to Jupiter and looping into orbit around Ganymede than it was to haul water from the oceans of Earth. The first stations set up on Ganymede were semiautomatic—meaning a few unlucky souls had to tend the machinery.

If they could survive at all. A man in a normal pressure suit could live about an hour on Ganymede. The unending sleet of high-energy protons would fry him, ripping through the delicate cells and spreading red destruction. This was a natural side-effect of Jupiter's hugeness—its compressed core of metallic hydrogen spins rapidly, generating powerful magnetic fields that are whipped around every ten hours. These fields are like a rubbery cage, snagging and trapping particles (mostly protons) spat out by the sun. Io, the innermost large moon, belches ions of sulfur and sodium into the magnetic traps, adding to the protons. All this rains down on the inner moons, sputtering the ice.

It was not enough to burrow under the ice to escape. The crew had to work outside, supervising robot ice-diggers. The first inhabitants of Ganymede instead used the newest technology to fend off the proton hail: superconducting suits. Discovery of a way to make superconducting threads made it possible to weave them into pressure suits. The currents running in the threads made a magnetic field outside the suit, where it brushed away incoming protons. Inside, by the laws of magnetostatics, there was no field at all to disturb instrumentation. Once started, the currents flowed forever, without electrical resistance.

Those first men and women worked in an eerie dim sunlight. Over half of Ganymede's mass was water ice, with liberal dollops of carbon dioxide ice, frozen ammonia and methane, and minor traces of other frozen-out gases. Its small rocky core was buried under a thousand-kilometer-deep ocean of water and slush. The surface was a thin seventy-kilometer-deep frozen crust, liberally sprinkled by billions of years of infalling meteors. These meteorites peppered the surface and eventually became a major facet of the landscape. On top of

Ganymede's weak ice crust, hills of metal and rock gave the only relief from a flat, barren plain.

This frigid moon had been tugged by Jupiter's tides for so long that it was locked, like Luna, with one face always peering at the banded, ruddy planet. One complete day-night cycle was slightly more than an Earth-week long. Adjusting to this rhythm would have been difficult if the Sun had provided clear punctuation to the three-and-a-half-day nights. But even without an atmosphere, the Sun from Ganymede was a dim twenty-seventh as bright as at Earth's orbit. Sometimes you hardly noticed it, compared to the light of Jove's nearby moons.

Sunrise was legislated to begin at Saturday midnight. That made the week symmetric, and scientists love symmetry. Around late afternoon of Monday, Jupiter eclipsed the Sun, seeming to clasp the hard point of white, light in a rosy glow, then swallowing it completely. Europa's white, cracked crescent was then the major light in the sky for three and a half hours. Jupiter's shrouded mass flickered with orange lightning strokes between the rolling somber clouds. Suddenly, a rosy halo washed around the rim of the oblate atmosphere as sunlight refracted through the transparent outer layers. In a moment the Sun's fierce dot broke free and cast sharp shadows on the Ganymede ice.

By Wednesday noon it had set, bringing a night that was dominated by Jupiter's steady glow as it hung unmoving in the sky. This slow rotation was still enough to churn Ganymede's inner ocean, exerting a torque on the ice sheets above. A slow-motion kind of tectonics had operated for billions of years, rubbing slabs against each other, grooving and terracing terrain, erasing craters in some areas.

In the light gravity—one-seventh of Earth's—carving out immense blocks of ice was easy. Boosting them into orbit with tug rockets was the most expensive part of the long journey. From there, electromagnetic-thruster robot ships lugged the ice to the asteroids, taking years to coast along their minimum-energy spirals.

AGRIBUSINESS IN THE SKY

"Ice might be nice, but wheat you can eat."

So began one of the songs of that era, when the asteroids were filling up with prospectors, then miners, then traders. Then came settlers, who found the cylinder-cities too crowded, too restrictive, or simply too boring. They founded the Belt-Free State, with internal divisions along cultural and even family lines. (Susan McKenzie, the first Belt Chairwoman, was three generations removed from her nearest Earth-native Scot relative. Not that Belters stopped to think about Earth that much anymore.)

By then the near-Earth orbital zone was as comfortable as a suburb, and as demanding. The few iceteroids available in the asteroid belt had already been used up, but ice from Ganymede, originally hauled to the asteroids, could be revectored and sent to the rich artificial colonies. As the colonies developed a taste for luxury, increasingly that meant food. No environment can be completely closed, so human settlements throughout the solar system steadily lost vapors and organic matter to the void. No inventory ever came up 100 percent complete. (Consider your own body, and try to keep track of a day's output: feces, urine, exhaled gas, perspiration, flatus, sheddings. Draw the flow chart.) The relatively rich inner-solar-system colonies soon grew tired of skimpy menus and the endless cycle in which goat and rabbit and chicken were the prized meats.

Inevitably, someone noticed that it would be cheap to grow crops on Ganymede. Water was plentiful, and mirrors could warm greenhouses, enhancing the wan sunlight. Since Ganymede was going to ship light elements to the asteroids and beyond anyway, why not send them in the form of grains or vegetables?

Thus began the Settlements. At first they were big, domed greenhouses, lush with moist vegetables or grain. The farmers lived below in the sheltering ice. Within two generations humans had spread over a third of the moon's purplish, grooved fields. In the face of constant radiation hazard, something in the human psyche said *mate*!—and the population expanded exponentially.

Robot freight haulers were getting cheaper and cheaper, since the introduction of auto-producers in the Belt. These were the first cumbersome self-reproducing machines, sniffing out lodes of iron and nickel and working them into duplicates of themselves. An auto-producer would make two replicas of itself and then, following directives, manufacture a robot ion rocket. This took at least ten years, but it was free of costly human labor, and the auto-producers would work in lonely orbits, attached to bleak gray rocks where humans would never last. The ion rocket dutifully launched itself for Ganymede, to take up grain-hauling chores. Every year there were more of them to carry the cash crops sunward.

Working all day in a skinsuit is not comfortable. Day-to-day routines performed under ten meters of ice tend to pall. Fear of radiation and cold wears anyone down. For the first generation Ganymede was an adventure, for the next a challenge, and for the third, a grind. One of the first novels written in Jovian space opens with:

Maybe I should start off with a big, gaudy description. You know—
Jupiter's churning pinks and browns, the swirling white ammonia

clouds like giant hurricanes, the spinning red spots. That kind of touristy stuff.

Except I don't feel like writing that kind of flowery crap. I'm practical, not poetic. When you're swinging around Jupiter, living meters away from lethal radiation, you stick to facts. You get so vectors and grease seals and hydraulic fittings are more important than pretty views or poetry or maybe even people.

The psychological profile of the entire colony took a steep downward slope. Even the kids in the ice-warren streets knew something had to be done.

In the long run no large colony could live with the death-dealing threats to be found on any of the Jovian moons. Therefore, erase the dangers.

All sorts of remedies were suggested. One serious design was done for an immense ring of particles to orbit around Ganymede, cutting out most of the incoming high-energy protons. Someone suggested moving Ganymede itself outward, to escape the particle flux. (This wasn't crazy, only premature. A century later it would be feasible, though still expensive.) The idea that finally won looked just as bizarre as the rest, but it had an ace up its sleeve.

The Ganymede Atmosphere Project started with a lone beetle like machine crawling painfully around the equator of the world. Mechanical teeth ground up ice and sucked it inside, where an immense fusion reactor waited. The reactor burned the small fraction of heavy water in the ice and rudely rejected the rest as steam. From its tail jetted billowing clouds that in seconds condensed into an ammonia-rich creek.

This fusion plant crept forward on caterpillar treads, making a top speed of a hundred meters an hour. Its computer programs sought the surest footing over the black-rock outcroppings. It burned off toxic gases and left a mixture of water vapor, ammonia, oxygen, and nitrogen, with plenty of irritating trace gases. The greatest danger to it was melting itself down into a self-made lake. A bright orange balloon was tethered to the top. If the crawler drowned itself, the balloon would inflate and float the plant to the surface, to be fished out by a rescue team.

The trick was that the fusion-crawler wasn't made with valuable human labor, but rather by other machines: the auto-producers. Decades before, the auto-producers had begun multiplying like the legendary rabbits who invaded Australia. Now there were hundreds of them in the Belt, duplicating themselves and making robot freighters. The Belters were beginning to get irritated at the foraging machines; two had been blown to fragments for trespassing on Belters' mines. Simple reprogramming stopped their ferocious reproduction and set them to making fusion-crawlers.

Freighters hauled the crawlers out to Ganymede, following safe, cheap, low-energy trajectories. The crawlers swarmed out from the equator, weaving

through wrinkled valleys of tumbled stone and pink snowdrifts, throwing out gouts of gas and churning streams. The warm water carried heat into neighboring areas, melting them as well. A thin gas began to form over the tropics. At first it condensed out in the Ganymede night, but then it began to hold, to spread, to take a sure grip on the glinting ice lands below.

The natives saw these stolid machines as a faint orange aura over the horizon. Crawlers stayed away from the Settlements, to avoid accidents and flooding. Their rising mists diffused the fusion torch's light, so that a second sun often glowed beyond the hills, creeping northward, its soft halo contrasting with the blue-green shadows of the ice fields.

HELP WANTED: MUTANTS

An atmosphere can blunt the energy of incoming protons and screen against the still-dangerous sun's ultraviolet, but to be breathable it has to be engineered. Once a tiny fraction of the ice plains were melted into vapor, a greenhouse effect began to take hold. Sunlight striking the ice did not reflect uselessly back into space; instead, the atmosphere stopped the infrared portion, trapping the heat. Once this began, the fusion-crawlers were a secondary element in the whole equation.

The fresh ammonia streams and methane-laced vapors were deadly to Earth-based life. A decade after the first fusion-crawler lumbered through a grooved valley, hundreds of them scooped and roared toward Ganymede's poles, having scraped off a full hundred meters of the ice crust. They had made an atmosphere worth reckoning with. Ice tectonics adjusted to the shifting weight, forcing up mountains of sharp shards, uncovering lodes of meteorites, which in turn provided fresh manufacturing ore for yet more fusion-crawlers.

The first rain fell. A slight mist of virulent ammonia descended on the Zamyatin Settlement. It collected on a dip in the main dome, dissolving the tenuous film on it. After some hours the acid ate through. A *whoosh* of lost pressure alerted the agriworkers. They got out in time, but these were farsighted people: they knew one accident wasn't reason to kill the project that gave them so much hope.

The only solution was to change the atmosphere as it was made. Further rains underlined the point—it became harder to work outside because the vapors would attack the monolayer skinsuits. The fusion plants were no help. They were hopelessly crude engines, chemically speaking, spewing out vapors that had been laid down three billion years before, when the moon formed. They could not edit their output. As they burrowed deeper into the ice fields, the situation worsened.

Io, the pizza planet, had once enjoyed a more active stage. Its volcanoes had belched forth plumes of sulfur that had escaped the moon's gravity, forming a torus around Jupiter that included all the moons. On Ganymede this era was represented by a layer of sulfur that occasionally found its way into the crawlers' yawning scoops. The result was a fierce yellow rain that seared whatever it touched. Fifty-seven men and women died in the torrents before something was done.

The fusion-crawlers had been a fast and cheap solution because of self-reproducing machines. The answer to bioengineering of the atmosphere lay in a tried-and-true method: self-reproducing animals. But these creatures were unlike anything seen on Earth.

The central authority on Ganymede, Hiruko Station, introduced a whole catalog of high-biotech beings who could survive in the wilds of near-vacuum and savage chemicals. Hiruko Station's method was to take perfectly ordinary genes of Earthside animals and splice them together. This began as a program in controlled mutation but rapidly moved far beyond that. Tangling the DNA instructions together yielded beings who could survive extreme conditions. The interactions of those genes were decidedly nonlinear: when you add a pig to an eel, flavor with arachnid, and season with walrus, do not expect anything cuddly or even recognizable.

There were gravel-gobblers, who chewed on rocky ices heavy with rusted iron. They in turn excreted a green, oxygen-rich gas. The scooters came soon after, slurping at ammonia-laden ice. These were pale yellow, flat shapes, awkward and blind on their three malformed legs. They shat steady acrid streams of oxy-available mush. Hiruko Station said the first plant forms could live in the bile-colored scooter stools. Eventually, plants did grow there, but they weren't the sort of thing that quickens the appetite.

Both gravel-gobblers and scooters were ugly and dumb, hooting aimlessly, waddling across the fractured ice with no grace or dignity, untouched by evolution's smoothing hand. They roved in flocks, responding to genes that knew only two imperatives: eat and mate. They did both with a furious, single-minded energy, spreading over the ice, which was for them an endless banquet.

Hiruko Station liked the results, and introduced a new form—rockjaws—that consumed nearly anything, inhaled ammonia vapor, and exhaled oxygen and nitrogen. Rockjaws could bite through meteorites. Metallic jaws were the key. The high-biotech labs had turned up a method of condensing metal in living tissue, making harder bones possible.

Rockjaws were smart enough to stay away from the Settlements (unlike the others, who constantly wandered into greenhouses and tried to eat them). At this point the long-chain DNA-tinkering of Hiruko Station ran afoul of its own hubris. The rockjaws were *too* smart. They were genetically programmed to think the loathsome methane ices were scrumptious, but they also saw moving around nearby even more interesting delicacies: gravel-gobblers. And they were smart enough to hunt these unforeseen prizes.

Hiruko Station later excused this miscalculation as an unfortunate side-effect of the constant proton sleet, which caused fast genetic drift and unpredictable changes. Hiruko Station pointed to the big inflamed warts the creatures grew and the strange mating rituals they began to invent—none of it in the original coding. The scooter flocks were showing deformities, too. Some seemed demented (though it was hard to tell) and took to living off the excretion of the gravel-gobblers, like pigs rooting in cowflop.

First Hiruko Station tried introducing a new bioengineered animal into the equation. It was a vicious-looking thing, a spider with tiny black eyes and incisors as big as your finger. It stood three meters high and was forever hungry, fine-tuned to salivate at the sight of any mutation of the normals. This genetically ordained menu was quite specific, so it was the first thing to go wrong with the ugly beast. Pretty soon it would hunt down and eat anything that moved—even humans—and Hiruko Station had to get rid of it.

That was what led to the solution. The only way to exterminate the spiders was by hunting them down. Men in the Settlements volunteered for the duty. After some grisly incidents, they had grudges to settle, and anyway it gave them a reason to get out of the domed regularity of their hothouse gardens and manicured fields. Thus was revived a subculture long missing from Earth: the hunt, with its male bonding and reckless raw life in the wilderness. As a novel of the time opened:

> They went out from Sidon Settlement in a straggling band, clanking and crunching over the hard-packed, worn-down purple plain. The ice near Sidon had been melted and frozen and remelted again and again by orbit shuttle landings and by the heater exhausts of passing crawlers, so that now it was speckled and mottled with rainbow splashes and big blotches of contaminants. Out over this crusty trampled land they went, and inside their wheezing and huffing machines they sang and shoved each other and early got into the smeerlop and whiskey, as they always did.

These disorderly bands exterminated the spiders within a year. Hiruko Station found it was cheaper to pay the hunters to track down and destroy aberrant scooters and rockjaws and gravel-gobblers, than it was to try for a technological fix. The Settlements were tradition-steeped societies—internal discipline is essential when an open valve or clogged feed line can kill a whole community.

A LARGER CANVAS

The atmosphere thickened. Hiruko Station added more mutant strains of quick-breeding animals to the mix, driving the chemical conversion still faster. The biotechnicians found a way to implant microprocessors into the animals, so that they didn't get out of control. That was expensive, though, so hunting continued, echoing the heritage of mankind that came down from the plains of Africa. Bounty hunters were hard to fit into the labor scheme, and the socioplanners kept trying to phase them out. Earthside 3D programs lapped up tales of the rough-'n-ready bountymen (and bountywomen), giving what the planners felt was a "false image." Mutation was rapid, however, and the biosphere was never truly stabilized. The hunters became an institution. To this day, they are an unruly crew who don't fit into orderly diagrams.

Rain lost its sulfuric tang. Steam rose at morning from the canyons, casting rosy light over the Settlements. The moon's first rivers cut fresh ravines and snaked across ice plains.

All this hung in delicate balance. Huge sodium-coated mirrors were spread in orbit nearby, to reflect unceasing light on the paths ahead of the fusion-crawlers. This speeded evaporation and was used also to hasten crops to ripeness. But Ganymede was, after all, an ice world. Too much heating and a catastrophic melting of the crust would begin. If the crust broke or even shifted, moonquakes would destroy the Settlements.

Thus it was a careful hand that started up the first Ganymede weather cycle. Solar heating at the equator made billowing, moist clouds rise. They moved toward the poles as colder air flowed below, filling spaces the warm air left. As they moved, masses of warm clouds dropped sheets of rain. This meant there was only one circulation cell per hemisphere, an easier system to predict than the several-cell scale of Earth. Rainfall and seasons were predictable; weather was boring. As many on Luna and in the asteroids had learned, low gravity and a breathable atmospheric pressure gave a sensational bonus: flying. Though Ganymede would always be cold and icy, people could soar over the ice ecology on wings of aluminum. Compared to the molelike existence of only a few generations before, this was freedom divine.

There came at last the moment when the air thickened enough to absorb the virulent radiation flux. Years later, a foolhardy kid stepped outside an airlock five hours before the official ceremony was to begin, and sucked in a thin, piercingly cold breath. She got back inside only moments before oxygen deprivation would have knocked her out, but she did earn the title she wanted: first to breathe the free air of Ganymede. Molecules locked up for billions of years in the ice now filled the lungs of a human. She was fined a month's labor credit by her Settlement.

By this time Europa's cracked and cratered face was alive with the tiny ruby dots of fusion-busters, chewing away at that moon as well. They crawled along the cracks that wrapped the entire moon, melting the walls away, hoping to open the old channels below the cracks. The churning slush below burst forth here and there, spreading stains of rich mineral wealth. Jove itself, hanging eternally at the center of the sky, was now the only face unmarked in some way by mankind.

Not to be outdone, the Republic of Ganymede hastened the heating of their air. They laid a monomolecular layer over the top of the atmosphere, spinning it down from orbit, letting it fall until it was supported by the pressure from below. This gossamer film stopped the lighter molecules from escaping first, keeping the chemical balance of the air and speeding the greenhouse effect. The designers left holes big enough for orbital tugs to slip through. From the ice fields below, Callisto and Europa and Io now carried a gauzy halo of scattered light.

The first lake on Ganymede formed in a basin of meteorite rock eight kilometers wide. This created a ready source of fresh water and an almost resort-like atmosphere to the spot. Sailing and even swimming became fashionable. Agribusiness boomed, driven by more and more mirrors that augmented the natural sunlight.

Trade with the asteroids increased. Stations around distant Saturn were supplied from Ganymede, and research satellites out as far as Pluto. The exploration of gloomy, ruddy Titan was complete, and some people were talking about trying to make a go of it at the bottom of that chilly organic soup. By then Ganymede was the luxury world of the outer system. The pioneers had moved on, long before the first Hilton went up.

Some moons were set aside as natural preserves, where selected tourists and scientific teams could see the way the ice worlds had once been. Other rocky moonlets were kept aside, in case future scientists had new methods of studying this primordial matter. The first ecological movements began, seeking to preserve the original bleak wastes wherever they remained.

As always, it was a battle of economics. The moons that later boiled off their atmospheres had to compete with Ganymede. Their most brilliant stroke lay in *not* applying the insulating monolayer. Without it, they could profit from the new asteroid importation business.

Some chunks of useful mass (nickel, iron, silicates rich in rare ores, the usual) orbited near or beyond Jupiter—the Trojan and Transjovian groups. Manufacturers argued that it was cheaper to make metal-rich products on Ganymede than to import them from the asteroids, particularly now that the McKenzie Conglomerate was upping the prices in a monopoly market. Trouble was, they needed the metals, and the McKenzies owned everything in sight.

But the Transjovians were there for the plundering, if only they could be cheaply moved to near-Ganymede orbit.

The Europa entrepreneurs jumped into the fray. Since their atmosphere did not have a monolayer cap, they could send asteroids zooming through it. On these flybys the asteroids lost a lot of their unneeded momentum, making them easy to slip into orbits in Ganymede's neighborhood. They also heated up Europa's air and provided a valuable tourist attraction, with their well-choreographed displays of burnt gold, electric blue, and ruby amber. As the pilots of these rockships became more graceful, they began to carry passengers. Later, atmospheric grazing in protected suits became popular. In the freewheeling ethical climate of the time, bookings were permitted (indeed, the rates were even lowered) for those who signed on as suicides.

Sometime later, a large Earthside foundation proposed capping the Callisto atmosphere. They intended the largest work of art possible—a gaudy, beribboned design of loops and swirls that could be seen (properly magnified) throughout the solar system. The glorious monolayer film would have changeable polarization and colors, so that later generations of artists could express themselves through it.

This idea was opposed by a rare coalition of environmentalists—Keep Callisto Clean—and business interests, who wanted to horn in on Europa's atmospheric deceleration franchise. The foundation lost its zoning permit. Undeterred, they set about to move Pluto into a long, looping orbit, which passed through the inner solar system. Suitably decorated, they said, Pluto would make a magnificent touring art gallery.

Soon there was talk of starting a power-generating plant on Io. Not the volcanoes there—those had already been tapped. This plan proposed hooking directly into the currents that ran between Io and Jupiter itself—six million amperes of electricity just waiting to be used. Work began. Soon they would harness the energy that drove the aurora.

The forward vector of humanity had by now passed beyond the Jovian moons. Near Earth, the first manned starship was abuilding, soon to depart for Alpha Centauri. Given the engineering abilities of humanity, the matter of whether an Earth-like planet circled there seemed beside the point. (As it turned out, there was no such world within sixty-three light years.) Humans could survive anywhere. Better, they would prevail and come to enjoy just about anything. Any place where sunlight and mass accumulated, there a human would find a way to form a roiling, catch-as-catch-can society—and probably make a profit doing it.

Of course, there was Jupiter itself. It and the other gas giant planets had formed the backdrop for all this drama, but that was all. Many a Ganymede native, perhaps as he lounged beside a lake in a heated skinsuit or banked and swooped through gossamer clouds, peered up at the swollen giant and idly wondered. Jupiter occupies two hundred and fifty times as much of the sky as Luna does from Earth; it was never far from the minds of the millions who lived nearby.

So it was inevitable. A physicist on Luna had developed a new theory of Jove's interior, accounting for all the latest data on pressure and temperature and chemical composition. She found that there had to be stratified bands of pure hydrogen metal near the surface of Jupiter. The hydrogen metal might be close to the outer layers of rock, near enough to mine.

Once squeezed into being by Jupiter's huge gravitational pressure, metallic hydrogen was a stable form. At great expense, laboratory tests created a few grams of the stuff. It was incredibly strong, light, and durable. It could even survive a slow transition to low pressure. If you could go down there and mine it . . .

The pressures deep in that thick Jovian atmosphere were immense. Where they were measured at all, the conditions were brutal. The technology for handling the mines was completely undeveloped. It was an insane idea.

They said, of course, that it was impossible. They always do.

SATURN

ESSAY BY
David Morrison

SPECULATION BY
Roger Zelazny

SATURN: A RINGED WORLD

David Morrison

BY 1980 SPACECRAFT had visited all of the planets known to ancient peoples. Human beings had placed their boot prints in the lunar soil, and robot spacecraft had landed on Venus and Mars. Only one more chapter remained in the initial exploration of the solar system, to be written by the Voyager encounters with Saturn.

Two years before, Pioneer 11 had made the first reconnaissance of the Saturn system, following a 1 billion-kilometer detour across the solar system from Jupiter. But the Pioneer spacecraft had only rudimentary cameras and a low-power data system. The main acts in the Saturn drama would take place in November 1980 and August 1981, when the two Voyagers made their historic flybys. Saturn had been the primary scientific target of the Voyagers from their inception a decade earlier, and close to $1 billion had been spent to accomplish these short weeks of exploration. For the engineers who had built the Voyagers, these encounters would prove the merit of their work. For the scientists, they would demolish cherished theories and provide the raw material for a decade of studies to follow. And for the press and the public who followed these events, the Voyagers would illuminate a mysterious and beautiful ringed world, a dream planet more enchanting than any other.

THE SATURN SYSTEM

Looking at Saturn, even through a small telescope, is an unforgettable experience. Although faint rings have now been discovered girding Jupiter, Uranus, and Neptune as well, Saturn remains *the* ringed planet. It also boasts the most extensive and complex system of satellites, with more than twenty known moons. The largest of these, cloud-shrouded Titan, is an appropriate topic for a chapter in itself; indeed, if Titan orbited the Sun alone, rather than as a part of Saturn's retinue, we would be proud to list it among the more interesting of the planets.

The most distant member of the solar system visible to the naked eye, Saturn requires twenty-nine years for a single circuit of the Sun. This time span, about equal to one human generation, was the longest natural interval defined by the heavens. It is no wonder, then, that Graeco-Roman astronomers named this planet for Kronos/Saturn, the ancient god of time.

In spite of its great distance from the Sun—about 1 billion kilometers— Saturn is quite bright, easily seen in the night sky as one of the brighter stars. Clearly, therefore, it must be a large planet. It is, in fact, the second largest planet in the solar system, sharing with Jupiter the designation of giant, or Jovian, planet. With its diameter of 120,000 kilometers, the volume of Saturn is great enough to encompass nearly 1,000 Earths. The density of Saturn, in contrast, is the lowest of any planet: 0.7 grams per cubic centimeter, or 70 percent the density of water. Saturn would float if you could find a big enough bathtub—but it would probably leave a ring! Such a low density is incompatible with compositions of metal, rock, ice, or most gases. Only a giant gasbag of hydrogen and helium, the two lightest elements, would have such a low density.

The rings of Saturn were first seen by Galileo in 1610, but his small telescope did not have sufficient power to reveal their true nature. Before the end of the seventeenth century Christian Huygens had identified the rings correctly, although it was not until the middle of the nineteenth century that scientists became convinced that they were made up of myriad small particles in individual orbits around the planet. In 1970 the composition of these particles was measured to be water ice, and a radar signal was bounced off the rings in 1974.

Outside the ring system, Saturn's family is dominated by Titan, the second largest satellite in the entire solar system. Discovered in 1655, it followed its orbit around the planet in relative obscurity until 1944, when it was found to have an atmosphere. A satellite with an atmosphere was a completely unexpected phenomenon! By the late 1970s, some astronomers even suspected that this atmosphere might be more extensive than that of our own planet.

Most of what we know about the Saturn system comes not from these telescopic studies but from the spectacular Voyager encounters in 1980 and 1981. The more distant a planet, the more there is to gain by observing it at close range from a spacecraft. The Voyager 1 spacecraft came within a mere 4,000 kilometers of the clouds of Titan, and Voyager 2 risked a daring plunge through the tenuous outer rings of Saturn. This chapter describes the results of those two exploration missions, results that are not likely to be challenged until the next millennium, unless efforts are made soon to mount another mission to this distant world.

THE PLANET

When we look down on Saturn, either with a telescope or with spacecraft cameras, we view an immense sea of clouds. There are no breaks in this canopy, and even if there were, we would glimpse no solid surface beneath, for there is none. Saturn is a fluid planet, with its atmosphere giving way at great depth not to a solid crust but to a liquid interior of compressed gas. The atmosphere we see is composed primarily of hydrogen, the most abundant element in the universe. Like Jupiter, Saturn has a "primitive" composition, consisting of the cosmically abundant elements left over from the formation of the solar system. Unlike the other, smaller members of the planetary system, Jupiter and Saturn are large enough and far enough from the Sun to hold on to these gases.

The clouds of Saturn are condensations composed primarily of crystals of ammonia. This ammonia cirrus forms a deep, planet-wide haze much thicker than that of Jupiter. Saturn also lacks the brightly colored chemicals that make the Jovian clouds so spectacular. Consequently, Saturn itself is a rather dull-looking planet, with a nearly featureless cloud layer of pale butterscotch hue.

Although the clouds look dull, the atmosphere in which they float is an active one. The primary feature of Saturn's weather is a giant equatorial jet stream blowing toward the east at nearly 2,000 kilometers per hour. This equatorial current is twice as broad and four times as fast as Jupiter's.

Until recently we did not know how fast Saturn spins on its axis. Because there is so little structure visible in the atmosphere, astronomers could not follow individual features through their telescopes to time the rotation period. Voyager, however, has provided the answer. As it approached Saturn, the spacecraft detected bursts of radio emission that varied periodically. Like the radio bursts from Jupiter, these emissions define the rotational period for the core of Saturn, which is where the magnetic field is generated. This is the true period of rotation, ten hours and thirty-nine minutes, almost as short as Jupiter's day. Interestingly, the two largest planets turned out to have the fastest rotation speeds.

Deep inside Saturn, the atmospheric hydrogen is transformed into a metallic liquid form unfamiliar to us on Earth. This interior is hot, and heat leaking upward supplies much of the energy to power the circulation of the atmosphere. We believe the interior heat is the result of two processes. One is a slow shrinking of the core; the other is the gradual separation of helium from hydrogen in the interior.

Deep in the liquid metallic core, the rapid rotation of Saturn generates electric currents and produces a strong magnetic field, which extends into the space surrounding the planet. Like Jupiter, Saturn has an extensive magnetosphere of charged atomic particles trapped in this giant magnetic field. The magnetosphere of Saturn is more modest than that of Jupiter, however, and the strength of its radiation belts smaller. The main reason for the difference is the presence of the rings and inner moons of Saturn, which absorb magnetospheric particles. The result is to eliminate most of the intense inner radiation belts, leaving an extensive but less powerful outer magnetosphere that stretches out several million kilometers from the planet, enveloping the rings and most of the moons.

THE RINGS

Surrounding Saturn is a disk of orbiting particles that has no counterpart in the planetary system. This disk is nearly 400,000 kilometers across, about the distance from Earth to the Moon, yet it is incredibly thin: no more than a few tens of meters. If we wished to build a scale model of the rings of Saturn, with the ring thickness represented by a sheet of paper from this book, the model would be forty city blocks across and the planet would loom above the rings as high as a hundred-story building.

Traditionally, three major rings have been identified by telescopic observers. With typical imagination, astronomers named these the A, B, and C rings. The one major gap in the rings seen from Earth, between the A and B rings, is called the Cassini Division, after the astronomer who discovered it in 1675.

Seen at closer hand from the Voyager spacecraft, however, the rings of Saturn take on an entirely different aspect. With increasing resolution comes increasing complexity. Although there are only about twenty true gaps, the entire width of the rings displays an intricate structure in the form of tens of thousands of concentric ringlets. Perhaps most remarkable is the observation that this fine structure is not fixed but varies with time and position. Seen up close, the vast flat plane of the rings looks more like the surface of a white sea of orbiting particles, with wave crests running across it in undulating currents.

Waves can form and propagate in the rings because of the mutual gravitational attraction of the ring particles. This gravitational bond couples each particle weakly to its neighbors, permitting a disturbance to move outward from its place of origin like ripples on the surface of a pool. From the spacing of the ripples, it is possible to calculate the thickness and density of matter in the rings. Typically, the waves form spiral patterns, like the grooves in a celestial phonograph record, wrapping repeatedly around the planet.

The disturbances that give rise to the waves in the rings are only partially understood. Many of the spiral waves appear to start at places where the rings are influenced by the gravitational pull of the moons of Saturn, orbiting beyond the ring system. At distances where a ring particle orbits Saturn in an exact multiple of the satellite period, repeated gravitational perturbations reinforce each other. Such a distance corresponds to a satellite "resonance." Most of the observed wave patterns in the rings have been identified with points of resonance with the inner satellites of Saturn.

Not even the Voyager spacecraft came close enough to the rings to see the individual particles. The phenomena photographed by the spacecraft cameras are ensemble effects resulting from interactions among the particles. But we believe from indirect evidence that yet another class of phenomena would be seen by a spacecraft that probed down to skim along the surface of the rings themselves.

Peering into the rings, such a craft would see myriad individual particles, ranging in size from a house down to a snowflake or, in some places, even smaller. Each particle would be made out of water ice or snow. Each would be following its own essentially circular orbit around the planet, completing one circuit in ten hours or so, depending on its location within the rings. Relative to its neighbors, which follow nearly identical orbits, it would not seem to be moving at all. The particles would be like a flight of birds, moving together on some greater mission while slowing and randomly weaving about among themselves.

If we looked closely, however, we would see occasional collisions, usually resulting in two particles sticking together. Through collisions, the particles would grow larger, and close examination of the larger particles would probably reveal that they are merely loosely adhering collections of smaller building blocks. But the particles will not grow forever. Rare collisions or other effects apparently break the largest ones apart, scattering their components and starting the cycle all over. Thus even on this smallest scale, the rings are constantly shifting as particles grow, break apart, and then grow again.

This process takes place in the denser parts of the rings, the best-known A and B rings, where they account for most of the fine structure. Other forces, however, give rise to the major gaps in the rings, as well as producing some remarkable features, such as kinky and braided rings.

The ring gaps represent true voids, places where something is sweeping away ring particles. Most probably, the sweeper is a small satellite, perhaps a few kilometers in diameter. Sometimes there is within a gap a single, narrow strand of ring material, often of an elliptical, rather than circular, shape. These narrow, eccentric rings are also attributed to hypothetical small satellites, although the exact processes at work are in dispute among ring experts.

The most remarkable of the rings of Saturn lies just outside the classical ring system. Called the F ring, it was discovered in 1979 when the Pioneer 11 spacecraft made the first visit to the Saturn system. The F ring, like the elliptical rings within ring gaps, is very narrow, a mere ribbon of material a few kilometers wide and more than 1 million kilometers in circumference. Narrow as the ring is, however, Voyager discovered considerable fine structure within the F ring, which is actually made up of several even narrower strands. In some places, these strands separate and then appear to twist around each other in a braided effect, although probably the ringlets do not actually wrap around each other in a configuration as complex as a braid.

Fortunately, we understand something about what gives rise to the F ring. Two small satellites, each a few tens of kilometers in diameter, have been found orbiting on either side of the ring. Apparently it is the gravitational influence of these satellites that confines the ring particles to a thin ribbon and even gives rise to the multiple structure. Because of their role in keeping the ring particles confined to a straight and narrow path, these two satellites are called the shepherd satellites of Saturn. The existence of the F ring shepherds, and a similar small satellite that defines the outer boundary of the A ring, provides part of the justification for the idea that small satellites imbedded in the rings themselves cause the gaps and eccentric rings. But no imbedded satellite has actually been seen, so the idea remains conjectural.

Where did the rings come from? Why does only Saturn have such an extensive ring system? In truth, no one knows. There are two possibilities. First, the rings may represent leftover material that never formed into a satellite. The second, and probably more likely, scenario involves one or more smaller inner satellites that formed early in the history of the Saturn system and were subsequently broken apart by impacts. We know from the observations of the remaining satellites that there were small icy bodies in this region, and it is quite plausible that some of these would have suffered catastrophic collisions long ago, when there was a great deal of debris left in the solar system. Presumably, then, the special thing about Saturn was the presence of icy satellites near the planet. Given such satellites, the formation of the rings follows naturally.

SATURN'S SATELLITE SYSTEM

Saturn has the most extensive, and perhaps the most complex, system of satellites. All but three of the twenty or so known moons are in circular orbits in the same plane as the rings, and presumably they were formed together with the rings and the planet itself. In all cases where composition has been measured, the satellites are at least half water and ice. Water ice also dominates on their surfaces, making these objects among the most reflective in the planetary system. But in spite of these general similarities, the moons of Saturn are a curious and varied lot.

One of the strangest things about the Saturn satellites is the presence of a number of objects in shared orbits. Generally speaking, it is not possible for two objects to follow the same orbit; eventually they interfere with each other, and one or the other is ejected into a different path. Only a few exceptions are theoretically possible, and several of these are found in the Saturn system.

Janus and Epimetheus represent the most interesting case of shared orbits; these two satellites circle the planet a few thousand kilometers outside the rings. These moons, each about 200 kilometers across, have orbits that are almost, but not quite, identical. As a result, the trailing one gradually gains on the leading one. But they cannot pass each other, since their orbits are only separated by about 50 kilometers. Instead, they begin to interact gravitationally as they approach, and this causes them to exchange orbits. With their roles reversed, they drift apart again. This complicated orbital dance is repeated over and over, within a period of about four years.

Another moon with a unique orbit is Hyperion, which inhabits the outer part of Saturn's satellite system. Hyperion is the only object in the solar system known to be in a "chaotic" rotational state, which means that its period of rotation is not fixed. As Hyperion follows its eccentric orbit around Saturn, its rotation speeds up and slows down in apparently random fashion. This strange behavior confused observers until a few years ago, when theorists came to the rescue with calculations showing that such chaotic rotation was possible.

The five larger inner members of the satellite system are icy bodies between 400 and 1,600 kilometers in diameter. In order outward from Saturn these moons are named Mimas, Enceladus, Tethys, Dione, and Rhea. In many ways Rhea is typical not only of these objects but perhaps also of the satellites of Uranus. It is composed about half each of water ice and rocky silicate minerals, and its bright, reflective surface appears to be made of slightly dirty ice. The surface of Rhea is heavily scarred by impact craters, resembling the cratered highlands of our Moon.

Because surface temperatures are very low at this great distance from the Sun, the ice that makes up the crusts of these moons is as strong and stiff as rock. That is why their surfaces look so much like those of the Moon or of other rocky bodies. Geologically, ice in the Saturn system behaves much like rock in the inner solar system.

Two of these icy moons are so unusual that they deserve individual description. The first of these is Enceladus, which is 500 kilometers in diameter. Enceladus is an icy moon par excellence, with a surface so bright that it reflects 90 percent of the sunlight striking it. To achieve this high reflectivity, the surface must be very special, probably covered with fine crystals of ice, acting somewhat like the glass beads on a movie projection screen. Enceladus is also associated with an extremely tenuous outer ring of Saturn called the E ring.

A montage of Voyager images of Saturn and its satellites (NASA photo; courtesy Astronomical Society of the Pacific)

This E ring is itself made up of very small ice particles, which are probably producing the reflective surface coating. But the origin of the E ring is a real mystery. Such a ring of fine particles is not stable for long time periods, so it must be the result of some recent event, perhaps an impact or eruption on the surface of Enceladus.

The geology of Enceladus is also remarkable. While the other Saturn satellites have surfaces heavily cratered from impacts, that of Enceladus bears evidence of large-scale volcanic activity. Over large areas the impact craters have been replaced by flaws and wrinkled ridges. Since this moon is composed primarily of water ice, the "lava" is almost surely liquid water, another case where water in the outer solar system plays the same role as silicate rocks for the inner planets. The mystery, however, arises from the fact that Enceladus is the only Saturn satellite showing evidence of recent internal activity. Why was this small satellite singled out for such activity? No one knows.

The other unique moon is Iapetus, which orbits near the outer edge of the satellite system. Iapetus is a two-faced object. Basically, it is an icy, cratered moon like Rhea and most of the others in the Saturn system. But one side of Iapetus, the side that faces forward as it orbits around Saturn, is much darker than the other. Specifically there is a huge, nearly circular black spot right in the middle of this leading hemisphere, apparently a deposit of some very dark mineral. While most scientists believe that this deposit came from the outside, no one has identified the mechanism by which nature could "paint" one side of an icy satellite in this manner.

A great deal of recent effort has gone into identifying the black spot on Iapetus. Black material seen elsewhere in the outer solar system is organic in nature, consisting primarily of complex carbon compounds that are loosely termed tars. Such compounds formed naturally under conditions present when the solar system formed. Specific telescopic studies of the dark face of Iapetus indicate that a coating of organic tars is present. Unfortunately, there is no obvious external source for such material, so this chemical clue does not help much in solving the mystery of this two-faced moon.

TITAN

One moon of Saturn deserves, and has received, special attention. Titan is by far the largest of Saturn's retinue, with a diameter of a little over 5,000 kilometers; in fact, it just loses out to Jupiter's Ganymede for the distinction of largest satellite in the planetary system. Much more remarkable, however, is the presence of an extensive cloudy atmosphere surprisingly similar to that of Earth.

Before the Voyager exploration of Saturn, Earth was thought to be the only place in the solar system with an atmosphere composed primarily of nitrogen. When we looked at Titan, however, we found that nitrogen was also the main constituent of its atmosphere. In addition, it turned out that the atmosphere of Titan was much more extensive than had been anticipated; in fact, this satellite has a nitrogen atmosphere about ten times greater than that of our own planet. Nitrogen is a transparent gas, however; therefore, since Titan is shrouded in perpetual haze, something more complicated must be happening.

Apparently, Titan's atmosphere is acting as a gigantic chemical plant. In addition to the nitrogen, the atmosphere contains methane and other more complex organic compounds made of carbon, oxygen, and hydrogen. Under the action of sunlight, these organic gases undergo a complex series of reactions, in the process creating various organic hazes—what we would call smog. These chemical processes, and the organic matter they produce, are thought to be similar to those that took place in Earth's atmosphere billions of years ago, before the advent of living things and an oxygen-rich atmosphere. Because of the low temperature and lack of water, this smog builds up to form an impenetrable haze surrounding Titan.

The ultimate fate of this organic smog is even more interesting. Eventually, it must settle from the clouds down to the surface, where it accumulates. In this dark, cold environment (about the temperature of liquid air), the organic sediment can remain intact forever. Thus the surface of Titan must contain a chemical record of solar system history. If we could examine this record, we could gain a unique insight into the early history of our own planet as well.

What would it be like to explore the surface of Titan? We don't know, since we cannot see beneath its ubiquitous clouds, but we can speculate. Titan is large enough to have experienced internal geological activity, so we might expect some interesting topography, including mountains; ancient volcanoes are also a possibility. Everything, however, will be blanketed by the organic sediment, in layers that may be from hundreds of meters up to, perhaps, several kilometers in depth. Oceans are also possible, although of course not oceans of water. The most likely candidates are liquid hydrocarbons, especially ethane, which would play the role of water for the frigid surface of Titan. Some have suggested that a probe to the surface of Titan should take the form of an automated boat, able to cruise the ethane seas of this remarkable object.

Titan is like an inner planet in deep freeze. It is an ideal storehouse for the chemical archives of solar system history. Not surprisingly, this remarkable object has a strong pull on the imaginations of planetary scientists. For many, Titan is second only to Mars as the most interesting and desirable place in the planetary system for additional missions of exploration.

As we discussed at the outset, the Voyager encounters with Saturn were the final act in the initial exploration of the solar system. They were the culmination of two decades of extraordinary accomplishment, during which humans first came to see other planets as worlds and our own world as a planet.

After the Saturn encounters, while the Voyager spacecraft continued in their lonely flights outward toward Uranus and the edge of the solar system, the enterprise of planetary exploration slowed almost to a halt. Technical problems with the shuttle and its upper stages contributed, but more fundamental was a failure of vision, an unwillingness to face the challenge of the exploration of other worlds. The second Voyager encounter, in August 1981, was appropriately called "the last picture show."

Five years later we are again beginning to explore the planets. In 1986, Voyager 2 will reach Uranus, a flotilla of craft launched by Europe, the U.S.S.R., and Japan will greet Halley's comet as it sweeps past the Sun, and the Galileo spacecraft will be launched toward Jupiter, with the first flyby of an asteroid along the way. New missions are also planned to Venus and Mars. And someday soon we may once again look out toward Saturn.

The next mission to Saturn will likely be focused on Titan and on the remarkable rings. At the top of scientists' priorities is an entry probe into the atmosphere of Titan, which will radio back to us measurements beneath the clouds and perhaps even from the surface. Radar can also probe through the clouds to build up images of surface topography. And a long-lived orbiter will allow extensive study of the rings and the other satellites, including returns to mysterious Enceladus and Iapetus. Perhaps most important, a new mission to Saturn offers the opportunity to make planetary exploration into an international, rather than a national, program. A joint mission has been proposed, involving both NASA and the European Space Agency, with possible contributions from Japan. Such a cooperative effort, in which the expenses as well as the rewards of space exploration are shared among the peoples of the world, may point the way toward a true golden era of space travel in the twenty-first century.

DREADSONG

Roger Zelazny

Saturn, two centuries hence . . .

I sat on a breastwork of rocks I had constructed behind my home and I stared into the night sky; I thought about Saturn, as it is now and as it might be. There was a cool wind out of the Sangre de Cristos to the northeast. Something was feeding in the arroyo behind me—a coyote, perhaps, or a stray dog. Above me, the stars moved imperceptibly in their great wheel.

The center of a system of satellites as well as some fascinating rings, Saturn has probably changed little save its position in eons. But the next 200 years are likely to represent a crucial time in the history of humanity, which, barring self-destruction or massive technological regression, is probably going to extend its influence through the solar system. What might we want of that giant primal ball of gases? What might we find upon it?

I live on a ridge, where I hear and feel all the winds. When the rains come they run off quickly, which is why I hauled stones to construct a breastwork, preventing erosion to the rear of my home. I changed the pattern of runoff by doing this. Different channels were formed. A neighbor's complaint to the city resulted in my constructing a bar ditch to deal with a problem this had caused him. The bar ditch created no problems that anyone has complained of, though it has benefited the growth of some plants by depriving others. What effect this has had on local animals and insects I do not know. But I was raised in the shadow of a depression and I recall the rationing of World War II. I grew up feeling it was almost sinful to waste food. I throw all scraps into an arroyo, to cycle them back into the food chain. Ravens will circle if there are any bones, descending finally to pick off shreds of meat. Later, something will carry the bones away. Breadcrusts vanish quickly.

Thus I alter the world about me in countless ways every day. Small things, these personal changes, hardly on a scale with those alterations wrought by industry or government projects. Yet the total of all our changes, from the burning of Amazon forests to provide grazing land for the cattle that fill our hamburger buns to the tossing of a few crumbs to local birds, produce a phenomenon sometimes called the Carson factor, named after Rachel Carson by writer William Ashworth to indicate the unforeseen secondary effects of primary human changes upon a part of our planet.

Yet—and even so—I am not a person who would like to see this or any other world embedded in Lucite for the benefit of future planetary archaeologists. Change is inevitable. Its alternative is death. Evolution is more and more a product of our own action or inaction. Living systems adapt constantly to the vagaries of our technological culture.

But what's to evolve on a gas giant or a barren rock that we should be mindful of it? I don't know, and things like that trouble me. I have spent much of my life creating scenarios. I even did it back when it was just called daydreaming—and this, too, I feel, is a very special part of the evolutionary process.

As a lifetime member of the L5 Society, I am in favor of space exploration and of cautious development of the solar system's resources. I am also leery of the Carson factor: We must avoid the extermination of any extraterrestrial life-form, from the smallest virus to some supercooled Plutonian blob, not only for its own sake but for the wealth of genetic material contained within it, material that would have evolved over eons, developing unique abilities for dealing with its problems and, by extension, our own.

In that we are not yet wise enough to maintain proper stewardship of our own planet, I am particularly happy that these large-scale endeavors lie far beyond the horizon. I also take consolation in the knowledge that if a government is involved, heels tend to drag, inertia maximizes in accordance with Murphy's, Max Weber's, and Parkinson's laws, and that the slowness which frustrates us so on the one hand provides time on the other, time for a measure of deliberation, for the development and pursuit of secondary concerns, for the occurrence of the proverbial second thoughts.

Yet Saturn's ice and volatiles will have a value. Its helium is very scarce on Earth—and the rare form, helium 3, could provide a potent fuel for nuclear fusion in power generation. Some of its less exotic materials will doubtless be desired one day for terraforming purposes elsewhere in the solar system. The materials of the outer satellites of the gas giants are more tempting than those that lie far deeper within the massive worlds' gravity wells. This means that Saturn's outermost moon, Phoebe, would be a likely candidate for mining. And Titan, more Earth-like than any other planetary body, may well be an ideal place to set up a permanent scientific base. Those scientists lucky enough to be first on the base will have the initial opportunity to observe—and exploit—whatever lies within Saturn's great interior.

Let us paint some fanciful pictures, then. Let us develop a scenario about Saturnian affairs some 200 years hence. And let us talk of life—the big question, the one which comes first to mind when considering an alien environment or when speaking of preservation: Will we find any life when we give close attention to that great ringed world?

If higher life had evolved in such a place, it would have to be able to survive in a great range of temperature and pressure scales or else be capable of holding itself at relatively stable levels within the atmosphere. The absence of a solid surface would require a creature able to control its buoyancy in ways analogous to some of Earth's sea creatures. It might achieve this by containing within itself enough of the hydrogen gas to match the density of the upper atmosphere. This would seem to indicate a tough-skinned balloonlike creature that could ride the planet's winds and rise and fall within certain limits.

To enter the world of such a creature is to discard our entire culture. But we've already come this far, so let's . . .

She drifted, browsing, amid canyons of steely cloud whence flowed lightning discharges like instant bright rivers. Songs of the others filled the air about her with soothing rhythms. Below, the beat of the Everdeep pulsed at the heart of mystery, nether pole of existence, eternal dreamdark presence. That one day, perhaps soon, she would join the mystery, toppling down the sky, broken-bagged, from heat layer to heat layer, spinning the last life equations through lanes of mist and crystal, songless, descrying the lower wonders at long last, she knew, as all of them knew, there in the zone of song which was memory and the marriage of minds, knew, and was incapable of avoiding, there in the shoals of life, moving in the timeless present.

And recently there had been certain twinges . . .

Rick had come to the station on Titan, Earth-alien carbuncle facing across the sea of darkness toward the ancient king in yellow, Saturn, there to behold the instruments of his trade in yet another chamber.

A highly specialized mining engineer, more mathematician even than technician, Rick seldom looked through the station's ports at the planet itself, preferring the cleaner picture, the precise representation of the mass and structure of that giant body as displayed by the section of monitoring instruments for which he was responsible.

He knew, for example, that the planet's heavier elements—primarily iron and silicon—were concentrated in its small core, along with most of the water, methane, and ammonia, held in the form of very dense liquids by the high pressures and temperatures. And he knew well of the separation of helium from hydrogen, with the helium forming drops and raining down to even deeper levels—for he personally programmed the "plows," those scoop-ships that harvested the exotic helium 3, which provided fuel for nuclear fusion in power generators.

Emerging from the dining room, he looked about quickly for a place of concealment. Dr. Morton Trampler—short and round, owl-eyed behind thick glasses—was approaching, and he was smiling, and aiming the expression in Rick's direction. For reasons known only to the gods of psychology, Morton had earlier chosen Rick for a confidante, cornering him often to deliver lengthy monologues on his pet theory and project. The fact that he had recited the same information earlier seemed not to bother him in the least.

Too late.

Rick smiled weakly and nodded.

"How goes it?" he said.

"Wonderfully," the smaller man replied. "I should have a fresh batch of readings in a little while."

"Same level?"

"No, a bit deeper than I've gone in the past."

"Still broadcasting synthetic whale songs?"

Morton nodded.

"Well . . . good luck," Rick said, edging away.

"Thanks," Morton replied, catching hold of his arm. "We could pick up something very interesting. . . ."

Here it comes, Rick decided. That bit about the layer below the frozen salts and ice crystals where the complex organic molecules form, to drift downward like plankton to that area where the pressures and temperatures are similar to Earth's atmosphere. . . .

"The probe is going through that area where complex organic molecules form," Morton began. "We've finally screened the transmitter against much of the static."

Rick was suddenly reminded of the wedding guest and the ancient mariner. But the guest had been lucky. He'd only had to hear the story once.

Now comes the biology, he reflected. I am about to hear of the hypothetical living balloons with gravity-perceptive *sensilla* and electrical broadcasting and receiving organs whose waves penetrate surfaces—giving them a "texture sense" as well as a means of communication. I guess everybody needs a hobby, but . . .

". . . And the possibility of a life-form streamlined for constant vertical adjustments of position," Morton was saying. "Point symmetry rather than line symmetry could well be the case, giving it a brain more like that of the

octopus than the whale. Radial rather than bilateral symmetry would eliminate the left-hemisphere–right-hemisphere separation of the higher creatures on Earth. What this would mean in terms of modes of thought would be a difficult thing to guess at."

A new twist. He was actually dashing after finer and finer illusory points of biology now. Seeing the opening simultaneous with Morton's pausing for an inhalation, Rick plunged, satisfying months of irritation:

"There is no such creature, and if there were, there would be no point in getting in touch," he said. "They could build nothing, they have nothing to experiment with. So there would be no technology. All of their culture would be within their weird minds, so they would have no history. If one of them ever had a great idea and none of the others appreciated it, it would die with him. They would know nothing beyond their sky, and not much about what's down below either. Their dead would just sink and vanish. They'd have no homes, they'd just wander. They would do nothing but eat, make noises at each other, and think incomprehensible point-symmetrical thoughts. I doubt we could ever find grounds for conversation, and if we did we'd find we had nothing to talk about. They'd probably be stupid, too."

Morton looked appalled.

"I have to disagree," he said. "There are such things as oral culture, and their communications could take the form of, say, a great oratorio. I would say it is impossible right now to imagine what they think or feel. Which is why it would be so great to communicate—to find out."

Rick shook his head.

"Morty, it's like the Loch Ness Monster and the Abominable Snowman. I don't believe they're there."

"And if they are, it doesn't matter?"

"They're not there," Rick said. "The universe is a lonely place."

Moving through food-fall to densest point. Eating here, singing location-vectors-coming-to-song. Crowding distant side spaces, clouds. Crackle song of storm far to rear. Flicker of storm in songs of other eaters there, arriving now, giving distance against sizzling.

Pain. More and more, with rising and falling, expansion, contraction, the notes of sharp, fiery pain ...

Grown, young of this voice, drifting, browsing free. Borne no more, bodyfed no more of this voice. To come forth no others; tightened, place of birthing; locking and dryness. Gone. With age the body-bag stiffens, weakness comes, song wavers. Long has it been so, this voice. Compute. ... Soon now, very soon, the time of collapse and sinking, the end-of-songtime will come.

Pain . . .

Pulsing, in the Everdeep, stronger, always stronger now. Voice of Everdeep, slow and steady. Calling, calling this voice to songs-end rest. Falling-to place of burst, stopped voices. Returning not ever. Never again.

Old, song of Returned Voice. . . . False song of very young? Or very old? Song of Reinflated, of fallen voices, rising, singing again, of Evercalm, of food-full skies in place of no mating, no birthing, no bagburst, strifeless and eversong perfect. False song? Returned Voice? Returning no more, sing it, stopped voices. True song? Returned Voice?

Stiffness, slow-filling bag, slow-emptying. Stiffness. Pain, everpain. Soon. Time-matrix, there. . . . Soon to enter Everdeep, fall-place of all food and voices. Songs-end.

This is now. Pain. Eating's cease.

To end song here? Drifting, filled . . .

No.

To fill one time more? Rising, passing hard-filled particle-clouds? Rising, singing, to high place of food-fall source? Indeterminate intersection, fall-angles axes. . . . Find it, somewhere, up. Cease singing there. Find it, feel it, know it and fall. To mount sky-high, singing, wind-dance, end-dance, touching textures. Feeling, thrusting, calling. Better to fall from high than from some middle height, knowing perhaps, telling . . .

Go then, high up, before bursting of bag. To know source. Understand mystery. Fall then, far, silent at last and knowing, down Everdeep, knowing. To have touched. Knowing source, life. Returned Voice? No matter. To know, at singing's last.

Inflating now. Like jagged lightnings in body, the pain. To open. Calling, young of this voice, "Go not. Go not now. Stay. Browse and sing."

Singing this, too, into storm and fall, counterpoint, inflating. Growing, pain like heat. To go. To go. High. To sense, to sing back, feeling . . .

Rising, slowly. Going. Rising. Hello, hello. Going. Good-bye, good-bye.

Touching, textures of cloud. Soft, hard. Warm, cool. Rising, tower of warm air, there. Join it.

Easier way, thus. Mounting faster. Fountain of warmth. Riding, rising. Higher. Through clouds. Up.

Bright cracklings, wind-pushed clouds, browsers, food-fall. Higher . . .

Soaring, expanding. Hot pains, creaking of bag. Faster. Tossed and spinning.

Song-dampening, clouds, winds, crackling. Voices tiny, tinier. There below, fire-flecked, cloud-dappled, wind-washed, fall-swept, small—young of this voice, listening. Listening.

Higher . . .

Singing back, this voice. Telling. Telling, of lift and drift. Of rising. Below, young of this voice, hearing . . .

Rising . . .

. . . into heat, into continuing food-fall.

"Voice here, voice here"—singing of this voice, to singers there.

Going, down the song? Hearing, some voice, somewhere? Above?

Higher . . .

Singing, more loudly now, within heat-rise. Reaching, reaching. . . . Expanding, creaking. Pain, hot and spreading.

Is heat, all . . .

Beat, beat, beat, beat, beat. Following, pulse of the Everdeep. Matching, pulse of this voice. Slow, steady. Calling. Sending song of this voice back down . . .

"Voice here. . . ."

Answers not.

Again . . .

"Returned Voice? Breaking soon, this bag, this voice. Sing back."

Answers not. Higher. Higher. So high, never. Below, all clouds. Evercloud. Smothered, songs of the young of this voice. Too far . . .

Above, tiny. Something, something. . . . Singing, strange voice, strange song, never of this voice heard . . .

Understanding not.

Higher. Hotter . . .

"Voice here. . . ."

Something, somewhere above. Far. Too far. Louder now, strange singing. Matching it, this voice, now. Trying. To it, "Mm-mm-mm-mm-mm? Returned Voice? To Everdeep, soon, this voice. Bear this voice, bodyfeed this voice, down. Down Everdeep, Returned Voice. To place of evercalm, food-full skies, no mating, no birthing, no bagburst, strifeless and eversong perfect. Hello, hello? Returned Voice? Returned Voice. Hello? Mm-mm-mm-mm-mm."

Above and tiny. Above and tiny. Fast-moving. Too far. Too far. Goes not up, the singing. Varies not the song from on high. No answer.

Shuddering, creaking, tearing. Heat, heat. Now, now the breaking.

The pain . . .

Buffeted, swept sidewise. Turned. Spinning. Collapsing. Grows smaller, skies, all. Falling. Falling. Smaller. Good-bye. The fall, the fall of this voice begins.

Down, twisting. Faster . . .

Faster than foodfall, through clouds, back, cooler, cooler, unvoiced, shrinking. Lights, fires, winds, songs, fleeing past. Loud, loud. Good-bye. Pulse of Everdeep. Hello. Returned Voice? Falling . . .

Spiral symmetry vectoring indicates—

Pulsing is all. . . .

After dinner Rick, vaguely troubled, walked to the control center. It bothered him now, having stepped on the other man's pet idea. Ten minutes' penance, he decided, should be sufficient to sop his conscience, and he could check his own instruments while he was in the place.

When he entered the bright, cool chamber he saw Morton doing a small dance to a sequence of eerie sounds emerging from one of his monitors.

"Rick!" he exclaimed as he caught sight of him. "Listen to this stuff I picked up!"

"I am."

The notes of the creature's death song emerged from the speaker.

"Sounds as if one of them rose to an unusual height. I'd figured them for a lower lev—"

"It's atmospheric," Rick said. "There's nothing down there. You're getting neurotic about this business."

He wanted to bite his tongue immediately, but he could not help saying what he felt.

"We've never picked up anything atmospheric at that frequency."

"You know what happens to artists who fall in love with their models? They come to a bad end. The same applies to scientists."

"Keep listening. Something's doing it. Then it breaks off suddenly, as if—"

"It's different, all right. But I just don't think anything could cut it down in that soup."

"I'll talk to them one day," Morton insisted.

Rick shook his head, then forced himself to talk again.

"Play it over," he suggested.

Morton pushed a button and after several moments' pause the buzzing, humming, whistling sequence started anew.

"I've been thinking about what you said earlier," Morton remarked, "about communication . . ."

"Yes?"

"You asked what we'd have to say to each other."

"Exactly. If they're there."

The sounds rose in pitch. Rick began to feel uncomfortable. Could there possibly? . . .

"They would have no words for all of the concrete things which fill our lives," Morton stated, "and even many of our abstractions are based upon the possession of human anatomy and physiology. Our poetry of valley and mountain, river and field, night and day with stars and sun would not come through well."

163

Rick nodded. If they exist, he wondered, what would they have that we want?

"Perhaps only music and mathematics, our most abstract art and science, could serve as points of contact," Morton went on. "Beyond that, some sort of metalanguage would really have to be developed."

"A record of their songs might have some commercial value," Rick mused.

"And then?" the smaller man suggested. "Would we be the serpent in their Eden, detailing wonders they might never experience directly, causing them some strange existential traumas? Or could it possibly be the other way around? What may they know or feel that we have not even guessed?"

"I'm getting some ideas for breaking this thing down mathematically, to see whether there's a real logic sequence behind it," Rick said suddenly. "I think I've seen some linguistic formulations that might apply."

"Linguistics?" Morton observed. "That's not your area."

"I know, but I love math theory, no matter where it's from."

"Interesting. What if they had a complex mathematics that the human mind simply could not comprehend?"

"I'd go mad over it," Rick replied. "It would snare my soul." Then he laughed. "But there's nothing there, Morty. We're just screwing around. . . . Unless there's a pattern," he decided. "Then we cash in."

Morton grinned.

"There is. I'm sure of it."

That night Rick's sleep was troubled by strange periodicities. The rhythms of the song throbbed in his head. He dreamed that the song and the language were one with a mathematical vision no bilaterally symmetrical brain could ever share. He dreamed of ending his days in frustration, seeing the thing cracked by brute computer force but never being able to comprehend the elegance.

In the morning he forgot. He located the formulations for Morton and translated them into a program of analysis, humming an irregular tune which never went quite right as he worked.

Later, he went to a port and stared for a long while at the giant ringed world itself. After a time it bothered him, not being able to decide whether he was looking up or looking down.

Uranus

ESSAY BY
Dale P. Cruikshank
FANTASY BY
Philip José Farmer
SPECULATION BY
Charles Sheffield

URANUS: DISTANT GIANT

Dale P. Cruikshank

IN THE LAST DECADE, our robotic eyes and ears have taken us deep into the distant reaches of our solar system where Jupiter and Saturn, the largest planets, hold court for their retinues of circling satellites. The Pioneer and Voyager spacecraft have revealed these worlds in stunning detail and with a clarity that had only been dreamed of by three centuries of Earth-bound astronomers, who tried to glean their secrets in the feeble light gathered from these bodies by their telescopes. Building upon this foundation of hard-won knowledge, spacecraft have recently shown us the intricacies of color and motion in Jupiter's ponderous atmosphere, with its Great Red Spot—the vortex *suprima*—and a gossamer ring of tiny particles circling its equator. The four Moon-size satellites discovered by Galileo in 1610 quickly emerged as worlds in their own right, one with active volcanoes, one with a frozen universal sea, and two others with the surface scars of cataclysmic impacts and crustal motions.

When Voyagers 1 and 2 reached Saturn 2 years later, plummeting across the vast distance separating the two largest planets, we scrutinized the ringed giant that has captured our imaginations for centuries. The three beautiful rings seen in telescopes from Earth blossomed into thousands of delicate ringlets under the close-up gaze of Voyager. The colored cloud bands of Saturn's massive atmosphere showed their whirls and swirls, and the family of satellites emerged as icy worlds with shattered and tortured frozen surfaces. Titan, the largest satellite, revealed a busy organic chemical factory high in its atmosphere, and two-faced Iapetus showed its icy and perhaps tarry hemispheres as the Voyagers sped past.

But what lies beyond Saturn? What have the astronomers seen with their telescopes, and what will Voyager 2 encounter in its race toward the edge of the solar system?

We stand with our hand outstretched toward a door through which we can presently see only hazily. Beyond the door lie the planets Uranus and Neptune, the outermost giants of the solar system, and one of the Voyager spacecraft is about to open that door and expose them with a fleeting but penetrating glance.

URANUS DISCOVERED

To the Greeks, the Egyptians, the Chinese, and all the ancient peoples who studied the sky, the "wanderers," or planets, included only those out as far as Saturn. All of the objects in the solar system beyond Saturn have been found only since the invention of the telescope in the very early 1600s. The first discovery was made by an amateur astronomer who was scanning the skies with his homemade 6-inch telescope. William Herschel, a German musician working in England, had become fascinated with the sky and learned to make small telescopes with which he systematically cataloged stars and comets and watched the planets. On March 13, 1781, he found a fuzzy object in the sky and at first thought it was a new comet. Subsequent observations soon showed that it was no comet, but a planet that had never been seen before!

Herschel's new planet, now known by the mythological name Uranus (after Urania, the Greek muse of astronomy), brought him good fortune, for he was appointed court astronomer to King George III and thus gained the leisure to pursue astronomy as his career. His legacy to astronomy grew to include larger and better telescopes and discoveries of many new things in the sky, not to mention his son John, an eminent astronomer himself.

Uranus orbits the Sun at a distance of almost 20 AU. One AU, or astronomical unit, is 150 kilometers, the distance of Earth from the Sun. Uranus's orbit is very close to a position that had been predicted by the Bode-Titius rule, an empirical rule for calculating the spacing of the planets. (According to this rule Neptune should have been orbiting at 39 AU, but in fact it orbits at 30.1 AU.)

THE INTERIOR OF URANUS

Through a telescope, even a very large one, Uranus and Neptune appear very tiny, distinguished from the background stars by their small, extended disks and faint colors. Uranus is greenish in color and Neptune is light blue. We now know that these colors are the result of the atmospheres of the two planets and the way that specific gases and clouds in the atmospheres absorb and reflect the sunlight that shines on them. Uranus appears in the telescope about twice the size of Neptune, but this is because Neptune is almost twice as far away. In fact, both planets are very nearly the same size, about four times the diameter of Earth.

Uranus is 50,800 kilometers in diameter. The spectrograph has revealed that it has a dense atmosphere composed primarily of hydrogen, but with about 10 percent helium and lesser amounts of methane and ammonia. It is the very strong absorption of sunlight by methane gas and the fact that the upper atmosphere is clear of any haze that gives Uranus its greenish color.

In the chapter about Jupiter, we saw that the giant outer planets, by virtue of the hydrogen and helium that comprise their bulk compositions, can be compared with the Sun. The Sun is, after all, a big gas ball of hydrogen that is slowly being converted into helium by the nuclear reactions in progress in its interior. The heat energy that radiates to Earth and the other planets is a by-product of this nuclear activity, but the overall composition and bulk density (amount of mass in a given volume) of the Sun is very similar to that of Jupiter and Saturn, which, of course, are very cold. Now, while the atmosphere of Uranus (and Neptune, as we shall see) is primarily composed of hydrogen, the bulk density of this planet is greater than either Jupiter, Saturn, or the Sun. This suggests that deep in the interior of Uranus there is some heavier material, perhaps made of the silicate minerals and metals that comprise so much of the smaller planets nearer to the Sun, such as Earth and Venus.

The core of Uranus, according to the best current estimates, is comparable to Earth in size and mass and is probably composed mostly of rocky material at a temperature of about 1,000°C or so. Surrounding this Earth-like seed is a mantle of mostly water, with some methane, nitrogen, and ammonia mixed in. While these materials normally form ices in their frozen state on the surfaces of the cold outer planets and their satellites, in the mantle of Uranus they are probably in a liquid or mushy, semisolid state. Above the mantle of slush is the deep atmosphere where the occasional clouds and haze form that we see with our telescopes and passing spacecraft.

Why are the unseen insides of a remote planet of any particular interest? One of the goals of planetary science is to establish the conditions under which the Sun and planets formed from the gas and dust accumulated in patches among the stars and called the interstellar medium. The compositions and structures of the Sun's family of planets are important keys to understanding the formation and subsequent evolution of the entire solar system, a question that has vexed scientists and philosophers at least since the time of the Greeks.

There is another reason for an interest in planetary interiors, for it is there that planetary magnetic fields are formed. Earth's magnetic field causes, among other things, the intense auroras that are seen in high northern and southern latitudes, and we now know that Jupiter has similar auroras in its polar regions.

But not all planets have magnetic fields, and this tells us that the interiors of some planets are very different from the others. Uranus has been studied not only with ground-based telescopes, but with remotely controlled observatories orbiting Earth as artificial satellites. From measurements made with these unmanned satellite observatories, we find that Uranus appears to have an aurora at its pole. This in turn implies that there is a magnetic field surrounding the planet, a field that is generated by fluid motions in Uranus's interior. Whether these fluids move in a molten rock-metal core (as is the case with Earth and its magnetic field) or in the mushy surrounding mantle is unknown, but this problem is one of great current interest to planetary scientists.

We know that both Jupiter and Saturn give off more heat than they receive from the Sun, probably because there is a continuing process in their interiors of settling out, or "unmixing," of the various kinds of materials there. Uranus appears not to have a heat supply in excess of that which it receives from the Sun, though our knowledge of this is presently incomplete. Why is Uranus different from Jupiter and Saturn in this regard? We don't know, but this fact is a clue to the interior composition and structure of the planet, and we can only hope that it will be unraveled as we continue our study of the giant bodies of the outer solar system.

A TIPPED PLANET

One of the great enigmas of Uranus is the fact that it is tipped over! Most of the other planets in the solar system have their rotational axes more or less perpendicular to the plane of their motion around the Sun. As a planet forms from a rotating and collapsing cloud of dust, gas, and large chunks of solid matter, its rotational axis should be more or less aligned perpendicular to the plane of the disk, and while Earth, Mars, and some other planets are tipped by a few or several degrees (23.5 degrees for Earth, a fact that gives us our annual pattern of seasons), Uranus is peculiar in that its axis lies very close to its orbital plane.

How this configuration came about is a subject of much serious thought on the part of scientists concerned with the formation of the planets. The best current idea is that toward the end of the formation period, when most of the solid material in the solar system had condensed into the major planets, there were many Moon-size, or even Earth-size, objects moving in orbits that took them near the major planets. Eventually, most of these bodies collided with the major planets, and in cases where the colliding object was sufficiently large or the planet sufficiently small, there was enough energy in the impact to cause the planet to tip its rotational axis. The experience we have all had of tipping a rotating gyroscope can give us some idea of the energy required to change the rotational axis of an entire planet, so the energy of the impacts postulated to tip over Uranus must have been prodigious indeed!

But what of the satellites in this scenario? Preexisting satellites could hardly have survived the big tip, especially in their present highly circular and orderly orbits. It is speculated that the impact that tipped the planet blasted off material from either Uranus or the impacting body (or both) and that this material condensed in the space around the planet to form the present system of five satellites (and possibly the rings as well).

RINGS AROUND URANUS

The rings around Saturn are known to every schoolchild, and every cartoonist's picture of the nighttime sky includes at least one planet with a ring around it. When Voyager 1 flew past Jupiter in 1979, it found a faint and tenuous ring surrounding that planet. Two years earlier, in 1977, astronomers flying in an airplane observatory high above the southern Pacific Ocean made the accidental and unexpected discovery that Uranus has a complex system of at least nine individual rings circling its equator. In stunning contrast to the broad, bright rings of Saturn, the nine rings of Uranus are very narrow—only a few kilometers wide—and are made of swarms of little black particles. Furthermore, while three of the rings are circular, six are not. Instead, they are elliptical in form, and these ellipses move around Uranus in a way that gives additional clues to the interior structure of the planet.

Saturn's rings consist of aggregates of billions of tennis ball-size chunks made mostly of frozen water. They form a configuration some 350,000 kilometers in breadth but only about 1 kilometer thick. Why, then, are the rings of Uranus so different in both form and composition? They are so thin and tenuous that our best theories say that the rings should have disappeared long ago. Yet, there they are. We do not know if they formed at the time that Uranus itself formed from the solar nebula some 4.6 billion years ago, or if they were created much more recently by dust that was knocked off one of Uranus's satellites, or perhaps captured from a passing comet.

URANUS'S FAMILY OF SATELLITES

Following Herschel's discovery of Uranus in 1781, telescopes improved rapidly in size and quality. Six years later, Herschel himself discovered two faint satellites around his planet, and subsequent studies over the last two centuries have revealed three more, for a total of five. Until the last few years, we have had to be content knowing just the number of Uranian satellites and a little bit about their orbits around the planet. This state of ignorance has changed dramatically, however, as scientists have begun to use large telescopes with advanced instruments attached to them to study the outer planets and their satellites.

Seen from Earth, the satellites are tiny points of light, even with the largest telescopes. They are some 2,000 times fainter than the faintest star visible to the naked eye. Yet with advanced electronic detectors on big telescopes, we can now determine the composition of the satellites, establish their sizes, and estimate what their interiors may be like.

The five satellites of Uranus all lie in circular orbits well outside the region where the rings encircle the planet. They are known by names taken from characters in Shakespeare's plays: Oberon, Titania, Ariel, Umbriel, and Miranda. Uranus and its satellites are about 3 billion kilometers from Earth, and the sunlight falling on them is so feeble that the surface temperatures of the satellites never exceed about −190°C. Nevertheless, the high-technology instruments of modern astronomy allow us to detect the heat radiation from the five Uranian satellites, cold and distant as they are.

The first such measurements were made from Mauna Kea Observatory atop a 4,200-meter volcanic mountain in Hawaii in 1981. From measurements of the heat flow of the satellites, it is possible to determine their diameters and the reflectivities of their surfaces. Because the satellites are so small and distant, the heat measurement is, in fact, the only way to establish their sizes until we can send a robot spacecraft to make direct observations. Each of the satellites is tiny by comparison with Uranus itself; the largest, Oberon, is less than half the size of the Moon, while Miranda, the smallest, is comparable to an average asteroid.

Studies of the near-infrared light from the satellites of Uranus begun in 1979 have shown that all five bodies have surfaces covered in large part by water ice. As we have seen, earlier work of a similar kind revealed that three of Jupiter's satellites have water ice on their surfaces, as do most of the satellites of Saturn. Water, then, is a very common substance in the middle regions of the solar system (from Earth out to Uranus), though beyond Jupiter it is frozen because of the very low temperature at large distances from the Sun.

Ice isn't the only substance on the Uranian satellites, for studies of the spectrum of light reflected from them show that some other darker material, either ordinary dirt or possibly black organic residue, must also be present, mixed in some way with the ice. The details haven't been worked out yet, and may not be until the Voyager 2 spacecraft visits Uranus and its satellites, but it is possible that the dark material contaminating the ice on the satellites is the same dark stuff that comprises the rings of Uranus.

There is an interesting clue that the satellites may be dissimilar from one another apart from minor differences in the way their surfaces reflect light and the distribution of the dark material in the ice. Observation of the effect that each satellite has on the motion of its neighbors over a long span of several years has made it possible to determine their masses. When combined with the new determinations of the diameters of the satellites, this new information makes it possible to calculate their bulk densities. The bulk density of a satellite of pure ice would be about 1 gram per cubic centimeter, as is the case with one of Jupiter's and one of Saturn's satellites. Two of the four largest Uranian satellites, however, have bulk densities of about 1.3, and the other two are about 2.6 grams per cubic centimeter. Ariel and Umbriel, with the lower densities, probably have a higher proportion of pure ice, while Titania and Oberon, with the higher densities, probably have larger amounts of rocky material mixed in with the ice in their interiors. They may even have rock cores surrounded by a liquid mantle of water that is frozen in a layer a kilometer or so thick at the surface. Thus, the satellites may fall into two distinct and different categories of composition and interior structure. For the time being we know very little about Miranda, but all that is about to change.

VOYAGER TO URANUS

On August 20, 1977, the Voyager 1 spacecraft was launched from Florida. Sixteen days later, Voyager 2 joined it on an odyssey that would take both spacecraft past Jupiter (in 1979), and past Saturn in 1980–1981. The flights of Voyager to these giant planets opened new worlds to the gaze of the scientists.

Having finished its studies at Saturn, the Voyager 1 spacecraft veered north and out of the plane of the solar system. Voyager 2, however, took a sharp left turn toward Uranus in order to continue the odyssey to the outermost reaches of the planetary system. While the minimum distance between Saturn and Uranus is about 1.5 billion kilometers, the spacecraft's trajectory is taking it over a path of 2.8 billion kilometers in the 4 years and 4 months required to make the journey. With an average velocity of some 40 kilometers per second, Voyager 2 will whiz past Uranus on January 24, 1986, at about 10 times the speed of a rifle bullet.

As we saw, Uranus is tipped in such a way that at the present time its pole faces the general direction of Earth and the Sun. Consequently, the view presented to the approaching Voyager 2 spacecraft is a polar view not only of the planet but of the satellites as well. The circular satellite orbits appear to Voyager as a bull's-eye with Uranus at the center. The celestial navigators here on Earth

172

have taken careful aim with their one and only shot at Uranus, pointing to a spot that will take the spacecraft closest to the inner satellite Miranda, missing by about 49,000 kilometers. At the same time, satellite Ariel will be well in view at a distance of 140,000 kilometers, but the other satellites will be substantially farther away at various points in their orbits. The closest approach to Uranus itself will be some 107,000 kilometers.

The cameras and other instruments aboard Voyager 2 will photograph the details of the clouds in the atmosphere of Uranus and will reveal geological structures on Miranda and Ariel with a resolution of about 2 kilometers. At that resolution we expect to see craters, ridges, and other structures similar to those seen on the icy satellites of Saturn. The number and form of craters and the character of the landscape on which they occur will tell us much about the formation and subsequent history of these satellites, for the experience with other cratered worlds has already taught us much about the bombardment suffered by planets and their satellites in the dim, distant past when they first took form. Do the Uranian satellites bear any scars of the cataclysm that caused the entire plant to tip over on its side?

The powerful infrared and ultraviolet instruments aboard the spacecraft will probe the atmosphere of Uranus, searching for specific gases that are clues to the origin and the evolution of the gaseous outer envelope. How much helium is there in the mostly hydrogen atmosphere? What is the nature of the aurora seen from Earth, and does it reveal a magnetic field generated within the planet? Are organic molecules being produced as a photochemical smog in the high atmosphere of Uranus, as is the case elsewhere on various planets (including on Earth, over big cities)? And what of the rings? Voyager's glance at them will give new information on their sizes and the packing of the particles comprising them.

We wait impatiently to see.

URANUS
OR
UFO VERSUS IRS

Philip José Farmer

"THEY JUST killed one of our babies!"

The tiny TV transmitter-receiver orbiting the mothership, *Herschel*, showed the bright side of the craft and, below, the blue-green oblate shape of Uranus. Though *Herschel* was in *epsilon*, the broadest of the planet's eleven rings, the TV viewers on Earth did not see *epsilon*. The coal-black particles composing the ring were too far apart and too small to appear solid at this close range. Nor did the rings cast a shadow on the planet. At this moment and for twenty years to come, Uranus was tipped so that its south pole was to the Sun. When the TV satellite circled to *Herschel's* other side, its camera would show the bright crescent that the Sun made on the planet's southern hemisphere.

"There's the Sun."

Rees, the anchorman for KPIT-TV, was talking from the Houston studio to his three billion viewers. "That tiny disk of intense light. Not much compared to our bonfire terrestrial Sun, but it's millions of times brighter than the great star Sirius. From Uranus, our Sun is a bright thought in the midst of many pale ones."

Throughout the special program, the statistics had been spooned to the mass audience because of its limited attention span, an estimated three and a half minutes. The viewers had learned, or at least heard, that Saturn was the seventh planet out from the Sun. It was a far-off celestial body, being nineteen point eighteen times the mean distance of Earth from the Sun. Way out.

The "jolly green giant," as the *Herschel* crew called it, was only one-fifth denser than water and was more massive than fourteen Earths. Its hot core of silicon and iron, however, was not quite as large as Earth's. The outermost layers of its enormous atmosphere were thin, cold hydrogen layers. A spacecraft descending through this (none had) would get warmer as it passed through

174

methane, hydrogen, and helium clouds into a thick fog of ammonia crystals. The warmth was only relative; you certainly couldn't use it to toast your marshmallows.

Below the crystals blowing at hurricane speed would be water vapor clouds. Then the fog would become slush and, later and deeper, hot liquid hydrogen. At a depth of approximately eight thousand kilometers, the temperature would shoot up to more than two thousand degrees Centigrade. Then the spacecraft would penetrate, if it could, a slushy or frozen layer of water and ammonia. The rock-metal core would be at seven thousand degrees Centigrade, hotter than the surface of the Sun.

At this statement, one of the three billion viewers had muttered, though in no terrestrial language, "A thousand kilometers above the core is hot enough for the third stage of growth."

Uranus, Rees said, had seven small moons. Puck and Bottom had recently been added to the long-known Ariel, Titania, Oberon, Umbriel, and Miranda.

Like Saturn, Uranus had rings around its equator, but these were not Saturn-bright. They were dark and much narrower, steeped in iron oxides and complex carbon compounds, which absorbed sunlight. These rotated in a thin gas of negatively charged electrons and positively charged ions.

Most of this data had slipped by or been forgotten by most of the viewers. They were absorbed in watching the *Herschel* matching its velocity and proximity with one of the larger objects forming the ring. This was black and about two meters long and three meters at the widest part. Its "body" was flattened out; its "wings" were almost as thick as the body. It looked more like a devilfish or batfish than anything, though it took some imagination to see the parallel. What made it so riveting to the viewers was that it was not the first such object observed. One hundred and thirty-nine had been photographed in this small sector approximately one hundred kilometers wide and ten thousand kilometers long.

"No theory has been advanced, so far," Rees said, "as to why these space objects seem to resemble artifacts. Nor has any scientist theorized why they're so evenly distributed."

"How about the need for living room, space to grow and feed in?" Agrafan said. Agrafan was one of the two viewers in three billion who could have enlightened Rees. Not that he was going to do so.

The *Herschel*, having matched its velocity exactly to that of the object, moved sideways toward it. The screen displayed to the Earthbound audience a closeup so that they could see the four "antennae," two slim spirals of seeming rocklike material projecting from the junction of "wings" and "body" and two pointing from the "belly." The remotely controlled TV machine revolving around the ship showed the cargo bay port swinging out from the hull. Then it showed the brightly illuminated bay and a long mechanical arm unfolding from its base on the hull. Its spidery metal "fingers" were opening.

Netter, one of the two viewers who knew what was happening, said. "About ten seconds to go."

"It's terrible, " Agrafan said. "And there's absolutely nothing we can do about it."

Agrafan, the more emotional of the two, discharged a mist of formaldehyde particles, its equivalent of human tears.

The mechanical arm stopped. Its fingers only needed to close to delicately grip the object.

"They can't be blamed," Netter said. "How're they to know?"

"That doesn't help," Agrafan said.

The fingers of the mechanical arm closed on the object. Only two of the three billion viewers were not surprised when the fingers and the object were briefly shrouded in blinding electricity. There was no explosive noise, of course.

The fragments of the object, impelled by the discharge, floated away. The fingers, half-melted, were frozen in their half-grip.

Startled and shocked, Rees cried out a four-letter word as pungent (socially speaking) as the product it referred to. Half of the citizens of the United States heard that, and less than half of that were offended. However, the network executives and millions of members of American religious organizations were outraged.

When the astronauts had recovered from their alarm, the captain explained what had happened. The *epsilon* ring was in a low-density plasma of relatively negatively charged electrons and positively charged ions. Since the electrons were less massive, they moved faster in the ring than the ions did. They collided more often with the rock debris in the ring. Thus, the pieces of debris built up, after a long time, a negative charge.

The astronauts had known this, but the *Herschel,* having been in the ring for thirteen months, had also collected a negative charge. Hence, they had not expected much of a discharge, if any.

The object they had tried to pick up must not have been in the ring long enough to pick up much of a negative charge. That had to be the only explanation possible. The object had been relatively positive to the arm, which, placed on the outside of the hull, had become positively charged.

The astronauts had assumed that the object had been in the plasma of the ring as long as the other space debris. Obviously, it had not. Where, then, had it come from? And when? And why were there so many similar objects that, for some unknown reason, looked as if they had been shaped by sentients?

Neither the astronauts nor the scientists on Earth were ever to advance the theory that the objects were living.

The only two on Earth who could have enlightened the theorizers were too shaken with grief at that moment to pass on their knowledge even if they had wanted to. They were flying—rocketing was a better description—around their huge room deep under a house. They were out of control, bouncing into the frozen carbon dioxide walls and ceiling and floors. Added to their grief were slight injuries from the impacts as their fierce discharges of formaldehyde droplets shot them here and there.

These expressions were matched by anchorman Rees's uncontrollable tears and howlings. Rees was giving vent in his human way to the news that he had just been fired. Moreover, the entire industry would blackball him.

Jeremiah Gnatcatcher, a district director of the Internal Revenue Service, sat behind his desk in the Detroit skyscraper and scowled. The three field agents standing before his desk looked away from his eyes, as cold and as blue-green as Uranus in their human way and shields for a soul as black as Uranus's rings. No one spoke for a long time; if Gnatcatcher had not been grinding his teeth, there would have been complete silence. It sounded to the agents like a shovel digging their graves.

At last, harshly, Gnatcatcher said, "What do you mean, Mr. Agrafan and Mr. Netter can't come here? Since when can any taxpayer refuse to come here?"

Smith, the boldest of the agents, said, "Well, chief, it's this way. Agrafan and Netter have notarized statements by three doctors that health reasons confine them to their house. So, like it or not, we have to go to them. Only . . ."

"Only what?" Gnatcatcher growled.

"Only . . . we can't go to them for the same reason they can't come to us. The doctors say that the allergies and poor immunity-protection systems of the two require them to live practically in quarantine. They're like those babies that live in isolation bubbles."

The three agents could not interpret their boss's peculiar expression. That was because he had not used that particular interplay of facial muscles since becoming district director. It portrayed frustration.

"Okay, okay. So we can't, for the time being, anyway, get them in here to sweat them or go to them for browbeating. What about their lawyers? They don't have any excuse not to come here to represent their clients."

"The firm of Reynard, Wolfgang, Mustela, and Scarab has been very co-operative," Brown, the second agent, said. "After we got a court order to seize their tapes."

"I know that," Gnatcatcher said impatiently. "You dummies never catch on that all my questions are rhetorical."

"Sorry, boss," Smith, Brown, and Jones said in unison.

"So what have our auditors found?"

The three were silent. Finally, Gnatcatcher barked, "What's the matter? You don't *know*!"

"We thought the question was rhetorical," Smith said.

"I'll tell you when they're rhetorical. So, what have they dug up?"

"A can of worms," Smith said. "The tape records look okay on the surface, and they are. I mean, they're not doctored. But still waters run deep. Some of the tapes, most of them, in fact, have codes, references to other companies and record tapes. We had to get a second court order to force the lawyers to explain their meaning."

Smith stopped talking and licked his lips. His eyes were glazed.

"Well?" Gnatcatcher said.

"We uncovered a pyramid of real corporations and dummy corporations, a maze of interlocking financial structures that was so complex that even the computer had to shut down and cool off for a while. Our auditors got dizzy; one of them went to bed with chronic vertigo. But we've uncovered what looks to me like a conspiracy to end all conspiracies, a super-super-conglomerate. The Justice Department is going to have a ball with antitrust suits. If we tell them about this. Personally, I think we should. Anyway, those two hypochondriacs, Agrafan and Netter, if they are only hypochondriacs and not something sinister, make Howard Hughes look like an inept extrovert. They're at the apex of the pyramid and the end of the maze. They own . . ."

Smith licked his lips again. Gnatcatcher said, "Well?"

"Interlocking global conglomerates and several Third World nations worth . . . ah . . . worth . . ."

"Spill it, man! Get it out!"

Smith's voice squeaked.

"Three trillion dollars!"

"That Walt Whitman knew what the universe was all about," Agrafan said. "Listen.

I celebrate myself and sing myself,
And what I assume you shall assume.
For every atom belonging to me as good as belongs to you.

How about that? An ignorant Earth-person sees intuitively that all is connected. The atoms of Earth's flesh ring from the impact of a meteor falling into Uranus. A temple bell tolls in India, and an entity on Arcturus IV wonders where that vagrant but novel and illuminating thought comes from. Wonderful! Yet, he was an oxygen breather!"

"It's not that simple," Netter said.

They were in the subterranean room beneath the mansion which the local natives had built long ago for them without understanding why or for whom. The locals had been satisfied with the pay, and, if they were curious about it, they had not pursued their nosiness. Nor had the house servants ever tried to find out why their employers never revealed themselves but always gave orders through the telephone. They had been happy with the extremely high pay, though those hired in the beginning had not known that the money was counterfeit. Later, the two agents of UFO, the Uranian Field Operation, had made real money from their investments with the fake.

The house has been built in A.D. 1900 in a suburb of Detroit. Operating from within it, making contact with their servants by telephone and with their business managers by phone and messengers, the two had worked hard for twenty-nine years. It was they who purposely brought about the stock market crash of 1929 and the Great Depression. Unfortunately, the Uranian science-art of calculating trillions of physical factors and trillions of mental vectors had not been as well developed then as it was in the early part of the twenty-first century. The effect of the depression had not been quite what they had calculated. The depression had brought about World War II and, thus, a great step forward in the development and use of rockets. This, in turn, had accelerated and intensified the drive of Earth people to conquer space. Agrafan and Netter would have done better if they had kept Earth's economy prosperous.

Since World War II, the two agents, collaborating with their Uranian colleagues via atomic-impingement waves, had brought event influencing and calculating to a higher level. Or so they hoped. This time, they would certainly set back space exploration for a long time and, hence, destruction of Uranian higher life-forms.

World War II had also caused the invention of the atom bomb much sooner than anticipated. Agrafan and Netter could have started nuclear warfare any time in the last fifty years. They had twelve different ways to bring this about. The danger to Uranus would have been removed forever. That it would also have caused their deaths did not bother Agrafan and Netter. They were willing to sacrifice themselves.

But, though so unhuman-looking and lacking much of the physical and emotional warmth of humans, the Uranians were moral. It was not *right* to destroy the entire life of Earth just to keep themselves from a possible extermination. All things connected, impinged, and transmitted. The ethical mathematics of the universe made such a deed not only a cardinal sin but an ordinal one.

No. The extinction of Earth people was not the way out. The Uranians must just delay the space projects for a long long time. Above all, they must halt the exploration around Uranus. And this must be done soon. Calculations of all verifiable data showed that the optimum time to complete this phase of their operation was three weeks from now. That delay might mean, probably would, the deaths of the strong-looking but fragile babies orbiting Uranus in the *epsilon* ring. The estimate was a loss of four hundred—if the *Herschel* crew continued pulling in the babies. They probably would. And they would know enough now to trickle-discharge the field on the babies before collecting them. Even so, four hundred babies would die, but that loss would not mean a serious break in the chain of Uranian reproduction and growth.

However, the crew might notice, probably would, the occasional ascent of fiery-tailed egg clusters from the green clouds into space and toward the *epsilon* ring. The *Herschel* might locate and take some of these into the bay. If they did, their examination of the eggs, which looked like small, rough rocks, might—probably would—reveal the embryonic life-forms within them.

Then there would be no stopping the scientists. They would probe the atmosphere of the planet with radar and laser, and the two forms of the adult Uranian, the flying colonies, would be known. What then?

The Uranians' observation at long distance of Earth and the reports of their two agents on Earth had convinced them that war was a deeply established terrestrial cultural trait. It would be a long, long time before the Earth people shucked that trait. The Uranians were willing to wait for that, but until then they wanted to keep Earth people far, far away from them.

Hence, the Uranian Field Operation.

Just now, Agrafan and Netter were watching a TV screen which displayed in infrared. This was connected to a conventional set in another part of the house, the warm part inhabited by the staff of servants and the butler, Goll. Agrafan's remark about Walt Whitman had been evoked by the name of a character, Lance Whitman, in the soap opera *Dinah Stye*. All things connect, impinge, and transmit. One thing leads to another, and then the whole universe is moving.

Another show, *The Signs of the Times,* had followed the soap opera. Rod de Massas, the host, was saying: "The wave of Aquarius started in 1998. Aquarius, as we know, is the sign of dreams and aspirations of betterment and ideals. So far, there seems to have been little of this because of the worldwide wars, revolutions, and violent agitation for social, political, and economic reform. These, however, have been motivated by idealism, the fierce desire to make changes for the better.

"Also, as I predicted in 1998—the stars never lie—the first fourteen years of Aquarius were still influenced by Capricorn. But that pernicious influence is a dying wave. The age of Aquarius is beginning to bloom. It will flourish as it never has before, will be far stronger now than at any time in the past. The world will begin its march toward Utopia. The Neptune factor will have ebbed to silence, and the times will be controlled by the ruler of Aquarius, the planet Uranus.''

"Half-right, half-wrong," Netter said.

"Mostly wrong, but he should be honored for the tiny fraction of right," Agrafan said.

Even in "empty" space, particles and radiation impinged on each other, resonated, bumped, and penetrated. The universe was crammed with shocks, small and big; everything affected everything else. Some things were, from the sentient viewpoint, more influential than others. Size, location, distance, and velocity of inanimate things and animate beings determined what was most influential. There were also the factors of weak and strong linkage and of intent.

Intent, of course, was possible only for animate beings, except the star Sirius and a rather far-off galaxy.

The Uranians knew that the total interconnectedness of all matter was a fact. But it was and probably always would be impossible to know the size, location, and velocity of every bit of matter in the universe. The data they could get about the solar system was a mere microfraction of what was needed for even gross influencing. Nevertheless, on Earth, the two agents had had considerable success in predicting and influencing on a rather gross level. It was, however, their ignorance on a fine-grain level that now threatened their plans. They did not know that Gnatcatcher had been suffering for a long time from a duodenal ulcer.

They could not be blamed for this. Gnatcatcher had not told anybody about it because he was obsessed with his power as district IRS director. If he went to the hospital for tests and, probably, for surgery, his assistant would take over his directorship. Gnatcatcher would be powerless for a long time. And who knew what machinations his assistant might resort to in order to oust his boss?

The increasing pain from the ulcer was, however, making him behave less cautiously than he should, not to mention less legally. The news about the secret global business empire of Agrafan and Netter and the suspicion that they might be—must be—cheating the IRS made his ulcer flare up like a sunspot and his anger explode like a nova.

"Get everybody and every machine on this! Drop everything else! Twelve-hour shifts! We won't stop until we've accounted for every penny they owe us!"

Agent Brown was tactful enough not to point out that there was no evidence whatsoever at this time that Agrafan and Netter had cheated Uncle Sam. Agent Smith also said nothing to his boss, but, an hour later, he phoned Goll, the butler. Smith told Goll all that had happened and was likely to happen. Goll thanked him and said that $200,000 in cash would arrive at Smith's mailbox tomorrow. Goll then phoned his employers.

"Gnatcatcher will be getting a court order to tap our phone lines," Netter said.

"How long before the taps are installed?"

"Within an hour."

Netter cut off the phone and spoke to his partner. "Some vital data is missing from our prognosticator. We have to revise our plans. Quickly."

Agrafan said, "I'm not sure that if we start Operation Trapdoor now, it'll be successful."

"There's nothing else we can do. Also, Gnatcatcher is acting irrationally. He insists on speaking to us. Not just through the phone but face to face on the screen. He won't take no for an answer. We . . ."

Agrafan answered the phone. He listened for a moment, then said, "Thank you, Goll." To Netter, he said, "Goll just got a call from Gnatcatcher himself. Gnatcatcher says that we must talk to him face to face. He has to see us, even if only through the screen."

"Why is he so adamant about visual contact?"

"Goll said that he thinks that Gnatcatcher suspects that we two don't exist. Or perhaps he suspects that someone or some group has murdered us and is posing as us. Goll calls it the Howard Hughes syndrome."

Netter sighed from a ventral tube and flapped his wings and wiggled his antennae. "Very well. Have Goll put us through to Gnatcatcher."

"No, first we pull the lever," Agrafan said. "One call to our chief representative in Wall Street, and it's done."

That having been accomplished, Agrafan made the arrangements for the video meeting. A minute later, Gnatcatcher's face, now a near-purple, though it just looked dark on the infrared screen, appeared. But, on seeing what he thought was the two (actually, he was seeing a video simulation), his jaw dropped, his eyes bugged, and the purple changed to gray. Then the screen went blank.

"A very strange and unexpected reaction," Netter said. "What could have caused him to cut us off?"

Agrafan said, "Obviously, we lack some data."

They had been watching TV ever since the first sets had been sold. Their favorites were old movie films, and they especially liked the antics of two film comedians who had made all their pictures before TV had become a mundane reality. Agrafan and Netter saw a parallel between their own early bumblings and mistakes on Earth and those of the two comedians. Because of their empathizing, they had used the two comedians as models for the simulations. Until now, however, they had not been forced to use these. All contacts with the world outside their room had been by phone.

How were they to know that Gnatcatcher, when he was a child and still undehumanized by forty years of IRS employment, had often seen and loved the ancient tapes of two Hollywood comics?

183

Brown, Smith, and Jones, burdened with fifty pounds of computer printouts, had just entered Gnatcatcher's office. Though the paper contained only a small fraction of the enormousness of what *must* be a communist plot, the three carried in their heads the summary of the terrifying and mind-spinning situation.

They were pale and tottery when they came through the door. Seeing Gnatcatcher's corpselike skin and wild eyes, they became even whiter and weaker. "What's the matter, boss?" they said in unison.

"Laurel and Hardy!" Gnatcatcher screamed.

"What?" the three said, again in unison.

Gnatcatcher did not explain. He roared. "Get me the White House! And get another court order! We're invading the house!"

"The White House, sir?" Smith said faintly.

"No, you imbecile! The house of Agrafan and Netter! Have our men armed, ready to shoot at the first sign of resistance! Can you get hold of bazookas?"

Smith said, "Yes, sir," and he staggered out to transmit the orders. First, though, he phoned Goll. The butler thanked him and said that another $200,000 would be in Smith's mailbox by tomorrow.

It was left to Brown to explain the situation to Gnatcatcher. Stammering slightly, swallowing saliva that was not there, he said, "I've never heard of or encountered such a case before, sir. It's absolutely unprecedented. I talked to their lawyers just before I came in; they explained the whole amazing business. They said that Agrafan and Netter are real patriots. They've been paying far more income tax, their businesses have, I mean, than they were required to pay. They—" He stopped.

"So what?" Gnatcatcher snarled. "We gave them the proper refund, didn't we? Nobody can say we're not honest. We always refund if we find we have to!"

"Well, it's this way, sir. Since 1952, every property they own has paid twice what they should have paid!"

"How in hell could they do that? Why didn't we catch it?"

Brown said, "Uh . . . their companies have been keeping two sets of books!"

Gnatcatcher's face was speeding toward a purple again.

"That's illegal! We got them now!"

"No, sir, it's not illegal to pay Uncle Sam twice what you should. The records we've seen showed one set of profits on which they paid taxes double what we should have gotten. Their other records, the ones we hadn't seen until now, showed the true profits, the smaller ones."

"I don't believe this!" Gnatcatcher screamed. Then, calming a little, "So what? They've just made a big donation to the Treasury, that's all!"

Very quietly, Brown said, "You forget what I said, sir. About the refund. They're calling in the chips. They want every cent of their overpayment. There's no time limit on it, sir, like there used to be. The good news is that they're not asking for interest earned on the overpayment, though I don't think it would do them any good to ask."

"That's fraud, collusion, and God knows what other hideous crimes against the state!" Gnatcatcher bellowed. "They can't get away with it! We'll take them to court! They'll get bounced so quick—no way is—" He paused, struggled for breath, clutched his stomach, then said, "What is the total sum of this alleged overpayment?"

Brown opted out of answering by fainting. While he was being revived, agent Jones said, "Uh, the exact sum is eight hundred billion, ninety-six million, twenty-seven thousand, six hundred and three dollars and thirty cents, sir!"

It was Gnatcatcher's turn to faint. When he came to, he muttered, "Rally around the flag, boys."

A minute later, having recovered somewhat, he said, "We've got to squash this, nip it in the bud. It's sheer nonsense, gibberish, mopery on a colossal scale. But the mere rumor that this situation existed would cause the stock market to crash. We'll keep this quiet among us, men. And we'll go out and burn the traitors' house down! That'll put a stop to it!"

"Their lawyers and whoever runs their empire for them know about this," Jones said.

"None of their underlings'll dare say a word about it or about a refund after I get through talking to them!" Gnatcatcher screamed. Still holding his belly, he said, "We're going to storm their house, drag them out, doctors' excuses or no excuses, slam them into jail, incognito! I mean incommunicado! Don't argue with me!"

"Their civil rights, sir?" Brown said.

"This is war!" Gnatcatcher shouted. "I'll get the President to declare a state of martial law, civil rights suspended during the emergency! Once he understands the full implications of this, even he, dumb as he is, will cooperate fully!"

The phone on Gnatcatcher's desk rang. Brown punched a button, and a face appeared on the screen. "Speak of the devil," Brown muttered. He turned. "The President, sir."

It was too late. If the IRS did not pay the refund, or if it fought the case in court, every company controlled by Agrafan and Netter was to unload its stocks and declare bankruptcy. That meant that the stock market would topple with a roar far louder than it had made in 1929. The world would sink into Great Depression II. All funds for space exploration, especially those for the tremendously expensive Uranus project would be cut off. Another generation, perhaps two or three, would pass before Earth endangered the life-forms of the great green planet again.

Meanwhile, Gnatcatcher and his IRS contingent were outside the house. With them were National Guard units equipped with tanks and rocket-launchers.

Agrafan and Netter radioed their farewells, knowing that they would probably be dead before the message reached home.

"Well, it's not so bad to end this," Netter said. "I've been suffering from the heat ever since I got here. Now, I'll be comfortable. Death is comfortable, isn't it?"

"We'll find out," Agrafan said. "Anyway, there's usually something good to say about any situation. Don't the Earth people have a word for that attitude?"

"Pollyanna."

"I had a teacher named that. No connection, of course."

"Don't die thinking that," Netter said. "It makes it seem that you've learned nothing, wasted your life. All things impinge. Nothing moves without being moved or moving other things."

Sorry," Agrafan said. "I've been here too long. I'm starting to think like *them*."

Agrafan punched a button. Its last thought was of home, of the deliciously cold clouds, of flying through them, of ecstasy felt when he had been young and foolish and had dived as deep as he could, coming dangerously close to the hot, liquid hydrogen layer. Earth people did not know what fun was.

The insulated room with its frozen carbon dioxide furniture and emergency bottles of methane-hydrogen-helium gas and the TV set with the infrared screen vanished in a gout of flame. Nothing would be left for the Earth people to identify Agrafan and Netter as nonterrestrials.

Gnatcatcher ran as fast as he could, but the heat, far greater than that in his belly, caught up with him and passed him.

DIES IRAE

Charles Sheffield

"Max Cotton?"

The man seated at the desk jerked around as his name was spoken. He nodded.

"I am Anton Lanj. Psych Corps. May I see you for a few minutes?" The stranger advanced slowly, holding out his hand.

"Do I have a choice?" Cotton made no move to shake hands, but he gestured to the other chair.

The man smiled, shrugged, sat down. "I suppose not." He was tall, and his broad shoulders stretched the severe black tunic. But the face on the long neck was a comedian's—wide, mobile mouth, startled blue eyes, and tangled, black curly hair. And the hands holding the folder were magician's hands, with long, flexible fingers.

Max Cotton swiveled his chair to stare at him curiously. "You're new to Cobweb Station, aren't you? I would have remembered you."

A bobbing nod. "Four weeks. Out from Europa. Last outpost of 'civilization,' if you believe their advertisements." The smile was a comical grimace. "Still getting my feet on the ground here. This won't be much comfort, but you are my first assignment."

He looked for a reaction. Nothing. Only the continuous nervous movements of lips and hands. Even with the sedatives indicated on the medical report, Cotton was on a high wire. His manner was casual, but the rapidly blinking eyes suggested a tension that could not be concealed.

"So what did they tell you?" said Cotton abruptly. "That I'm wicked and dangerous? Or just crazy?" He stabbed savagely at the console in front of him. The display screen took up a full wall, and now it filled with an image of Uranus, the whole swirling gray-green ball of the planet. "That I'm scared to go down there? That I'm ready for the retirement home? That I'm suffering delusions?"

"That you are . . . disturbed. That you no longer wish to serve as a Monitor—even though you are the best there is. That you have refused the opportunity to return to the Inner System for rest." The clown's face distorted, one bushy eyebrow raised, the other lowered. He pulled at his fingers, snapping the joints one by one. "And that you are suffering badly from insomnia. But I must admit I find nothing unusual in that." Lanj smiled. "If poor sleeping is the criterion, I share your disturbance. And I too have no wish to see the Inner System again. Seventy billion people . . . a few too many for my comfort."

"That's all? That's all you were told?" Cotton's hair was dark and frizzy, receding from his forehead. He scratched now at the balding temples, then knuckled his eyes. "That idiot Trustrum. She doesn't even listen—'loneliness, alienation, solitude, harshness of the Uranian environment.' Bullshit! That's why I'm here, for God's sake. Just answer one question. Will you run an Erga Monitor with me? *She* wouldn't. And if you won't, you may as well leave now."

"Run an Ergatandromorph Monitor with you? You mean . . . with one of those?"

"How else?" Cotton picked up the headset. It was a hollow sphere of light metal, designed to make feather contact at eyes, ears, nose, and mouth. "Yes, with one of these. That's just like Trustrum. Didn't she even give you a briefing? Typical. Go away, then, and come back when you know what you're talking about." He lifted the set, ready to place it over his head.

Lanj bit at his upper lip. "I will monitor an Erga with you. If you want me to. And if you will tell me how to do it."

Max Cotton placed the headset back on the console. "My God. What's this? A psych tester with guts. Where did they dig you up?"

Lanj did not speak. He looked at Max with pleading blue eyes, waiting.

"Hell, I was only joking." Cotton laughed without humor. "If you just arrived here, you shouldn't try an Erga Monitor. Not first off. Didn't Trustrum tell you that we Erga Monitors have been going mad? Yes, I'm sure she did. It's a tough experience."

"Try me." The comical face was no longer humorous. It was full of dignity and intensity. "I am less ignorant than you think. I have worn a Monitor set on Europa. I was connected to a Cephalorphine there, psych-testing the crews for the deep-ocean work."

"Not the same thing at all." Max Cotton again picked up the headset, fiddling with the strap. "Monitoring an Erga is different from monitoring other organisms. You should begin with a Diver. I could show you how. If that went all right, maybe we'd plug into an Erga later."

His voice had veered from angry to conciliatory. Lanj could hear a terrible longing in it, a need to trust. He reached for the second headset. "Find me a Diver."

"*Now?*"

Lanj nodded. "If you are willing." The bushy clown's eyebrows raised to give Max Cotton one beseeching look; then Anton Lanj brought the set down firmly over his head. After a few seconds Cotton took a deep breath and put on his own equipment.

"Hear me all right?" Cotton's voice was deeper than usual, missing some of the high frequencies. "There's nothing to see yet, but the audio should be working."

"Yes." Lanj sounded only slightly apprehensive.

"All right. This will take a little while. I'm moving into the search mode."

Cobweb Synchronous Station orbited the equator of Uranus within a period of a little less than eleven hours. It hovered thirty-six thousand kilometers out, always above the same point on the Uranian equator. The probe signal scanned the surface of Uranus in an expanding spiral from the nadir point. Cotton explained that the Monitor set was tunable for different life-forms, but not for individual members of a species. They would contact a Diver, but chance decided which Diver it might be in the five hundred million square kilometers of Uranus visible from Cobweb Station; the inflexible constraints of signal-to-noise ratio greatly favored contact with one near the nadir.

After a thirty-second pause there was a brief buzzing in the headsets and a flicker of blue-green light. ("Locking in," said Cotton. He sounded better, less tense. "There. We've got one.") There was one dizzying moment of disorientation, then Anton Lanj was looking out on a clear sea of pale green. His ears heard a steady swish from behind and what seemed to be a soft murmur of contentment from somewhere within.

("We're diving now," said Cotton. "Hear that? It's happy, it likes to dive. There's almost no sensory feedback from us to the Diver, but let me try! I'll see if we can make it turn its head.")

After another pause, the field of view changed. Instead of a featureless sea, Lanj was looking at a circle of rainbow patterns, centered on one point of light and broken in a few places by darker intrusions.

("Good," said Cotton. "It turned its head. See the diffraction disk? That's the way the Sun looks to a Diver. The dark breaks are our signal beacons on Ariel and Miranda. We use them for navigation, and that tells us the depth we are at. We've still quite a way to go before we get to operating levels. Look on the left. That's the main load.")

Lanj was still adjusting to the visual signal. He realized after a few moments that the dark, amorphous mass on the extreme left of his field of view was actually the body of the Diver itself. He could see the outline of a long, jointed body and, behind it, the turbulent jet sent out by the Diver's powerful rear syphon. And off to the side was the cargo, a bulky oblong of opaque material.

("What's the outside temperature here?" Lanj was feeling a little too cool for comfort.)

("I'm not sure. About one-thirty Kelvin, for a guess." Cotton sounded amused. "Don't worry, you'll feel better in a little while. You're picking up the Diver's own temperature sensation. They prefer it a little warmer, closer to the center. We're near an inversion point now. But we won't go *too* deep. There's a rock-and-metal core to Uranus, a little bigger than Earth. Temperature there is up near a thousand degrees—that would kill the Divers and the Ergas. Down there we have to use inorganic Moles.")

The Diver's head had turned again to track its path downward. Lanj tried unsuccessfully to make it look back at the cargo.

("We don't seem to have any control at all," he complained. "How did you make it turn its head?")

("Food thoughts. But I'm not letting any inputs from you go through our headset, anyway, so don't waste your time. You're quite right, though, the control we have over the Divers is minimal. It's never any better than this. They're pretty brainless. They were designed that way, to do one job perfectly, over and over. Ninety percent Arachnida DNA, nine percent Mollusca, at most one percent human—and that little bit was only put in to make communication easy with our Monitor sets. But there's no way we could make this Diver turn back, no matter *what* signals we sent out. It's making a delivery. We might as well just sit quiet and enjoy the ride. As soon as the cargo is dropped off we can break contact.")

("What's the cargo?")

("The usual—fusion plant components. The procedure is automated now. The Uranian lift system is shipping two billion tons of volatiles a day off-planet and directing it to the Uranian satellites and Inner System. Plus a fair fraction of that in waste products coming down.")

Anton Lanj peered out through the Diver's eyes into the mushy mantle of ammonia, water, methane, and nitrogen. The Diver was "seeing" by means of a combination of visual input and ultrasonics, and the result was astonishingly clear. They were plunging now through a layer of tangerine cloud, in which uneven masses of dark green were floating. The Diver skillfully avoided those, zig-zagging down vast emerald-walled canyons and through sharp-sided amethyst crevasses. The speed was dizzying, and the downward pace never slackened. Finally they emerged to a region of clear light blue and the Diver's thirty-meter body went to a straight vertical descent.

("Look ahead." The tension was suddenly sharply back in Max Cotton's voice. "See them? Those are Ergas. I think it's time we broke contact.")

Far below lay a cluster of dark moving objects, surrounding a massive central sphere. The Diver was driving itself purposively toward it.

("What happens next?")

("It waits there by the fusion assembly until the Ergas have unloaded the cargo. Then they release it. It rides back to the higher levels and waits for the next load of components.")

("Don't you want to watch them unload?")

("No. That's it." Cotton's voice was urgent, almost panic-stricken. "We're going back.")

The scene in front of Anton Lanj suddenly blinked out. He lifted the Monitor headset off and peered around him. After the great Uranian vista, the room he was in with Max Cotton was cramped and claustrophobic. He shook his head.

"Phew. That's a different experience, all right. It was nothing like that on Europa. No wonder you Monitors have a high emotional disturbance rate."

"You don't understand." Cotton was sweating profusely. "Maybe you will. But not today. Come back next shift, and I'll introduce you to the Ergatandromorphs. They're the real builders and shapers down on Uranus." His smile was ghastly, just a glint of teeth through pale lips. "Was your own basic training in biology?"

Lanj hesitated for a moment. The wrenching change of subject had caught him by surprise. "My original training? No. Not biology. Why?"

"Because the DNA combination for the Ergas is unique: twenty percent Insecta, five percent Mollusca—and seventy-five percent *Homo sapiens*.. I think you will find them . . . surprising." Cotton wiped his brow with a green cloth, then stood up abruptly and headed for the door. At the threshold he paused. "You're not a biologist, and you're not an engineer. And you don't sound like a medic. So what the hell were you before you became a psych tester?"

The broad mouth drooped mournfully, and puffy eyelids came down to cloak the bright blue eyes. "For seven years I was a priest in the Inner System. First on Earth, then in the Belt and the Venus Habitats."

"Why did you change."

"I decided that I was . . . unsuited for such work." A weak smile. "Perhaps, like you, I found seventy billion of God's charges rather too many for me. And the inner worlds are too neat for my tastes, I thought there might be more need for me in the Outer System."

Max Cotton nodded. "There might be. Tomorrow you may understand my feelings about my own work." He strode out, leaving the other man alone with his sad clown's face and secret thoughts. Lanj came to Cotton's crowded work quarters late in the next shift. The other man was sitting at his desk making no attempt to work. He was simply waiting. Without invitation Lanj sat again in the other chair.

"No sleep?" he said.

Cotton looked at him but did not speak.

"Me neither." Lanj leaned forward, laced together his long fingers, and rested his chin on their fulcrum. "I have been wondering, since our last meeting, about life on Uranus. You have been there more times than any other Monitor. Tell me, have you ever seen any sign of *native* life-forms?"

Cotton shook his head. His eyes were black-rimmed and bloodshot. "Never. Uranus was barren when humanity first came to this system. It remained so until we seeded it. Plants and animals—if those terms can be applied to Uranian life-forms—both were planted there. Why do you want to know?"

"I wondered if our actions on Uranus might be destroying native life that was there before us. As we did by accident on Europa and by design on Titan."

"No. Quite the opposite. The synthesizers found it hard to construct life-forms that can survive down there. Before the Ergas and the Divers, there were over forty failures. And for some of them we still do not know why they failed to flourish."

Lanj closed his right hand surreptitiously on the miniature condition sensor that he was holding in his palm. It was tuned to Cotton and provided tactile readout of his heart rate and blood pressure. The questions so far had produced no unusual reactions. Max Cotton's pulse was steady at seventy-five, and blood pressure at one-thirty over eighty-five. "But the Divers and the Ergas *are* flourishing?" he said. "Even without human aid?"

"Very much so. There is no census for the population on Uranus, but every Monitor will tell you that their numbers are growing rapidly. Four years ago you would seldom see more than half a dozen Ergas near a fusion plant during construction. Now I have seen as many as a hundred of them—and there are far more fusion plants in operation."

Cotton was toying with the Monitor headset as he spoke, lifting it from the table, hesitating, and putting it down again.

"Today we will monitor an Erga," said Lanj. He had noticed the tremor in Cotton's fingers. "Unless you feel too unwell."

"No. Let's get it over with." Cotton picked up the headset again, shivered, and placed it quickly over his head. His jaw muscles were clenched as they disappeared from view inside the hollow sphere. After a few moments Lanj donned the second set and sat there in darkness, waiting.

"This time it will take a little longer," said Cotton tightly. "The probe has started, but the Monitor lock to an Erga is more complicated than to a Diver or a Mole." Lanj could hear his rapid breathing. He still held in his right hand the condition sensor. The other man's pulse rate had jumped to around one hundred and thirty, and blood pressure was one-eighty over ninety-seven.

There was a burst of static in Lanj's ears, then a flashing stipple of colored lights blinded him for a moment. ("We have contact," said Cotton. "Now we're locking in.") His pulse was one hundred and fifty. A rolling sea of turquoise suddenly flooded into Lanj's eyes, turned through sixty degrees, then steadied. He was looking up at a familiar diffraction pattern, and again there came the hiss of a syphon from behind. The Erga was cruising along beside a half-constructed fusion plant, carrying a water-ice component in its forelimbs.

It was like monitoring the Diver, but also enormously different. A series of emotional sensations came from the Erga that had been absent the previous day, and the bonding was far more urgent and immediate. Lanj could feel the Erga's dedicated focus of attention. *Find place,* it said. *Find place, find place, find place.* The component it was carrying belonged at one point in the assembly, and one alone. Until that location was found, there could be no room for any other thought and no interest in any other activity.

Even as the Erga's thought flooded through him, Lanj heard a grunt of relief from Max Cotton. Some great knot of stress had been cut in the other man. The tactile readout in Lanj's palm told him that Cotton's pulse rate was dropping rapidly toward normal, and his blood pressure was also drifting down.

("I recognize this plant," said Cotton's voice suddenly. The tension had left it. "They've been working on it now for almost three weeks. Another few days, and it will be ready for operation.")

("What happens to the Ergas here when it starts up? Won't they be boiled alive?")

("No. They know they have to get well away before operations begin. After the last component goes in, they'll take off. They'll be a hundred kilometers away before power goes on.")

The Erga they were monitoring had found the place it was looking for. It slotted the long tube it was carrying into position and began to use its forelimbs to tighten the connection. It was working side by side with two other Ergas, and Lanj had his first chance for a close-up look.

He saw a twelve-meter-long dark carapace, jointed at the head. At the other end of the ergatandromorph's body was the flexible syphon, arranged so that the outgoing jet could be pointed in any direction. Of the three pairs of limbs, two could be used for manipulation, and one was only for locomotion. Respiration was a secondary function of the syphon, which pumped aerated fluids through the long body and out through apertures below the limbs and head. The ultrasonic generator and eyes were on the top of the head, well away from the mouth and olfactory antennae. As Lanj watched, he saw that the other Ergas were using their two compound eyes and sonic generators to look at the host Erga. The ultrasonics that bathed the long body created a strange feeling of contentment and peace.

("They know of each other's presence," he said to Cotton. "Do you think they know that we are here, too?")

("I think they do not. We have a little control over their movements, but they have no idea of that. So far as they are concerned, they have complete freedom of action. We implanted in them only three basic desires: to survive; to breed; and to build the fusion plants from the components that the Divers bring them. Beyond that, they are free to do as they please.")

The tension was creeping back into Max Cotton's voice, and again his pulse was rising.

("Do you want to break contact?" said Lanj quickly. "If you don't feel good, let's go back.")

("No. Believe it or not, I'm actually enjoying this. Look how well they work together and handle obstacles. Do you think a human team would do it any better?")

The fusion plant would sit deep in the mantle of Uranus, well below the level where water, methane, hydrogen, helium, and ammonia formed a multiphase interface of atmosphere and ocean. It would provide another element of the Uranian lift system, designed for a final efflux capacity of forty billion tons of volatiles a day and targeted on the needs of the Inner System. Anton Lanj had asked how long the system could operate before Uranus itself began to be depleted of mass. Cotton had thought for a moment before answering. "Uranus is a big planet. Including the atmosphere but leaving out the rocky core, you're talking of a mass of over ten to the twenty-second tons. At the rate we're removing material, there's enough volatiles on Uranus for another billion years."

It was a reassuring answer, but from the tone of Cotton's voice Lanj suspected that he had asked the wrong question. The right question was difficult to discover. He had been studying the pattern of Cotton's emotional responses for two days. Stress seemed unrelated to the events that he had seen. So if *observable* events were not causing stresses, then it must be anticipation of events to come. And if those events didn't materialize, Max Cotton again became calm.

The Ergas had finished their task, and the small group gathered round to rub carapaces and exchange gratifying bursts of ultrasonics. *Good work, good work, good work.* It was like a warm bath of mutual approval. Lanj allowed himself to relax for a few minutes. Max Cotton had become completely silent. Finally Lanj realized that he was more than relaxed. After a sleepless night he was postively drowsy.

("Cotton! Time we broke contact and went back. I'm falling asleep.")

("No problem." The reply was slow and comfortable. "I've done that before when I was in Monitor connect. Nothing bad happens. You stay connected

194

until you wake up, then break as usual.")

But he was already responding to Anton Lanj's request. First came the loss of the ambient warmth, then vision and sound departed. Anton Lanj was once more sitting in a chair with a metal helmet over his head, strangely empty and alone.

"Was that it?" he said, as soon as Cotton emerged from his headset. "The depression that Trustrum talked about—it comes when you leave the Ergas?"

"I guess. Some of it." It didn't sound convincing. Away from the soothing Erga influence, Cotton had again become evasive and edgy. Lanj leaned back in his chair. He had thin, gangling legs that sprawled right across the small room. He was absent-mindedly cracking his finger joints again.

"Mind if I talk to you for a minute?"

Cotton shrugged. "Talk on. That's your job."

"Part of my job. Let me tell you what I'm seeing, then you fill in the details—if you're willing. I think you have a classic problem. You want to talk, and you need to talk. But you have a block of some kind. And it's all tied into the Ergas."

Another shrug. "No prizes for that."

"When we tried to lock onto a Diver, you didn't mind at all. Even seemed to like the idea. But as soon as the Diver saw the Ergas, you got uncomfortable. Then today, before we got the Monitor unit tied to the Erga, you were uncomfortable again—worse than uncomfortable, sweaty-palm-panicked. But as soon as we had the lock, you were all right again. Understand, I'm not giving you a *theory* about that. I'm telling you facts, things I've been able to observe directly. Do you want to argue with any of it?"

Cotton was staring straight ahead. He shook his head. His face was greenish-white, with dilated nostrils.

"All right. So now we move to speculation. You dread coupling the Monitor to an Erga. But when you *did* couple, everything was all right. So what does that say? It says that *sometimes* when you hook the Monitor to an Erga, you don't get what we got today." Lanj leaned forward. The clown's face was scowling, the dark eyebrows a line of authority. *What do you get?*"

"I get—" Cotton started to speak, then shivered and leaned back in his seat. He stared at Lanj. "I made recordings. I tried to get Trustrum to sit in on one of those recordings ten different times. And I got nowhere. Do you *really* want to experience one of them—do you want to feel the way I do at night?"

Breakthrough. The change in relationship of the two men was subtle, but it was real. Anton Lanj could hear a new dependence in Max Cotton's voice. "What makes you think that your nights are worse then mine?" he said quietly. "Are an agnostic's nightmares worse than an atheist's? Show me what you have found." His voice was low and persuasive.

Cotton hesitated, then finally nodded. He leaned forward, pulling a data cube from a box and jamming it into the Monitor set. "Put your headset back on." He was speaking fast now, almost gabbling. "I told you, when we do a Monitor connect we know which species we will get, but we don't know which *individual* we'll connect to, or even which Erga colony. There are four or five hundred different colonies down on Uranus, each in its own geographic area. Ninety-nine times out of a hundred, when I connect I find the sort of thing you heard today—'*make connection, good work, feels good, take food*', that primitive level of communication. But the *hundredth* time is different. There's one special colony, somewhere down there on the surface of Uranus. I made recordings of them." He picked up his own headset. "Remember, this will be sound and vision only. There's no way of recording other sensations, so some of this won't make easy sense. But I'll be tagging along, and I'll explain whenever I can. And don't expect continuity. I've done editing—God, how I've done editing. I've sweated and agonized over it, worried if I was adding false meaning. I've spent days and nights and nights and days. But I'm still not sure."

The headset was hissing softly when Lanj slipped it on. He heard Cotton's voice cut in over a faint unintelligible chanting sound: ("Ask me when you have questions. I can stop the recording anytime.")

Vision had bled in on his final words. They were looking at a group of about fifteen Ergas, gathered round one of their number. The Erga that Cotton had monitored and recorded was on the periphery of the circle. All the creatures were smaller and lighter in color than the ones that Lanj had seen before, and their forelimbs had an extra protuberance close to the thorax. The Erga at the center of the group was the smallest of all. The scene was almost dark, lit by a strange monochrome that gave to everything an odd two-dimensional appearance. ("Ultrasonics only," said Cotton's voice. "Night on Uranus. Listen.")

"The light in the sky has gone." The voice was flat, without inflection or emphasis. "The Master is here. Four times we have met. Soon the Master will leave us."

("Master, Teacher, Leader." Cotton spoke jerkily, emotionally. "I don't know which word is the right one.")

("Cotton! They're self-aware!")

("I know.")

("But this is a fantastic discovery.")

("Maybe. Keep listening. Remember, this is my transcription, but it is *not* my invention.")

The group of Ergas clustered more tightly around the smaller central figure. A powerful beam of verbal signal came from it. "The World was here before the People. The World will be here when the People are gone. You have asked, *why* do the People live? Where did the People come from? When the People die, where do they go? The Master says, the World was made by one Great Being. It created the People, and everything in the World. The People were created to serve the Great Being. If the People give service, that is enough reason for existence. When the People die, they become part of the Great Being.''

"Master, the World is changing.'' It was a new voice, from one of the circle of Ergas. "The People make the Burners, more and more Burners—'' ("Fusion plants.'' Cotton's voice was calm. "A hundred new ones going in this year, to power the lift system.'')

"—but the People cannot live near them. And there are more and more of the People. Some day there will be so many Burners, so many People. And no places. What will the People do?''

("So many'—they don't have a vocabulary for numbers yet.'')

"The Master tells the People, this question cannot be answered. Only the Great Being knows. There will be so many Burners, so many People. When that time comes, the Great Being will provide for the People.''

The same voice. "Master, some of the Small People are not shaped correctly. They cannot feed. What should the People do?''

"Leave them. The Great Being will care for them.''

Another voice. "The Burners make dirt, and it fills the World now. It touches us. It is harder to breathe. Some of the People are sick, some of the People are dying.''

"All things die. Nothing in the World promises that life must be easy. Sometimes the pieces of a Burner do not fit together, and the People must struggle to make the fit. The whole World is a struggle, also. Like the Burners, there will always be trouble and difficulty. The Great Being made the World that way.''

("The fusion plants are killing the Ergas?'' said Lanj. "I didn't know that.'')

("Nor did I, until I heard it there. Sounds like a radiation problem.'') There was a click, and the visual signal disappeared. Cotton had halted the recording. "The fusion plants must be less clean than we thought. Nobody up here bothered too much with that—we've been using Uranus as a dumping ground for waste products anyway, so a little more didn't seem to make any difference. The Ergas must be radiation-sensitive. Any more questions, or are you ready to back the recording?''

"No!'' Anton Lanj had jerked his headset off. He reached over and pulled at the Monitor sphere on Cotton's head. He did not like the look in the other man's eyes. There was a blankness there, a coldness. "Who have you shown this recording to?''

"No one." Cotton gave a gruff laugh. "You're the first. Don't you understand? I *tried* to find an audience here—and no one gave a damn."

"But that's ridiculous. Look at the significance of what you've found. Completely unknown to us, down there in the darkness, we have a whole new species—intelligent, self-aware, and with a religious sense."

Max Cotton was shaking his head wearily. "You're missing the main point. If it were a native life-form down there, one that had evolved on Uranus, you'd have exobiologists all over Cobweb Station. There would be real interest. But we *created* the Ergas. We put them there ourselves. They're more than three-quarters human, so is it a surprise if they share the human drives and satisfactions—work, play, procreate? That's what you'd be told by people here, or on the Titania and Ariel settlements."

"But we're doing the Ergas real harm. The fusion plants are killing them."

"Sure they are. You think the settlers care much about *that*? They need the supply of volatiles that comes up the Uranian lift system—they would die without them. They won't worry about a few 'animals,' not with their own existence at stake."

"*But they're not animals!*" Anton Lanj's eyes were agitated, and his long hands curled and rubbed at each other like white spiders.

Cotton looked at him coldly. "I hear you. But do you think you can persuade the rest of the Outer System—or even people here on Cobweb Station?"

"You know they're not animals. You agree with me."

"I'll tell you what I think. And I'll say again, you're missing the whole point. We gave the Ergas intelligence—for our own reasons. We wanted them to be able to build the fusion plants. But we gave them no knowledge of their own orgins, and we gave them an environment where greater intelligence and curiosity would be an asset. See, we created the Ergas in our own image—not physical image, but mental image. We ought not to be surprised if we hold the mirror up to them and see our own faces."

Lanj sat motionless for a moment and struggled to gain full control of himself. He thought that he understood what was happening. When Max Cotton found the emotional burden intolerable, he had done his best to pass it on to Lanj. But the meeting had taken a strange turn. He had to bring Cotton back to full involvement.

"You may pretend it doesn't matter to you," he said at last. "That you can let the Ergas continue to build our plants and then die. But I don't believe it. It doesn't explain why you are so upset by your meetings with the intelligent Ergas. And you *are* upset—don't try to deny it."

Cotton looked up. His eyes were filled with a sudden, blank despair. "Did I ever suggest that I was not upset? I am more upset than you are—but for different reasons. You were a priest, so you tend to see everything through priest-colored glasses."

"And what the devil does *that* mean?"

Cotton shrugged. "You want to credit the Ergas with immortal souls and feel anguish at their death without salvation. There is another message here, a cause for greater sorrow. Before you came here you lived in the Inner System. Why did you leave?

"I told you already." Lanj was fidgeting in his seat. "I felt uncomfortable with so many people."

"Right. Billion after billion, swarming over everything. But you know what? Not one of those billions is living in a *natural* habitat for a human. We took that whole, wild, haphazard collection of planets and moons and asteroids, and we changed it. Now the Inner System is neat, organized, and sanitary. And a priest should *like* people. Will you tell me the truth this time. Why didn't you want to live there, back on Earth or Mars or Ceres?"

Lanj shook his head. He was looking into Max Cotton's eyes, and they were disturbingly rational and despairing. "I don't know."

"I do. It's not a place where *any* human can live comfortably anymore. You had a way out, you could leave. Most people lack that opportunity—or they would leave, too. And soon we'll have the Outer System the same way."

"But even if you're right, what in God's name does that have to do with the Ergas?" Anton Lanj was making a last effort at self-control. "Why do they disturb you so terribly?"

"Because of their message. The Ergas are changing Uranus for our convenience. And that will kill them. We *made* them intelligent—in our mental image—so they could build the Uranian lift system. When that's finished, they won't be able to survive there. Do you see their message now?"

Anton Lanj could not speak. He shook his head and touched his fingers to the hidden crucifix beneath his dark tunic.

"We're changing the whole solar system. *We're getting it ready.*" Max Cotton was staring at Anton Lanj, and his eyes were no longer sane. "You were a priest. Are you still a priest?"

"Yes." The word was a whisper.

"So tell me this, priest. *In whose image are we created?*"

Who in their right mind would write a story about Uranus in 1985? Might as well write a book about the American Revolution in 1774, or the Civil War in 1860. For in January 1986, the Voyager 2 spacecraft will fly by the Uranian system. If the experiences of the Voyager flybys of Jupiter and Saturn are any guide, after that our ideas of Uranus will never be the same again. We should know vastly more about Uranus and its satellites in late 1986 than we do today.

In fact, our overall gain in knowledge from the Uranus flyby may exceed that obtained in the case of Jupiter and Saturn. The difficulty in observing a planet from the surface of Earth depends on three factors: the planet's size, its distance from the Sun (illumination goes as the inverse square of distance), and its distance from Earth (apparent area goes as the inverse square of distance). Putting these factors together, it is 2,200 times as difficult to observe Uranus from Earth as it is to observe Jupiter. A planetary probe makes an object's distance from Earth irrelevant, and object size of secondary importance.

All this tells us is that is it even more foolhardy to write of Uranus today than it was to write of Jupiter and Saturn in the middle 1970s. In the next year, we should know much more about the rings of Uranus; about its interior composition; about its satellites (chances are that Voyager 2 will discover at least one additional satellite, and my money is on more than one); about its magnetic field; and about conditions in its atmosphere.

From a fictional point of view, there are only two safe courses: either write an outright fantasy (Uranus the Magician, perhaps, drawing from Gustav Holst's The Planets *and caring not at all for any physical constraints or current knowledge of the surface and interior of the planet); or, if that does not appeal, set the story far in the future, when technology, following Arthur Clarke's dictum, will be indistinguishable from magic to today's eyes, and such things as large-scale modification of the outer solar system will not be unthinkable.*

How far in the future is "far"?

That is an excellent question. The population numbers quoted in the story are of little help. It took all of Earth's history for the human population of this planet to reach 1 billion about the year of 1800. We reached 2 billion by 1930, 4 billion by 1975. If that curve is extrapolated with a cubic exponential fit, there will be 70 billion humans before A.D. 2080. I hope that projection is wrong, and I feel pretty sure that it must be. Simple-minded curve fitting (especially with exponentials!) is an excellent road to self-delusion.

Here is another way to look at the question. The outer regions of the solar system seem to have roughly a fifty-year cycle for interesting new events and discoveries. Beginning in 1781, with Herschel's discovery of Uranus, the idea that there was another and more distant part of the solar system became a reality.

Fifty years later, in 1830, Alexis Bouvard's tables of motion for Jupiter, Saturn, and Uranus showed that Uranus was not where it ought to be. Another planet was suspected, and the search for Neptune was on, culminating in its discovery in 1846.

The year 1880 saw—

No, I'm writing this on Washington's birthday, 1985, and I refuse to tell a lie. It would be stretching it to say that I know of any significant event related to the outer solar system in or near 1880; but fifty years later, in 1930, Pluto was discovered. And in 1980, give or take a year, we had those spectacular sight-seeing tours of the Jovian and Saturnian systems, already referred to, that multipled by many times our knowledge of those planets, satellites, and ring structures.

By 2030, we should have permanent colonies in space, a base on the Moon, and manned exploration of Mars. But I don't think we will have large-scale industrial development out as far as Saturn and Uranus or be mining the Oort cloud for water, ammonia, methane, and liquid hydrocarbons. We must look farther out in time.

I place this story in the year 2180. A population growth of 1.4 percent per year (the current annual growth rate is more like 2 percent) would bring us to 70 billion people. Technology should have advanced accordingly—for good or evil. Do I really believe that by 2180 we will be using Uranus as the coal-field and junkyard of the solar system? I don't know. Two hundred years ago North America was unspoiled, and its resources must have seemed endless and indestructible. Go out today, and look on dust bowls, acid rain, toxic landfill, and strip mines. Then prove to me that it can't happen again somewhere else in the solar system.

I don't expect to see that proof. For, of course, a story set in 2180 has another advantage. Even with the most optimistic assumptions as to my own longevity, I do not expect to be accountable for its inaccuracies.

NEPTUNE

ESSAY BY
Dale P. Cruikshank

SPECULATION BY
Jack Williamson

NEPTUNE: FARTHEST GIANT

Dale P. Cruikshank

THE DISCOVERY OF URANUS prompted a natural speculation at the possibility of a yet more distant planet at the position predicted by the Bode-Titius rule, about 39 AU. The speculation was heightened when continued observations of Uranus showed that its orbit was not perfectly regular, as predicted by the mechanics of the solar system discovered by Isaac Newton a century before.

Observations of the motion of Uranus continued into the 1800s, and by about 1830 it was clear that some other undiscovered body must lie farther out in the solar system. But where should astronomers point their telescopes to look for the supposed new planet?

The problem attracted the interest of the English mathematician John Couch Adams, who by 1843 had worked out a preliminary solution. Adams himself could not go to the telescope to search in the part of the sky where he thought the new planet might be found, and following the protocol of the day, he communicated with the Astronomer Royal of England, George Airy. Airy was indifferent to Adams's prediction and did nothing to search for the supposed new planet. At the same time, however, the French mathematician Urbain Leverrier made calculations similar to those of Adams and presented his results to the French Academy on June 1, 1846. But the French astronomers seemed as uninterested in Leverrier's predictions as was Airy in Adams's, and it was finally the German J. G. Galle who located the new planet on September 23, 1846, searching in Leverrier's predicted position with the 9-inch telescope of the Berlin Observatory. It was quickly learned that Neptune circles the Sun at a distance of 30.1 AU, about 1.5 billion kilometers beyond Uranus, substantially less than that predicted by the Bode-Titius rule. The discovery of the new planet within a degree of the position predicted by Leverrier (and almost equally close to that predicted earlier by Adams) proved that the supposition of an external planet affecting the motion of Uranus had been correct.

At at time when mathematical astronomy dominated observational astronomy, the prediction and discovery of Neptune was a stunning success of mathematical deduction—when computers did not exist and all calculations were done by hand.

Neptune had in fact been seen before Galle found it with the Berlin telescope, but its nature as a planet rather than a background star was not recognized. Research into Galileo's observations in 1612, just after the telescope had been invented, has revealed that in December of that year the Italian noted an object near Jupiter that we now know was Neptune. Galileo saw that the "star" moved in the course of a few nights, but there is no evidence that he thought that it might be another planet.

As it happens, observations of Neptune showed that it too was moving in an irregular way, suggesting that yet another planet outside its orbit was nudging and pulling it slightly off its normal path around the Sun. The search for the trans-Neptunian "Planet X" is a story for another chapter, but even the discovery of Pluto in 1930 hasn't solved the problem of Neptune's motion: Pluto is too small and insignificant in mass to move the much greater Neptune. Searches for additional "Planets X" continue to this day. There remains the possibility of other planetary bodies beyond Neptune, but we think that anything big enough to perturb the orbit of a major planet would have been discovered by now.

THE INTERIOR OF NEPTUNE

Superficially, Neptune is similar to Uranus in composition, size, and density. Its atmosphere is mostly hydrogen and helium, but methane gas is also present, contributing to the planet's blue color. But Neptune must be quite a different place from Uranus. Its axis has not been tipped in the same way as has that of Uranus, and apparently it has only two satellites, each with its own peculiarities.

Among the most striking differences between Uranus and Neptune is that Neptune, like Jupiter and Saturn, appears to radiate excess heat. The first measurements of the temperature of Neptune were made from that same Hawaiian mountaintop observatory where so many other planetary temperature measurements have been made. The feeble heat from Neptune was detected in the infrared in 1972 at Mauna Kea Observatory, and it was quickly seen that the temperature of the planet was a couple of degrees warmer than that predicted from the known intensity of sunlight falling upon it. It appears, then, that something is happening inside Neptune, perhaps a slow separation of different chemicals, with the heavier elements falling toward the center and releasing energy as they do so. The situation may be far more complex, however.

We know so little about Neptune and its environment that the range of possibilities for the generation of excess heat is very large. The density of Neptune is a little higher than that of Uranus, and as a consequence its core may be solid. Yet the excess heat suggests that convection (the rising of hotter materials) or some other fluid motion is occurring somewhere in the interior, and that this may be going on in a liquid or slushy mantle of the kind of "icy" materials already described for Uranus. Perhaps mantle convention is also generating a magnetic field.

A major problem in understanding the interiors of things as big as planets is that they have pressures and temperatures far beyond the range of conditions that can be reproduced in the laboratory. As a result, we do not understand well the properties of materials under the conditions that occur inside planets. This is not a problem that will be readily solved by spacecraft or telescopic observations, but one that depends upon additional laboratory investigations and the theoretical studies of the properties of matter under extreme conditions.

RINGS AROUND NEPTUNE?

We used to ask the question, "Why is Saturn the only planet with rings?" Since 1979, however, the question has changed. "Why is Neptune the only outer planet *without* rings?" We have already seen that rings of one sort or another encircle Saturn, Jupiter, and Uranus, but to understand why we think there are no conventional rings around Neptune, we have to look for a moment at the way astronomers search for and study rings around distant planets.

All the planets change position in the sky from night to night, moving slowly against the background of distant stars. Occasionally, a planet will pass in front of a star as seen from our vantage point on Earth, causing the star to be eclipsed or *occulted* for a few minutes or even a few hours. Astronomers have found ways to observe these occultations of stars by planets in order to study the atmospheres of the planets. They have also learned how to predict such occultation events several weeks in advance, giving them time to get their telescopes and other equipment ready.

It was during the observations of an occultation of a star by Uranus in 1977 that astronomers were waiting for the star to disappear behind the planet as Uranus moved closer and closer. But several minutes before Uranus moved to cover the star, the light from the star blinked out several times, just for a fraction of a second or so. The starlight had been blocked by something near Uranus that could not be seen through the telescope, and it was quickly determined that invisible rings of dark, opaque material were circling the planet. Since that first discovery, which was confirmed by several astronomers working simultaneously from different observatories, the occultation technique has become our most powerful means of studying the rings of Uranus and for searching for rings of Neptune.

What, then, do we find when we watch an occultation of a star by Neptune? There have been several opportunities to search for rings around Neptune in the past few years, but there are no clear or confirmed positive observations that can be attributed to rings in the conventional sense of the word. For example, rings around planets are symmetrical, so a ring occultation of a star on one side of the planet should be when the star appears to pass on the other side of the planet as well. There are no such observations.

A few occultation events have been seen near Neptune, however, and we will discuss these when we consider the satellites.

A STRANGE PAIR OF SATELLITES

Triton, the largest of Neptune's two satellites, was found within a few weeks of the discovery of the planet itself in 1846. Several things were soon apparent. First, Triton is quite bright, given its great distance from the Sun; that is, it is reflecting quite a bit of light. This means that it must be fairly large, comparable to our own Moon. Second, Triton moves in an orbit around Neptune in the *reverse* direction compared to other satellites around their planets; that is, the orbit is retrograde, and opposite the direction in which Neptune itself revolves on its own axis. Third, the orbit is almost exactly circular, and the time it takes Triton to make one circuit of Neptune is about 5.9 days (our own Moon takes 27.3 days to circle Earth). This means that the satellite is relatively close to Neptune.

We will return to Triton, but we can state all we know about the second moon of Neptune is just a few lines. A small, faint satellite moving around Neptune in a highly elliptical orbit in a peculiar configuration was found in 1948 and named Nereid. A full circuit of Neptune by Nereid takes 360 days. We know virtually nothing about Nereid except where it is, for it is too faint to be studied with present astronomical instruments. Our best estimates are that its diameter is about 300 to 1,000 kilometers, comparable to the large or medium-size asteroids. We have little idea what it is made of.

Because Neptune and its satellites are 50 percent farther away than Uranus, astronomers have had difficulty in studying them, even with the largest telescopes. The improvements in detecting equipment made in the mid-1970s, however, have begun to change this situation. The first rudimentary spectral measurements of Triton were made in 1978 in order to begin to understand what materials it is made of. Without even knowing how big Triton was, and in the absence of fundamental information of any kind about it, we began to unravel a picture of its surface chemistry and structure that promises to be very interesting indeed, and perhaps even unique in the solar system.

The first spectral measurements were expected to reveal very cold water ice, as had been found on the satellites of Jupiter, Saturn, and Uranus, but they did not. There is, instead, strong evidence for frozen methane—ice and snow formed from freezing the kind of gas that we use for cooking here on the warm Earth! Methane, as we have seen, occurs in the atmospheres of the outer planets from Jupiter to Neptune, and in 1976 we found evidence that methane ice occurs on distant Pluto. But the discovery of methane on Triton caught scientists by surprise. Its presence tells us that the conditions for formation and evolution of planetary satellites were very different at Neptune's distance from the Sun in comparison with those conditions all the way from Jupiter to Uranus, where water ice is the dominant chemical substance on the surfaces of the large satellites.

Perched back on their cold mountaintops, astronomers have continued the study of Triton and have found evidence of another substance on its surface. The spectrum of the satellite indicates that covering at least part of the surface is a sea of liquid nitrogen. Nitrogen is the main component of Earth's atmosphere, but here where it is warm, nitrogen remains a gas. At the low temperature of Triton, nitrogen is a liquid or a solid, depending on a variety of factors; on the part of Triton we can presently see in our telescopes, it appears to be a liquid. The temperature of liquid nitrogen is about 196°C; conditions on Triton are harsh indeed.

An important consequence of the discovery of methane and nitrogen on Triton is that the satellite has its own atmosphere. The atmosphere of Triton may in fact be quite similar in some respects to that of Saturn's much warmer satellite Titan (even astronomers confuse the names!). Triton's atmosphere is mostly nitrogen with traces of methane, and the pressure at the surface is only one-tenth of the atmospheric pressure on the surface of Earth. Of course, it is vastly colder on the surface of Triton than on any other solid body in the solar system except even more distant Pluto. Strong winds of 100 kilometers an hour or more are quite possible.

We cannot presently tell whether the nitrogen seas on Triton are shallow or deep. The astronomical evidence says only that the layer of liquid must be at least several centimeters deep and that it must cover about half of the visible surface.

There may be other substances on Triton's surface, either deposited on the expanses of methane ice and snow or suspended in the nitrogen sea. We can see from our Earth-based observatories that Triton is reddish in color, but neither nitrogen nor methane are this color. They are distinctly white or colorless. What then is giving Triton its red hue? We know that the effect of sunlight on methane and nitrogen can produce complex organic molecules that stick together to form fine reddish dust. Such is the case on Saturn's Titan, and we have similar examples of photochemical smog on Earth. Possibly Triton's white snow is contaminated by organic dust produced by the action of sunlight (or the subatomic particles astronomers call cosmic rays) on its tenuous atmosphere.

Neptune's rotational axis is inclined with respect to the plane of its orbit around the Sun by about 29 degrees, giving it a range of seasons similar to Earth, though the Neptune year is 165 Earth-years long. The orbit of Triton is tipped a little farther relative to Neptune's equator, so the range of seasons on the satellite is fairly extreme. This means, for example, that the south polar regions of Triton are presently in permanent (or long-term) darkness, while the north pole is enjoying permanent sunlight. The same effect occurs on Earth, of course, but the duration of the seasons here is much shorter. The strong seasons of Triton must have a profound effect on the surface and atmosphere because of the very strong effects of temperature on methane and nitrogen. The nitrogen sea, for example, may exist only in the particular polar region exposed to long-term sunlight, while the sea is frozen solid at the dark pole. The atmospheric pressure in the sunny regions may be much higher than in the dark, and there may be strong winds that carry gases evaporating from the sea and ice fields to the colder dark hemisphere. The thin atmosphere should be cloudless, but there may be wisps of cirrus and a variable haze that changes with the seasons over various parts of the satellite. And slowly gliding across the dark blue sky of Triton is Neptune itself, taking nearly three days to go from the western horizon to the eastern and appearing fifteen times larger than the full Moon appears to us in our sky.

What of other possible satellites of Neptune? On a few occasions when astronomers were searching for rings around Neptune during occultations of stars there have been brief blinkings of the star indicative of something near the planet. On at least two occasions, two different observatories working separately reported the same occultation event, but for various reasons it does not appear that there is a conventional ring around Neptune. The likelihood that an occultation of a star by a satellite would be observed even once is very small, and that two separate such observations would be made is infinitesimal. Some scientists are therefore suggesting that Neptune has a belt of small satellites, perhaps millions in number, but much more widely spaced than are the much smaller particles in the rings of either Saturn or Uranus. The wide spacing would mean that occultation of a background star would occur only sometimes, but would be far more probable than for just one or two individual satellites in orbits close to the planet.

Clearly, then, Neptune and its system seem to hold some mysteries for us to ponder. Is there a magnetic field and an aurora in the high atmosphere of

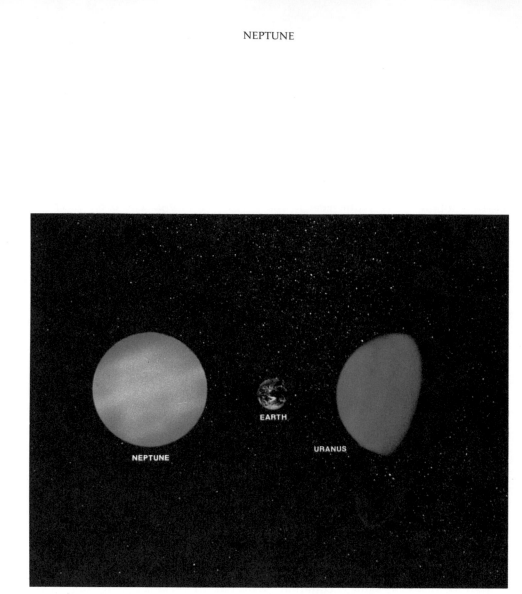

Neptune, Earth, and Uranus to scale (Diagram by S. Meszaros; courtesy Astronomical Society of the Pacific)

the planet? What is the cause of the excess heat that Neptune radiates? Is there a belt of small satellites? What is the nature of Nereid? Triton may be among the most interesting bodies in the solar system with its seasonally dependent atmosphere and surface. What about the possibility that its surface is contaminated with organic compounds, possibly even very complex ones?

Again, we wait impatiently in our warm little corner of the solar sytem while Voyager speeds toward Neptune for a close-up look.

VOYAGER AT NEPTUNE

On August 25, 1989, when Neptune is high in the sky over the giant circular antennas of the Australian tracking station that are part of the Deep Space Network, Voyager 2 will slide past Neptune in a sharp curve taking it within 32,000 kilometers of the planet. Just five hours later, it will sail past Triton with its cameras clicking and its instruments buzzing in the last flurry of activity of a robot spacecraft that was launched from Earth nearly twelve years earlier.

If its instruments are still working properly, as Voyager approaches Neptune after its 3-year, 7-month journey from Uranus, its cameras will record the patterns in the clouds and its sensors will probe for a magnetic field, measure the heat radiating outward, and search the atmosphere for new gases. The cameras will search for undiscovered satellites—either individuals that have escaped detection from Earth or the band of satellites suspected from the occultations described earlier. While we can anticipate some of the discoveries that Voyager will make at Neptune, we are likely to be in for some surprises as well. We are about to open the window on a world that has been glimpsed only dimly and imperfectly.

It is a curious and embarrassing fact that we have been unable to measure the diameter of Triton with satisfactory accuracy, yet we have so much information about its surface chemistry. Pictures from Voyager should solve that problem, as well as allow us to determine the mass of the satellite (also presently unknown). Voyager will probe Triton's atmosphere in great detail and search for organic molecules formed on the surface or in the tenuous air surrounding it. Through the eyes of Voyager we may see icy continents and a glint of sunlight reflected from a liquid sea. There may be the outlines of giant craters formed by impacts of meteorites and comets and ruined by the dynamics of the intense seasons of Triton.

After a few backward glances at Triton and Neptune, Voyager will have accomplished its main mission and will cruise deeper into space, eventually leaving the solar system, a speck of man-made dust in the void of the galaxy.

AT THE HUMAN LIMIT

Jack Williamson

"NEPTUNE?" The Tycoon snorted at the would-be explorer. "Forget Neptune! Too far beyond the human limit."

That historic hoot had seeming reason. Smallest of the four giant gas planets, Neptune swings through eternal icy twilight thirty times Earth's distance out, six times Jupiter's. Its Sun is only a star, somewhat brighter than Earth's full Moon but yielding no perceptible heat.

For humanity, Neptune promised nothing better than cruel hardship and killing difficulty. Yet the very next century bred pioneers bold enough to go there. Space rangers, they liked to call themselves, hardy souls who regarded stay-at-home Earth folk with an inborn scorn.

Evolution had already begun remolding them to dare a new human limit. Not through any startling new mutation, but rather through selecting the best genes for space. Testing themselves through half a dozen generations, the rangers had terraformed Mars and the major moons of Jupiter, moved on from there to occupy Saturn's icy satellites and prospect the meager moons of Uranus. Though still completely human, they were already a new human breed.

People fit for Earth had stayed there, people willing to endure stifling congestion and savage competition for the scant resources of a wasted planet. Or those unfortunates who simply lacked the means and nerve to get away.

With a new mix of genes winnowed from the vast human pool, the space rangers were people at home on the new frontier; people born with improved endurance for different gravities and rough accelerations; people with a better tolerance for synthetic atmospheres and hard radiations and long years of flight in free fall; people at ease in the limitless emptiness of space, who even relished its awesome splendors.

Knut Gunnarson led the way to Neptune. A tough-minded egoist, he claimed descent from the Viking rovers of an earlier Earth. He and his venturesome

handful sealed themselves into a single tiny rocket for four bleak years, flying out from Phoebe, Saturn's outermost moon.

They bypassed Uranus because too many others were already reaching their own limits there, too many Martians and Jovians and prospectors from the Belt, strangers crazed, so Gunnarson felt, with too many changing notions of faith and business and politics and justice.

Gunnarson wanted none of the new religions sweeping the decadent Sunward worlds. He hated the tightening grasp of the Sun Tycoons. In the aftermath of skirmish with a new Company governor bringing new laws, he took off too hastily, too poorly equipped and supplied.

Barely half his tiny crew were still alive when at last they looped close around Neptune and Triton and finally climbed back into orbit around Nereid, the outer satellite. Their first years there were as cruel as the voyage had been.

Neptune itself was mockery and menace, hanging dim and balefully blue green in the starry dark, offering nothing they knew how to reach. Its deep gravity well was a dangerous trap, its atmosphere a noxious smog, mercilessly cold at the surface, its hurricane winds and shifting magnetic fields hinting of enormous unknown forces at work in its unplumbable depths. With neither time nor gear to probe those haunting mysteries, they could only wonder.

They bypassed Triton, the massive inner moon, deep in its own hazardous gravity well. Seen from space, it showed them only crater-fanged highlands white with methane frost and lowlands pooled with inky seas of liquid nitrogen. Yet it tantalized them with its own hints of untouchable wealth.

Massive as the Earth's Moon, and denser, it had to be rich in the heavy elements so rare and precious at this vast distance from the Sun. But it must have been molten, at least at the core, early in its history. Most of the heavy elements had separated out and sunk far from any easy reach.

Nereid, now their chosen home, was only a big snowball, perhaps a captured comet. Just as stark as the Saturnian moonlet they had left, it was small enough to let them land and leave again, and it offered the food and fuel they needed so desperately.

Raw stuff of the cosmos, those dirty snows were a blend of water ice, ammonia ice, and methane ice, salted with all the lighter elements. Refined, they could yield reaction mass for the rockets and feedstocks for the hydroponic gardens. They were raw stuff, too, for the plastics that would be essential here, where the heavier metals were so rare.

Scratching grimly just to stay alive, the colonists converted empty mass tanks into a narrow habitat and stripped every possible scrap of metal out of their craft to improvise a crude refinery to feed their crude hydroponic garden. Too crude to save most of them.

Ironically, that quick victory defeated the expedition. Most of the captured engineers were refugees from Earth who found old school friends in the Tycoon's fleet. Their reunions led to a mutiny. One cruiser surrendered to the colonials and the crews of two others refused to fight. The loyal officers had to bargain hard for their lost ship, and all they took home was a proposed commercial treaty. The indignant Tycoon refused to sign the treaty, but he did agree to a limited diplomatic contact, sending missions intended to spy on the colonists.

Luther Chou came out as a cipher clerk with the first ambassador. He was an able physicist and a secret rebel, embittered by the quota system then in effect, which denied him the laser-burned Sunmark of Company citizenship.

Chou deserted the mission and invented the pressure cell. That was a multilayered sphere of superconducting kwanlon, enormously strengthened by magnetic effects of his own discovery. It could be made selectively reflecting to control internal temperatures and strong enough to resist the enormous pressures of Neptune's depths.

Chou built a robotic probe, shielded in the first experimental shell and equipped with recording telemetry. Its operating power came from Neptune itself, generated by atmospheric gases flowing through magnetohydrodynamic generators into empty pressure cells carried down by heavy ballast.

Dropped off the skywire, the descender was soon lost in the bluish murk. Its radio signals faded and went out. It could never return because the atmosphere at the bottom of the skywire was too thin to float it, but he hoped it would get back into radio range.

Waiting for that took a long time. Chou monitored the spot where it had vanished, listening for anything. Seven months went by—Terran months; the colonists still measured time by the clocks and calendars they had brought from old Earth. His hopes were fading before the transponders picked it up again.

Random drift had carried it five thousand kilometers east. It was still invisible, floating below a layer of ice-crystal clouds. Even its radio signals were muffled and dimmed, garbling its recorded data. Chou was able to pick up fragments of only a few transmissions before it went abruptly silent.

Searching for it with the satellite's telescopes, his assistants never found it, but they did report a perplexing observation. At the moment it stopped sending, they saw a vast dark shadow that leaped and whirled and vanished again, disturbing the thin ice-cloud.

"What?" Chou wrote that unanswerable question in his notebook, and underlined the words. "What could it have been? I suppose one might imagine a creature curious enough to follow our descender up out of the depths and large enough to swallow it. But what manner of thing could digest that kwanlon shell?"

Many of the recorded radar and lidar and kinescope images had been lost, but he kept his computers reprocessing the intact fragments and piecing them together until he had a record of the voyage complete enough to keep him more than ever tantalized.

The descender had dropped fast at first. The green dusk faded into utter blackness, lit only by the stroboscopic flash of the searchlights. Savage near the surface, the winds grew sluggish, then violent again in convective storms where blue lightning burned and thunder jarred the instruments.

As the atmosphere thickened, the descender settled ever more slowly through ammoniac rain that evaporated again as temperatures rose. It sank through ice-crystal clouds, through a level of great, slow-floating flakes of something the telemetry failed to identify. Now and then, there were radar images of something stranger: vague and distant shapes too far for the camera and lidar lenses to reach, too far even for the radar to pick up any clear detail.

Chemical clouds? Density contrasts, perhaps due to temperature anomalies in convective columns? Or fleeting glimpses of something—something unknown and maybe unknowable? Wondering again what had silenced the first descender, Chou ran those tapes again and again. He could never be sure.

External pressures grew enormous, overloading the heat pumps that cooled the kwanlon shell. Internal temperatures climbed so high that the shell had to be driven to total reflectivity, opened for only the briefest flashes of incoming radiation.

Only a handful were left alive when Sam Kwan-Liang arrived with another fugitive crew. He was a renegade plastics engineer in flight from charges of treasonable conspiracy against the Sun Tycoons. False accusations, so he claimed, fabricated to protect the Company monopoly on kwanlon.

That was a nearly miraculous stuff, invented and perfected by earlier generations of his own family. A synthetic mix of carbon and silicon, kwanlon could be spun into monomolecular filaments approaching quantum limits of tensile strength. Skywires fabricated of it had linked geosynchronous satellites with the surface of Earth. Lifting cargo to space stations and dropping the gathered wealth of space back to the mother planet, it had woven the vital fabric of the Company.

Its uses were endless. Kwanlon bubbles could form immense and safe enclosures for space habitats. Properly doped, it became superconducting. Wound into the magnetic elements of fusion engines and fusion drives, it generated energy and drove spacecraft.

Kwan-Liang brought skills to make and spin and dope and anneal it, skills that meant life for the dying colony. The dusty snows of Nereid were rich enough in nitrogen and oxygen to make atmospheres for new orbital habitants, rich enough in everything to feed new hydroponic gardens.

Leading the way back down toward Neptune, Kwan-Liang built Triton's first geosynchronous satellite and dropped a skywire to its impact-pitted snows. It had cooled too fast for crustal tectonics to deposit heavy metals near the surface, but a crew began drilling through the silicate mantle toward the richer ores they hoped to find somewhere beneath.

At first that pit went fast, but the metal-poor crust proved unexpectedly thick. The waste rock grew too difficult to lift, and temperatures increased until the walls of the shift began to crack and creep. Men and women died, but at last they began striking workable ores. Year after year, the stubborn survivors kept inventing new equipment, kept on digging.

More refugees arrived. Still dreading the ruthless reach of the Sun Tycoons, the colonists tried to keep themselves concealed. Most seemed happy enough with their hard frontier, sufficiently absorbed in coping with its penalties and promises, yet there were malcontents.

The younger generation, those who had never felt the cruel reins of Company law, had always been entranced by the stray radio and TV signals picked up from toward the Sun. Dreaming of the richer and more varied ways of life they imagined on the older worlds, a few rebelled. Seizing a survey ship, they took off for Earth.

Alarmed, the settlers put sentry satellites into orbit and dug fortresses into the ice cliffs of Nereid, but the final outcome was not entirely bad. One who went back had been Kwan Gunnarson, a nephew of Sam Kwan-Liang and a grandson of the first pioneer. Welcomed by the Tycoon as a willing informer, he was allowed to earn science degrees at Kwan Tech. Recruited later as a secret agent for the Company, he infiltrated another band of dissidents and returned with them to Neptune on a hijacked space freighter.

At first only pretending to repent, this renegade Gunnarson set up a secret radio station to carry his reports back to the Company. He married a colonial girl and set up a new observatory in geosynchronous orbit around Neptune itself. That project may have been planned only as a cover for his spy work, but it soon began to absorb him completely.

Neptune's dim and hazy face was still a hostile mystery. An unending sea of dull-blue gases, roiled with never-ending storms. What lay beneath it was all unknown, but the traitor's calculations had convinced him that there ought to be some sort of solid center, probably fractionated into a surface of mixed ices over a rock-and-metal core.

His only data came from the thin and frigid winds he could observe, but even in them he found enough to fascinate him. Flow patterns changed in unexpected ways, and the planet radiated more energy than it received from the Sun.

"I dreamed last night," he wrote in a private diary. "Dreamed I had an answer to the riddle of the planet. An answer I can't forget, though this morning

217

it seems unbelievable. It's a notion common prudence may never let me publish, but I want to record it here, to be examined again when my mood has cooled.

"In the dream, I discovered that those perplexing disturbances in the wind flow are caused by moving objects. A notion nobody else is likely to care for. This morning, anchored to my desk here in the free-fall lab with the planet's cold blue-green gloom shining up around me through the ports in the floor, I can't quite imagine anything big enough to cause those enormous eddies, solid enough to hold its shape in these hurricanes, yet light enough to climb to the levels we can observe. The answer dazed me when I found it in the dream, and it still rocks my sanity.

"In the dream, I found evidence that they were alive.

"Awake, I can't see any sane hypothesis to explain how that could be. What could be their cycle of life? Where their energy source? Perhaps that mysterious flow of excess energy out of the core? Nothing I think of makes much sense.

"Certainly, no such creature could have anything in common with anything we know. Nothing evolved from anything like Terran protoplasm could survive an instant in these storms of noxious gases. Yet I can't help reflecting that even back on old Earth, thriving life was found in toxic jets of superheated water ejected from undersea volcanoes.

"All I can do is keep a careful silence. I suppose I shouldn't even think about it, but the riddle will always tease me."

More new fugitives kept on coming, slipping past Company bans with outlawed knowledge and updated technologies. Some of them joined the observatory staff to drop a skywire from it into the surface turbulence of Neptune itself.

Used at first only to support telemetric gear, that experimental line was soon redesigned to tap the planet's gravity for energy. With field effects reversed, the same motor cables that lifted elevator cars became dynamos. Waste mass, loaded into magnetic buckets sliding down the motor line, transformed gravitic force into power for transmission out across space to all the orbital habitats, to those miners still toiling toward the heart of Triton, even to far Nereid.

New explorers, impatient with the slow progress of the pit, had gone out to claim another source of ores, a small asteroid somehow tossed from its origin in the metal-rich regions nearer the Sun. They lost it to a Company fleet. A new Tycoon dispatched a cruiser squadron to tame the colonists and restore the kwanlon monopoly. Unarmed, the salvage crew had to surrender themselves and their prize.

Yet, tested to such extremes, the descender endured everything. It passed the one-thousand-kilometer level. Still intact, it fell through the two-thousand-kilometer level. Instruments open for only milliseconds by then, it passed twenty-five hundred kilometers. At two thousand eight hundred and sixty, the radio altimeters indicated a solid surface still thirty kilometers below.

A surface!

Chou felt the jolt of that, almost as if he had been aboard the robot craft. His own computer models had given him conflicting pictures of Neptune's interior. Summing them up, he had come to expect a semiliquid transition zone between gaseous and solid states, possibly scattered with floating bergs of crystal hydrogen. Certainly nothing like these perplexing images.

Any sort of surface should have been level, so he had thought, smoothed with layers of chemical snows precipitated from above. Amazingly, the few recorded images showed a seemingly endless slope littered with broken boulders, some of them enormous.

Two kilometers above them, the pilot computer had released ballast to check the descent. The atmosphere here was too dense for any rapid motion, but a sluggish current carried the descender slowly up that boulder-slope. With the heat pumps at the brink of failure, the lenses had been opened for only half a dozen more exposures.

The briefest possible flashes, those traced the probe's drift across a towering upthrust from which the boulders must have somehow been shattered. Beyond it, the surface dropped sharply toward a floor so distant that haze obscured it.

One revealing frame had caught a mountain-sized fragment at the brink of the pit in startling detail. It looked crystalline, seemingly transparent, illuminated with its own prismatic reflections of the strobes.

At that point, the computer had cut the mission short. It jettisoned a series of experiments designed to drive test holes for crust specimens and dropped all the remaining ballast to climb back to safer levels.

The final radar image, the most perplexing of all, showed something looming out of the dark ahead of the drifting descender, something almost on its own level and many kilometers above that far-off floor. Chou spent many hours trying to coax any definite detail out of the haze-veiled shape and came to no firm conclusion.

"Only a cloud?" He wrote that question into his notes. "Perhaps." He underlined perhaps. "At that level, however, under the recorded conditions of temperature and pressure and chemistry, I can't imagine what would condense into a cloud.

"Something—I shrink again from what lunatic dream—something alive?

"It must have been twenty kilometers away, drifting at the extreme limit of the prevailing radar range. It was huge! Most of it must have been too far for the beam to reach it. The image is too badly blurred even to hint at wings or limbs—if the thing *was* a being with wings or limbs or any other comprehensible organ.

"I can't imagine—"

The entry closes with that phrase, bold-stroked for emphasis. Later notes record months of effort to enhance and interpret that fragmentary record. Studying the images of those unexpected crystal masses, he recalled an old conjecture about the heart of Neptune, the notion that its core might be armored in diamond.

Diamond!

Ancient astronomers had speculated that most of the carbon compounds in the native cosmic mix that formed the planet must have precipitated out and settled in a thick layer around a mostly metallic core. Baked clean of all volatiles as temperatures and pressures rose, the carbon should have fused and finally crystallized into a solid shell.

A romantic daydream? The evidence for it, that image of a whole mountain range of shining diamond, was too dazzling to be denied. It must have crystallized far below, he had to suppose; some volcanic cataclysm of the planet's youth must have thrown these shimmering fragments up through a crust of lighter stuff.

A world-sized diamond!

The vision kindled a fever in him. Men on the home worlds had enslaved themselves and murdered one another for diamonds small enough to swallow. Here, near enough for the robot almost to touch, was treasure that could change the fortunes of the colony and alter human history in ways he hardly dared imagine.

If it could be recovered—

That problem baffled him. His own resources were used up. Any recovery effort would take a far more sophisticated device than his lost descender. He was wary of asking for help. Even a rumor of his discovery would surely bring Company fleets to snuff out precarious freedoms and claim his diamond strike for the Sun Tycoons.

Yet he resolved to try. He hid most of his recordings, enciphered the best computer transmissions, and applied for a Terran visa. The next ship to call took him home. He had two children there, born to a wife who refused to share his exile. Twins, a daughter and a son, infants when he left.

Yang and Yin—yielding to one final whim of his, his wife had let him name them. She was remarried to a Company shareholder. He doubted that she would want to see him, but he had kept in affectionate touch with the twins. Now coming of age, they were completing their engineering degrees at Kwan Tech.

He revealed his discovery to them, then to some of their friends, sons and daughters of Earthside industrialists who had been denied their Sunmarks. Working in secret, his first small group recruited physicists and engineers, designed new equipment, secured materials to build and equip two new descenders, and finally returned to Neptune on a craft cleared for Pluto.

A year and a half on the long voyage out, even on faster modern craft, they used the time to assemble the first descender. All its external equipment was robotic or remote-controlled, but its tasks would be too demanding for any computer. It was to be manned, though by only a single crew member. Both twins volunteered for the mission.

"No! Neither one!" He was dismayed. "I've gotten to know you too well. I love you both too much. There are others enough who want to go."

Yang agreed that it was too hazardous for a girl. Not, however, for him. Hotly, Yin challenged that. He had always been shorter and slighter than she, the result of an old infection with one of the mutant viruses forever infesting the crowded Earth. She had led and protected him through their childhood, and she still felt fitter than he.

"We'll toss a coin."

Yang produced a bright new Sun dollar, let her toss it, and called heads. It fell with the new Tycoon's golden head glinting at her.

"Sorry, Sis." Grinning at her, he picked up the dollar. "Don't fret for me. I beat the shaking fever, and I can beat anything I happen to meet down toward the core."

With Chou's protests overwhelmed, the project went forward. They installed a new skywire extension to lower the descender to a level where they might hope to pick it up again. Preparing to go, Yang seemed coldly silent, totally absorbed. But when he gripped Yin's hand and turned to climb aboard, tears filled his eyes.

"See you, Sis," he called though the closing hatch. "With enough diamonds to make the Tycoons cry."

The short day was ending before the descender fell away into Neptune. She followed it down, a bright fleck dwindling into dull bluish dusk turning swiftly dark. Its strobes came on, winking like the fireflies she had known at home, slowly dimming until she lost them.

"My poor, dear brother," she wrote that night in her journal. "Always risking everything, because he always wants to beat me. I'm sorry for him. Terrified now. And suddenly I wonder why he seemed so sure when he called the coin. Was he somehow cheating?"

They waited for him, waited for his signal capsules, waited a year.

"A crazy dream," her aging father told her. "We've followed it far enough. No hope for him now. I'm giving up."

"I'm not." She had been assembling the spare descender. "If he doesn't get back, I'm going after him."

"I can't let you—"

"Here's why you must." She showed him a bright Sun dollar. "I found it last night in his room. Look at it." She turned the coin to let him see the new Tycoon's golden head shining through the plastic on one face and then on the other. "He cheated, and you've got to let me go."

Before her craft was ready, they picked up transmissions from a signal capsule that told Yang's story. Sinking for months as the unmanned probe had done through ammoniac rain and chemical snows, through calm and fury, he had come at last to the stagnant surface of a tar-colored sea.

"Liquid methane." Her brother's voice, faint and distorted, but still her brother's crisply careful voice. "Stained, I imagine, with carbonaceous pollution. The power cells are almost gone, but I can use wind motion. Drifting now."

He drifted for many days.

"Cliffs ahead!" In that later report, excitement lifts his voice. "Tall and jagged. Could be the floating continent of solid hydrogen the old theorists expected. Dropping ballast to climb over it. No sign of diamonds anywhere."

Next day. "Dropped more ballast to clear a second line of cliffs. Ice below me now seamed with pressure ridges and crater-marked where I think ejecta fell. Dived again to study impact masses. Hard black stuff. High carbon content, but no crystals visible."

"Diamonds!" That was four days later. "Here at last, too huge to believe! Too splendid to be true! An endless field of diamonds bigger than buildings, covering a slope that reaches as far as my lenses can see. The slope, I suppose, of the volcano that ejected them. Fracture planes glittering under the probes. Wait, Sis, and I'll make you richer than anybody!"

Sealed inside the pressure cell, he couldn't touch that treasure. Hoping to raise what he could with remote-controlled devices attached to flotation cells, he dropped anchors to hold him over a shimmering boulder that looked small enough to lift. Before his gear was attached, his long-silent radio crashed into life.

"Bursts of long-wave radiation," he reported. "Nothing resembling the static I got coming through the storms. This is modulated into repetitious patterns. Signals? From what? I'd like to know, but lifting this rock will take everything I can muster. No time or power to waste on talk."

He worked on. The signals grew stronger, until his radar picked up a moving image.

"A native getting curious?" Yang had seldom shown emotion, but Yin caught a tremor in his thinned, far-off voice. "Something sized to fit the planet. Now near, so near it ought to show a shape—but the radar reveals no shape. I'm trying the searchlight on it now.

"Something—" The tremor was stronger when he went on. "The near edge of it not a dozen kilometers away. And still no detail. When I narrowed

222

the beam, it burned right through—through whatever it was. That stopped the signal. The radar still showed the same dim cloud. Ragged where the light had cut it. Fading fast till it vanished altogether. A funny thing! I'd like to know all about it, but no time to wonder now."

He went back to work, but found himself stopping to stare at the glory of his chosen diamond blazing under the strobes. Nearly too large for his gear, it must weigh more, he thought, than all the gem diamonds men had ever mined. Absorbed in its burning splendor, he was slow to hear the beep of his radar alarm.

"Something coming. Something else I've no time for," he reported from the monitor. "Smaller than that queer shadow-thing. Coming low up the slope behind me." His wispy voice quickened. "I've got it in the searchlight now. Something dark and solid, that light doesn't dissolve. Coming straight at me. Already too near—"

The object exploded against the descender. The rest of his reports were breathless fragments. A heavy concussion had dazed him. He found no other injury, but the instrument lights were dead. Groping in the dark, he started the emergency generator and discovered his bleak situation.

The descender had been powered by the flow of gas into five generator cells. Two had already been used up and jettisoned. Now two more were dead. The fifth, though still attached and working, had sprung a leak that filled it fast.

His first thought was to finish securing the lift cell to his prize, but all the external gear was dead. With no strobes flashing, not even to let him inspect the damage, all he had time for was to gasp a few final words into his computer log and launch it in the Mayday capsule.

"Sorry, Sis. This time, I really hoped to show you—"

Max Lind was sitting with Yin in the satellite lab as she played and replayed the recording. He had been her fellow student back at Kwan Tech. The son of a Company director, a golden Sunmark blazing on his cheek, he had thrown away the promise of a fine career in the Tycoon's service to come with her to space. He tried hard now to dissuade her from following her brother into Neptune.

"A monstrous trap," he told her. "Baited with a prize unreal as a dream. Those diamond boulders aren't for us. Too far down beyond what that old Tycoon called the human limit."

"Maybe so." She shrugged. "Maybe not. I've got to go, because I should have been where my brother is. He tricked me and died for it. I mean to do better."

The second descender was nearly ready, but she delayed the launch to install radio gear designed to retransmit those enigmatic signals her brother had chosen not to answer.

"Yang was always too impulsive," she told him. "He wasn't always wise. I think he should have tried to talk to those creatures—if that's what they are. Ignoring them, he must have puzzled and alarmed them. Meaning no harm, he seems to have let his searchlight destroy one of them. I'll try to make peace."

Her old father embraced her before she went aboard, sobbing forlornly. Max Lind kissed her and gave her a modest Terran diamond his mother had worn. Her descender dropped into the frigid surface winds, flickered down into darkening smog, vanished into Neptune.

She dropped it safely toward the diamond-slope where her brother had died. When her altimeters read two hundred kilometers, she blacked out her strobes and began retransmitting the signals he had recorded. They were answered from somewhere farther up the slope. She slowed her descent and echoed those answers, still showing no lights. Her radar caught no motion, but as she came lower it began to image something that amazed her.

"A wall?" She was recording a log. "Some sort of barrier ring? Nothing I can understand. Nothing solid, certainly—the radar penetrates it to image things beyond. It's circular. Enclosing the spot where my brother died. Maybe a kilometer thick and twice that high, the area inside perhaps forty kilometers across. Intended for defense? Set up to contain the danger they felt in my brother's descender? Probable enough, but I'm not going to test the notion.

"Yet I wonder. Wonder what it is. Wonder about the laws and the limits of matter and energy, down in this queer hell. About the energy cycles, and the evolutionary processes—if whatever got my brother is even akin to life and mind. Nice riddles for physics and biology, if I get home with them. But now, like my poor brother, I'm here for diamonds."

She had brought five flotation cells. With no move to approach that shadow-barrier, she landed near the flat-crushed fragments of Yang's descender and secured her first cell to the fire-bright boulder where his lifting slings were still in place.

Nothing attacked her. The cell secure, she dumped its ballast to let it rise. Driving herself against iron limits of time and power, she lifted four more enormous crystal masses. Lacking any special gear to gather or move her brother's remains, she left them where he had died, those diamond crags to be his monuments.

She reached the surface safely, long months later, with no further contacts to report. Luther Chou picked up her signals, and Max Lind was aboard the first explorer craft to reach her with the kwanlon lines to tow her and her prizes to the low-level station.

"What are they, really? What are they like? What do they want?" Lind asked her that, while she was still in his arms.

"What are we to them?" Brooding over the enigma, she never found a better answer. "Sharing so very little, I doubt that we can ever know each other. They must fear us, as we fear them. I believe they have given us the space and the diamonds inside that barrier. A token, I think, of their desire for peace. I doubt they'll ever let us land anywhere outside it."

Time, confirming that intuition, has told us very little more about them. More descenders have been allowed to land inside the ring, lift diamonds, and rise again—but only one by one. Any second craft, diving before the last has completed its voyage, has been invariably lost. Though a good many adventurers have tried, no expedition toward any other section of the core has ever returned.

Neptune's later history, and the later lives of Max and Yin, could fill another volume, though one with little to rival the drama of that first diamond strike. Though the Tycoons have tried, none of their own diamond seekers has ever got back from testing those implacable limits. They have granted the colonists at least a nominal autonomy, with Sunmarks to symbolize all the rights of citizenship, brands few have ever cared to wear.

On all the planets, the discovery has had vast impacts. Though long-established gemstone values were shattered overnight, rich new technologies have made up the loss many times. Diamond-based semiconductors have created a dazzling array of new solid-state devices.

Diamond chips make up the computer brains of the robots now on their way out to search for the dark tenth planet whose position they have recently computed, that remote and sinister planet whose wanderings through the comet clouds seem to have caused such hails of cosmic stuff as the one that killed off the dinosaurs.

PLUTO

ESSAY BY
Robert Silverberg

SPECULATION BY
Robert Silverberg

PLUTO: OUTERMOST

Robert Silverberg

THE UNKNOWN PLANET

MUCH OF WHAT WE KNOW about the small and distant world of Pluto is only newly emerged from the realm of speculation. Pluto's moon Charon was discovered as recently as 1978. Our information on the surface temperature of Pluto is just a few years older than that, as is our scanty knowledge of the sparse Plutonian atmosphere. Even our information about Pluto's size and mass and gravitational pull was being debated vigorously by astronomers in the early 1970s, and to this day some of the readings are far from certain.

But that we should know so little about the outermost planet of the solar system is hardly surprising. Worlds such as Mercury, Venus, Mars, Jupiter, and Saturn were familiar to the ancient Sumerians and Egyptians and probably even to the more primitive cultures that preceded them. But Pluto has been part of our fund of scientific knowledge for barely more than half a century. When Herbert Hoover became president in 1929, the solar system still had just eight known planets. However, there was good reason to think that an unknown ninth planet did lie somewhere in the depths of space. Mathematical calculations indicated the strong likelihood of its existence—the same sort of calculations that had led to the discovery of the eighth planet, Neptune.

Uranus was the first planet to be discovered in modern times—by the British astronomer William Herschel, who spotted it while scanning the heavens on March 13, 1781. Astronomers quickly calculated the probable orbit for this distant world, 2.9 billion kilometers from the Sun; but as Uranus moved through its eighty-four-year-long journey along that orbit, it could be seen to stray from its predicted path. Some unknown force was disturbing its motions, pulling it thousands of miles off course. The most plausible explanation was that Uranus was subject to the gravitational pull of some unknown planet even farther out, the presence of which had not been taken into account in the calculations of Uranus's orbit; and in 1845 the French astronomer Urbain Leverrier was able to work out the likely mass and orbit of that hypothetical planet. Acting at Leverrier's suggestion, Johann Galle of the Berlin University Observatory began a search for the new planet, which he found on September 23, 1846. It was discovered that Neptune has an average distance of 4.5 billion kilometers from the Sun, considerably less than that predicted by Leverrier.

Not only did Neptune's orbit fail to fit the conventional mathematical expectations, but its mass was not great enough to account for the disturbances that had been noted in the orbit of Uranus. Obviously still another unknown planet lay somewhere in the outer reaches of the solar system, and by the late nineteenth century a serious quest for it was under way. Two astronomers in particular—the Americans William H. Pickering and Percival Lowell—devoted much of their careers to finding the ninth planet, which they independently calculated should lie about 8.4 billion kilometers from the Sun. But neither had any success, and each eventually abandoned the search. Using Pickering's calculations, Milton Humason of the Mount Wilson Observatory, California, conducted an extensive hunt in 1919, also fruitlessly. No further attempts were made to find the hypothetical ninth planet over the next decade.

But the invention by a German optical firm of a device called a "blink comparator" greatly simplified the task. In this instrument, two astronomical photographs are placed side by side and viewed through a single eyepiece. First one picture is lit, then the other; the mind retains the image of the first picture during the split-second jump to the second one, and, to an experienced operator, any object that is in a different place on each photograph will appear to leap back and forth with each blink of the lighting.

In 1929, a 23-year-old Illinois-born astronomer named Clyde Tombaugh joined the staff of the Lowell Observatory in Arizona and took up the task of finding the ninth planet. He spent hours each day checking photographs in the blink comparator. On the afternoon of February 18, 1930, while blinking photographs that he had taken on January 23 and 29, Tombaugh suddenly noticed a faint object "popping in and out of the background . . . as first one plate and then the second was visible through the eyepiece. 'That's it!' I exclaimed to myself."

He was right. During the next few weeks the Lowell Observatory checked and rechecked until there could be no doubt, and on March 13, 1930—the one hundred and forty-ninth anniversary of Herschel's discovery of Uranus—the announcement was made of the finding of an "object beyond Neptune" that was apparently a planet. An 11-year-old British girl suggested a name for the newfound world: Pluto, for the Roman god of the dead, brother to Jupiter and Neptune, who presided over a realm of eternal darkness.

THE ENIGMA OF PLUTO

Darkness and mystery indeed are the hallmarks of Pluto the planet. So distant and faint is it that it is four thousand times too dim to be seen with the naked eye; only the most powerful telescopes are able to see it at all, and not even they can perceive it in much detail. Most of the information that scientists have been able to collect about Pluto is highly approximate; in fact, aside from its orbit, nearly all aspects of Pluto are matters of doubt and controversy.

Determining a planet's orbit is largely a matter of mathematics, and the procedures have been understood since Kepler's time. Pluto's orbit turned out to be the most eccentric of any of the planets—bringing it as close to the Sun as 4.4 billion kilometers at one point, carrying it as far away as 7.4 billion kilometers at another. The mean distance of Pluto from the Sun is about 5.9 billion kilometers, making it the most remote of the planets, traveling on a track so vast that Pluto requires some 248.5 years to make a single revolution around the Sun. Yet because of the eccentricity of its orbit, Pluto spends a short period of each Plutonian year closer to the Sun than the ostensible eighth planet, Neptune. That is the situation at present: Pluto crossed the orbit of Neptune in the winter of 1978–1979 and will remain within it until the spring of 1999, when it will make its closest approach to the Sun and begin moving outward again. (There is no danger that the two planets will ever collide during one of these orbital crossings; not only is Pluto's orbit extraordinarily eccentric, it is also inclined at an angle of more than 17 degrees to the rest of the solar system. The closest Pluto can come to Neptune is 387 million kilometers.)

The bizarrely elongated orbit of Pluto mystified astronomers. Some denied that Pluto was a planet at all and insisted it was merely a trans-Neptunian comet or a giant asteroid. Others suggested that it was a moon of Neptune that had escaped into a solar orbit of its own, which may yet be proven to be so. But within a few years of its discovery the new heavenly body was generally accepted as a planet—although one vastly different from its neighbors in the outer reaches of the solar system.

For one thing, Pluto did not appear to be in the proper place in the heavens. There are formulas of celestial mechanics that have traditionally allowed astronomers to predict the most probable spacing of undiscovered planets. Those formulas do not *dictate* that spacing; they simply correspond to the actual distribution of worlds between Mercury and Saturn. Uranus had turned out to be right where the formulas said it should be. Neptune was not in the proper place, by a margin of 1 billion kilometers. In Pluto's case, though, an even greater divergence from what was expected was found: as we have seen, calculations had indicated that the ninth planet should be in an orbit 8.4 billion kilometers from the Sun, but Pluto's mean distance was found to be just 5.9

billion kilometers. That huge discrepancy remains a puzzle to this day. It seems that the traditional laws suggest patterns that do not correspond with the actual orbits of the outermost planets. On the other hand, some astronomers believe that Pluto is in fact not the ninth planet that the calculations of Pickering and Lowell indicated, and that at least one more major world in a more distant orbit remains to be discovered.

Then there is the problem of Pluto's size and mass. Pickering believed that a body capable of disturbing the orbits of Uranus and Neptune to the extent that had been observed would have to have a mass about twice that of Earth; later Lowell calculated that the ninth planet would need to have seven times Earth's mass to account for the known orbital effects. Early attempts at measuring Pluto's actual dimensions were stymied by the remote planet's faintness: it shows no visible disk, appearing in telescopes and on photographic plates merely as a pinpoint of light much like a star. If Pluto were really as tiny as it appears to be—the best early guesses gave it a diameter of about 10,500 kilometers, only slightly less than that of Earth—then it would need to have an average density about thirty-eight times as great as water's in order to be as massive as Lowell's figures demanded. There is no element as dense as that except in the cores of stars.

Then in 1950, Gerard Kuiper, using the 200-inch Mount Palomar telescope, succeeded in viewing Pluto more clearly than anyone had done before and reported that its diameter was even less than first thought—about 5,800 kilometers, about equal to that of Mars. Which worsened the problem: if Pluto was less than half as great as Earth in diameter but had seven times Earth's mass, then it would need to be more than fifty times as dense as water—if not an impossibility, then certainly a huge implausibility.

One way around the dilemma was the notion that Pluto might actually be a very large planet which reflects light in a deceptive way. This was the billiard-ball theory. Consider a highly polished black billiard ball, some astronomers said, that sits on a table in a dark room into which the light of a single candle comes through a slot in the wall. All that we would see of the billiard ball would be a point of light reflected from its glossy surface; this would give us no hint of the ball's true diameter.

Suppose, then, that Pluto is covered with a sheet of ice that reflects the feeble light of the distant Sun just as the billiard ball would reflect a candle's gleam. Through our telescope we would see a glint of brightness—the zone of reflection, having, perhaps, the 5,800 kilometer diameter Kuiper observed. The rest of the planet would be shrouded in darkness. Pluto might well have a diameter of 32,000 kilometers or more, most of its surface invisible to us; and in that case, it would not be necessary to bring forth issues of unlikely densities to account for the gravitational effects it exerts on its neighboring planets.

But the billiard-ball theory had to be discarded in 1965, when Pluto's path took it between Earth and a star in the constellation of Leo. If Pluto had been any larger than 6,815 kilometers in diameter, the star would have been completely hidden for a short while. The star remained visible, though, and thus an upper limit to Pluto's size was established.

Meanwhile Pluto was steadily moving closer to the Sun, with the result that it was now nearly twice as bright as it had been at the time of its discovery in 1930. And astronomers now had new tools at their disposal, such as computers and more sensitive measuring devices. By 1971 it was evident that Pluto must be a very small world with a mass no greater than one-tenth of Earth's. Whatever is perturbing the orbits of Neptune and Uranus, it is *not* the little planet we call Pluto.

How insignificant Pluto actually is was demonstrated in September 1978, when James Christy of the U.S. Naval Observatory noticed an odd bump jutting out of the side of Pluto's image on his photographic plates. Checking older photographs, Christy found similar bumps—always in the same position. The best explanation was that Pluto has a smaller body in orbit around it at extremely close range; to our astronomical instruments, planet and moon would appear to be a single entity. Careful observation at several other astronomical stations confirmed Christy's discovery; Pluto's moon has been named Charon, after the ferryman who brings the souls of the dead across the River Styx to the god Pluto's domain.

The known presence of a moon permits very precise mathematical analysis of a planet's mass, by application of the Newtonian and Keplerian laws of planetary motion. And Pluto turned out to be insignificant indeed—its mass is actually just .0024 that of Earth. Charon itself, though it is large—40 percent as big as Pluto, making it the largest moon of the solar system in relation to the size of its primary planet—accounts for only one-tenth of the total mass of the pair. Its distance from Pluto is just 17,000 kilometers or so, and its period of revolution around Pluto has been determined to be approximately 6.39 Earth days. Since Pluto rotates on its axis every 6.39 Earth days—as was shown in 1955 by photoelectric measurements of fluctuations in Pluto's brightness—Charon must remain constantly in the same position in Pluto's sky, probably as a giant presence above the equator.

(The very long Plutonian day is an oddity in itself. The other planets rotate once every 25 hours or less, except for Mercury and Venus, which are slowed by special gravitational conditions that are caused by their proximity to the Sun. Pluto's relatively slow period of rotation seems more like that of a moon than that of a planet: Neptune's Triton rotates once every five days, twenty-one hours, and Uranus's Titania every eight days, sixteen hours, and so on. Since Pluto is unquestionably in orbit around the sun, not around some other planet, it is by definition a planet. But its slow rotation lends strength to the argument of Gerard Kuiper and others that Pluto may once have been a moon of Neptune that somehow escaped and took up independent orbit while retaining its moon-like rate of spin.)

COMPOSITION

Now that we are certain that Pluto is a lightweight world smaller than our moon, we have a better chance to solve another of its mysteries: its chemical composition. Gone is the need to speculate that it is a ball of some fantastic superheavy substance. Spectrographic evidence indicates that the surface of Pluto is made up of frozen water, methane, and ammonia. Indeed, Pluto and Charon are so light that Clyde Tombaugh has suggested that the entire planet and its moon are constructed of nothing else—"two huge icebergs, the ices consisting of solid water, ammonia, and methane." Other astronomers believe it more likely that Pluto has some sort of solid core of silicate rock, perhaps constituting a quarter of its mass. About this, it has been proposed, may lie a thick blanket of water ice, accounting for nearly all the remaining mass, with a thin shell of frozen methane covering the surface, mixed to some extent with ammonia. A different speculative picture places the methane layer at hundreds of miles in thickness.

The presence of *frozen* methane is a clue to the terrifying coldness of Pluto. Measuring the surface temperature of a planet whose very mass and size were controversial just a few years ago is no simple project. But we know that even on so chilly a world as Neptune, where the surface temperature is −184°C or lower, methane remains a gas and is an important component of Neptune's atmosphere, providing that planet with its characteristic greenish hue. The methane on Pluto, sensitive instruments have shown, is a solid frost. Therefore the temperature of Pluto may be less than −200°C much of the time, approaching the absolute physical limits of coldness.

But even on Pluto there is a Plutonian equivalent of night and day, and a sort of oscillation between winter and summer. These factors probably bring a relatively wide range of temperatures even to that awesomely frigid world. We have seen that Pluto's distance from the Sun varies between 4.4 billion and 7.4 billion kilometers over the course of its 248.5-year period of revolution. Because the orbit of Earth is somewhat elliptical, our distance from the Sun varies during the year too, but that is not at all a factor in our climate; we are actually closer to the Sun in winter than in summer. (The true determining factor for us is the angle at which the Sun's rays reach us—more obliquely in the cold months than in the warm ones.) For Pluto, though, with its far more eccentric orbit, the variation in the impact of solar radiation that reaches it during its long year is extreme, and beyond doubt the ninth planet grows warmer as it moves toward the inner reaches of its orbit.

That may cause the methane to shift from the frozen to the gaseous form—giving Pluto an atmosphere at least some of the time. As Clyde Tombaugh wrote in 1980, "Wouldn't it be interesting if astronomers began to observe methane-gas absorption in the spectrum of Pluto in the next two decades as it warms up a little more while Pluto is inside the orbit of Neptune? In other words, will the methane frost be transformed into a methane atmosphere? If so, then after the year A.D. 2000, Pluto's methane atmosphere would be precipitated as frost again on its surface, with a winter season lasting for over 200 of our years."

Or perhaps the cycle is even shorter than that: a thawing of some of the methane during the long Plutonian day and a freeze again when the planet swings around to show its other side to the Sun. Some scientists think that Pluto has a scant but permanent methane atmosphere, perhaps containing heavier gases such as argon as well, with methane constantly evaporating at the planet's surface during the daylight period and falling as frost when the bitter night returns.

At its coldest—during night periods at those times when the planet is at its farthest from the Sun—Pluto's temperature may drop to just 30 to 40 degrees above absolute zero, −459.67°F (-200°C). The odds against the existence of any sort of life on inhospitable Pluto are colossal.

FUTURE INVESTIGATIONS

In any event the mysteries of Pluto are apt to remain mysteries for centuries to come. That perplexing little globe in the depths of space will go unvisited by the Voyager spaceships as they swing onward through the solar system in the years ahead, and even after the resumption of manned space missions it seems unlikely that Pluto will be very high on anyone's priority list for exploration. The distance is enormous, after all, and will be increasing all during the next century. A journey to Pluto and back under present technology would require close to a hundred years for the round trip. Doubtless the spaceships of the future will be much swifter than ours, but, even so, going to Pluto is not likely to be anyone's idea of a casual jaunt at any time in the foreseeable future. Then, too, the temperatures that explorers must endure on Pluto will probably be a hundred degrees or more colder than anything encountered on our Moon even in the darkest part of the lunar night. Insulation against the Plutonian chill will not be the main problem, but rather the tendency of many materials to change their physical properties entirely as temperatures drop toward absolute zero. Some metals perfectly suitable for vehicles used in the exploration of the Moon and Mars will become hopelessly brittle on Pluto; most plastics will turn to powder. The vehicles that carry explorers over the surface of Pluto will have to be made of materials capable of withstanding the lowest temperatures in the solar system.

Yet the enigmas of the ninth planet will surely pull spacefarers to its grim shores eventually—and beyond, to the tenth planet that may lurk in the darkness at the borders of our solar system. Something is perturbing the orbits of Uranus and Neptune, and we know now that Pluto is not massive enough to be doing it. The search now centers in the region about 11 billion kilometers from the Sun, which astronomers have calculated is the most likely site for the orbit of Planet X. Perhaps a vast, dark giant world moves slowly through that outer darkness, a frigid world from which the Sun appears as a small dot of light and where a year is five hundred of our years in length, a world which receives and reflects so little sunlight that it is invisible from Earth.

Perhaps. Perhaps the first explorers who reach Pluto may stare outward toward worlds yet unknown. Our ancestors spoke knowingly of "the five planets"—Mercury, Venus, Mars, Saturn, Jupiter. Our tally has reached nine. (Unlike the ancients, we count our own world as a planet among planets, and we have added Uranus, Neptune and Pluto to the original list.) There may be more to find. But for the moment Pluto marks the outermost point in our knowledge of our small corner of the galaxy.

SUNRISE ON PLUTO

Robert Silverberg

W E HAVE WAITED OUT THE NIGHT, and now at last we will go forth onto the frozen face of Pluto. One by one we take our places—Leonides, Sherrard, Gartenmeister, me—and ready ourselves to clamber down the ladder to the icy surface of the outermost of worlds.

Soon we will have an answer to the question that has obsessed us all during this long night.

Night on Pluto is six point three nine Earth days long, and that night is blacker and colder than anything any of us has ever known. It is a true dark night of the soul, a dismal time made infinitely more terrible by our awareness of the monstrous distance separating us from all that we love. That distance imposes a burden which our spirits can scarcely carry. God knows, the dark side of Luna is a bleak and terrible place, but one never feels so wholly crushed by its bleakness as we have felt here. On Luna one need make only a brief journey to the edge and there is the lovely blue Earth hovering overhead, close, familiar, beckoning. But here stand we on forlorn Pluto, knowing that we are nearly four billion miles from home. No one has ever been so far from home before.

Now at last the fierce interminable night is ending. When we made our touchdown here the night was half spent; we used what remained of the dark hours to carry out our preliminary observations and to prepare for the extra-vehicular journey. Now, as we make ready to emerge, there comes the first trembling hint of a dawn. The utter and absolute and overwhelming darkness, which has been made all the more intense by the chilly glitter of the stars, is pierced by a strange pale glow. Then a sudden astonishing burst of light enters the sky—the light of a giant star whose cold radiance is hundreds of times as bright as that of the full Moon seen from Earth.

It is the Sun, *our* Sun, the well of all warmth, the fountain of life. But how sadly its splendor is altered and diminished by those billions of miles! What reaches us here is not the throbbing golden blaze of summer but only a brilliant wintry beacon that sends glittering tracks of dazzling merciless brightness across the stark ice fields of Pluto.

We move toward the hatch. No one speaks. The tension is rising and our faces show it.

We are edgy and uneasy, but not because we are about to be the first humans to set foot on this world: that is trivial, entirely unimportant to us, as I think it has always been to those who have carried the great quest outward into space. No, what concerns us is a mystery that no previous explorers of the solar system have had to confront. Our instruments, during the long Plutonian night, have been recording apparent indications that living creatures, Plutonian life-forms, are moving about out there.

Life-forms? Here, on the coldest and most remote of worlds? It seems absurd. It *is* absurd. Nowhere in the solar system has anyone ever found a trace of extraterrestrial life, not on any of the explored planets nor on any of their moons. Unless something unimaginable lurks deep within the impenetrable gaseous mantles of Jupiter or Saturn or Uranus, our own small planet is the sole repository of life in the system, and, for all we know, in the entire universe. But our scanners have picked up the spoor of life here: barely perceptible electromagnetic pulses that indicate something in motion. It is strictly a threshold phenomenon, the most minimal trace-output of energy, the tiniest trickle of exertion. The signal is so faint that Sherrard thinks it is nothing more than an instrumentation error, mere noise in the circuitry. And Gartenmeister *wants* it to be an error—he fears the existence of extraterrestrial life, so it seems, the way Pascal feared the eternal silence of the infinite heavens. Leonides argues that there is nothing that could produce such distinct vectors of electromagnetic activity except neural interaction, and therefore some sort of living beings must be crawling about on the ice fields. "No," I say, "they could be purely mechanical, couldn't they? Robots left behind by interstellar explorers, say?"

Gartenmiester scowls at me. "Even more absurd," he says.

No, I think, not more absurd, merely more disturbing. No matter what we discover out there, it is bound to upset deeply held convictions about the unique place of Earth in the cosmos. Who would have thought it, that Pluto, of all places, would harbor life? On the other hand, perhaps Sherrard is right. Perhaps what we have imagined to be life-forms emitting minuscule flickers of electrical energy is in truth nothing more than deceptive Brownian tremors in the atoms that make up our ship's sensors. Perhaps. Soon we may have an answer.

"Let's go," Leonides says.

We swing downward and outward, into the cheerless Plutonian dawn.

237

The blackness of the sky is tinged with green as the distant sunlight bounces through the faint wispy swirls of methane that are Pluto's atmosphere. Visible now overhead, hovering ominously close, is the dull menacing bulk of Charon, Pluto's enormous moon, motionless and immense. Our shadows are weird things, sharp-edged and immensely long. They seem to strain forward as though trying to escape from us. Cold tendrils of sunlight glide unhurriedly toward the jagged icy cliffs in the distance.

Sunrise! Sunrise on Pluto!

How still it is, an alien sunrise. No birds sing, no insects buzz and drone. We four have seen many such sunrises—on Luna, on Mars, on Titan, on Ganymede, on Iapetus: standing with our backs to the rising Sun, looking out on a harsh and silent landscape. But none so silent as this, none so harsh.

We fan out across the surface of Pluto, moving lithely, all but floating: Pluto is the lightest of worlds, its mass only a few hundredths that of Earth, and its gravitational grip is less secure than those of some of the larger moons. What do I see? Ice. A joyless methane sea far away, shining faintly by the dull light of dawn. Fangs of black rock. Despair begins to rise in me. To have come billions of miles, merely for the sake of being able to say that this world, too, has been explored—

"Here!" Leonides calls.

He is far in front of us, almost at the terminator line beyond which the Sun has not yet reached. He is pointing ahead, into the darkness, stabbing at it with the beam of his light.

"Look! I can see them moving!"

We run toward him, leaping in great bounds, soaring, gliding. Then we stand beside him, following the line of his light, staring in awe and astonishment toward the darkness.

Yes. Yes. We have the answer at last to our question, and the answer is a stunning one. Pluto bears life. Small dome-shaped things are scrabbling over the ice.

They move slowly, unhurriedly, and yet one somehow feels that they are going as fast as possible, that indeed they are racing for cover, pushing their bodies to the limits. And we know what it is that they are struggling to escape; for already the ones closest to us have been overtaken by the advancing light of day, and as the rays touch them they move more slowly, and more slowly yet, and then they fall entirely still, stopping altogether between one moment and the next, like wind-up toys that have run down. Those that are in sunlight now lie stranded on the ice, and those ahead of them are being overtaken, one after another.

We hasten to them, kneel, examine them. None of us says a word. We hardly dare look at one another. The creatures are about the size of large crabs, with thick smooth waxy-textured gray shells that reveal neither eyes nor mouths. They are altogether motionless. I touch one with a trembling hand, nudge it, get no response, nudge it a bit more forcefully. It does not move. I glance at Leonides. He nods, and I tip the creature on its side, which shows us a great many small jointed legs that seem to sprout from the shell surface itself. What a simple creature! A mere armored box!

"I don't believe it," Sherrard mutters.

"You still think it's an error in the circuitry?" Leonides asks him gently.

Sherrard shakes his head. Carefully he gathers one of the creatures into his gloved hands and brings it close to his faceplate. "It doesn't move at all," he says quietly. "It's playing possum, isn't it?"

"It may not be able to move," says Leonides. "Not with anything as warm as you so close to it. They're tremendously sensitive to heat, I imagine. You see how they start to shut down the moment the sun strikes them?"

"Like machines," says Sherrard. "At the wrong operating temperature they cease to function."

"*Like* machines, yes," Leonides replies. "But surely you aren't going to try to argue that they *are* machines, are you?"

Sherrard shrugs. "Machines can have legs. Machines can have shells." He looks toward me. "It's like you said, Tom—robots left behind by explorers from some other part of the galaxy. Why not? Why the hell not?"

There is nothing to gain by debating it out here. We return to the ship to get collection chambers and scoop three of the creatures into cryotanks, along with liquid methane and lumps of frozen-ammonia ice. The discovery is so wholly unexpected and so numbing in its implications that we can hardly speak. We had thought we were making a routine reconnaissance of an unimportant planet; instead we have made one of the most astonishing discoveries in the history of science.

We store our finds in the ship's lab at a temperature of two or three degrees Kelvin. Gartenmeister and Sherrard set about the job of examining them while Leonides and I continue the extravehicular exploration.

The crab-creatures are littered all over the place, dozens of them, hundreds, scattered like jetsam on a beach. They appear to be dead, but very likely Leonides' notion that they are extremely heat-sensitive tells the real story: to the native life-forms of Pluto—and how strange it is to have a phrase like that running through my mind!—the coming of day must be an inexorable signal bringing a halt to all metabolic activity. A rise of just a few degrees and they are compelled to stop in their tracks, seemingly lifeless, in fact held in suspended animation, until the slow rotation of the planet brings them back, in another

6.39 Earth days, into the frigid darkness that they must have in order to function. Creatures of the night: creatures of the inconceivable realm at the borderland of absolute zero. But why? It makes so little sense: to move by night, to go dormant at the first touch of the life-giving sun! Why? Why?

Leonides and I explore for hours. There is so much to do: collecting mineral samples, drilling for ice cores that may yield data on earlier epochs of Pluto's history, searching for other forms of life. We move carefully, for we are not yet used to the lightness of the gravitational field. We prowl in a slow, systematic way, as if we are going to be the only expedition ever to land on this remote outpost of the solar system and must take pains not to overlook anything. But I see the fallacy in that. It is true that this is the first time anyone has bothered to visit Pluto, although centuries have passed since the earliest human voyages into space. And it is true also that when we planned this expedition it was under the assumption that no one was likely to have reason to come this way again for a long time. But all that has changed. There is extraterrestrial life on this world, after all. Nowhere else is that the case. When we send back the news, it will alter the direction of virtually all scientific research, and much else besides.

The impact of our find is only just beginning to sink in.

Sherrard peers out of the ship's lab as Leonides and I come back on board. His expression is a peculiar one, a mixture of astonishment and—what?—self-satisfaction?

"We've discovered how they work," he announces. "They operate by superconductivity."

Of course. Superconductivity occurs only within a few degrees of absolute zero: a strange and miraculous thing, that resistance-free flow of current, the most efficient possible way of transmitting an electrical signal. Why *not* have it serve as the energizing principle for life-forms on a world where nighttime temperatures drop to two degrees Kelvin? It seems so obvious, now that Sherrard has said it. But at the same time it is such an unlikely thing, such an *alien* way for living creatures to be designed. If, that is, they are living creatures at all, and not merely some sort of cunning mechanisms. I feel the hair lifting along the back of my neck.

Gartenmeister and Sherrard have dissected one. It lies on its back, its undershell neatly cut away and its internal organs exposed to view. Its interior is lined with a series of narrow glossy green and blue tubes that cross and meet at rigid angles, with small yellow hexagonal bodies spaced at regular intervals down the center. The overall pattern is intricate, yes, but it is the intricacy of a well-designed machine. There is an almost oppressive symmetry about the

arrangement. A second creature, still intact, rests unmoving and seemingly lifeless in its holding tank. The third has been placed in an adjoining tank, and it is awake and sullenly scrabbling about like a trapped turtle trying to climb the walls of its bowl.

Jerking his thumb at the one that is moving, Gartenmeister says, "We've got it at Pluto-night temperature, just a notch above absolute. The other tank's five degrees warmer. The threshold is very precise: when the temperature rises to seven degrees above absolute zero they start to go dormant. Lower the temperature and they wake up. Raise it again, they stop in their tracks again. It's like throwing a switch."

"It's *exactly* like throwing a switch," says Sherrard. "They're machines. Very neatly calibrated." He turns on a projector. Glittering cubical forms appear on the screen. "Here: look at the crystalline structure of one of these tubes. Silicon and cobalt, arranged in a perfect matrix. You want to tell me this is organic life? These things are nothing more than signal-processing devices designed to operate at supercold temperatures."

"And we?" Leonides asks. "Are we not merely signal-processing devices also, designed to operate in somewhat warmer weather?"

"Merely? *Merely?*"

"We are machines of flesh and blood," says Leonides. "These are machines of another kind."

"But they have blood also," Gartenmeister says. "Of the sort that a superconductive life-form would have to have. Their blood is helium II."

How startling that is—and yet how plausible! Helium II, that weird friction-free fluid that exists only at the lowest of temperatures—capable of creeping up the side of a glass vessel in defiance of gravity, of passing through openings of incredibly small size, of doing all manner of unlikely things—and of creating an environment in which certain metals become capable of superconductive propagation of electrical signals. Helium II "blood," I realize, would indeed be an ideal carrier of nutrients through the body of a nonorganic creature unable to pump a conventional fluid from one part of itself to another.

"Is that true?" Leonides asks. "Helium II? Actually?"

Gartenmeister nods. "There is no doubt of it."

"Helium II, yes," says Sherrard, sullenly. "But it's just lubricating fluid. Not blood."

"Call it what you like," Gartenmeister tells him. "I use only a metaphor. I am nowhere saying yet that they are alive."

"But you imply—"

"I imply nothing!"

I remain silent, paying little attention to the argument. In awe and wonder I stare at the motionless creature, at the one that is moving about, and at the dissected one. I think of them out there on the Plutonian ice fields, meandering in their unhurried way over fields of frozen methane, pausing to nibble at a hydrocarbon sundae whenever they feel the need for refreshment. But only during the night; for when their side of Pluto at last comes round to face the Sun, the temperature will climb, soaring as high as seventy-seven degrees Kelvin. They will cease motion long before that, of course—at just a few moments after dawn, as we have seen, when the day's heat rises beyond those critical few degrees at which superconductivity is possible. They slip into immobility then until night returns. And so their slow lives must go, switching from ''on'' to ''off'' for—who knew?—thousands of years, perhaps. Or perhaps forever.

How strange, I think, how alien, how wonderful they are! On temperate Earth, where animal life has taken the form of protoplasmic oxygen-breathing beings whose chemistry is based on carbon, the phenomenon of superconductivity itself is a bizarre and alien thing, sustainable only under laboratory conditions. But in the unthinkable cold of Pluto, how appropriate that the life-forms should be fashioned of silicon and cobalt, constructed in flawless lattices so that their tissues offer no resistance to electrical currents. Once generated, such a current would persist indefinitely, flowing forever without weakening—the spark of life, and eternal life at that!

They still look like grotesque crabs to me, and not the machines that Sherrard insists they must be. But even if they are animals rather than machines, they are, by comparison with any life-form known to Earth, very machinelike animals indeed.

We have spent a wearying six hours. This discovery should have been exhilarating, even exalting; instead we find ourselves bickering over whether we have found living creatures or mere ingenious mechanisms. Sherrard is adamant that they are machines; Gartenmeister seems to lean in both directions at once, though he is obviously troubled by the thought that they may be alive; Leonides is convinced that we are dealing with true life-forms. I think the dispute, now overheated and ugly, is a mere displacement symptom: we are disturbed by the deeper implications of the find, and, unwilling thus far to face them directly, we turn instead to quarreling over secondary semantic technicalities. The real question is not who created these beings—whether they are the work of what I suppose we can call the divine force or simply of other intelligent creatures—but how we are to deal with the sudden inescapable knowledge that we are not alone in the universe.

I think we may just have settled the life-versus-machine dispute.

It is morning, ship-time. Gartenmeister calls out sharply, waking us. He has been on watch, puttering in the lab, while we sleep. We rush in and he points to the Plutonian that has been kept at superconductive temperatures.

"See there? Along the lower left-hand rim of its shell?"

I can find nothing unusual at first. Then I look more carefully, as he focuses the laser lamp to cast its beam at a steeper angle. Now I observe two fine metalic "whiskers," so delicate that they are barely visible even to my most intense scrutiny, jutting to a length of five or six millimeters from the edge of the shell.

"I saw them sprout," he says. "One came half an hour ago. The other just now. Look—here comes a third!"

We crowd in close. There can be no doubt: a third delicate whisker is beginning to protrude.

Sherrard says, "Communications devices, perhaps? It's programmed to signal for help when captured: it's setting up its antenna so that it can broadcast to the others outside."

Leonides laughs. "Do you think they get captured often? By whom?"

"Who knows?" Sherrard responds. "There may be other creatures out there that prey on—"

He stops, realizing what he has said. It is too late.

"Other *creatures*?" I ask. "Don't you mean bigger machines?"

Sherrard looks angry. "I don't know what I mean. Creatures, machines—" He shakes his head. "Even so, these might be antennae of some sort, can't they? Signaling devices that protrude automatically in time of danger? Say, when one is trapped by an ice slide?"

"Or sensors," offers Leonides. "Like a cat's whiskers, like a snail's feelers. Probing the environment, helping it to find a way out of the tank we've got it in."

"A reproductive organ," Gartenmeister says suddenly.

We stare at him. "*What?*"

Unperturbed, he says, "Many low-phylum life-forms, when they are trapped, go automatically into reproductive mode. Even if the individual is destroyed, the species is still propagated. Let us say that these are living creatures, yes? For the sake of argument. Then they must reproduce somehow. Even though they are slow-growing, virtually immortal, they must still reproduce. What if it is by budding? They take in minute quantities of silicon and cobalt, build up a surplus of nutrients, and at a certain time they put forth these filaments. Which gain in size over—who knows, a hundred years, a thousand, ten thousand?—and when they have the requisite minimum mass, they break free, take up independent life, foraging for their own food. The electrical spark of life is transferred automatically from parent to offspring and sustains itself by means of their superconductivity."

We look at him in amazement. Obviously he has been pondering deeply while we were sleeping.

"If you tell us that they metabolize—they eat, they transfer nutrients along the flow of helium II, they even reproduce," says Leonides, "then you're telling us that they're living things. Or else you're asking us to redefine the nature of machines in such a way as to eliminate any distinction between machines and living things."

"I think," says Gartenmeister in a dark and despondent tone, "that there can be no doubt. They are alive."

Sherrard stares a long while at the three tiny filaments. Then he shrugs.

"You may be right," he says.

Leonides shakes his head. "Listen to you! Both of you! We've made the most exciting discovery in five hundred years and you sound as though you've just learned that the sun's going nova tomorrow!"

"Let them be," I tell him, touching his arm lightly. "It's not easy."

"What's not?"

"A thousand years ago everyone thought Earth was at the center of the universe, with everything else moving in orbit around it," I say. "It was a very comfortable and cozy and flattering idea, but it didn't happen to be true, as Copernicus and Kepler and Galileo were able to prove. It was such a hard thing for people to accept that Galileo was put on trial and forced to deny his own findings, wasn't he? All right. In time everyone came to admit that Earth moves around the Sun, and not vice versa. And now, for centuries, we've explored space and found it absolutely lifeless—not a smidgeon of life, not a speck, no Martians, no Venusians, no Lunarians, nothing. *Nothing.* Earth the cosmic exception, the sole abode of life, the crown of creation. Until now. We have these little superconductive crabs here on Pluto. Our brothers-in-life, four billion miles away. Earth's last uniqueness is stripped away. I think that'll be harder to swallow than you may think. If we had found life right away, on the Moon back in the twentieth century, on Mars a little later on, it might have been easier. But not now, not after we've been all over the system. We developed a sort of smugness about ourselves. These little critters have just destroyed that."

"Even if they are machines," says Gartenmeister hollowly, "then we have to ask ourselves who built them."

"I think I'd prefer to think they're alive," Sherrard says.

"They *are* alive," I tell them. "We're going to get used to that idea."

I walk to the hatch and peer outside. Small dark shapes lie huddled motionless here and there on the ice, waiting for night to return. For a long while I stare at them. My soul is flooded with awe and joy. The greatest of miracles has happened on this planet, as it had happened also long ago on Earth; and if life has been able to come into being on dismal Pluto, I know we will encounter it on a million million other worlds as we make our way in the centuries to come beyond this little solar system into the vast galaxy. Somehow I cannot find anything to fear in that thought. Suddenly, thinking of the wonders and splendors that await us in that great beyond, I imagine that I hear the jubilant music of the spheres resounding from world to world; and when I turn and look back at the others, I realize that they also have been able to move past that first hard moment of shock and dismay which the loss of our uniqueness has brought. I see their faces transfigured, I see the doubt and turmoil gone; and it seems to me that they must be hearing that music too.

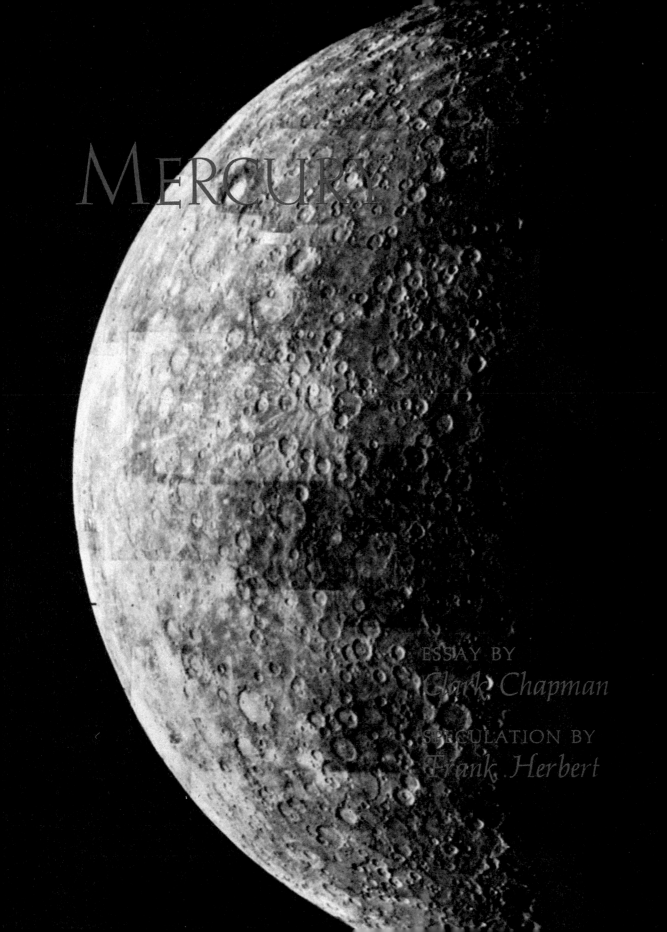

MERCURY

ESSAY BY
Clark Chapman

SPECULATION BY
Frank Herbert

MERCURY: THE SUN'S CLOSEST COMPANION

Clark R. Chapman

A WALK ON MERCURY

A spacefarer trying to survive on the surface of the planet Mercury would have to deal with one of the harshest environments in the solar system. The Sun hangs hugely in Mercury's black sky, its fierce heat baking the rocky ground to temperatures as high as 430°C. In such a furnacelike environment, lead and zinc would melt and elements like mercury and sulfur would boil away. Eventually sunset would bring temporary relief from the heat, but waiting for nightfall might be frustrating indeed. Like ten Suns merged into one, the bloated orb would drift toward the horizon at an excruciatingly slow pace. For relief from the broiling heat, one would have to wait for many Earth days, even weeks. Just when it would seem about to settle below the mountainous horizon, the Sun might temporarily rise again for a few extra days of torture, before finally relenting. Even the arrival of night would bring short comfort: within hours, the temperature would plummet toward bitter cold. Before sunrise, Mercury's soil would be so frigid that the familiar gases we humans breathe would liquefy on contact!

There are never any liquids on Mercury, however, for there are no gases to liquefy. Mercury's "atmosphere" is hardly more than a perfect vacuum, with a barometric pressure less than a billionth of a millibar (a millibar is one-thousandth of sea-level atmospheric pressure on Earth). It is hardly surprising that Mercury lacks air, since it is difficult for the gravity of a small planet—especially one as hot as Mercury—to keep gases from evaporating away into space. Lacking any air, water, or other abundant liquids, Mercury's landscape closely resembles the surface of the Moon. There are no clouds, rivers, dust-storms, or other aspects of weather beneath its jet-black sky. The light-rays from distant stars shine unimpeded onto Mercury's surface, although during the lengthy day, the blazing brilliance of the solar inferno would blind our spacefarer to the firmament beyond. At night, stars emerge from the glare, along with a few unfamiliar, exceptional ones: a gleaming double star is the Earth and its Moon, while the even more brilliant planet Venus casts shadows on Mercury's ground, like a surrogate moon for this moonless world.

What would a spacefarer see, walking across the broiling surface of Mercury? It would be a rather flat, monochrome terrain, not unlike the Apollo landing sites on the Moon. The surface would seem rather dusty, perhaps with pebbles and even a boulder or two strewn about. Here and there one would encounter the gentle raised rims of impact craters, bowl-shaped excavations in the ground like Meteor Crater in Arizona. In some provinces on Mercury there is more impressive topography—mountain ridges, deep canyons, and hilly regions. Most impressive are the great mountain ranges, over 3,000 meters high in places, that ring the immense Caloris Basin, a great impact crater about 1,300 kilometers across. Occasionally, a traveler crossing the broad Mercurian plains would encounter an obstacle peculiar to Mercury, one of the great escarpments that testify to epochs long ago when the crust of the whole planet shriveled up like the skin of an old apple. These great cliff faces range from 300 to 3,000 meters high, and some of them extend across the plains for tens to hundreds of kilometers. Apart from these uniquely Mercurian escarpments, the gray landscape would seem distinctly lunar to our spacefarer. Perhaps the most noticeable difference, apart from the heat, would be the greater gravity. Although gravity is less on Mercury than on Earth, one could not take the great bounding leaps that are possible on the Moon.

MERCURY'S MOTIONS

Mercury's surface is obviously a very dangerous environment for human beings. It is not easy to conceive of a practical life-support system that could refrigerate an astronaut for long or protect against the dangerous ultraviolet and other lethal rays from the immense, nearby Sun, unshielded by even a wisp of cloud or air. Before leaving the surface of Mercury to return to the comparative safety of an orbiting spaceship, let's turn our attention once more to the omnipresent Sun. Traversing the planet from the Caloris province to the various plains and cliffs, our spacefarer might have noticed interesting differences in the size and motions of the Sun. Mercury is an unusual world, where its solar day (the time from noon to noon) is twice as long as its year (the time it takes the sun to circle once through the familiar constellations of Mercury's zodiac). A solar day on Mercury lasts 176 days, nearly six Earth-months, while it takes Mercury just 88 days to circle the Sun. Actually Mercury's true day (as distinct from a solar day), measured by the time it takes stars to circle the sky and come back to the same position, is just 58.6 days: that's how long it takes the planet to spin once on its axis. But because the little planet is revolving so swiftly in its orbit about the Sun, and turning in a direction that tends to keep the Sun from appearing to move, it takes three spins before the Sun is back where it started.

The motions of the Sun aren't the same everywhere on Mercury, however. This is largely due to the great eccentricity of Mercury's orbit, which is more oblong in shape than the orbit of any other planet or large satellite in the solar system, except for distant Pluto. As the small planet swings around the Sun every 88 days, the Sun appears larger as Mercury nears perihelion (closest point in its orbit to the Sun), then shrinks toward aphelion (farthest point), and once again begins to expand. Mercury's orbit is so oblong that the planet actually receives about twice as much sunlight when it is close to the Sun as when it is far away. Furthermore, the rate of the Sun's motion across the sky, while always slow by Earthly standards, varies a lot depending on where Mercury is in its orbit. Throughout most of a Mercurian year (88 days), its somewhat faster spin (58.6 days) keeps the Sun moving westward in the sky. But as the laws of celestial motion require, Mercury zips around the Sun especially rapidly near perihelion—so rapidly, in fact, that the orbital revolution gets ahead of the spin and the Sun appears to move back eastward in Mercury's sky for a while before resuming its lumbering westward motion. This little backward oscillation in the sky always happens when the Sun is largest and brightest, causing a burst of excess heat for a planet that needs no more.

There are two places on the equator of Mercury, called its "hot poles," where this maddening oscillation of the bloated Sun occurs at high noon. The average temperatures are much lower at longitudes a quarter of the way around Mercury where a shrunken Sun is zipping most swiftly across the sky at noon. At these "warm poles," the Sun expands and does its dance near sunrise and sunset. Apart from the respites of the long, frigid nights, it would be difficult indeed to escape the Sun for longer than a few months, unless one kept constantly on the move. It is just possible, however, that there are a few craters near the north and south poles of the planet that are deep enough to be in perpetual shade. If there is ever to be a manned base on the surface of Mercury, it might well be in the middle of such a crater, warmed and lit by the reflected light and heat from the crater walls, as the swollen-then-shrunken Sun skims around the horizon just out of view, beyond the crater rim.

MERCURY FROM SPACE

Let our imaginary spacefarer leave the surface of the innermost planet and ascend into space to look back on it as a globe, as a whole world. Mercury whirls rapidly around the Sun, as if chained to it by a tight spring, blistering under the onslaught of its radiance. Mercury is locked to the Sun in more ways than one. The great tidal forces exerted by the nearby Sun wax and wane as Mercury's orbit brings it nearer to and farther from the Sun. These forces, tugging at slight bulges in the planet's topography over billions of years, have slowed Mercury's axial spin and finally captured it in what scientists call two-thirds its spin-orbit resonance. (Multiply Mercury's 88-day orbital period by 2, then divide by 3. It is no accident that the result is precisely Mercury's spin period of 58.6 days.)

Looking down across the planet, we don't see such prominent features as the continents and oceans of Earth, or even the bright highlands and dark mare basins of the Moon. Some areas are a bit darker than others, but Mercury is a pretty uniform gray. There *are* topographic provinces, however. Perhaps the most prominent one is the immense Caloris Basin. Ringed by towering mountain ranges, its relatively crater-free floor is cracked by large canyons and criss-crossed by sinuous ridges. A giant bulls-eye, Caloris resembles some of the great impact basins on the Moon, on Mars, and on several of the moons of the outer planets. Evidently it was formed eons ago when a large asteroid crashed into Mercury. Beyond the encircling mountain ranges are sculptured terrains and ridges radiating away from the center of the impact. It is not certain whether the smooth plains beyond Caloris were formed by materials ejected from the center of the impact and deposited at great distances, or by great volcanic lava flows triggered by the catastrophic event. Perhaps they were formed at another time, but there is more than adequate evidence that the Caloris impact was the last great event in the geologic history of Mercury. The quakes resulting from the impact apparently were so strongly focused on the side of Mercury directly opposite from Caloris that all preexisting topography was destroyed, creating an anomalous province of closely spaced hills and mountains.

Much of Mercury is covered with large impact craters, rather like the cratered highlands of the Moon. In places, the craters are so numerous, overlapping each other, as to suggest that they resulted from a saturating bombardment by comets and small asteroids. There are much more widespread provinces on Mercury than on the Moon, however, which are deficient in the larger craters. Such "intercrater plains" grade into even more lightly cratered plains. Some relatively small regions, called "smooth plains" are entirely lacking in moderate-sized or large craters. Nevertheless, a close look reveals that there are small craters—a few kilometers across and smaller—all over Mercury, just as on the Moon. A global view of Mercury also reveals that the uniquely Mercurian scarps we mentioned earlier occur all over the planet, at all longitudes, from equator to pole. Viewed from above, the escarpments are not straight, but bulge in places. Geologists call them "lobate scarps."

Mercury is a small planet (only Pluto is smaller) but it exerts a surprisingly strong pull on our orbiting spaceship. The fact is that Mercury is surprisingly massive for its size. The bulk density of Mercury is so large, indeed, that it is certainly composed of the densest combination of materials of any of the planets. Given what we know about the abundance of chemical elements in the cosmos, there is no reasonable alternative to the conclusion that Mercury must contain a very large proportion of iron. If the iron is all concentrated in a central core—and later we will see some evidence for thinking that it is—then the iron core is immense, indeed. Extending outward about 75 percent of the distance from the center to the surface, Mercury's core alone is larger than the whole of our Moon! Mercury's rocky mantle forms a comparatively thin shell around the core, unlike all the other rocky planets. The presence of this enormous metallic core within Mercury has manifestations on the surface of Mercury, as we shall see, and perhaps in the space surrounding the planet as well.

Invisible to the eye, but no less real than the brightly lit landscapes below our spaceship, is a large magnetic field surrounding Mercury. Apparently connected to the planet, this roughly dipolar field is much weaker than Earth's magnetic field but strong enough to deflect the wind of charged particles from the Sun that would otherwise impinge on the surface of the planet. This solar wind streams around Mercury and continues on outward into the solar system. As we scan around Mercurian space, it looks very empty, filled only with the brilliance of the Sun. Unlike most planets in the solar system, Mercury lacks any moon of appreciable size. It endures the Sun's heat alone.

EARLIER VIEWS

The picture of Mercury I have just portrayed is from the perspective of the 1980's. Don't be fooled, however, into thinking that what I have described is anything like a complete or correct picture of what a real spacefarer may find when a voyage to Mercury ultimately takes place, well into the next century. Past embarrassments have taught students of the planet Mercury to be somewhat tentative in asserting what is truly known about the small innermost planet. An account of Mercury written twenty-five years ago would probably have been quite positive in tone but very different in content from what we think is true today.

Mercury hasn't changed in twenty-five years, but thanks to new kinds of telescopes and instruments, as well as to the Mariner 10 spacecraft which reconnoitered Mercury three times in the mid-1970s, we have learned that a lot of the earlier "facts" were not just incomplete but plain wrong. There were lots of scientific articles written in those days about Mercury's appreciable atmosphere and about the clouds drifting across its surface. Scientists were positive that Mercury spun on its axis once each time it went around the Sun; that is, its day was thought to be 88 days instead of 58.6. The thinking was that it always kept one face to the Sun, just as the Moon keeps one side always facing the Earth. Thus one side of Mercury was thought to be perpetually baking in the sunlight, while the "dark side" of this innermost world was, ironically, considered to be the coldest place in the solar system, warmed only by the light from distant stars and by whatever heat radiated up from the ground.

Other "facts" about Mercury, patiently learned by generations of science students, began to bite the dust in the 1960s when the new telescopic instrumentation was turned to Mercury.

The world's largest radar telescope is suspended between the hills in Arecibo, Puerto Rico. Precisely-tuned radar pulses were aimed at Mercury in the mid-1960s. Many minutes later, faint echoes bounced off Mercury were received by the same huge radar dish. The Doppler effect should have broadened the pulses (detuned them) because one side of Mercury's globe is rapidly approaching Earth, and the other side receding, as the planet spins on its axis. The weak pulse echoes were amplified and examined; they turned out to be broadened, all right, but by the *wrong* amount! It turned out that Mercury spins in just two-thirds the time once thought. Astronomers hastily rechecked the old data and came up with plausible rationalizations for why they went astray. Mercury is, after all, very difficult to observe from Earth because it stays so close to the Sun. It can be seen only during particular short intervals in the dawn or dusk, and it happens that for years on end, astronomers would see the same parts of Mercury at the same times whether the rotation period was 58.6 days or 88 days (or some other periods as well). So the data—glimpses of fuzzy patches on Mercury's surface—were *consistent with* an 88-day spin, but the careless astronomers failed to notice that the data were also *consistent with* 58.6 days. The familiar case of the Moon keeping its same side to Earth lulled them into thinking they had the right answer. This is neither the first nor the last time that planetary analogies have lead observers astray.

THE MARINER 10 FLYBYS

The real revolution in knowledge of Mercury came in March 1974 when the American spacecraft Mariner 10, having completed a successful reconnaissance of Venus, made the first close encounter to the innermost planet. It snapped a sequence of close-up pictures of Mercurian landscapes and made a variety of other measurements of near-Mercury space. By means of a kind of celestial pinball wizardry, Mariner 10 was able to make two more passes by Mercury within the next year or so (only a single encounter had been planned originally). The early Mariners lacked instruments capable of measuring the chemical or mineralogical composition of planetary surfaces. But Mariner 10's discoveries were spectacular enough. Perhaps most surprising of all was the discovery that Mercury has a dipolar magnetic field, resembling a weak version of our own planet's magnetic field. This was unexpected because scientists had a prejudice that planetary magnetic fields were produced by dynamo effects deep within a planet. Dynamo action was thought to require a molten core within a rapidly spinning planet, quite impossible for a planet like Mercury, spinning nearly sixty times slower than Earth. Furthermore, a small planet like Mercury would have cooled off long ago if it ever had a molten core, the theorists reasoned. As happens often in science, theory had to come to grips with the facts. In the case of Mercury, more than a decade of subsequent thinking about Mariner 10's discoveries has still not yielded a clear understanding of what's going on inside the planet.

At first sight, Mariner's collection of Mercury pictures was unremarkable. Mercury looked a lot like the Moon. A decade earlier, when Mariner 4 flew past Mars, scientists and lay people alike were shocked to find that Mars had craters and was "as dead as the Moon," a view modified considerably by subsequent exploration of Mars. Anyway, finding another planet with craters on it was becoming commonplace by the mid-1970s. The scientists charged with the task of interpreting Mariner 10's pictures suggested that most of Mercury's craters, and those on Mars too, were formed at the same time as most lunar craters. Laboratory age-dating techniques applied to Moon rocks returned to Earth by Apollo astronauts had pinpointed the heaviest cratering on the Moon as occurring about 4 billion years ago, toward the beginning of solar system history, but a significant 0.5 billion years after the actual formation of the Earth and other planets. So there must have been a lot of asteroid-size chunks flying around the solar system way back then, the Mariner scientists reasoned, and they collided with all the terrestrial planets. After the temporary population of these "late-heavy-bombardment" projectiles had become depleted, there has been a continued low level of cratering over the ensuing four eons by small asteroids and comets. (The extremely active geological activity on our own planet—including plate tectonics and continental drift—long ago destroyed any terrestrial record of such ancient craters, but we believe they must have been formed on Earth as well during this early epoch.) The topography on Mercury revealed by Mariner 10 shows evidence of little geological activity—volcanism, faulting, or any other kind—in the time since the Caloris Basin formed, apparently toward the end of that cataclysmic epoch of bombardment. Mercury, in this view, has been a quiescent, geologically dead world for nearly four eons.

SOME MYSTERIES REMAIN

In the years since the first and, so far, only spacecraft mission to Mercury, scientists have continued trying to unravel that small planet's secrets. There is little new information. Mercury remains hidden in the glare of the Sun. Even the great ground-based and orbiting telescopes planned for the future are unlikely to contribute much; the large, orbiting Hubble Space Telescope may not even be allowed to turn toward Mercury, for fear of burning-out its sensitive instruments. There now exist some crude radar maps of the surface of Mercury, including views of the hemisphere never seen by Mariner 10. But most of the new ideas are being developed simply by sifting through past data and running new theoretical calculations through the computer.

Not everything makes sense. Consider Mercury's giant metallic core. The small planet probably didn't form with a core. Like other rocky worlds, Mercury presumably was formed from a mixture of rocky and metallic grains that condensed from the original solar nebula, that immense cloud of hot gas and dust from which the Sun and all the planets were born. We have meteorites in our museums—rocks fallen from the skies—that are composed of just such a mixture of rock and metal. These so-called ordinary chondrites are thought to represent the compounds, in their original cosmic proportions, from which the Sun and planets were made. The only substances missing from these meteorites are the gases and other volatile materials that never could condense at the warm temperatures of the inner solar system. Mercury, being in the warmest location of all, might be expected to lack not only gases but also volatiles that are present within Earth, like water and sulfur. Even some rocky minerals may have been too volatile to be incorporated into Mercury, but others, like olivine, and all of the iron metal should be part of Mercury. This view of the different condensation temperatures at the locations of the different planets explains Mercury's high density and its presumably enormous iron content.

So is Mercury now composed of material like the iron-rich types among the ordinary chondritic meteorites? Perhaps it once was, but scientists don't think it has remained so. Instead, they believe that in the distant past Mercury was heated to near its melting point so that the heavy, dense iron grains could coagulate and sink toward the center of the planet. (Just such a process of core formation took place within Earth.) One piece of evidence is that the detailed colors (the spectrum) of the light reflected from Mercury's surface look very similar to spectra of the lunar surface. And we know, from the explorations of Apollo astronauts, that the lunar surface is composed of volcanic lava flows and other rocks devoid of metal. Even more convincing, Mariner's treasury of pictures reveals many landforms on Mercury similar to volcanic landscapes on Earth, the Moon, and other planets. Volcanism is the geological expression of intense heat within a planet: If Mercury's surface is partly volcanic, as appears to be true, then the planet *must* have heated and formed a core. Of course, Mercury's magnetic field also indicates the presence of a core, indeed a core that is still molten today.

That raises another problem, however, for it is barely possible that the measured traits of Mercury's magnetic field could be due to frozen-in magnetization by an ancient dynamo, no longer active (if Mercury's core has now cooled and is solid). It is not easy to understand how such a remanent magnetization could be retained in Mercury's metal-depleted mantle and crustal rocks. But some scientists are motivated to look for ways to avoid having to accept the apparent existence of a still-molten core within Mercury, for the following reasons: If Mercury heated up and formed a core, it must have done so very early in its history. In particular, the core must have formed *before* the late heavy bombardment, 4 billion years ago; otherwise, the process of core formation—a veritable turning of the planet inside-out—would have destroyed all of the craters formed on Mercury during that epoch. Although Mercury is such a small planet that it would normally not be expected to heat up and form a core until several billion years after its formation, there *are* several processes that could have heated small bodies like Mercury (or even some asteroids!) and these could have been active very early in solar system history. So it is quite reasonable to believe that Mercury's core must have formed early in its history.

But if Mercury's core formed so long ago, it is difficult to understand why it wouldn't have frozen solid shortly afterward. Earth still has a molten core, but our planet is much larger than Mercury and is thus able to retain its abundant heat longer than Mercury can. Furthermore, some radioactive elements responsible for continued heating of the Earth's interior (like potassium 40) are quite volatile, and few scientists expect them to be abundant within Mercury. Those radioactives that *were* incorporated into Mercury, moreover, would not have a chemical affinity for the metallic core, but rather would be incorporated into Mercury's thin shell of mantle and crustal rocks. In short, most of these theoretical considerations mean that Mercury's core—if it formed early in the planet's history—must have long ago frozen solid.

We must not be hasty, however, in dismissing the notion that Mercury has a molten core and an active dynamo. There is an even more powerful reason for believing that the core has not yet solidified. Everyone is familiar with the fact that water expands when it freezes into ice. Most materials, however, *contract* upon solidification and cooling; unlike water, the rocks of Mercury's mantle and the metal in its core are no exceptions to this general rule. Calculations suggest that the diameter of Mercury's whole globe should have shrunk by about 40 kilometers if the planet has entirely solidified and cooled off. Indeed, as we saw, Mercury's surface is crisscrossed by the network of lobate scarps, which are just the kind of topography one expects to find on the surface of a shrinking planet. As the planet shrinks, blocks of land are thrust up on top of others, forming so-called thrust faults, which often have lobate shapes as viewed from above. The discovery of such lobate scarps on Mercury would seem, at first glance, to be a remarkable geological confirmation of the theoretical thermal-history calculations. But only to a point! The scarps have been measured, and the total shrinkage implied is only about 4 kilometers, not 40 kilometers. That is the amount of shrinkage expected if Mercury's rocky mantle and crust had cooled off, but *not its core*! This implies that Mercury's core must still be molten; otherwise Mercury would have ten times as many fault scarps as it does!

Wait a minute, a skeptic might say. Suppose the core mainly cooled before the late heavy bombardment, before the time that Mercury's surface geology began preserving the scarps that are still visible today. Then Mercury's core could have formed early and solidified rapidly (somehow preserving a remanent magnetic field in the rocks), and the uniquely Mercurian scarps record just the tail-end of the planet's shrinkage. The problem with that hypothesis is that it is difficult, then, to understand how all the volcanic plains were formed. Generally a planet is volcanically active only when it is possible for rifts or cracks to form in its crust, which serve as escape vents for the molten lava below. When a planet's crust is compressed by shrinkage, the vents will be squeezed shut and volcanism will cease. Unless planetary volcanologists are greatly mistaken about the connections between volcanism and tectonics, or unless the Mariner photo-interpreters are wrong about Mercury's plains being volcanic, we must suppose that those expansive plains were formed chiefly *before* the planet began to shrink very much. Since the volcanic plains postdate the heavily cratered terrains of the late heavy bombardment 4 billion years ago, we are left with a dilemma: Mercury's core must still be molten, despite the inability of scientists to understand how it could remain molten so long after it formed.

Some scientists have challenged the accepted view of Mercury's geological chronology in order to solve this problem. Contrary to prevailing opinion they suggest that all of Mercury's surface geology is of comparatively recent origin. All evidence of the late heavy bombardment was destroyed by more far-reaching subsequent events. There were no magical early heat sources, these scientists suggest, and the planet's core took eons to form. Finally turning itself inside out only 1 or 2 billion years ago, Mercury is still settling down from that traumatic episode. Its core is still molten and its volcanism has stopped only recently as the planet begins to cool and shrink. The problem traditionalists would have with this scenario is this: What formed all the craters on Mercury so recently? The unexpected answer is that Mercury may have its own private source of bombarding projectiles! Maybe there is something akin to an asteroid belt orbiting inside Mercury's orbit that only encounters Mercury. Theoretical calculations of how the orbits of such bodies—left over from the original epoch of planetary formation—might evolve show that such bodies inside Mercury's orbit might last for billions of years. This is because of the rare times that the continually changing shape of Mercury's orbit permits it to penetrate that sizzling region of space and collide with any small bodies that may be there. Telescopic searches for such intra-Mercurian bodies—dubbed "vulcanoids" after the mythical inner planet Vulcan—have turned up nothing, so far. But the nearby sunlight is so bright that any putative belt of vulcanoids may remain hidden from our view until the next generation of orbiting telescopes is designed and put into space.

The vulcanoid hypothesis is not the only escape hatch from the contradictions presented by Mariner 10's data about Mercury. Maybe better pictures taken by some future spacecraft will contradict the widely accepted view that Mercury's surface is volcanic. Maybe new theories about how planets gather together from smaller bodies and how their temperatures evolve will solve the problem of how Mercury's core could have formed before the late heavy bombardment but still be molten. Maybe today's scientific understanding of the nature of planetary magnetic fields is flawed. Maybe the picture of planetary shrinkage begetting lobate scarps is oversimplified. These, and any number of other apparent "facts" and interpretations of Mariner data about Mercury may be found to be as wrong as were earlier "facts" about Mercury. But this is all part of the scientific process. Scientists are trying to understand what this small planet, hidden in the glare of the Sun, is like as a real world and how it came to be different from our own planet. The challenge is to design machines and instruments to measure the planet's characteristics, to collect the data, and then to *try* putting it all together into a coherent understanding of Mercury, consistent with our knowledge of the other planets. The apparent contradictions inspire more scientific research and exploration. Some day, eventually, men and women may live in a Mercurian base settlement, nestled beneath the walls of a polar crater. By that time, perhaps the puzzles that confound us today will be resolved. Surely, by then, other tasks will confront the ingenuity of the new generation of Mercury's explorers, and they will thank us for being interested in this small, metal-rich world way back in the 1980s.

TRANSCRIPT: MERCURY PROGRAM

Frank Herbert

TALENT: Murray Murray of *You* and Carol Boswei of
Other Places

Log # G-21-RO   Three cuts for promos; Holo
Quality AAA

MURRAY. Hello, everybody out there in the human universe! This is your old
buddy Murray Murray of *You*, and no, I am not stuttering. We are bringing
you a special program, something extra special that I've wanted to do ever
since I started working on the holo channels. We call this program "A Vision
from Mercury in the Year 2383." For those of you buzzing along on other
calendars, that's the Standard Solar Year 2383, and everything we refer to
here will be dated SS. This marvelous person seated beside me is Carol Boswei. Yep, *the* Carol Boswei, whose program, *Other Places,* is known to most
of you. I . . . do I need an introduction, Carol?

CAROL. Only to those people who haven't seen a holocast in the past fifteen
years. I don't know how to thank you, Murray, for inviting me to do this
program with you. We are, indeed, on Mercury—*the* Mercury of the solar
system—and I've had to pinch myself several times to make sure I'm not
dreaming.

MURRAY. Look at this studio! It's really one of the VIP lounges they rigged
up for us. That golden wall behind us is part of the deflector system. When
the big show starts, it'll open up to give you a ringside seat at the most
awesome display in the universe. I kid you not. We are right here in the
front row.

CAROL. Camera Two, swing around and give them a complete look at this place.
Those things over there, those two metal mounds, are our personal servos.
They're supposed to keep us out of trouble. Mostly, they guide us in a way
that always keeps us behind the deflectors.

MURRAY. And do we ever need deflectors! This place can get hotter than Pulao Town on Fleet Night. These chairs we're in, if you want to call them that, are also servos. They can snap more deflectors around us in an emergency. The cameras—why don't you four cameras look at each other?

CAROL. They don't look much like our ordinary cameras.

MURRAY. They're so big because they had to be fitted with special servos and their own deflectors. Can't have the transmission shut off by hard radiation. Once you get inside the Mercury fittings, though, they're standard and they are, as usual, keyed to our voices and controlled from Joel's remote mixing studio. How we doing, Joel?

JOEL [Voice-over]. We're getting you loud and clear here on Mars, and you're going out strong on the Big Booster. It's just like *You*-sual!

MURRAY. *You*-oooooooooo said it! Hey! Cameras! Look at us. You're supposed to keep track of the talent.

CAROL. Isn't it the first law of *You* that you can't trust a machine?

MURRAY [Laughing]. Wye-Oh—*You* are right! Say, Carol, there are a lot of young people out there who may not know about Mercury. Some of them may not even have heard of it.

CAROL. Never heard of Mercury? Come on, Murray!

Far inside Mercury's orbit, a lone space tug falls toward the Sun. This little ship, of a type designed for near-planet orbital operations or short interplanetary hops, is out of place in the glare-filled night between Mercury and the Sun. It has been heavily insulated and coated with thermal-ablation blocks— a crude, jerry-rigged job. Weeks before, the ship had been one of an armada of tugs in orbit, servicing the Mercury bases and this year's solar feeding operation, not to mention the ragtag army of reporters who were gathering. Now the ship contains a single ninety-five-year-old woman. She is ill. She has, well, stolen the ship. It is the only thing she feels guilty about. Feeling old but not ancient by the standards of her society, she is fiddling—game playing, really—with the controls of a filter-visor system that she wears over her face as she peers out a quartz-shield window. Ludmilla Santiana, solar astrophysicist, planner of this year's solar feeding, grand old lady of the astrosciences, mutters to herself.

Her monologue had started out as a careful record dictated to a recording unit she had left in orbit around Mercury when she took the ship. The golden, spidery antenna protruding from the communications bay on the tug points back to Mercury, linking her with the electronic diary. She is sure the recorder will be discovered sooner or later; she has set it to start beeping tomorrow. The diary was meant to be an orderly record of what she saw. Already it is turning into a spontaneous record of what she feels because now she is caught

up in her adventure. Now she is muttering about everything.

Far below, lost in the glare, a million cannisters the size of small asteroids have been falling toward the dazzling, diffuse, ghostly grained surface of a sunspot. The seething spot, brewing its solar storm, waits. . . .

Ludmilla speaks. "Now, my little electric daughter-recorder, listen: There comes a time for the end of theory and the beginning of experience. I am now closer to the Sun than anyone has ever been."

She adjusts the filter-visor system. "The filter-visor is wonderful. It adapts to any wavelength you want, any passband. A little narrower passband, I think, so I just see the Doppler-shifted part of the hydrogen alpha radiation. . . . There! Behold, the Sun! Thirty degrees across. No one's ever experienced it like this! I can see the upwelling—like a boiling—around the sunspot, where the flare will break out. Some things you experience only once. Ah, perhaps everything you experience only once. Each experience unique. Mars, I remember, and the white fog in Valles Marineris swirling and slithering up the pink cliffs. There was a sight for these sore old eyes. . . .

MURRAY. It says right here in my program notes that we're supposed to give our viewers a brief rundown. Of course, they can look in any standard atlas under "solar system" for the details, that Mercury's the closest planet to "Our Mister Sun," that sort of thing. But Joel tells me our audience share at this moment is eighty-two percent, and that's nine hundred and thirty-four trillion people! We're supposed to give them a feeling of being here. What's it like being right here inside Mercury and this close to the BIG show.

CAROL. No complicated stuff. Technical backgrounds warp me.

In the tug, falling toward the Sun, Ludmilla Santiana mutters to herself and to her tape recorder. "Closer, closer . . . I've studied her all my life. Why shouldn't I rush into her embrace at last?"

Her flight of fancy makes her suddenly self-conscious. "Well, a sick old woman has the right to wax poetic if she wants! Listen, I want to tell you about the theory. The theory is extraordinary, as you will soon see. Or rather, as you will have seen by the time you find this recorder and publish it. As I was explaining earlier, I've been working out the theory for the last three years. It's the high point of my career."

She pauses, wondering whether to censor what comes to her mind next. "The only thing I regret about it is, well, I just wish I had had more time to work on the problem of the gamma-ray opacity. If you look at the theory, you find where I stated the assumption, 'sigma equals 0.5.' I had to state it as an assumption, because I couldn't prove it, and there haven't been adequate experimental measurements. Well, it had to be close to 0.5. . . . Still, with a little more time, I might have . . . I might have . . . Oh, well, there's no use speculating on might-have-beens. It must be nearly right."

By now, Ludmilla has dictated most of what she had intended to put onto the tape. Since purloining the space tug from the armada of official project vehicles in orbit above the Sun-and-crater-blasted surface of Mercury, she has been thinking (trying to convince herself), "What's one tug more or less? The project has so many of them, they can't even keep track of them all." She has also been dictating in fits and starts, imparting to future generations the whole mathematical structure of her new theory of solar-flare reactions. She wants the theory not only to show how the Sun works but also to demonstrate that creativity need not stop after a person reaches her nineties. She wants to leave both a legacy and an example. The theory describes how atoms accelerate and smash together in the midst of the sunspot's raging storm, how the temperature rises, how the magnetic field coils and writhes like a serpent waiting to strike. . . .

MURRAY. Carol speaks three hundred migration languages at least and can even talk to the n'Krini, and she says she doesn't like the complicated stuff. Listen, folks, if you've never caught her *Other Places*, you've probably been unconscious for at least ten years. Carol goes places where it makes me sweaty and terrified just watching her on holo. I mean, she just walked outside on Aldeprak wearing nothing but a jumpsuit. I tell you, if those beetles had been hungry!

CAROL. You're very kind, Murray, but if we don't come back to talking about Mercury, they'll think we're trying to fill.

MURRAY. We *are* filling, but stay with us. Honest, folks, it won't be long before you'll be looking out there at the greatest show in the universe. I tell you, I'm as excited as Carol. I've entered every lottery for a Mercury pass for the past twenty-six years. Zilch. And now—we're here and we've been shown all through the planet.

CAROL. Mercury's mostly hollow, you know. It's . . .

MURRAY. Hold it there, Carol. Let's not say hollow. It's not a hollow planet.

CAROL. But all those tunnels. There must be more tunnel than rock.

MURRAY. Right. Look around your room, folks. Got anything made of metal? Chances are, it came out of a tunnel in the mantle of Mercury. Either there or some asteroid that the Spacers brought back.

CAROL. The way I hear it, the whole planet is one giant ball of metal ores. Mercury's getting cleaned out. Tunnels, all full of equipment. They say Mercury's one gigantic robot, staffed mostly by servos. The only full-time human occupants are the scientists and other researchers and, of course, the techs who oversee the robotechs. But the planet itself is really an extremely complex . . . well, I suppose you'd have to call it a machine.

MURRAY. Another reason for the complexity is that Mercury's the primary base for the solar experiments: the old "feeding station," as the human staffers call it.

CAROL. We're talking about a solar feeding project that goes back more than a hundred SS years.

MURRAY. Do you want to close your ears, Carol, while I give them some of the complicated stuff?

On board the tug, Ludmilla idly flips on the holo. It carries the glib banter of Murray and Carol. Reacting to their style without hearing their content, Ludmilla is about to turn it off when she realizes they are talking about the solar feeding project. She pauses, surprised that Murray and Carol hype her scientific project as the biggest media event in the solar system, and even more astonished that the show is being presented to what Ludmilla condescendingly thinks of as the ignorant masses. Ludmilla watches and listens.

CAROL. Let me tell the story. The solar feeding project isn't really a *feeding* project. People somehow got a false idea that dumping material into the Sun was feeding the solar fires. Especially after the astronomers began to use it to produce the spectacular effects we're going to see in a little while. It's more of a garbage disposal project, really. It was started after Rachelle Carson published *The Noisy Year*. She pointed out that while Earth was being restored to its original Edenic state, the number of meteors visible in a given night had grown to ten times what people might have seen in prespace days.

MURRAY. Space junk.

CAROL. Right, Murray. The inner solar system was becoming a junk pile. You couldn't fly once around the Sun without picking up at least a few micropits on your windows.

MURRAY. There was a public outcry. Strict regulations to confine all refuse from space manufacturing . . . to avoid the fate in space that Earth itself suffered a century earlier.

Ludmilla Santiana sputters to herself. "It was aesthetics, really, when you come right down to it. An aesthetic judgment. They could have rocketed all the garbage out of the solar system more easily than driving it into the Sun. That argument about cluttering space. . . . The Clear Space people simply didn't appreciate the volumes involved. A political judgment, really, to keep the masses happy. What a delusion! Trying to keep space clean. The irony is, it'll all be blown back out again someday . . . in the wink of a cosmic eye. It just won't be in nice, neat dumpsters. Naked ions . . .

CAROL. So some farsighted people, like the great Pander Oulson . . .

MURRAY. And I'm sure you've all read about him in your history classes.

CAROL. Who hasn't heard about him? The astronomer who cleaned up space and allowed us to learn more about the universe's ultimate energy sources, all at the same time. What incredible vision! He rallied public support for the feeding program, helped design the instrumented dumpsters, assembled the astrophysical panel to plan dumps of carefully chosen size and composition, set up the Mercury Base Project to track and guide the dumpsters into selected incipient-flare spots on the Sun's surface, until they could induce flares and alter Z-particle reactions at will. . . .

MURRAY. Think of it! Controlled plunges into the Sun!

"Interesting old coot, Pander Oulson must have been. What a con man!" Ludmilla gazes thoughtfully at the mottled sunspot. "Wish I'd known him. Conning the public and *the government into a ridiculous garbage-dumping program as a means of initiating a new field—experimental astrophysics— for which he never even got credit. If the astronomers had ever come to the public and said they wanted to play games with the solar surface, the whole idea would have gone down in flames faster than a dumpster falling into the Sun. They didn't even dare to coin the term "experimental astrophysics" until fifty years after the program started. . . . It's getting warm. Come on, thermal-ablation panels, do your stuff!*

CAROL. Mercury is a robotic wonder. On our tour today, we saw some of the most sophisticated instrumentation in the universe. Most of it went in here to help the astrophysicists keep the solar system clean. I'll be showing you that tour another time on a special *Other Places* program—a tour through Mercury Observation and Guidance, which around here they call MOG. Watch for it on your holo calendars: *Other Places*—"MOG".

MURRAY. That's how it started, kids. They wanted to save the space, environment, learn the secrets of solar energy, and save Museum Earth—all at the same time.

CAROL. Museum Earth! Do you know, Murray, that's still my most popular *Other Places*. The network says that throughout the universe, it's being run once an hour.

MURRAY. That's wonderful, Carol. Six hundred million tourists visit Museum Earth every year.

CAROL. The visitors come from the farthest frontal wave of humanity's expansion across the universe. The first time I went there, I felt as though I were going home. I was going back to where we all originated. It was like a pilgrimage.

265

MURRAY. But isn't it funny, Carol, how fate works? They started the project to save Museum Earth. And now Earth has become the secondary attraction. Everyone wants to come here to Mercury.

CAROL. But they don't want to come here any old time, Murray.

MURRAY. Nope. They want to come during the once-a-year feeding of the Sun. Which, I've just been told through this little gadget in my ear, will begin in about ten minutes. They'll give us a three-minute alert and then a one-minute alert and a thirty-second countdown.

CAROL. Oh, Murray, I'm so excited!

MURRAY. With good reason. The little brochure they give you when you come to Mercury calls the solar response "the most spectacular fireworks display in the universe."

CAROL. The pyrotechnics that accompany the feeding, even when you only see them on holo, are far more awesome than a nova . . . and we all know why. The controlled violence lets you come right up here for a close view.

"More awesome than a nova! Baloney! If they ever saw a real nova up close, they'd have a real story to report! I've had enough of novas and 'Museum Earth.' " Ludmilla flips off the holo.

"Museum Earth! This old lady's come a long way from there. I'll be the first to go from the Earth to the Sun! It's been a long trip. I suppose there was one bit of luck to it, and that was pirating this ship away from the ISC. By the time they figure out where I've gone, they'll know the brilliance of what I've done. Wait till they read my paper. The whole conception will hit them all at once: To predict the reaction from raw theory alone, choose the correct composition and mass for the feeding, send in the manuscript, and then swoop down into the midst of the holocaust. . . . From luck to unluck to luck: that's my story. Brilliant astrophysicist; to learn that I'm being cut down at only 95 by brain cancer; and then to get the chief experimenter slot on this year's dump, just when I've completed the theory, and to have this ship fall into my hands. Not that I didn't pull a few strings. . . . I can afford to pull all the strings I can when I'm not coming back. All in a good cause. . . . I'll set an example of human courage in the face of an implacable universe. . . ."

MURRAY. According to the press release from Ludmilla . . . Ludmilla . . .

CAROL. Santiana.

Ludmilla finishes her thought as her name is beamed across the solar system. "Implacable universe? What euphemistic nonsense, old lady! Death is what I'm talking about. Death from brain cancer . . . or death from fire. I choose the universe! I choose fire."

MURRAY. Right, Carol. Ludmilla Santiana, the head of the feeding team this year, says they expect thirty-three days of fireworks display this year, which means those lucky few who won a Mercury Pass in the lottery are being divided into six groups. They'll be rotated through the viewing cubicles here on Mercury—five days for each group.

CAROL. We have time to give them a look at the cubicles, Murray. Can we run that now while we're waiting?

MURRAY. Good idea. Give us that short clip, will you, Joel? There! That's a bank of cubicles, folks—one person in each cubicle. Those are really life-support tanks. Every occupant has to strip mother-naked and be plugged in . . . but it's worth it. I promise you, it's worth it . . . and when you see the holos in a few minutes, I know you'll agree.

CAROL. I wonder if there are any deceivers in that group, Murray?

MURRAY. There could be, Carol. A valid Mercury Pass is worth a lotta money. Our news side says there's still an active black market. Mostly, it's rich people looking around for a "look similar" who might want to sell.

CAROL. I hear they use plastic surgery and very clever forgery.

MURRAY. It's pretty sophisticated, all right.

CAROL. I also hear there have been a few fortunes made by selling a valid Mercury Pass. I wouldn't sell mine, I know, but . . .

MURRAY. I think Von Lutzow was the last one caught. And he got the full treatment—brain erasure.

CAROL. It makes me shudder. Von Lutzow paid twenty-three million—and then there were all those bribes!

MURRAY. A lot of people lost their jobs and went to correction. Kids, you should understand there's a reason why the Mercury Pass is nontransferable. The lottery is the biggest tax supplement in the universe. Governments depend on it, and it has to be kept honest.

CAROL. Look at that woman there in left center, Murray. She looks like she's praying.

MURRAY. She could very well be praying. Even today, Carol, followers of the Islamic faith count Mercury as a necessary stop on the pilgrimage to Mecca.

CAROL. There is something like a religious experience about coming here. It's quite different from the visit to Earth.

MURRAY. This is more than just the observation platform of choice for the solar pyrotechnics.

CAROL. You're right, Murray. The pyrotechnics of the feeding are a kind of celebration, a human celebration of what we're preserving here. [*Chuckle*] Even the black market in Mercury Passes, I guess, is part of that thing, which hasn't changed.

MURRAY [*Laughter*]. Carol, you're something else. I never thought of it that way, but you're right.

CAROL. I like what Pander Oulson said when he found out about the illegal trade in passes. You remember it?

MURRAY. Yep. I sure do.

CAROL. Oulson said: "The hoary platitude that there's nothing new under the Sun places the truth in its proper location. Where but on Mercury—more under the Sun than any other place in our universe—where else could you expect human foibles to keep their museum quality?"

MURRAY. A wise old man, he was. Look at those cubicles we're seeing now, Carol. Those are the low-number winners.

CAROL. God, they *are* Spartan.

MURRAY. They have to be—so many people wanting to come here. You notice how the rather primitive accommodations on Museum Earth become even more basic as you move closer to Sol?

CAROL. I found Earth fairly comfortable. Those sleeping cubicles in underground stacks were kind of amazing, but at least you had your own place and you could move around during visiting hours. Terraformed Venus is more like what you see here on Mercury.

MURRAY. Those Mercury cubicles you're looking at right now, folks, are where you stay for five days. We're lucky. Our chairs, which are really our cubicles, can move around. But when you get into one of those viewing cubicles, like that one we're seeing closeup now, you're plugged in, and that's where you stay the full five days.

CAROL. Observation station, living quarters, toilet and shower, cafeteria, exercise machine, and diagnostic system. That's the way it has to be.

MURRAY. If you get the idea that it's dangerous to be here . . . well, it is in a way, but every precaution has been taken to make your visit safe.

CAROL. The fiery eruptions we're about to see are controlled in the sense that they are located precisely on the solar surface. You've all seen holos of the great flaming arches and the incandescent towers. . . .

MURRAY. Sometimes they lift a full solar diameter before falling back.

CAROL. The resulting shock waves flood the solar system with high-energy particles. . . .

Constantly adjusting her filter-visor system, Ludmilla is now peering intently at the solar surface below, watching for the first signs of flare development, as predicted by her theory. "Strange to think that a million dumpsters of heavy nucleon residue contain as much mass as the disturbance-generating core of a flare region. If I'm right about the gamma-ray opacity in the Z-particle flux tubes. . . . Holy Mary! Look at the braided spicules building around that spot! You could induce lithium burning in a flash, just there, where the magnetic fields pinch. . . .''

MURRAY. Joel, let's have a clip of a converter-collector. There! That's Museum Earth and its satellite, folks. There are nine human-occupied planets and satellites in this solar system, all of them waiting to see what you're about to see. We've just had the three-minute alert.

CAROL. Joel, give them a close-up of that collector on the left. There it is. That's a forerunner of humankind's present electron-driver systems. These collectors are maintained in their original operating condition because . . . well, they are historical oddities, but they still work, and work very well. The solar system uses a lot of energy.

MURRAY. Especially Mars.

CAROL [Laughing]. Honeymoon on Mars! In spite of the disputes, I'm sure Mars will remain a honeymoon center. The archaeologists and other researchers are not going to make it off limits. There has to be an acceptable compromise.

MURRAY. I'm sure there will be.

CAROL. Murray, I'm so excited! I wonder if we'll see a coronal pillar this time.

MURRAY. Or a ghost cloud.

CAROL. Look at the way I'm shivering. We could even see a roller or a statue.

MURRAY. Camera one—give us a close-up of Carol. She's really shivering, folks. See there. To tell you the truth, so am I. What I hope to see is a ghost cloud.

CAROL. I think I agree. They look so deceptively gentle.

MURRAY. And the way they paint strange shapes on the void. It's one minute, folks!

CAROL. We're stopping at Museum Earth on our way back, but I don't think I'll watch the rest of the display from there.

MURRAY. An anticlimax after what we're about to see.

CAROL. I don't want my memories of this to be dimmed by some other view.

MURRAY. This is the real thing. No holo can give you this. No other view can give you this.

CAROL. Not even theater-in-the-round?

MURRAY. That's what everybody says. Thirty seconds and counting, folks. Give them the audio, Joel, and put us on reflectors. Ladies and gentlemen, the big show is about to begin! Our deflectors are pulling back. . . .

MOG CONTROL. Sixteen, fifteen, fourteen. . . .

MURRAY [Voice-over with countdown behind]. Words can't describe it, folks. You are there!

MOG CONTROL. Seven . . . six . . . five . . . four . . . three . . . two . . . one. . . .

Ludmilla, transfixed by the sun, has forgotten her recorder. What began as mathematical theory is ending as stream of consciousness. "There! The surface is heaving upward, a giant dome. There's the lithium flash, just as predicted. Expanding over a larger area than I thought. . . . Damn! It's getting hot in here. Not that I didn't warn you, old lady. Well, as they say, if you can't stand the heat, stay out of the Sun."

The ship falls onward.

CAROL. God in Heaven! Look at that. It's coronal pillars, a whole progression of them. Look at them!

MURRAY. At least a solar radius high.

EDITING [Twenty-second pause in audio].

MURRAY. It's . . . it's a ghost cloud. Carol, it really is!

Ludmilla Santiana adjusts her filter visor to a new wavelength. "Look at those granules, collapsing in on the target spot! The flare is erupting, just as the model predicts! This will prove the theory once and for all! And it'll be the biggest flare they've ever seen! If anything, it's even bigger than I predicted! What a wondrous thing, to be able to stick a few field and composition matrices into the computer and make sense of the photospheric chaos—the turmoil that makes life possible in the solar system! At last, to see into—to predict—the heartbeat of life. . . . Half a league, half a league, half a league onward. . . . It's getting hot. . . ."

MURRAY. There it is, folks, the biggest, brightest ghost cloud there's ever been! You're seeing it here, live, on Wye-Oh-You.

CAROL. It's so close!

MURRAY. It's like a gigantic face . . . an old woman.

CAROL. So beautiful. . . .

MURRAY. It's changing. . . . Now it's like an explosion of stars.

CAROL. And even closer! Murray, I think we're going right through that one. We . . . what happened? I can't see!

MURRAY. Our deflectors snapped into place. My monitor says they're still getting visual at the studio, so we're still going out.

CAROL. Oh, yes, but I want to see it live.

MURRAY. So do I. Look at that . . . a fountain of fire.

CAROL. My grid says it's six times the diameter of Earth.

MURRAY. I find it hard to imagine the size of those things.

CAROL. Look at that little greenish streak, right on the front edge of that wave. . . like a little green comet.

MURRAY. Maybe it is a comet, or a little asteroid with some weird metal vaporizing, or whatever they do. The technical handouts said there's stuff falling into the Sun all time. Look at those colors, folks. Remember, it takes only two and a half minutes for the radiation to get from the flare to us on Mercury. The rest of you outliers will have to wait a while longer. We're the first! Numero uno!

CAROL. Our deflectors are pulling back. There! What are those globs breaking away from the Sun's surface?

MURRAY. My monitor describes them as firedrops. Each one is several hundred times the size of a terraform planet. Look! There's one like a teardrop.

CAROL. Waves . . . a surf. Firesurf. Can I call it that?

MURRAY. Why not? My monitor says it's a brand new phenomenon. Particle count has reached a new high.

CAROL. My monitor is overprinting: "Flash Red." What does that mean . . . oh, yes . . . Murray!

MURRAY. Carol, I'm afraid neither of us will be able to have any more children. And that goes for everyone down there in the viewing cubicles, too. The deflector system was not engineered to take this high a count. We've really been hit, but the show goes on, folks. Look at it!

CAROL. I don't like making history but . . . you're right. The show goes on.

MURRAY. And what a show it is! That fountain in center screen is a diameter and a half tall.

CAROL. And my firesurf. Can you imagine riding a surfboard on that?

MURRAY. Look at that thing off to the left. It's like a cliff rising out of the Sun. They really must've given her *some* feeding this time.

CAROL. I see the count's going down. We must be over the peak of particles.

MURRAY. I sure hope so. I don't fancy spending all those months in decon. You want to do an *Other Places* from a decon hospital?

CAROL. That might be interesting. Look! Your cliff is even closer.

MURRAY. And there are vertical seams in it. Those black lines. Look at them. Each one's three or four times an Earth diameter.

CAROL. And the fireshower overhead! There's never been a display like this! Aren't we lucky?

MURRAY. Carol! I think it's going to . . .

EDITOR. End transmission.

APPROVED COMMENTARY. You have just seen the remarkable final Mercury Display, which, as you know, ended in the virtual destruction of MOG. There were no human survivors, and the robotics were so disrupted that their records are considered unreliable. The official judgment is that the Solar Replacement Series set up an unexpected harmonic feedback, which created gigantic solar waves. One of these waves is believed to have come within only a few thousand meters of Mercury, not actually striking the planet but overriding all deflectors and cooling systems. Only the core survived, and, of course, there were no humans at the core. Records made from Venus and Earth confirm this diagnosis.

VENUS

ESSAY BY
Lawrence Colin

SPECULATION BY
Marta Randall

VENUS: THE VEILED PLANET

Lawrence Colin .

DESCENT TO VENUS

THE FIRST VISITORS TO VENUS will encounter a world hellish and deadly, yet strangely beautiful, with temperatures high enough to melt lead and a dense atmosphere that turns the surface into a dull, shimmering landscape of pink and orange. Until recently, the thick cloud cover around Venus has hidden that world from our view. Only with the planetary probes in the 1960 s and 1970 s did we have our first glimpse of what lies beneath the clouds—and what we might encounter if we were to dive beneath them.

During the whole of their four-month flight, astronauts bound for Venus will see no more of the planet than we can see from Earth—merely a creamy yellow mask of clouds. Only when the spacecraft descends into the clouds will the visitors begin to experience what Venus is really like. At about 70 kilometers above the surface, where the clouds begin, the meteorological conditions are much the same as they are in the clouds of our own planet: the temperature is $-25°C$ and the atmospheric pressure is 0.1 bar—but of course the clouds on Earth are only about 8 kilometers high. Also, the clouds above Venus are rather hazy, like a thick fog, and visibility is just a few kilometers. They are composed not of water, as on Earth, but mainly of sulfuric acid—more commonly known as battery acid.

A descending craft will pass through three distinct cloud layers. The middle and thickest layer is quite turbulent, and would severely buffet any craft passing through. The entire region of clouds, including the haze above and below the three main decks, is at least 40 kilometers thick, compared to perhaps 6 kilometers on Earth.

Finally, at about 44 kilometers, the spacecraft will break through this cloud cover into relatively clear air, through which the surface remains invisible below. This atmosphere is a mixture of carbon dioxide and nitrogen, quite unlike Earth's nitrogen-oxygen mixture. (From our perspective, you might say that Venus has an even more severe pollution problem than Los Angeles!) The atmosphere is so dense that the small amount of sunlight that does manage to seep through the thick yellow cloud decks is dispersed in all directions. As a result, the sky looks much like the whiteouts seen at Earth's polar regions. Every once in a while there are light flashes—familiar to our Earth-bred astronauts as lightning.

At an altitude of about 10 kilometers, the astronauts will be able to spy the surface. It looks like some of the more barren regions on Earth, although there seem to be several volcanic constructs, which are actively spewing material from their caldera. One advantage of the thick atmosphere is that no fuel is needed to slow the descent for a safe landing, and the shock of a 35-kilometer-per-hour impact will be easily absorbed by the deployed landing gear. During the spacecraft's one-hour descent the crew can prepare to face the deadly conditions on the surface of Venus.

The temperature on the surface is about 465°C—twice as hot as a kitchen oven. Atmospheric pressure is ninety-five times greater than on the surface of Earth, equivalent to the pressure found several thousand feet below the surface of our terrestrial oceans. So conditions for life on the surface of Venus are literally deadly, and without special air-conditioned pressure suits, an oxygen supply system, and perhaps a propulsion system to aid in mobility, our Venus explorers will not survive.

And what would these hypothetical astronauts see as they stepped onto the Venusian surface? Because of the thick atmosphere and clouds, the Sun cannot be seen on Venus, and even daytime is rather dark—like a foggy, winter late afternoon in San Francisco. The air and ground are peach-colored, however, due to the peculiar filtering effect of the air on the blues and violets of the Sun's light. Although it is not possible to see very far horizontally, the landscape looks strangely distorted, as if viewed through a fishbowl. One scientist has predicted that if you could see far enough on Venus you could see around the entire planet to the back of your own head!

Navigating directions on the surface will be a bit difficult, since the absence of a magnetic field on Venus will render a compass useless. The surface terrain will be rather boring compared to Earth's: radar probes have shown that some 95 percent of the surface is rolling plains with modest highlands and lowlands. There are only two or three continental-sized features that contain mountain peaks as high as those on Earth. These are the sites of most of the active volcanoes.

On Venus the Sun rises in the west and sets in the east every day, just the reverse of what we are all used to on Earth. Even more strange, a Venus day lasts 117 Earth days, half of which is daytime and half nighttime—and the temperature does not change more than a few degrees from day to night. In fact, there is little change in temperature from the equator to either of the poles. There is no place that a Venusian visitor can go to escape the blazing heat!

Venus is such a forbidding planet that such a journey is not likely to be made for a long time, if at all. Still, the probes we have sent to Venus in the last two decades have given us a much better understanding of our sunward neighbor. Let us briefly examine how Venus changed from a mere point of light in our sky to a world we have at last begun to explore. Mankind has been curious about Venus since antiquity. For thousands of years we had only our eyes for plotting its course across the sky. It was recognized that Venus's movement differed from that of the bright stars as least as early as the time of the Babylonians, who recorded its motions and supposed influences on society, around 3000 B.C. It is clearly recorded in the astronomical chronicles of other civilizations, including those in China, Meso-America, and Greece. Galileo turned his little telescope to Venus in 1610 and recognized that Venus shows phases, like the Moon. Thus he realized that the planet is not itself luminous but is visible to us because it reflects sunlight. He wrote: "Cynthiae figuras aemulatur mater amorum"—"The mother of love [Venus] emulates the figure of Cynthia [Moon]."

Those who followed Galileo with the simple telescopes of the seventeenth and early eighteenth centuries confirmed the phases, and some detected spots on the nearly blank, white illuminated face. Some attempted to time the rotation period of the planet by the variable appearance of the markings, not realizing that they were seeing a cloud-shrouded planet and not the surface. Later, other extended low-contrast markings were reported by observers with better telescopes. Early in the twentieth century much higher contrast markings were seen through telescopes equipped with ultraviolet filters. These were clearly correlated with the visible spots and markings and led to the correct conclusion that the white face of Venus was actually clouds. Of course, clouds are not possible without an atmosphere. The Venusian atmosphere had been detected earlier—in the 1760's, in fact, during a rare transit. As Venus passed across the face of the Sun, a gray halo was observed around the planet that behaved peculiarly as the planet crossed the Sun's circular edge. Other measurements of Venus were also made during transits, giving us its diameter, for example.

By the early decades of the twentieth century, it was known that Venus had an atmosphere and clouds, its size was not much different than Earth's, and it was our nearest planetary neighbor. These obvious similarities led many people to call it "Earth's twin sister." It was natural to assume that its atmosphere must be similar to our own and that its clouds were made of water. It was then a simple step to conclude that life must exist there. Today it is clear that much of this was unfounded speculation, but it did provide much grist for the science fiction writers of the period.

EXPLORATION FROM EARTH

The early 1930's witnessed the birth of new astronomical techniques, radiometry and spectroscopy, which permitted the first measurements of atmospheric composition and temperature structure in remote planetary atmospheres. Venus's atmosphere was found to consist mainly of carbon dioxide, very unlike Earth's. Even the composition of trace constituents was unlike that of Earth. Water vapor, for example, was found to be much less abundant on Venus than on Earth. The composition of the clouds remained elusive well into the space age. (It wasn't until 1975 that infrared observations taken from a high-flying aircraft showed that the clouds were composed of sulfuric acid.) However, microwave observations did allow us to "see" below the clouds for the first time. In 1961 these observations enabled us to measure the direction and rate of rotation of Venus. Microwave also enabled us to measure the atmosphere's temperature, density, and pressure and to get some idea of the topography of Venus.

Despite these major findings, our knowledge of Venus was still seriously limited in the early 1960s prior to mankind's first rendezvous by spacecraft. In 1961 competing views of Venus could be classified in seven broad categories:

1. moist, swampy, teeming with life
2. warm, enveloped by a global carbonic-acid ocean
3. cool, Earth-like, with surface water and a dense ionosphere
4. water, massive precipitating clouds of water droplets with intense lightning
5. cold, polar regions with ice caps 10 kilometers thick and a hot equatorial region far above the boiling point of water
6. hot, dusty, dry, windy global desert
7. extremely hot and cloudy, with molten lead and zinc puddles at the equator, seas of bromine, butyric acid, and phenol at the poles

From this list it is not obvious that scientists were all describing the same planet. For those who are impatient about the outcome, speculation 6 appears to represent most closely what we now think Venus is like.

SPACECRAFT EXPLORATION

The exploration of our solar system has been dominated in the last twenty years by the missions of scientifically instrumented robot spacecraft which could examine the planets and their satellites from nearby. Shedding the limitations of the Earth-based telescopes, which had served ground-based astronomers so well for over 300 years, a new generation of scientists from the United States, the Soviet Union, and other nations have been systematically and steadily re-writing the textbooks about our cosmic neighborhood. Initially, the planets were studied using spacecraft that quickly "sounded" the planet from a distance as the craft flew by. Observation times for these soundings were greatly increased by subsequently substituting orbiters for the flyby craft. Finally, both the United States and the U.S.S.R. developed the capability of making *in situ* observations, with the use of atmospheric entry probes and surface landers. The Soviet Union has concentrated its planetary exploration program on a series of Venera probe-lander missions to Venus. After a series of early failures at both Venus and Mars, recent Soviet missions to Venus have been highly successful. The United States has taken a more balanced, and thus complementary approach, not concentrating on any one planet or type of spacecraft. The first U.S. entry probe-lander was at Mars with Viking in 1976 and then at Venus with multiple-probe entries by Pioneer Venus in 1978.

Why have these missions to the planets been so effective in capturing the imagination of both the scientific community and the public at large? A key ingredient is that they allow us all to be there along with the robot craft we send. Through the eyes of the cameras and through the other complex instruments they carry, all of us can examine a strange, complex, and alien world. Those of us who have been fortunate enough to have participated directly in sending spacecraft and scientific instruments to these wonderful bodies have been there vicariously and have left part of ourselves. Some have spent more than ten years laboriously and methodically developing instruments that return but one hour of scientific data! But what an hour. Few people get as much return in a lifetime.

All in all, the United States and U.S.S.R. combined have launched almost two dozen spacecraft to Venus from 1962 to 1984. These have included close flybys, orbiters, entry probes and landers; their number has far exceeded the number of visits to any other planet, a tribute to the intrinsic interest and excitement Venus holds for us. Some of the results from these missions have merely confirmed what we knew from ground-based observations, while other results have provided entirely new information and knowledge.

In light of the spacecraft missions it has become apparent how far Venus is from being Earth's twin. Only their sizes and bulk properties are truly comparable. Venus is slightly smaller than our own rocky planet. It is the most spherical of the planets. Its mass is about 81.5 percent that of Earth's mass and its average density is nearly 97 percent that of Earth's. Thus any object on the surface of Venus would weigh about 91 percent of what it weighs on Earth.

Similarities between the two planets end here. Whereas Earth exhibits a sizable magnetic field, Venus has almost none at all, for reasons that are not known. It has no satellite. It completes its revolution around the Sun in 224.7 Earth days, as opposed to our own 365.26. Earth completes its daily rotation in almost 24 hours, spinning about its axis in a counterclockwise direction, so that the Sun rises in the east and sets in the west. Venus, on the other hand, takes 243.01 Earth days to complete its rotation and spins in a clockwise (retrograde) direction. We do not understand the reason for Venus's peculiar backwards rotation. The fact that Venus takes longer to rotate on its axis than to go around the Sun leads to an interesting effect on its cycle of light and dark. Here on Earth, the length of daylight is little affected by our revolution about the Sun, because Earth's rotation is so much faster. But Venus makes a very significant part of its turn around the Sun as it turns on its axis. Thus both the planet's rotation and its revolution determines when the Sun is seen to rise or set from the surface of Venus and the result is not obvious without making a calculation. It turns out that the periods of sunshine and darkness on Venus are each about 58 days long.

Finally, Venus's axis is barely tilted (2.6 degrees), whereas the tilt is 23.45 degrees for Earth. It is this tilt which is primarily responsible for the major seasonal variations on Earth. Even if Venus did not have a thick atmosphere to even out temperature differences, it still would not have very dramatic seasons.

SURFACE FEATURES

Very recent radar from spacecraft probes, supplemented by ground-based radar observations, have provided a detailed, though low-resolution, look at the surface characteristics of Venus. Extremes in relief extend over about 13 kilometers. The terrain can be divided into "upland" rolling plains (about 65 percent of the surface), highlands (about 8 percent), and lowlands (about 27 percent). The plains that make up most of the surface are generally flat, although we have identified numerous dark, circular features which may be lava-filled impact basins. In some areas, a series of ridges and troughs suggest the kind of tectonic motion that created the mountains, valleys, and continents of Earth. Granitic rocks discovered in one region likewise suggest ancient crustal material. However, an integrated pattern of ridges and valleys together with continental plates, so common on Earth and indicative of active plate tectonism, has not been identified. Venus's crust is probably relatively static, whereas Earth's crust is marked by constant relative motion of the plates.

Two continent-size regions, Ishtar Terra, at northern high latitudes, and Aphrodite Terra, near the equator, compose most of the highland region; their highest peaks rise 5 to 10 kilometers above the plains. Ishtar Terra is made up of a great volcano plus an uplifted plateau containing the highest mountains on Venus, the Maxwell Montes, which reach an altitude higher than our own Mount Everest above sea level. Aphrodite Terra, spreading across an area the size of Africa, is much larger than Ishtar Terra, but not nearly as high. Consisting of wide valleys and rugged mountains, it also displays some features which may be volcanic. A third highland region, Beta Regio, appears to consist of two side-by-side giant volcanoes, both of which may still be active. The radar studies suggest that Venus's crust has a basaltic, rather than granitic, composition around Beta Regio.

The predominance of rolling plains and flat lowlands marking the Venusian topography and the absence of plate tectonism suggest a history for the interior of Venus quite different from that of Earth. This is quite unexpected, given the similar sizes and bulk properties of the two planets, and scientists are still puzzling over the cause.

THE ATMOSPHERE

The atmosphere of Venus may be divided into three levels, each with distinct characteristics: (1) the upper atmosphere, from 100 kilometers to about 250 kilometers above the surface; (2) the middle atmosphere, from about 80 kilometers to 100 kilometers above the surface; and (3) the lower atmosphere, or troposphere, which extends from the surface to the cloud tops. The middle atmosphere is highly stable and the temperature remains the same. In the upper atmosphere the temperature changes greatly over the course of a day; this is the only place where the temperature is *low* relative to Earth: about 27°C on the day side and an extremely cold −173°C on the night side. As we noted in our imaginary flight to Venus, there is a gradual increase in temperature and pressure in the troposphere, from Earth-like conditions in the cloud layer to an unbearable surface temperature of 465°C and a pressure of 95 bars.

The ubiquitous, creamy-yellow clouds are rather tenuous by terrestrial

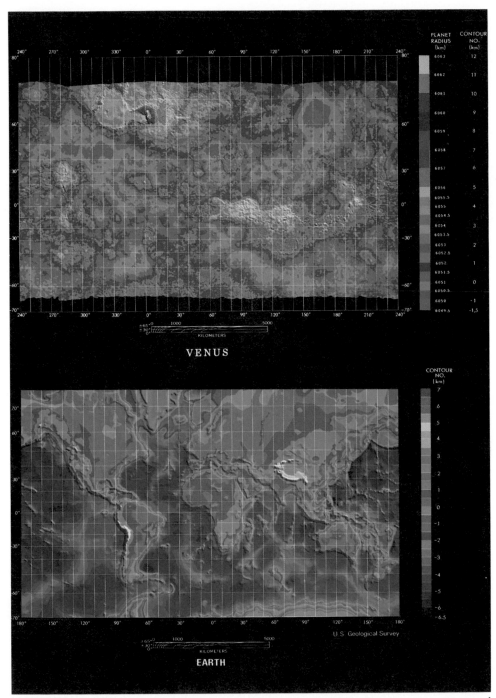

Radar Maps of Venus and Earth at the same scale (From *Worlds in Comparison;* courtesy of the Astronomical Society of the Pacific)

standards. Visibility within the cloud layer is quite good. As on Earth, meteorological processes conspire to produce precipitation. On Venus, the result is entirely "acid rain." As the sulfuric acid droplets fall toward the surface, they evaporate in the continually increasing temperatures, and the gas rises to return to the cloud layers. Thus, while always falling, the acid rain never reaches the surface.

Lightning originating at unknown locations below the clouds has been confirmed. The physical and chemical makeup of the clouds seems incompatible with lightning of cloud origin. There have been suggestions that the lightning sources are correlated with volcanic-looking features on Aphrodite Terra; if true, there is the possibility of active vulcanism on the planet today.

Ultraviolet pictures taken of the clouds over periods of several days have revealed another surprising fact about Venus—the upper atmosphere and the clouds rotate sixty times faster than the planet beneath it. The longest-lasting ultraviolet markings are found to move around the planet in about four days. The principle direction of motion is westward over the entire globe, increasing from about 1 meter per second near the surface to about 100 meters per second in the clouds and then steadily decreasing above. There may also be secondary, weak, north-south motions of the lower atmosphere. Explanations for the circulations are highly controversial and hotly debated by scientists.

The chemical composition of the air remains the most controversial aspect of our knowledge of the Venusian atmosphere. Carbon dioxide is by far the most abundant gas on Venus, constituting 96.5 percent of the lower atmosphere. It is followed by nitrogen at 3.5 percent. Other trace gases, such as water vapor, oxygen, hydrogen, chlorine, sulfur, carbon monoxide, sulfur dioxide and others, exist only in the parts-per-million range, yet are vital to understanding Venus's cloud structure and the resulting climate and meteorology. Furthermore, these and other trace gases, particularly the so-called noble or rare gases like neon, argon, and krypton, are vital to understanding Venus's evolutionary history. The noble gases are inert; in other words, they are chemically inactive, so they have remained unaltered in amount within the atmosphere since it formed. They thus give us direct clues to what Venus's atmosphere was like billions of years ago.

The most interesting, scientifically important, and controversial constituent of the Venusian atmosphere is water vapor. Very little water vapor exists on Venus today. Clearly, no large body of liquid water could survive in such high temperatures. Overwhelming evidence suggests that in its past Venus had much more water, perhaps as much as on Earth today—a whole ocean. If it did, why did the water disappear? During its 4.6 billion years, the Sun has gradually been getting hotter, as it follows an evolutionary path driven by nuclear reactions in its interior. This has in turn increased the amount of solar energy radiated out to bathe the planets and other bodies of the solar system. We can speculate that the comparatively temperate climate Venus had in its youth may have disappeared as it became hotter and hotter, and the surface water evaporated into the atmosphere. This evaporation was probably accelerated by the single most important factor in Venus's evolutionary history—the greenhouse effect—until the planet became the dry, torrid place it is today.

THE GREENHOUSE EFFECT

The temperature at the surface of any planet with an atmospheric envelope is enhanced by a phenomenon known as the greenhouse effect: the atmosphere captures and contains heat in much the same way as the glass roof over a greenhouse. Most of the Sun's energy that reaches the surface of a planet is contained in the visible portion of the electromagnetic spectrum, from red to violet. Both Earth's and Venus's atmosphere are transparent over this range of wavelengths, so a large percentage of the available solar energy reaches their surfaces to heat them. The surfaces then cool by reradiating energy back into space. They do so, however, not at visible but at infrared wavelengths. Atmospheres are not transparent in the infrared, however; instead they absorb some of the radiation, blocking its return to space. The heated atmospheres then reradiate themselves, some energy escaping out to space and some returning to the surface, again reheating it. Eventually a balance is reached, and the surface attains an equilibrium temperature that is higher than it would have been in the absence of an atmosphere.

The reheating cycle operates the same way on Earth as it does on Venus. On Earth, the temperature has been raised some 24°C by this natural greenhouse, resulting in the relatively mild climate we know today. On Venus, however, the temperature has soared hundreds of degrees higher than it would be without an atmosphere. Why this dramatic difference? Because some gases absorb more infrared radiation than others. The nitrogen and oxygen which constitute 99 percent of Earth's atmosphere absorb radiation less efficiently than the carbon dioxide on Venus. Carbon dioxide is not the only culprit, though; sulphur dioxide and water vapor are also excellent absorbers of thermal radiation. The temperature at Venus's surface is hot simply because the primary gases on Venus work together to trap heat as effectively as any oven door.

The greenhouse effect on Venus was further accelerated because of the ways in which planets obtain, and then retain, their atmospheres. Initially, the planets probably form with gaseous envelopes. During the early stages of planetary evolution, these so-called primordial atmospheres were largely lost through mechanisms that permit the gases to escape to space. At some stage the planets begin to outgas material from their hot interiors, and a secondary atmosphere is formed. Outgassing continues to this day, most visibly through the volcanoes active on Earth and, we think, on Venus. Volcanoes vent many different gases into the atmosphere, primarily carbon dioxide and sulfur compounds. On Earth, thanks to cooler temperatures and the presence of liquid water, also the result of outgassing, the carbon dioxide dissolved and eventually reacted with the oceanic rocks to form limestone. On Venus, this natural sink was not available, and the carbon dioxide has remained largely in the atmosphere.

It appears that this difference in atmospheric evolution is responsible for the increased temperature and atmospheric pressure on Venus: surface reheating by the atmosphere causes more outgassing of carbon dioxide, which leads to greater infrared absorption and greater surface heating, and so on. This upward spiral, which we have labeled the "runaway greenhouse effect," eventually reaches an equilibrium temperature which is quite high.

That Earth and Venus actually contain the same amount of carbon dioxide emphasizes the delicate balance between a poisonous and a life-sustaining environment. If Earth had been just a bit closer to the Sun, carbon dioxide now locked into carbonic rocks would have been released into the atmosphere, which would then have absorbed more infrared radiation and heated up Earth—and we know the rest of the story. Our use of fossil fuels, as well as natural outgassing, is at present increasing the amount of carbon dioxide in our atmosphere, and there is measurable evidence that this increase is causing a rise in temperatures around the globe. In Venus we have a frightening lesson in the effects of a runaway greenhouse, and we must take this lesson to heart by controlling the atmospheric level of carbon dioxide if we are to survive.

TERRAFORMING

Terraforming—deliberately and permanently modifying the atmospheric environment of a planet to resemble the life-sustaining environment of Earth—has been suggested for many years by scientists and nonscientists looking for places we may eventually want to colonize. Venus is clearly a logical candidate. After all, it is our nearest neighbor; this would simplify transportation problems associated with colonization. And it has sufficient solar energy for all the energy needs of the colonists. The scientific principles for terraforming are well known. All it takes is the injection of the correct chemicals and catalysts into the atmosphere of Venus to cause chemical reactions to occur that yield new, permanent gases, in the correct amounts, thus approximating Earth's air. The process is similar to the cloud-seeding operations used for agricultural applications. However, there are certain prohibitive difficulties. First, the chemistry between naturally occurring and added components must be precisely understood, and the required relative amounts of the interacting mixtures accurately known. Our knowledge of chemistry for this extremely large array of interacting particles is not nearly sufficient, nor is it clear that it ever can be. Second, we are talking about changing a massive atmosphere on a global scale, not on a regional basis. This would require equally massive amounts of added chemicals. The ability to produce, deliver, and inject this burden far surpasses current technological capabilities. It must be remembered that Earth's atmosphere is continually supplied with massive amounts of injected gases and particles, naturally from outgassing volcanoes and other surface fissures, and from many, many manufactured sources. The atmosphere shows lots of resiliency, fortunately, and it bounces back wonderfully, in general, from most short-term perturbing forces. However, there is clear evidence of permanent damage accumulating over many years from constant influxes of manmade pollution. The difficulty we have in understanding what is happening to our own atmosphere is a clue to the difficulties of terraforming.

The reader should not conclude that we know most of what we need to know about Venus. There is much to learn and humanity will continue to take small steps toward that understanding in the future. Will we personally visit Venus? As a scientist limited by twentieth-century-technology perspectives, I think not. There are other interesting places to go that are easier to get to. However, given the ingenuity with which we have explored the most remote areas of our own planet, I would not be surprised to be proven wrong.

Color view of the Venus surface taken by the Venera 13 lander in March, 1982 (Courtesy USSR Academy of Sciences)

BIG DOME

Marta Randall

GOOD EVENING. *This is Lindsay Yukio-Grimaldi for Public Expressions, made possible by a grant from Mutual Interplanetary, which invites you to join with it in sponsoring these continuing communicasts of interest to all the colonies of the Terran Exile.*

We have always had stories of people who escaped or evaded the notice of Central Census; what you are about to view is the story of an entire population about which, for over five centuries, Central Census knew nothing at all.

This blasted landscape was the surface of Venus, five hundred years ago. Barren, hot enough to melt lead, beset with sharp depths and sudden jagged mountains, dim under its mantle of sulferous clouds—a thoroughly unpleasant place and an unlikely candidate for terraforming.

As reclamation efforts show, Earth was not entirely poisoned, but waste toxins were so embedded in the system that by the middle of the twenty-first century, nothing was untouched. If you doubt the extent of the damage, you can come here, to the pre-Disaster exhibits in the Luna libraries. These two-dimensional photographs show the people of an earlier time; the faces and bodies look quaint and remarkably homogeneous despite the differing shades of skin, the different eyelids, the color or texture of hair. We don't find them particularly attractive, but this is how we used to look before radiation and other toxins fiddled with our gene structure. How strange and innocent they seemed—and how much damage they did.

When we began to work on Venus we had no reason to believe we would ever live on Earth again. We honeycombed the Moon with our cities; peppered interplanetary space with hub worlds, planted colonies on Mars—still our population grew, as did our desire to live in an environment that at least simulated our home world. Free atmosphere; free water; open sky—it was a dream

that increasingly obsessed post-Disaster society, until the terraforming of Venus became a necessity.

The first terraforming crews established a self-contained dome world here, near the slopes of Maxwell Montes on Ishtar Planum, and called it, with lamentable lack of imagination, Big Dome. A semipermanent population of scientists and workers moved in and, for sixty years, charted every pimple, wart, and scar on, above, and under the Venusian surface. The dome was self-sufficient; powered geothermally, it produced its own food, water, oxygen—a paradise of farmlands, forest, and towns banded about the central lake. There was only one drawback: It was hot. Not as hot as the hellish surface, but hot enough to compare to the Terran tropics, and humid, and lush. And, as you can see from these archival holotapes, astoundingly beautiful.

Terraforming began with the seeding of hardy algae into the upper cloud layer. The algae broke down the atmospheric CO_2 by photosynthesis, releasing oxygen and depositing carbon on the planetary surface. Hydrogen was introduced to react with the oxygen and create free water, followed by iron to scavenge the excess oxygen and prevent burning of the planetary carbon deposits.

Before the carbon deposits could grow too deep, Big Dome was abandoned in favor of an orbiting colony, called, with equal lack of imagination, Skyhome. That is, it was assumed that Big Dome was abandoned. We can only speculate on what actually happened during those last few months, for the original colony's logs are suspiciously silent. In any event, the majority of Big Dome's population emigrated to Skyhome, and for five hundred years it was assumed that Big Dome was a ruin, disintegrating on the harsh Venusian surface.

After five centuries of fine tuning, it appeared that the rains would fall at last, shallow oceans would form, and the highlands and arctic areas of Venus would at last be able to support human life. Then, in the year 2694, a survey crew from Skyhome rediscovered Big Dome, intact under its blanket of carbon dust; more astoundingly, they found the descendants of the original group of dissident workers, their history turned to mythology and their technology to magic, living in the overgrown jungle that Big Dome had become. Perhaps most importantly of all, the crew found Runner, one of the most remarkable humans you will ever meet.

FIRST THING FIRST

First thing first, in Big Dome it is all times with danger. There are light boxes up high on top like in Safe Place, but in Big Dome it makes light sometimes and sometimes not, you can't tell. In Big Dome it is raining at all times, but the most of danger in Big Dome is the growing stuff that eats; it is called Weed, I hate it because it kills. Also are moving-by-themselves things, they are called creatures, they eat growing stuff and sometimes they try to eat me but I am crafty-fast and sometimes I eat them. I do not hate them but I hate Weed because it tries to kill me more.

My name is Runner; I run it is what I do. There are two Safe Places with Big Dome between and I run from Near Safe Place to Far Safe Place; I bring stories, I bring the magics of Far Safe Place that heal or the magics of Near Safe Place that taste good, this is called Trade. My brother was Runner, and my father, and my grandmother I did not know her; Weed ate my brother as Weed ate my grandmother, but my father had a sickness and Near Safe Place people would not help him and he died, so I only am Runner now.

Safe Places people hate me because I run through Big Dome; they think Big Dome is evil and they will not go there, but they make me run through Big Dome and for this they hate me and think that I am evil also. They are foolish, for if I do not run they will have no healing magic in Near Safe Place, no good-tasting spice in Far Safe Place, and they know this. When one time I was sick I needed Far Safe Place healing magic, they made much talking but they gave it to me anyway. They have to, I am the only Runner and my Girl is too tiny to run Big Dome.

This story is of one run that I ran, I will tell it to you it because it is my story, and it is true.

Big Dome bottom is flat and round, and all around there is Wall, coming up and over and down again, like a bowl inside. Halfway up Wall at Near Safe Place there is a notch cut in Big Dome Wall, this is the Inbetween where I stay; behind it there is another wall and behind that is Near Safe Place. My place at Inbetween is all made-stuff, nothing growing, nothing with colors; I do not love it but it is mine, I live there with my Girl. My Girl has a mother and a father but I do not know them; people gave her to me as they gave me to my father, gave my brother to my father, gave my father to my grandmother. My Girl has pretty hair long like silver, she will be a good Runner when she is grown.

One day at Inbetween we are eating fruits; Safe Places people have fear of everything in Big Dome and will not eat the fruits, so only Runners eat them. Sometimes too I catch Big Dome creatures, tiny ones, they are good to eat but Safe Places people will not eat them either, because Safe Places people are foolish.

Two people come to us, a bigger one and a smaller one, and the bigger one says, My name is Kinner. This is Mian. We are come to your Inbetween for we want you to run. It is an important Run and you must do it.

I say, It is not time, I cannot make a Run, I have been on a Run, I have gone in I have come back, it is not time yet again.

They sit all shifting; a Runner does not all times fidget so, we are still until we have to move, then we all times move until we stop, then we are still again. Safe Places people, their still is all move, their talk is all broken, it is a waste. Kinner bigger one says, We are sorry. We know it is not time but this cannot wait. It is important.

I say, I will not run again without a because. I have another fruit and they look at it fast then away fast, it makes me smile.

Mian smaller one says, Do not waste time arguing with him. Make him do it. It is what he is for.

I say to them, You cannot ask a Run without a because, tell me your because then maybe I will do it if that is what I think.

Mian little one opens his mouth and Kinner bigger one touches him hard so that he yelps and shuts up. My Girl gives me another fruit; I eat it and Kinner pulls her mouth down at it.

Kinner says to me, There is a long story. It is of times many times far ago. It is not short.

I say, That is okay to me I can listen to a long story. Mian puts his face together like a sour taste and my Girl laughs at him.

Kinner says to me, First thing first there were people here. They did not come from here. They came from someplace else far away. It was a different planet.

Then I know this story and I know that Kinner tells me because she thinks I am stupid and I do not know it. But Runners know all the stories, Near Safe Place stories and Far Safe Place stories, and also Runner stories that Safe Places people do not know. I think to stop Kinner, but I have not told this story to my Girl yet, so I let Kinner talk. She tells it in Safe Place talk that is bunched in pieces, it is not pretty.

Kinner says, This different planet it is called Earth. There were people. Macus brought them here to this place. It is called Venus. The people built Big Dome. They built Near Safe Place and Far Safe Place. Macus told them to plant growing stuff in Big Dome. We do not know why. That was when people lived in Big Dome. The growing stuff stayed where Macus put it. Macus stayed in Big Dome he was happy. The people came to Venus and went to Earth and came again many times.

I say to my Girl, Macus was First Father, he made Big Dome and Near Safe Place and Far Safe Place, that is what they say in Near Safe Place.

Mian little one says, That is what is true. Macus did those things and many other things. Don't you believe that?

I say to him, I am Runner, I believe what I have to believe, it is what I do.

Mian wants to argue but Kinner yelps him, and he makes his hands go up and his mouth go closed.

Kinner says, Many times they came and went. Then it was told to them, you must all leave. You cannot live in Big Dome any more. You must go to Skyhome. Macus was not happy. He said, I do not want to leave Big Dome. We will stay in Big Dome where we are happy. Skyhome people did not like this. They tried to make people leave Big Dome. But Macus took his people that believed him. They hid in Big Dome, in secret places that Macus made for them. Soon Skyhome people went away. They left Big Dome. Then Macus brought his people out. They put together all the things that Skyhome people took apart. They made Big Dome to grow and be good. And Macus was happy again.

Kinner says, After then was Domer. He lived in Big Dome. He was all times angry. He said to the people that Macus lied. He said Macus made for them to stay in Big Dome. Domer said for that there was no reason. Domer said Macus was the evil.

Kinner and Mian make the sign over shoulder, but I and my Girl just eat fruit; Mian makes his face all together in bunches.

Kinner says, Then people did not come to Domer at all. And Domer's hate was many times bigger. He came to live alone in middle Big Dome in the growing stuff. He said, I will change the growing stuff. I will make it hate people. I will make it to eat people. Then they will have to leave Big Dome. They will do what I want. He changed the growing stuff. He put his hate inside it. Then the growing stuff became Weed. It moved out of where Macus told it to stay. The people fought with it but they could not stop it. Macus said, It is Domer his making. It must be stopped. And Macus alone went to middle Big Dome. He came to Domer. Macus had great magic but Domer his anger also was great. Weed did not stop. It moved until people had to go to Near Safe Place and Far Safe Place. They did not see Macus ever again. But Macus's magic was strong to keep Near Safe Place and Far Safe Place. And they are free from Weed.

Kinner and Mian again make the sign over shoulder; they look at me and look at my Girl, my Girl says, Father is this true?

I say, It is what they say is true, you can believe it if you want; in Far Safe Place they tell a different story, it is like this story sometimes, sometimes not.

Mian says, It is not a true story then. This is the true story. It is the only truth.

I shrug, I say to Kinner, This story is not a because, it cannot make me run.

Kinner says, The saying of this story is not ended. This is only the first thing first part. I have not said the second thing next part. For that part you must come with me to inside Near Safe Place. It is important for you to come.

Now I am surprised; they are not happy when I go to Near Safe Place and sometimes they try to hurt me there, so when I must I go only to Near Safe Place Market that is near the Wall, and go no further. I do not like it there but I am curious. I take my stick that is my Runner stick but I leave my Girl, she has fear of Near Safe Place because they throw things at her sometimes as they did to me, the children throw things and also the adults. Kinner says, You can come with me. You will be safe. Mian will come too for second thing next part.

I say, That is okay to me I can stand him. Kinner goes first, then me, and Mian comes behind; he does not like it, I hear him all times mutter mutter.

This ends first thing first part.

SECOND THING NEXT

Behind Inbetween is Wall, then there is Gate, then there is Near Safe Place as I told you. Gate is three parts, you go in first one first to wait, go in second one second to wait, go in third one last then you are in Near Safe Place market. The Runner story says that once there were great made-stuff birds in Near Safe Place, before the people came from Big Dome to live in Near Safe Place, but Near Safe Place people say that Macus made Near Safe Place to keep them safe from Weed. I will not tell them a different story; they are too foolish to listen and will say only that it is a lie.

We go through Gate into Near Safe Place; nothing grows here, it is all made-stuff places that are mostly round and black and grey with stairs; it is a Runner story that Near Safe Place people live in the dead made-stuff birds, but this, too, I will not tell them. Also here there is a heavy, thicker smell like air that is too old; my Inbetween is ugly but Near Safe Place is uglier. There are many Safe Place people, when they see me they make ugly faces with ugly eyes but they do not come near me, I want to make a face back to them but I don't.

We go through Near Safe Place until we come to a far place by the Wall where there is a square-builded place and Kinner stops there.

Kinner says, This is the start of the second thing next part. It is inside this building. I will show you.

Inside we go down many stairs then again down, I don't like it, it is too close. When we stop we are in a big empty place with carts and tools; there is nobody, just us, like everyone went fast away from everything, I do not like it either.

Kinner says, This is where the food comes from. They change it here. They make it into food we can eat. They do it in tanks. First it is in Big Dome. It is growing stuff. It grows near the bottom gate. It can't get through. The magic keeps it out. The food makers cut it. They bring it in with long scoops. They kill it. When it is dead they clean it. They put it in tanks. It grows and is food. It is what we eat.

I just look at her; she goes to a big door and opens it, she says, Come look.

Behind the big door is another room with holes in the bottom, some with white growing stuff in them. It is what Safe Place people eat, I have tasted it, it is awful. Some holes have no white stuff, only black stuff that looks dead and rotting; some holes have white and black stuff together. It has a smell worse awful than awful.

Kinner says, That is the second thing next part. Macus's magic is stopping. The magic that makes the growing-by-itself stuff become food. It is not working anymore.

Kinner and Mian make the sign and go away fast, I go also and Kinner closes the door.

Mian says, Domer is winning. Macus is losing. We have to help him or we will die.

Kinner says, In the place where Macus fights Domer there is a magic. It is a magic of Macus to make food. In the first time part the people came to Near Safe Place and Far Safe Place. They had the magic from Macus. It fed them. Now the magic is gone. We must go to Macus, we must help him to fight Domer. If we help him he will give us the magic.

Mian says, We need you to run to middle Big Dome where Macus fights Domer. We need you to take a power to Macus to help him. Macus will give you the magic. And you will bring it back. And we will eat.

Kinner says, If you do not do this Near Safe Place will be dead and so will you. It is important.

I shake my head, I say, I can live at Inbetween, there is food for me and water, I can hunt in Big Dome. Why should I do this for you?

Mian says to Kinner, I told you so. I told you not to trust Runner. He won't do it. He hates us.

I say, I hate you for you hate me, your hate came first. If you are hungry you can eat evilfruit, you can hunt, you can live Inbetween as I do you, you can run.

Kinner says, We cannot hunt. We cannot run. We cannot go to Far Safe Place. There is Big Dome between, it would kill us.

I say to her, Now I must think for a while it is important that I do this. Then I think that all I know of Big Dome is near the Wall where I run between Safe Places, that I do not know Big Dome middle at all or what is there, or how much danger it has. Also I think about Inbetween where Runners must stay, I think about how my Girl cannot come to Near Safe Place for they throw things at her, I think about how my brother died running, and how they would not give my father the healing magic when he was sick, I think about how Safe Place people need us to run but they hate us because they make us run. I think of all these things, and I do not like them. Then I look at Kinner and Mian that are Safe Place people, foolish like all Safe Places people, and I am angry.

I say to them, No. You made me what I am, you hate me for it, and for this I will not make this run for you. You can learn to hunt in Big Dome, learn to run as Runners must do, for we must hunt or we will starve. I will not help you now.

I take my stick and go up, then Kinner and Mian come behind me they do not talk. I do not trust them for they have made themselves helpless, then they come to me to make it better; they are not so good as they think they are. I do not like that they follow me but they will not stop, and together we go through Near Safe Place and I do not talk to them, they do not talk to me, it is silence.

I come to Inbetween with Kinner and Mian behind me and I call my Girl but she doesn't answer; I call all over Inbetween even by the edge to Big Dome but she doesn't answer. I turn to Kinner, I am scared-angry I say, Where is my Girl, where have you put her?

Mian smiles he says, We have her where she is safe. Until you return from middle Big Dome. Then you can have her again. If you do not go, we will keep her. If you do not come back, she will die.

Then I know them how they lie and I hate them as I hate Weed; I grab Mian by his neck I want to kill him, but Kinner she cries, Runner do not do this. If you do your Girl will die.

So I do not kill him but I hold him tight until his face is red; I shake him and throw him down and I put my stick to him, and I say, You are making me to run and so I must, but I will not forget this. If there is something not right when I come back I will kill you; if there is something not happy with my Girl I will kill you, do you understand?

I press my stick to him until he nods, he says, I understand. She will be safe. His voice is rough.

There is hate in him as there is hate in me; he stands to hold his throat and I turn away, I will not look at him. He says in a voice all rough, All runners are part Domer. It is what they are. They can go through Weed, that is the proof.

Kinner takes a sack from her clothes she gives it to me, she says, This sack has power in it. Do not open it until you reach middle Big Dome. For if you do that the power will not work.

I want to hit her too but I do not, I do not talk, I take the sack it is not heavy.

Kinner says, In middle Big Dome there is battle always. Macus and Domer have fires to their hands, they throw them. There is much noise and heat and light. You must take the magic power sack. You must hold it over your head when you are there. Then you will be safe.

I think, I will be safe when I am back and my Girl is not hurt, then I think another thought and I say to them, Mian says that all runners are part Domer and this is true. If my Girl is not safe when I come back, if you have changed her, I will bring Domer magic, I will bring it to Near Safe Place, then there will be Weed in Near Safe Place and Near Safe Place will die, and this also is true.

Kinner looks scared and Mian too, they are foolish and they will believe anything, but if they hurt my Girl I will kill them and this is all times true. I take my stick and my sack and her sack, I put them over my shoulder and I go down ropes into Big Dome and I go.

This ends second thing second part.

THIRD THING THIRD

I go down the ropes into Big Dome; here beside Wall there is a little space with no growing stuff and it is most times safe. After then comes growing stuff, some tall called Tree, some small called Bush; these are Runner words, Safe Place people do not know them. Safe Place people think all growing stuff is Weed, all is evil, they are foolish for they stay all times in one place they cannot learn. So there is a Tree and Bush place, then more and more places where there is Weed. Weed is fast, it hides then comes of a sudden to grab with arms and eat, I have seen it do this to creatures and they all times die.

It is important to go fast faster so Weed cannot grab and this is how I run. Sometimes there is a place that is okay, sometimes there is a place that was okay but now is with Weed and there I have to jump and climb and be crafty, and when I am come to my Runner rest I sit until my breathing comes easier again. Runner rest is a made-stuff place as high as Trees, there is no Weed there and it is safe; when my Girl is bigger I will bring her here so she can have a safe rest when she runs.

There is a Runner old thing called Map, it says where things are; my grand-mother had it, then my father, then my brother, now it is mine and when I am dead it will be my Girl's; Runners mark on it where they are and how they got there. Safe Places people do not have Maps, they do not care where they are or where the rest is. I sit on top of my Runner rest to look at Map; there is a Bush here with fruit growing so I eat some fruit while I look.

Runners mark only where Runners go, so when I see middle Big Dome on map I know Kinner was not all times lying, so I take fruit and I put my knife in my belt and I go.

Far Safe Place people name this Mother Jungle; they say that in middle Big Dome it is not Mother Jungle it is something else, they do not say what, but they never come here so they cannot know. In Mother Jungle there is Weed but also there is Tree and Bush with colors stuff called flowers, also there is fruit some good, some not. The most of danger is light, you run in light then light is gone, you can't tell when or why, and you can't see; some-times dark is short, sometimes long, you cannot trust it.

A Runner story says that long time back there was light in Big Dome that was not box light, that first there was nothing on top of Big Dome outside, just sky, and that light fell from the sky for many days, then there was dark many days, and box lights they were for that dark time. But the First Part people wanted to change Venus so they put growing stuff called algae in clouds that are in the sky outside of Big Dome, and the algae made dust to fall from the sky. The dust fell and fell and now it is over Big Dome, so there is no light from outside, just box light that is sometimes light and sometimes not, and that makes it dangerous. I believe this because it is a Runner story, and Runners tell truth to Runners when they know it or they don't tell at all. But I do not know how falling dust can make Venus change, except to make it very dirty. Safe Places people are foolish often, but First Part people were very strange.

The path to Far Safe Place goes through the growing stuff until it comes to the made-stuff bridge that fell; under the bridge is a deep place that has a big water noise in it, it is called Ditch. Here the path goes away toward the Wall, and here I must leave the path and the part of Big Dome that I know. I go over a big growing-stuff wall that is not Weed, then I am where it is new to me. I go on a made-stuff flat place, it is called Road Broken; I am a little scared of this new place so I am careful-curious and I look around.

I see creatures of colors moving in air, they are called birds; they dance through rain and sing like water, I have not seen them so near before. Some colored dancing birds are in Trees, also in Trees are flowers they have many colors. I look careful then I stop, for here I see only big Trees and colors dancing birds and flowers. I hear a quiet of noises: deep Ditch water, rain falling, water on Trees, singing of birds—also a manyness of color, of green Tree, brown Tree, colors dancing birds, flowers of many colors in gray rain like a magic come slowly dancing. I stand on Road Broken in the little rain and my fear goes from me, for I did not think it would be so beautiful with singing colors, that it would be so fine.

I am made stupid from beautiful, for I do not see the arm of Weed cross Road Broken and wrap on my leg; it throws me down. It pulls and I see more arms of Weed come fast from Ditch; I grab for my knife but it is tangled, then the Weed cuts my leg. This it does all times before it puts in poison and I am greatly scared, but I fight it with my Runner stick until I can get my knife, I cut the arm of Weed until it breaks, then I am free but other arms are coming, and I run for Tree and go up fast-faster-fastest, the colors dancing birds scream and fly, and I hold to Tree until my breathing comes. Weed is two parts, one part is arms that hold and poison to make creatures stiff but not to kill or eat; that is for the second part where the arms start. Second part of Weed is all white with mouth and teeth, it eats creatures that is how it kills them, it is awful.

Weed arms move on Road Broken waiting for me, and I am angry mostly to myself, it is my fault for being stupid with beautiful. When my breathing comes easier I open my sack, I take a strip of cloth and put it on my cut; it is not bad and it has no poison in it.

Weed will wait for long time, so I go up again until Tree touches the next Tree, and there I go across with breath tight. Old Trees groan, bending, then I am in next Tree, then next Tree, then next until Weed lies behind on Road Broken where I cannot see it. Weed cannot come up Tree, so I rest and mark upon Map of Ditch with Weed, then I eat fruit and stretch and sleep.

When I awake I come through tops of Trees to Road Broken again, but here there is no Ditch and no Weed, and I am pleased. I eat some fruit from the Tree, then I come down; Road Broken is wider here, with tiny growing things like leaves called Grass. I walk until Trees stop, then there is a place of falling down made-stuff buildings, but not like Safe Place places that are dead made-stuff birds; these buildings have flat sides going up far, and where some are broken the pieces lie around them like skirts. They are on Map, but Map doesn't tell of all the colors, for they are red and blue and green and yellow, not like Near Safe Place that is gray and black; here it is bright with flowers brightness, it is okay to me.

I go through this place on Road Broken where it is covered in Grass. The wind is like tiny breathings, there are clouds with tiny rain falling, it is quiet but not like Mother Jungle quiet for here there is nothing moving; it is strange. Through this I go for a long time; I stop to eat and drink, then I go for a long time again all day. Sometimes I see creatures, they are with caution to me as

I to them, but there is no Weed and for this I feel a little better, but not too much. Then I see where the buildings end; beyond is more Grass, then Bushes, then Trees, like a second Mother Jungle. It is not on Map, but I am too tired for more strangeness this day, I will wait to sleep for rest.

There is a building near that looks safe, it is empty inside with small lights in boxes, some bright some dark. Also there are stairs; I go up them to a place where there is a window broken and stuff in bunches underneath it, like leaves that are dry, it is safe. I go to second Mother Jungle for dead Tree stuff and I make a fire inside by window broken, for creatures and Weed fear fire and they stay gone. After I eat, I sit by the fire and I think of my Girl that they should not hurt her, of Near Safe Place that they lie to me, of the Runner stories that do not tell of all the singing or dancing or colors that are in Big Dome, where it is away from the Wall. Also I think of the Macus magic that Kinner told of, I do not know to believe or not, it is a puzzle.

In Far Safe Place they say before Macus was Seeder, he came and builded Big Dome to find things out; then he made for it to change slow-slowly outside where Big Dome is not. Also Seeder builded Skyhome, up beyond Big Dome; he said for people to go to Skyhome for it was time. Then Macus argued with Seeder, for Macus was a worker, he worked in Big Dome and he loved it. So Macus his people hid, they stayed in Big Dome, and Seeder his people went to Skyhome, and that is where they are. Far Safe Place people say Seeder will come back, he will bring Big Rain to wash Big Dome and wash all outside that is Venus, so people can go there and be safe. They want this, but still they will not go into Big Dome, and this also is a puzzle.

Far Safe Place people say also that there were many people like Domer that wanted to leave Big Dome, and that Macus's people fought with Domer's people and there was much death. They say that Domer made Weed to win this fight, but Weed ate Domer's people and Macus's people both, it was not particular. Near Safe Place people say Macus was First Father, but Far Safe Place people say Seeder was First Father. But Safe Places people do not know Big Dome, for they never come here, and I think maybe they do not know Seeder or Macus or Domer, that it is all just a Safe Place story and it is not true, is what I think, maybe, I don't know. Then I think I will know when I get to middle Big Dome, I will know if the stories are true, if Macus and Domer are there with fire throwing, and it makes me scared so I put Kinner's magic power sack under my head, for luck.

My fire goes low and I sleep, but in the middle of sleep the builded place wakes up; it groans and makes tiny shakings and hissings and I am halfway in air when I wake, so scared I yell and grab my stuff and run fast to outside of there. I run to Trees fast like birds, I go up a Tree fast-faster and there I sit shaking all over, and I look back.

The building stays put, groaning and hissing, then a cloud comes from the top of it. I look up at it and I see all the lights in boxes every place in Big Dome are shining, and all the smaller lights in boxes in the builded places are shining, and the light along Road Broken are shining, and I think that maybe they shine because the building hisses and makes clouds, but that is foolish; it is a mystery and I don't like it. After a long time I take my Map and mark of this, then I come down and move quick until I am away from there.

I do not want to sleep again for I am scared, also it is good to move while there is light, for the light may go away, and so I walk through Second Mother Jungle. Here the Trees are mostly in rows with some fruit, some not, and little Bushes not too many, and no place for Weed to hide. Second Mother Jungle is smaller than Mother Jungle, for soon I am out of it again and there are more made-stuff places; they are not hissing but still I have no trust, for the hissing place was quiet too before it woke up, maybe to eat me.

I do not want to go on, for fear of buildings that might hiss, but to go back I must go by the building that does hiss, and so instead I sit at the edge of Second Mother Jungle and I think many thoughts. I am almost to middle Big Dome, for Big Dome top here is highest, then it goes down again. I think about Macus and Domer throwing fire, but I also think that if I go back, Near Safe Place people will know I did not go to Macus and they will hurt my Girl. I do not see light or hear noise from fire throwing, but there is much I do not know here, and if buildings wake up to eat people, maybe Macus and Domer do fight in middle Big Dome, maybe it is not just a Safe Places story and maybe they will throw fire at me and I will die. And if I die then I cannot return to Near Safe Place and they may kill my Girl, and then what is the use? Then I am scared and I feel a blackness, like a dark time when there is much danger but it is too black to be safe, and there is nothing I can do.

I think then, I am Runner; I have run farther than my brother or my father or my grandmother, maybe farther than any Runner. I have seen colors dancing birds and flowers and hissing clouding places, I have seen the danger of middle Big Dome that it is stranger than strange and greatly beautiful. And I am scared, and I am tired, but I am still alive, I am not hurt, and I am not like Safe Places people that think all strange is deadly and all beautiful is bad. And I think, this strange run is *my* story, my Runner story that only I can tell, but I cannot tell a coming-back-not-finishing story, a story with no end. I am still scared, but the blackness is not so bad in me now. So for that, and for my Girl that I love her, I take my stick and sacks, I touch my knife in my belt, I stand and for luck I make the sign over shoulder. Then I go in.

This ends third thing third part.

Fourth Thing Last

Here in middle Big Dome the made-stuff buildings are bigger on the bottom, then smaller, then smaller like steps going up, and all glowing white with flowers down the sides bright as colors dancing birds with a sweet smell. These places have windows some broken some not, and some with words but I cannot read them. I am more careful than careful here, for there is no Weed but there may be other things, and I am cautious-curious and make myself to walk without noise. There is a new quiet of noises, of rain and tiny wind breathings and something also like a bigger breathing, beat to beat to beat, like a heart. I stop to listen to it; it makes my skin go cold, so I put Kinner's magic power sack over my head before I go on.

I walk slow, then slower, to the middle; soon I see where the buildings stop and I am even more slow. I hide at a corner of the last builded place, for the beat to beat is stronger here, and I hold my breathing, then slow-slowly do I look.

There is Grass, then there is dirt, then there is water, like in a cup but a muchness of it, gray-blue water that is just water moving by itself, beat to beat to beat against the dirt, and far away there is more Grass across the water, and more builded places, and that is all. I come slow around the last builded place and I look with great carefulness, but that is all there is in middle Big Dome, just Grass and water moving gray under clouds, and small rain falling. No Macus, no Domer, no Seeder, no fire-throwing fights; middle Big Dome is empty, they are all gone, there is only me.

I say, very quiet, Macus? Water goes beat to beat, that is all. I say, louder, Domer? There is no answer. I find a piece of dead Tree by the water and I throw it in, it makes a splash but nothing happens. And I think, is it for this that I have come, for a muchness of water and rain falling, and nothing else? I find a piece of rock and throw it, and nothing happens; I find a bigger piece and throw it, then a piece of fallen made-stuff that is huge and I throw it, and I yell for Macus, for Domer, for Seeder, for anyone, and the water goes beat to beat and nothing happens, there is no one in middle Big Dome but me, there is no magic here, there is no help.

Then I am with great anger, and I take the magic power sack, I rip it open. Inside there is only a piece of broken window tied with ribbon, and some paper with writing, and some powder that is blue and red and yellow; wind takes it from my hand to the water and it is gone, and that is what Safe Place people think is magic, for they are foolish, they live in lies. I throw Kinner's big magic into the water and throw the sack in too, and the water moves beat to beat to beat and nothing changes. All the things that I have seen, all the things that I have learned, are a waste; Safe Places people will die and I will die, there will be an end to Runners and to all stories, for there is no magic in middle Big Dome and I think there never was. I do many foolish things then, beside the water, until I cannot move again and cannot think, and a darkness comes.

When the darkness goes my anger goes also. I know that I must go back to Near Safe Place, I must tell them that there is no magic for them, and there is a great sadness in me, for I think now that I hate the Safe Places people but I cannot live without them; and they have come to me when they hate for help, their fear is so great they have forced me to help, but I cannot save them. I take my Runner stick and my sack, I walk not looking to the builded place; I think of my Girl that I love her and want to hold her, and I put my face with tears up to the rain, and then I see the Sign.

I know this Sign, in Near Safe Place they name it Macus Sign, in Far Safe Place they name it Seeder Sign but it is the same sign. The Safe Places Signs are dull and do not move, but this sign moves in the wind and it has colors that dance, it changes and glows, it is like a magic by itself. I see it on a made-stuff piece that sticks from a building it looks like this:

I stop and stare, for it is beautiful and strange and I do not understand what a Safe Places Sign does here in middle Big Dome. I touch it, it is real, it is smooth and cool, and first I think that maybe it is a Sign from Macus that there is help, but soon I know that is not so. That was just a story, I know that now, but still the Sign dances with colors and I cannot move from it, there is something here that I need to know. For if there is no Macus or Seeder or Domer, then there are only people and we must make our own magic, it is for us to do.

Then I sit and I think hardest of all times. I think of all the stories, and I think that when the First Part people went to Skyhome, some people stayed in Big Dome, for they knew it was good and beautiful. But they fought and made Weed and Weed kept them from Big Dome. And now they fear all of Big Dome and will not live here, and that is foolish, for here is where we belong. In Big Dome there are fruits and creatures for people to eat, not the white awful stuff that is Safe Places food; there is water and rain, there are buildings to live in. It is a stupid thing to die in Safe Place, when there is so much in Big Dome to help us live. And I think, there is also much to learn here, there is the hissing building, there is the muchness of water like a beating heart. There is danger, but in all things there is danger; there is much that is strange, but strangeness is not an evil thing.

Then I take the Sign, it comes easy into my hands, it makes colors between my fingers. I will take the Sign to Near Safe Place and Far Safe Place, I will tell the people that the Sign is Macus magic and Seeder magic that they gave to me. I will tell them that Seeder and Macus say it is time to come to middle Big Dome, or they will starve; I will tell them that the black food-killing magic also is a sign for them to come. I will have the Sign and they must believe it, or they must say that Seeder, Macus, Domer are a lie. And if Seeder, Macus, Domer are a lie, then people have no reason to stay in Safe Places, and again they must come. Then they will live, and my Girl will live, and we will be where we belong.

I put the Sign in my sack, I take my Runner stick, but before I go I take the Map and mark upon it, Here is the Sign place where it said, Come home.

Then I go.

ASTEROIDS AND COMETS

ESSAY BY
William K. Hartmann

SPECULATION BY
Paul Preuss

THE BILLION OTHER PLANETS: ASTEROIDS AND COMETS

William K. Hartmann

DICTIONARIES AND MANY ASTRONOMY BOOKS SAY that there are only nine planets. This may be right according to classical definitions, but it presents a misleading view of the solar system. To begin with, there are more than 3,000 other bodies moving in *known orbits* around the Sun. Based on statistics of their orbits and discovery rates, astronomers estimate a total population of more than 1 billion objects still to be discovered! They are small, but each is its own world. Some are rocky; others are predominantly icy. Long regarded as only distant curiosities or omens of astrological superstition, they are now coming into their own, due to recent discoveries and resulting new interest from planners of space exploration. They are the asteroids and comets.

Asteroids and comets are the rocky and icy debris left over from the formation of the planets. Most of the measured worldlets are about 2 to 60 kilometers across. But several dozen asteroids span hundreds of kilometers; the largest, 1 Ceres, is 1020 kilometers wide. (Asteroids are properly referred by their catalog number, listed in order of discovery and name.)

Historically, asteroids and comets have been treated quite separately. Although they look different and were initially considered totally different phenomena, the history of their study has slowly shown us that they are connected.

Comets were discovered in prehistoric times by naked eye. Their name comes from a Greek root for "long hair." The appearance, every decade or so, of a bright comet in our skies was regarded superstitiously as a portent. When it appeared in A.D. 66, Halley's comet was said to have heralded the destruction of Jerusalem in A.D. 70. After five trips around the Sun, it returned in 451; Europeans thought it marked the defeat of Attila the Hun. In 1066 it presided over the Norman conquest of England. In 1456 its appearance coincided with a threatened invasion of Europe by the Turks; Pope Calixtus III urged prayer for deliverance from "the devil, the Turk, and the comet."

How did humans make the transition from thinking about comets as ghostly celestial beacons to thinking about their actual, physical qualities? A first step was understanding their distance, their place in the solar system. Seneca, the Roman contemporary of Jesus, wrote "Some day there will arise a man who will demonstrate in what regions of the heavens the comets take their way." Merely phrasing the question was a giant advance over speaking about mysterious celestial omens! The man in question turned out to be Tycho Brahe, who in 1577 correctly concluded that comets were more distant than the Moon, based on his inability to detect any stereoscopic effect (or parallax, as astronomers say) when he observed the same comet from widely separated locations.

HOW ASTEROIDS WERE DISCOVERED

Asteroids were recognized later, in a series of discoveries around 1800. In the late 1700s, two German astronomers, Titius and Bode, discovered a simple mathematical relation that expresses the spacing of the planets. It seemed just a mathematical curiosity until Uranus was discovered in 1781, just in the place "predicted" by the rule. Taking the rule more seriously, astronomers now realized that there was a "gap" between Mars and Jupiter, at 2.8 AU from the Sun. The Titius-Bode rule predicted a planet at this distance. Bolstered by the Uranus discovery, several astronomers started searching this region betweeen Mars and Jupiter. On the first night of 1801, Italian astronomer Giuseppe Piazzi discovered Ceres just at the predicted distance of 2.8 AU! Initially, he regarded it as a new planet, but its small size and faintness, just at the limit of naked-eye visibility, troubled astronomers. Another problem emerged in a few years. Between 1802 and 1807, three more small planetlike bodies were found, also between 2.3 and 2.8 AU. They were even smaller and fainter. As more astronomers searched, more objects were discovered, mostly in the same region. Since they were small and there was more than one, it hardly seemed appropriate to call them planets. A new name was given: asteroids.*

By 1890, 300 asteroids were known. In 1891, German astronomer Max Wolf began using photography to search for them, and the number discovered shot upward. In the twentieth century, they have been discovered both during purposeful searches and accidentally, as astronomers photographed various parts of the sky. A discoverer gets the privilege of naming them, and so they bear names covering a wide range of human interests, from mythology (1915 Quetzalcoatl, an Aztec god) and politicians (1932 Hooveria!) to spouses and

---

*Once they were also called "planetoids," which makes more sense, since "asteroids" means "little star." But the word "planetoids" has virtually died out.

other lovers. Only those whose orbits are precisely known are given permanent catalog numbers and names; nevertheless, this list passed the 3,000 mark on February 17, 1984!

Unknown to the astronomers who discovered the first asteroids, another series of discoveries around 1800 clarified the nature of these worldlets. Through the ages there have been reports of stones falling from the sky, but "sensible" people knew that this was merely myth. Then, in 1794, German physicist E. F. Chladnie reported a detailed study showing that these stones were, in fact, different from normal stones but similar to each other. He concluded that these objects, called meteorites, actually *had* fallen from the sky and were not terrestrial rocks. Now a great controversy began among naturalists, even spreading to the fledgling United States. Naturalist and politician Thomas Jefferson reportedly remarked that it would be easier to believe that Yankee professors lie than that stones would fall from heaven. (The story may be merely apochryphal.)

The august French Academy, scientific establishment of the day, dismissed celestial stones as superstition. They were overly skeptical, probably because many meteorites had been taken by their peasant finders to the nearest local center of authority, the provincial church. A Yugoslavian fall in 1751, for example, had been carefully collected by the bishop of Zagreb and sent to the Austrian emperor. Champions of rationalism, the French academicians were inclined to treat priestly curiosities as products of superstition.

As if in answer, the Great Meteorite Maker in the Sky arranged for a large meteorite to explode over a French town in 1803, pelting the area with stones. The Academy sent the noted physicist J. B. Biot to investigate. His report is a historic document of science, methodically constructing an irrefutable chain of evidence, using eye-witness accounts, measurements of the 2-by-6 kilometer impact area, and specimens of the meteorites themselves. This report established that stones do, in fact, fall from space. (This episode has often been quoted by pseudoscientists in defense of the proposition that UFOs, dragons, or whatever are also real, just because the scientific establishment refuses to accept them. The analogy is not good, however, because Biot was able to come up with much better physical evidence than the defenders of alien spaceships or monsters.)

Some decades later, scientists began to understand a related celestial curiosity—meteors. Distinct from meteorites, which are rocky objects that hit the ground, meteors are the fleeting "shooting stars" that burn in the atmosphere but do not hit the surface. They are tiny dust particles, but like meteorites, they collide with Earth from space. As early as 1861, the astronomer Daniel Kirkwood, better known for the discovery of gaps in the asteroid belt, argued that meteors are debris from comets. By 1866, the Italian astronomer G. V. Schiaparelli, who achieved fame as the discoverer of the so-called canals on Mars, proved that Perseid meteors, a group encountered by Earth each August, are objects scattered along the orbit of comet Swift-Tuttle. Thus, by the end of the nineteenth century, scientists knew that most meteors are dust particles dislodged from comets, and they recognized the four classes of interplanetary debris: comets, asteroids, meteorites, and meteors.

During the twentieth century, the links among these classes grew stronger. We now know that meteorites are fragments of asteroids and, perhaps in a few cases, of comets. All four types of objects are examples of debris left over from the formation of planets.

Several lines of evidence support this. For instance, chemical studies can show that meteorites formed 4.6 billion years ago, the date of formation of the Earth and Moon. The same studies show that meteorites have had a history of collision and fragmentation. Studies of mineral chemistry in meteorites—showing the pressures and temperatures at which the minerals solidified—reveal that many types of meteorites originated inside parent bodies that must have been the same size as the larger asteroids, a few hundred kilometers in diameter. Some meteorites, such as the nearly pure nickel-iron types, have come from larger bodies that were molten. When the interiors of the asteroids melted (possibly heat produced by radioactivity), the iron drained to the centers and rocky mantles floated to the surfaces of the asteroids, just as iron sinks in a smelter vat while the rocky slag floats. Other meteorite types preserve primitive minerals that never melted. These minerals often have a high water content and appear to be unchanged from the days when our solar system began.

Various chemical properties show that the meteorites came from several different types of parent bodies, rather than from a single exploded planet, as was once thought. For instance, many meteorites are jumbled rocks composed of different types from different sources. An iron piece may be cemented next to a piece that was never melted. Such rocks probably formed during collisions of asteroids, as fragments blew apart, mixed, and fell back to form a new layer on the asteroid surface. They were then cemented together by pressure inside the asteroid to form new rocks. Many asteroids may have their entire interiors formed in this way; they may be rubble piles of mixed cemented rock fragments, chips, and dust. Later collisions broke many of them, producing the meteorites now in our museums.

In support of these findings, astronomers have calculated from the number of asteroids in the belt that asteroids must collide occasionally. Many of the original one hundred-kilometer-class asteroids have been broken, producing the thousands of small asteroids and meteorites—their fragments. Geochemists can determine the dates of the collisions that sent shock waves through many meteorite specimens and broke them into their present sizes. These dates are scattered randomly every few hundred million years during solar system history, confirming that the major asteroid collisions were sporadic.

In the 1970s, astronomers began to add new detail to the asteroid story. With more sophisticated instruments they were able to take spectra of the sunlight reflected from a variety of asteroids—that is, to break the light down into a spectrum and analyze information in the light about the materials which reflected it. Their spectroscopic studies showed different classes of asteroids with different spectral, or color-reflecting, properties. Some asteroids have almost exactly the same spectra as some meteorites. This confirms the theory that many meteorites are pieces of asteroids and allows us to estimate the actual composition of certain asteroids. We can match spectra and then say that a certain asteroid has rock types like the similar meteorite specimens. Scientists even think that in a few cases they can say what asteroid a particular meteorite came from.

EARTH-CROSSING ASTEROIDS

These discoveries raise the question of how the asteroid fragments could get from the parent asteroid to Earth. This question was answered some decades ago with the discovery of a class of asteroids called Apollo asteroids. They are named after the first known example, 1862 Apollo. Their special characteristic is that their orbits cross Earth's. Asteroids of this type have the potential for colliding with Earth, at least if their orbit crosses Earth's orbit close enough to our orbital plane. Many of these so-called Earth-crossers swing back toward the asteroid belt and may have their farthest point from the Sun in, or even beyond, the belt. Such an arrangement suggests that they were originally thrown out of the belt. A mechanism for doing this has now been discovered; the gravitational influence of nearby Jupiter, the most massive planet, can disturb the orbits of certain asteroids and fling them into the inner solar system. Apparently this happens occasionally, so that a constant supply of new asteroid material is brought into the inner solar system from the huge "reservoir" in the belt. Further confirmation of this idea comes from orbits measured from photographs of a few meteorites falling into the atmosphere: They were on orbits like Apollo asteroids' orbits.

More and more spectroscopic matches are turning up between Apollo asteroids and meteorites. For example, a common type of meteorite matches the spectrum of asteroid 1685 Toro, and some researchers believe that these rocks may be debris blasted off Toro by impacts. Another interesting match is between a rare type of meteorite and a small, obscure, Apollo asteroid tentatively called 1983 RD (it was discovered in 1983 and is not yet cataloged with a number and name). These meteorites and 1983 RD, in turn, match the spectrum of one of the largest asteroids, 4 Vesta, located in the belt. Researchers suspect that 1983 RD might be a kilometer-scale fragment blown off Vesta, reaching an Earth-crossing orbit, and that the meteorites might, in turn, be pieces of 1983 RD. Relative to these meteorites, then, 1983 RD might be the parent body and Vesta, the grandparent!

We've said that both asteroids and comets are examples of the debris left over when the planets formed. We can see now how this statement applies to asteroids: In the planet-forming process, planets grew by aggregation of asteroid-size bodies called *planetesimals*. Apparently this process never went to completion between Mars and Jupiter—the "gap" where the Titius-Bode rule predicted a planet. Instead, the gravitational forces from Jupiter tended to disturb motions in this region and keep those particular planetesimals—now called asteroids—from aggregating. This is lucky for us, because the asteroids now offer us a frozen tableau of the solar system's formative days.

But where do comets come into the story? How do they relate to planet-forming debris? Why do comets look so different from asteroids, if they are related?

COMETS AND THE SOLAR SYSTEM

The short answer is that comets are asteroidlike planetesimals, but they are the ones with a lot of ice, because they formed in the colder, outer parts of the solar system. Part of this answer has emerged from direct observations of comets seen from Earth. Gases given off by comets could only come by sublimation* of ices, such as frozen water (H_2O), frozen methane (CH_4), and frozen ammonia (NH_3)—materials known to be common in the cold regions of the outer planets beyond the asteroid belt. Among the atoms and molecules in comets, revealed by spectroscopes, are fragments of these ices: carbon, hydrogen, and OH (called hydroxyl). The fundamental definition of a *comet*, then, is this: a small body with high ice content, which can come close enough to the Sun for the sunlight to sublime the ice so that the object can give off gas. The

---

*Sublimation is a word for the transition from a solid state (ice) directly to gas, without passing through the liquid phase. It is similar to evaporation, the familiar transition from liquid to gas. In space, heated ices yield gases directly. A familiar example of ice subliming is dry ice, which changes directly into a gray mist, CO_2 gas.

reason that comets look different from asteroids is that comets give off gas and asteroids don't. But, interestingly, when a comet gets far enough from the Sun—beyond 4 AU or so—it gets too cold for the ice to sublime and spends much time looking like an asteroid. This causes some problems and confusion for observers, as we will see in a moment.

Where, then, do comets come from? Most newly discovered comets are entering the inner solar system not on orbits that come from among the giant planets but from orbits that come from beyond Pluto! This suggests there is a reservoir of inactive, frozen comets beyond Pluto. How did it get there? The chain of evidence to answer this question starts with observations of the variations of composition among planets and asteroids. Recent asteroid observations show a zonal pattern of compositions in the belt: The asteroids near the inner edge of the belt are generally rocky, with familiar lava rocklike minerals. Many probably have considerable metal content. The outer belt is dominated by a different kind of rocky material, with unfamiliar minerals. These are black minerals, probably carbon-rich, which means that these asteroids are blacker than a blackboard. We can call them carbonaceous asteroids. They seem similar in composition to a type of black meteorite, called carbonaceous meteorites (or, more correctly, carbonaceous chondrite meteorites.) Both carbonaceous meteorites and carbonaceous asteroids have water (H_2O molecules) chemically bound in their rock-forming minerals. Beyond the outer belt, circling the Sun in Jupiter's orbit, are two more groups of asteroids. One group lies ahead of Jupiter, and the other behind. They are called Trojan asteroids, because they are named after heroes of Homer's epics of the Trojan wars. The Trojans are also very dark but most have reddish-black or reddish-brown colors, instead of the more neutral outer-belt objects. We'll call them reddish carbonaceous asteroids. Their colors are believed to come from organic compounds, rich in carbon (C), hydrogen (H), oxygen (O), and nitrogen (N) atoms. From Jupiter's region outward, spectra show that most small bodies—the moons of the giant planets—contain a large fraction of ice.

Now note the progression of compositions as we go out from the Sun. *Inner* planets are made of metal and rock. *Inner belt* asteroids are also rocky and metallic. *Outer belt* asteroids are richer in carbon minerals and water. The reddish carbonaceous asteroids have water and additional organic compounds. Most of the satellites of nearby Jupiter are made partly of carbonaceous or reddish carbonaceous material and partly of ice. Satellites of planets *beyond Jupiter* are made mostly of ices. Chemists who have examined this progression realized that it goes from minerals that can form only at high temperatures to minerals that form at low temperatures.

After the Sun formed, the leftover gas around the Sun was cooling from initial temperatures of perhaps 2,000°C. As the gas cooled, mineral crystals condensed, just as snowflakes condense in cooling clouds above Earth. Far from the Sun, the gases got so cold that literal snowflakes—crystals of ice—were the dominant material to condense. Nearer the Sun, the gas never got this cold, and only crystals stable at higher temperatures, like rock-forming minerals, could condense. In fact, it never got cold enough in the inner solar system for ices to condense, although minerals at intermediate temperatures (from Earth's region to the outer asteroid belt) could trap certain amounts of water in their crystals.

Now we have explained why the solar system goes from rocky bodies near the Sun to icy bodies far from the Sun. Asteroids lie near the transition zone. According to these facts, the primordial solar system must have looked like a giant asteroid belt, but the planetesimals in the outer region were icy.

THE ORIGIN OF COMETS

Now we are ready to ask again: Where did the comets come from? When the giant planets formed, there must have been many icy planetesimals—dirty, floating icebergs of ice and reddish carbonaceous dirt—drifting among them. These could not last for long. Some collided with giant planets, blazing into their vast, dark atmospheres, never to be seen again. Many others had near misses. The gravity of the giant planets then deflected their orbits, just as Jupiter sent the Pioneeer and Voyager space vehicles toward Saturn and interstellar space. The surviving icy planetesimals then ended up being thrown into a swarm of bodies with orbits that spend most of their time beyond Pluto. This swarm has been called the Oort cloud, after the astronomer who first suggested its presence. The Oort cloud is the reservoir of comets! More than 1 billion icy planetesimals—inactive comets—are estimated to be in the Oort cloud. Hence the name of this chapter.

If comets are mostly in the Oort cloud, how do we ever see them passing near us, among the inner planets? An inactive comet in the Oort cloud barely feels the tug of the Sun. Over centuries, however, its orbit may be disturbed by the gravity of a nearby passing star, much father still from the Sun. So an occasional comet finds itself deflected onto a new orbit falling toward the Sun.

Initially in deep freeze in the Oort cloud, the comet is warmer as it approaches the Sun and the inner solar system. The ices start to sublime, emitting gas directly from the surface and perhaps building up gas pressure in subsurface cracks and layers of dust. Different ices sublime at different temperatures and distances from the Sun: water ice (frozen H_2O) is probably the major active component in most comet activity that we witness in the inner solar system.

Eventually the pressure of the gas may blow off sections of the dusty, ice-depleted, crusty layers on the surface, explaining observed outbursts of dust and gas in approaching comets. Closer to the Sun, the ice sublimes more furiously, and whole pieces of icy comet may break away; we have observed the breakup of some comets into several separate subcomets, some of which burn out. This also explains a radar observation of a close-approaching 1983 comet, which revealed not a single asteroidlike planetesimal at its center but rather a whole swarm of various-sized particles. All the time the comet is blowing off gas, the gas carries away dust particles weathered out of the dirty ice—particles that have been frozen in the ice since the dawn of solar system history. This explains meteor streams and showers—they are the dusty debris left scattered along the comet's orbit, as the gas dissipates into space. Finally, the comet rounds the Sun and heads back out into distant space, where it once again becomes cold and inactive.

Another fate can befall certain comets. On its way in or out, a comet can encounter a giant planet again and get thrown onto yet another new orbit that keeps it in the inner solar system. The most famous of all comets—Halley's—is an intermediate case. It is on an orbit that reaches out only a little beyond Neptune, bringing it back every 76 years. In the more extreme cases, perhaps after several near-encounters with planets, the orbit can end up looking like an Apollo asteroid's orbit, crossing the orbit of one or more inner planets.

A CONNECTION

Now we find an interesting tie-in between asteroids and comets. Recall that Apollo asteroids also arrived on Earth-crossing orbits because of the gravitational forces of Jupiter and may have been further altered by near-encounters with inner planets. A comet may undergo similar near-encounters. Thus, orbital evolution can produce both asteroids and comets on nearly indistinguishable types of orbits.

Having arrived as a new resident of the inner solar system, such a comet may have enough ice to remain active only for 1,000 trips around the Sun. But then what? When the ices are gone, there may be a residue of rocky and dusty debris, forming an inert body. This so-called burnt-out comet may have a surface of soil, a dust-ball aggregate interior, and possible pockets of hidden ice. From the outside, it may look just like an Apollo asteroid! Not only telescopic observers on Earth would have a hard time telling the difference; even as astronaut in a nearby spacecraft might have difficulty telling whether the seemingly asteroidlike object contained hidden residues of internal ice. Perhaps spectroscopic studies would reveal the difference, or closeup geologic studies might reveal that a burnt-out comet had fewer craters on its surface, since its surface is relatively young—dating to the time since the last cometary activity. Most asteroid surfaces, in contrast, have been battered for billions of years.

Indeed, current research abounds wtih controversial suggestions of specific objects, now cataloged as Apollo asteroids, that may be burnt-out comets. One interesting example is Apollo asteroid 2201 Oljato. It crosses the orbits of both Earth and Venus. When the planet Venus approached Oljato's orbit, detectors in the Pioneer spacecraft orbiting Venus picked up odd signals, reported by scientists in 1984. These signals could be explained if gas ions were being detected. Oljato itself was not nearby, but in a different part of the orbit. Thus, the observations imply that debris might be spread along Oljato's orbit (like meteors in a comet's orbit), and that these debris are emitting gas! Oljato may be a nearly burnt-out comet, still containing ice pockets and occasionally blowing off bits of ice-impregnated debris. The debris would travel in adjacent orbits and emits puffs of gas, as detected by Pioneer. In support of this interpretation, Oljato has spectral properties unusual compared to most asteroids, according to data assembled by Maryland astronomer Lucy McFadden in 1984.

MINING THE ASTEROIDS

Our understanding of asteroids, comets, and interplanetary debris is not merely of academic interest. Slowly space exploration planners are realizing that supposedly empty interplanetary space is richly dotted with thousands of worldlets fertile with resources. These resources should interest not only astronauts, but anyone concerned about Earth's future. As I have discussed in more detail in my book *Out of the Cradle* earthbound society faces severe depletion of metals, petroleum, and other natural resources in the next century, based on current growth trends, even if geologists find several times the presently known deposits. Yet we are discovering that we are surrounded by drifting space resources—fragments of the interiors of other worldlets. Some are nearly pure nickel-iron, like the iron meteorites that fall on Earth; these are remnants of metallic cores of once-melted asteroids. Others are rock resembling common types of stone meteorite, containing not only iron flecks but concentrations of extremely valuable platinum-group metals. Still others contain water-bearing minerals, from which water could be collected by mild heating; burnt-out comets may contain ice.

Examples of all these types probably cross Earth's orbit. Several dozen Apollo objects are already known, mostly ranging from 1 to 30 kilometers across. Searches for smaller, fainter ones are underway. Among asteroids, as you decrease the size by a factor of 10, you get about one hundred times as many objects. Thus, astronomers expect eventually to find hundreds or thousands of Apollo objects in the size range of 100 meters and up. Many will pass quite close to Earth. Apollo asteroids are already known which are easier to reach and return from (in terms of total rocket fuel or energy) than the Moon! Modest-sized individual objects of selected types (say, of kilometer scale) contain selected resources adequate to supply Earth's needs at present use rates for years! These modest objects would have incredible economic values of billions of dollars, comparable to the costs of going out there, finding them, and mining them. As we on Earth use up the last reserves of our own resources, digging ever deeper for ores and burning ever lower-grade fuels that cause more pollution, the costs of Earth resources will increase. Meanwhile, as we develop shuttles and space stations, costs of space operations will decrease. Thus, space resources will become ever more attractive economically.

There is an additional attraction to space resources. If we can set up giant orbiting processing facilities, powered by giant solar panels that collect "free" sunlight as an energy source, we can begin processing the space resource in space. Instead of dumping industrial pollution—coal smoke, toxic wastes, radioactive materials, strip-mine debris, refinery tailings—into our own air and waters, we could begin to move industrial production off Earth. Space wastes, in the form of gases and fine dust, would be swept out of the solar system by the ever-cleansing stream of solar gases, called the solar wind.

Space production might occur partially at the asteroid or comet being mined, and partly in Earth orbit, where materials are brought back for final processing. Note that moving such materials around in space is often much cheaper than bringing materials "up" from Earth, because much energy is required to lift material "uphill" from Earth, while very little is required to escape the tiny gravity of an asteroid. Planners have suggested ways of mounting engines on small (100-meter class) asteroids and moving them into Earth orbit, where they could then be processed. One such method is the mass driver, an engine that electromagnetically accelerates packets of asteroid dust off the asteroid at high speed, thus using waste material from the asteroid itself as the rocket fuel to drive the asteroid slowly forward. Over a period of months or years, the asteroid could be slowly maneuvered out of its original orbit, brought toward Earth, and placed into a new orbit around Earth.

The products of space production could be used in two ways. First, some materials might be returned to Earth; this would especially apply to materials like platinum, with extremely high value in dollars per pound, making it cost-effective to bring it back to the ground. Second, some materials would be used to expand space stations, solar collectors, and industrial facilities in space, so that humanity could accelerate the process of reducing our industrial ravaging of Earth while producing a productive economy in space.

There are many dangerous forks in the road leading to this dream. If individual nations attempt to grab space resources for themselves, they will increase the economic gap between rich and poor nations and thus reduce world stability. But if we can figure out a way for the advanced nations to proceed with acquisition of space resources while spreading the benefit throughout the world economy, we will increase the stability and peace of the world. If we develop energy resources such as solar energy and find metals and other materials distributed through space, then Earth's nations may no longer have to pursue deception and militarism to control strategic areas like the Persian Gulf. In *Out of the Cradle*, I proposed a Golden Rule of Space Exploration:

Each step in space exploration should be carried
out in such a way as to decrease, not aggravate,
tensions on Earth.

To implement such a golden rule is a social problem, not a scientific problem. It requires that the politicians and writers and molders of public opinion be just as involved in space exploration as the scientists.

We have learned that Earth is a Hawaii in the midst of a planetary system of beautiful, but forbidding, Siberias. If we have the necessary vision, we may learn to use the asteroids and comets to begin to allow the whole Earth to revert to its beautiful and natural state while expanding humanity into a vigorous interplanetary civilization.

HALLEY'S COMET

William K. Hartmann

B Y THE 1700S ASTRONOMERS had learned how to calculate orbits of comets after observing them cross the sky from night to night. When the English astronomer Edmund Halley (1656–1742) studied records of historic comets, he found something strange. A comet that had been seen in 1682, when he was 26, followed the same orbit as comets seen in 1456, 1531, and 1607. This comet seemed to return every 75 or 76 years! Halley predicted it would be seen again in 1758. It was indeed spotted on Christmas night in 1758, sixteen years after Halley died. Astronomers named the comet in Halley's honor and memory.

In 1910 the comet returned in a particularly favorable way. Not only did it pass near Earth as it looped around the Sun; Earth passed through its tail in mid-May. On May 6, a shower of meteors—debris from Halley—hit Earth and burned in the atmosphere. As seen from Earth in 1910, the comet's head was as much as two-thirds the size of the Moon and approached the brightness of the brightest stars. The tail reached angular lengths exceeding 90 degrees on some days; that is, it stretched halfway from horizon to horizon. Thus, Halley's comet became a synonym for spectacle in the twentieth century.

But when it returns in 1985–1986, we will not get nearly as good a view as in 1910. In any pass through the inner solar system, a comet is most active only when it is closest to the Sun. When this happens in February 1986, Halley's comet will be on the side of the Sun farthest from Earth. The comet will be closest to Earth in late December 1985 and in March 1986. At these two times, however, the comet will not appear spectacular, especially to observers in the Northern Hemisphere. It will be seen in early January evening skies in the southwest, but it will only be as bright as the fainter stars. It will again be visible in March and early April in southeast evening skies, a little brighter but very low on the horizon.

For these reasons, we are using our generation's space technology to get a better look. In the early 1970s and 1980s, scientists in several nations began planning to send unmanned space probes toward the comet's mysterious nucleus. First came the race to see who could find the returning visitor. This race was won by Cal Tech astronomers on October 16, 1982, when they used state-of-the-art equipment bolted on the Palomar 200-inch telescope to photograph the exceedingly faint object on its way toward the Sun, at a distance beyond the orbit of Saturn.

Meanwhile, international scientists readied a fleet of probes. The simplest probe of the fleet is the Japanese Planet A probe, containing cameras but designed to go only within perhaps 100,000 kilometers of the nucleus. More sophisticated are two Russian probes, called Vega. They will swing by Venus first, drop instruments there, and then be deflected by Venus's gravity on toward Halley's comet. They carry cameras and other instruments and may obtain data from within 10,000 kilometers of the nucleus. They were successfully launched in December 1984.

Finally, the European Space Agency has proceeded with a probe called Giotto, after the Renaissance painter, who portrayed the comet as it appeared in 1301. The probe Giotto will carry cameras and other instruments into the heart of the comet, probably within 1,000 kilometers of the nucleus. It may even be destroyed by comet debris, such as ice chunks or meteoritic grit.

This international fleet of probes is scheduled to arrive in mid-March 1986, and the cameras are designed to record features as small as a few hundred meters across. And, in addition to designing these probes, the world's Earth-bound astronomers have planned an International Halley Watch—a coordinated program to obtain simultaneous worldwide observations with a variety of instruments on preselected dates. Cameras and other instruments that are sensitive not only to visible light but also to infrared and ultraviolet rays will collect data and thus help build an integrated picture of Halley's activity.

U.S. scientists had begun to build their own Halley probe mission but were disappointed when government budget cutters, in spite of enormous deficit spending, killed the mission. Columnist George Will, usually a defender of the administration, declared that "David Stockman should stop sacrificing science on the altar of parsimony. . . . If our curiosity . . . atrophies, so will our humanity." The United States is planning a special mission of the space shuttle to observe the comet, but its efforts pale when compared to those of other countries. Still, humanity in general should know considerably more about the primordial icebergs of space by the time Halley's comet is on its way out of the planetary system in late 1986.

SMALL BODIES

Paul Preuss

WALTER NORRIS PULLED HIMSELF hand over hand to the edge of the open bay and looked out. Almighty God, there were a lot of stars.

For a moment he thought everything was going to be all right. They'd warned him he would have to look straight over his head to see the asteroid—the trouble was he forgot which way was supposed to be up. He looked and there was nothing there except a hundred thousand stars. And then he was falling.

An oxygen-parched voice hissed in his ear: "Okay, Walt, you can come on over now."

He was falling. Backwards. No, sideways. He scrabbled for a handhold. The aluminum panel fifteen centimeters from his nose had not moved, and through his faceplate Walt could plainly see his gloved hands desperately clamped around two worn handgrips.

The dry voice, David Cohen's, queried him: "Pastor?"

"Be right with you," he whispered. "I was . . . I caught on something."

"Do you need assistance?"

David's voice was calm, betraying concern only by its quick response, and it was succeeded instantly by that of Trudy Berg, who stood by fully suited inside the ship: "You want me outside?"

Walt moved his head until he could see an edge of metal and a field of steadfast stars beyond. So many of them. . . . Deliberately, cautiously, he craned his head back, following the edge of the cargo bay, until beyond the top of the open hatch he found an inky shadow blotting out a patch of the starfield; there was the asteroid.

"On my way now." He could barely voice the words.

He wasn't falling, except in the technical sense, the sense in which he and the ship and the asteroid were falling around the Sun together, and his inner

319

ear was once more persuaded that he could take a step without fear of plummeting into endless nothing. He clipped his lanyard to the coiling safety line, floated free of the bay, and shoved off with his fingers. It all came back to him now, just as he'd practiced it a dozen times at Mars Station; even without the reassuring presence of a planet filling half the sky, the laws of physics held.

A blast of gas from his jetpack sent him diving past the prow of the *Martian Sidewinder,* moving out across a hundred-meter strait of vacuum, leaving the compact little survey ship effortlessly keeping station behind him. He came into sunlight—light from a bright spark of a sun, tiny and far away. At his feet was the galaxy, its brilliance undimmed by window glass or the thinnest haze of atmospheric gases. It slanted across the night, ablaze with uncounted suns. Walt stared at it, fascinated.

Almighty God, there were a lot of stars.

This time the voice in his ear was urgent and a little annoyed. "Heads up, Norris!"

He jerked his head back. He was soaring into blackness, diving headfirst into a hole in the sky. He swung and tucked and aimed his toes and seconds later struck dust, the soles of his boots pushing waffle tracks into a viscous surface. Puffs of powder, black as the space into which it vanished, flew up from the impact. His knees bent as far as his suit would allow and a startled gasp escaped his lips, but as he rebounded he remembered to grab the anchored line and hold on.

He snubbed himself safely, floating like a man-shaped helium balloon, feet aloft.

Finally David spoke, his voice calm again. "Try not to break your neck. Who'd believe me if I claimed it was an accident?"

Walt had the grace to laugh at that, even as he reeled himself back to the surface. "Really, am I that much of a threat to secular science?"

He got no answer. He took his first close look at the asteroid: its nearby horizon could have been the edge of a cliff, overhanging a chasm full of stars. Greasy black dust, blacker than anthracite and with the same rainbow shimmer, lay smoothly over innumerable craters of all sizes, down to spatters that looked like fossil raindrops. "This thing really is black, isn't it?"

"That's why it's our first stop," said David. "It has the lowest albedo in the sector." David was the white shape floating above the asteroid's surface a dozen meters to the right and drifting slowly toward him. The smaller, more distant white figure was Rupert Harley, busy with his core sampler.

"I didn't expect this much dust." It coated every ridge and hummock, softening the ragged contours.

"Micrometeorite erosion," said David. "Sandblasting by particles too fine to leave craters. Took billions of years."

Walt tilted over and carefully took a handful of powder from the surface. "Now wouldn't that depend on how many grains of sand there were, in the beginning?"

David had come within a few meters, controlling his position by exquisitely precise puffs of gas from his jetpack. "Well, but see, it's in the craters. It accumulated *after* the beginning."

Walt freed a plastic baggy from the pouch at his belt and, putting it over his other hand, tried to shake the black dust off. Most of it clung to his glove.

"You don't have to do that. Rupert'll give you all the samples you want," said David.

"Thanks."

"Be sure to clean that stuff off when you get back aboard."

"Sure. I'd like to look at the tar pit. Okay with you?"

"In fifteen or twenty minutes. I've got to finish with this." David gestured to the instrument he towed behind him, a gyro-stabilized theodolite.

"Don't you trust me alone?" Walt said casually.

"I don't distrust you," David replied seriously. "But I'm responsible for your safety."

"I'm not as practiced with the pack as you, but I can use it. I promise, no more somersaults."

David hesitated, then said, "Check in every five minutes, or I'll come after you."

The asteroid was an oblong mass that in some cosmic confrontation had lost a big bite out of one end, the end presently opposite the Sun. The resulting crater was the size of an open-pit mine, its shadowed interior even blacker than the rest of a very black lump of rock.

Walt flew toward the rim of the crater, keeping his eyes on the surface. The stars still tugged at his concentration.

He flew over the rim and peered into a void. A puff of gas slowed his flight; he tapped his wrist controls, switching on the powerful lamp mounted atop his helmet, but he saw nothing. The beam was invisible in vacuum, and whatever it was hitting—it must have been hitting something down there—was so black it reflected no light. He strained his eyes. He was not sure where they were focused.

The darkness became palpable. His earlobes began to burn and he had an urgent desire to scratch his beard. It occurred to him that it was dangerous to be drifting where he could see nothing. He should roll over and find the stars.

Before he could move, the terror rushed at him out of the blackness. He had no means to resist. He only had time to cry out, "Help me! Please help me!"

He came slowly back to consciousness. He was in his sleep restraint, inside his cramped private compartment. His tongue was furry and his head throbbed.

David's gaunt face was peering at him from the doorway. It was a young face, darkly bearded, already lined by responsibility; his features had the deceptive fragility of all native-born Martians. David asked him something, and he must have given the right answer, for David smiled and went away, closing the door behind him.

Hyperventilation, vertigo, loss of consciousness—pure panic. Humiliating, but physically he was none the worse for it. Thank God he hadn't thrown up in his suit.

Later, freshly washed, a clean white jersey stretched over his expanse of chest and belly, Walt fixed a broad smile on his red-whiskered face and headed for the upper decks.

As he rose slowly through the hatch into the tight, dimly lit wardroom the others broke off a whispered conversation and turned to stare at him, leaving food trays stranded in midair. David nodded distractedly. Trudy Berg gave him a faintly contemptuous look; on her high cheekbones were patches of red. Walt had gotten used to the reedy blonde's constant, low-grade hostility, but he'd never seen her anger so close to the surface.

Rupert Harley, however, winked at him out of a wrinkled brown face, as if this sort of mishap was merely an initiation rite that everyone had to get through. "Hungry?" Rupert asked. "Good smoked turkey." He smacked his lips emphatically.

Walt was grateful for Rupert's sympathy, though he wondered if the little *pan sapiens* had ever in his life experienced a moment's severe spatial disorientation. He shook his head. "Still queasy. Maybe a beer."

Trudy glared; she disapproved of his calling, but Walt noticed she seemed to disapprove even more when he didn't behave the way she thought a clergyman ought to. In other circumstances he would have been amused.

Pushing himself off the ceiling, he angled past her to remove a canister of Martian lager from the cold locker. A twist of its green dome released the pressure; when it was safe he peeled off the dome and sipped at the plastic nipple. "Mmm. Stomach feels better already." He attempted a smile. "I want to thank all of you. I apologize for my childishness. I hope it did not seriously interrupt your work."

"It was my fault," said David.

"It won't happen again," said Walt.

"Yes, well . . . but I can't let you go off on your own any more, Walt"— David had yet to learn the trick of giving orders without apology—"I'm afraid

322

your schedule is going to have to fit into ours for awhile."

Walt shrugged, a motion that sent him gently toward the ceiling.

Abruptly Trudy launched her tray on a flat trajectory across the room. It sailed into the hooded washer unit and rebounded, caught there. Hands on hips, she faced Walt. "Pastor, pardon me for asking a dumb question"—

He nodded, though she had not paused.

—"what are you really doing here? We all listen to those sermons you send out on the video link every week, you know. They don't make a whole lot of sense to us. We're here on a resource survey, plain and simple. We're looking for hydrocarbons, fixed water, ores. You claim *you're* on some great expedition to investigate the facts of creation."

Quietly, Walt said, "I think you understand, you just don't approve." He sucked on the nipple of the beer can.

"Oh, well, if you say so. . . ."

"And they aren't sermons, Trudy, only reports to the membership of the Genesis Society."

"But what I really *don't* understand is how you keep a straight face when you make those so-called reports."

"Hey, give me a chance, all right?" Walt's white teeth smiled through his bristling beard. "When you look at the carbonaceous chondrite out there you were kind enough to pull me away from, you see a mass of materials that accreted at the formation of the solar system. Well, so do I. We differ as to the date of that event, that's all."

"That's *not* all." Her fair skin glowed pink with feeling. "You and your kind don't play fair. You call yourself a Scientist for Christ, but you ignore scientific data, you distort what scientists really say . . ."

David said, "Trudy, there's no need . . ."

She turned to him. "You know I'm right, David. It's not enough that this man keeps us from doing our job, he's planning to make us look like fools. To him this mission is a publicity stunt."

Walt shook his head gently. "I assure you . . ."

But she cut him off, turning on him so quickly her straight blond hair swung in a flat arc and wrapped itself around her face. "I knew Bob Hewitt. He thought you were a nice guy"—she hooked her hair out of her mouth— "when he took you down into the Valles Marineris. You had to get your life saved there too, didn't you?"

Walt's face grew warm. "I'll always be grateful for Bob's help. That does not mean I'm forced to agree with his interpretation of the data."

"You mean *his* data. You had nothing to do with it."

"Of course," he said quietly.

"He hates you," she said. "He says you made him a walking joke. Nobody lets him forget he helped you 'prove' the Valles Marineris was carved out in a thousand years."

Rupert Harley whistled and grinned. "A thousand years! Good trick."

"But not a miracle," said Walt quickly, grateful for the pan's interruption. "And not one thousand, ten thousand. I can show that rates of sediment flow, uplift . . ."

"Spare us," said Trudy. "We all know you believe God created the universe yesterday. We all know you think the dinosaurs drowned in the Flood." She pushed away from the wall and flew to the washer to clean up her tray, turning her back on the others.

The silence stretched awkwardly. David said, "It would have been better if you'd made your feelings clear before the mission started, Trudy."

"If I had I wouldn't be here," she said, swiping at the metal tray. "And you'd have had to choose between me and a ship of your own. Norris would be here, though. The vice commissioner of the Survey Corps is his church buddy."

This truth, hitherto unspoken although known to all, was followed by another silence. Walt glanced at David and then pushed himself back into a dark corner, trying to break off the conflict without leaving the room. Only Rupert seemed unperturbed by Trudy's emotional display, looking at the others with cheerful pongid curiosity.

David sighed. "We have a long trip ahead of us," he pronounced, talking to nobody in particular. "We must all do our best to keep tensions at a manageable level."

Rupert considered this and smacked his lips.

Trudy turned away from the washer hood. Her energy seemed to have drained away. "I apologize, David. I shouldn't have brought it up this way. Emergencies always leave me a little hung over." She looked at Walt then, and from her eyes he had some inkling of the fear he must have put in all of them—what it must have been like for them to search for him in that black pit, to rush his limp body back to the ship, to rip open his suit, to wait, wondering if the injections would bring him around in time.

"One more thing before I drop the subject, Pastor." Her words now were cool as stones. "Use the Bible for a textbook if you want, but don't try to buttress the Word of God with my numbers. Stay out of my lab."

Walt floated in his cell, his heels braced against the bulkhead, his ear pressed to the ceiling.

He could have challenged Trudy's territorial claim. His status as an observer gave him the run of the ship; the vice commissioner had made that explicit.

324

But there were long months in the asteroid belt to get through before the *Martian Sidewinder* fell back toward Mars, and Walt did not wish to be the cause of offense to his neighbors.

Meanwhile, it was a very small ship. Only a layer of honeycombed magnesium separated his private quarters from the laboratory.

Trudy had been in the lab for over an hour; the long silence was occasionally interrupted by clicking sounds Walt identified as a computer at work. Then someone else came into the room, and after awhile Walt heard David's voice: "That's very active chemistry."

"At least four dozen amino acids, including the whole protein kit." Trudy's voice had an excited lilt. "Plus nucleotides, sugars—"

"Which sample is this?"

"From the tar pit," she said. "But half the samples show the same spectrum."

"That stuff splashed around a lot. Rupert says we struck oil."

Trudy laughed. "How right he is, David. Look here."

The computer clicked and spat again.

"Remarkable. I've never seen anything that heavy," said David.

"Not in asteroids."

"What do you mean?"

"I had to look it up myself. Have you ever heard of hopanes? Long-chain hydrocarbons. Coal and crude oil are loaded with them."

"Coal? Petroleum?"

"That's right, fossil fuels. Hopanes are thought to be the debris of primitive cell membranes. Bacteria, algae."

The silence that followed went on so long that Walt thought the two must be whispering. He pressed his already-tender ear closer to the panel. Listening, Walt closed his eyes, and a chill seemed to seep into his bones. She was wrong, dead wrong. . . .

Finally Trudy spoke up—she could not have been more than a few centimeters from the other side of the panel—her voice booming: "Life is life, David. Do we have a monopoly?"

"Well, see, that's an open question. Isn't it?"

"Rupert's doing electron micrographs. They might tell us more."

"Rupert's work is always impeccable." There were meaningless sounds—somebody fiddling with knobs, doodling, mere displacement activity—then David spoke again. "I want you to do a new series, the highest resolution possible. I want our work to be impeccable too."

David must have left the room then, for Walt heard nothing more. After a long while he allowed himself to drift away from the ceiling.

He was exhausted. The emotional fatigue had been building up ever since he'd stepped out of the airlock. And he didn't know what to think.

He wrapped himself in his sleep restraint and reached into the net bag on the wall for his worn Bible. Its first pages were soiled and fragile but untorn—they had never been handled with anything but reverence. As he had uncounted times before, he turned to the first verse of the first chapter of the first book: "In the beginning . . ."

He read no more than a few words before he was asleep.

The darkness took on form, great wooden ribs like the bottom of a boat arching away overhead. In front of him was a wall of polished walnut and there was a giant figure coming to stand beside him, the wine was on her breath, it was his mother—glowing with heat, radiant—they were in the church in Louisville, the stars were streaming in at him through the wooden ribs, the altar was rising on a column of light, the Ark was sinking into phosphorescent seas, she was here but going away where he could not follow or understand, perhaps his father had taken her, but she said it was the Son. . . .

Walt was falling into the pit. He knew the terror, and this time he knew it for what it was. It was not space sickness. It was not even fear of death. Then he awoke, to silence and darkness.

His glowing watch told him it was Sunday morning.

He no longer felt helpless. Neither did he feel innocent.

He dressed, the black suit, the dog collar. It was just for the service, then he'd change to what the crew wore until this evening when it was time to send the message, but until then he was on his own. He reached into the net bag and opened the velvet case; he carefully set out the chalice, the wafers, the altar cloth, arranged the Bible and the prayer book. All floated before him, suspended in air. Whispering, conscious of the thinness of the walls, he began: "In the name of the Father and of the Son and of the Holy Ghost. . . ."

From each crisis of faith Walter Norris had emerged newly strengthened in belief. He believed God had brought the universe into being at a stroke. He believed the account of creation in Genesis was factual, given only a few minor uncertainties of terminology. Yet the methods of science were powerful, they had fostered the human exploration of all the planets out to the moons of Saturn, they had brought civilization to Earth's Moon, to Mars, to the frontiers of the asteroid belt.

Plainly God had not given men minds only to forbid them to think. Before he'd turned to the ministry Walt had set out to be a scientist himself, obtaining a degree in electrical engineering, and nothing he'd encountered in the laboratory had suggested that science was opposed to religion. It was an article of Walt's faith that the methods of science could be put at the service of God's word. To Walt's mind the difference between Creation and the Big Bang was a matter, mostly, of timing.

Of course the world wasn't created "yesterday," not even in 4004 B.C.— Trudy's charges were typical humanist distortions—but still, according to Walt's calculations and those of other scientists in the Genesis Society, the world wasn't much older than a hundred thousand years or so. And obviously the dinosaurs hadn't drowned in the Flood! Walt's research had helped prove that the Flood was perhaps the greatest in a series of great catastrophes, not all of them explicitly described in the Bible, because the Bible, after all, was *not* written as a textbook but was concerned with the relation of God to man. Science had long ago established that the dinosaurs were destroyed by an asteroid; obviously early humans had been spared in some fashion the Bible had not bothered to report.

His explication of such topics, his effortless dissolution of the apparent conflicts between science and religion by the application of simple logic and a few facts, had gained Walter Norris an enormous radio and television audience on all the inhabited worlds. Trudy could scoff, but he was proud of his reputation as a Scientist for Christ.

Unfortunately, these were not the sorts of issues one could debate with opponents as emotional as she. Although Walt had had great fun thrashing matters out with his geologist friend Bob Hewitt. . . .

He paused in his whispered reading of the Gospel, conscious that the pertinence of the passage was escaping him. From long experience he knew the fault was not the Bible's but that of his wandering attention. No congregation waited on him, so best deal with the distraction now—the hard kernel of guilt lodged in his craw.

He still thought of Bob as a friend, and it saddened him to think that Bob had suffered because of him.

Five years ago he had stood, pressure-suited, on a pinnacle midway down the vast depths of the Valles Marineris. For the first time he had felt himself transported, his spirit virtually carried out of his body. Great indeed were the works of the Lord.

At that moment he had fainted, and Bob had saved him from a mile-long fall. A long fall, the kind that in metaphor is preceded by gross pride.

What if, in his pride, a man goes beyond God's truth and creates his own? Had Walt, in his debater's enthusiasm, cheated Bob? Cheated himself? Cheated God?

He had suppressed the incident on Mars. Then yesterday he saw the naked stars, he gazed into the carbonaceous pit. These sublime spectacles could not threaten his belief. But for five years now the fear had been quietly growing in his mind that his conception of God was, perhaps, too small. . . .

He would go no further. He continued the quiet service, blocking all else from his mind. He raised the lonely communion cup to his lips. He would have liked to share the bread and wine, but two of his shipmates denied belief, and one had no soul.

Rupert hooted softly when Walt appeared in the wardroom. "Good morning. Hungry?"

Walt smiled. "Famished."

"Good scrambled eggs."

"I'll try them."

"Like beer better?" Rupert bared his teeth.

"Not before noon," said Walt. "Where are David and Trudy?"

"Outside. More samples."

"Oh." Walt busied himself at the food locker. Here was an opportunity. Trudy might not let him look at her numbers, but surely his friend Rupert wouldn't mind if he peeked at the electron micrographs.

He and Rupert got on quite well, a fact that might have been mildly shocking to many members of his broadcast audience. But Walt thought Rupert was living evidence for the argument from design: Rupert Harley, a credit to his race, hadn't *evolved* into a scientist, he'd been built that way.

Walt thoughtfully ate his flash-heated scrambled eggs. Looking up from his tray, he said, "How is your work going, Rupert?"

"Okay. Tomorrow I will have good micrographs of core samples."

"Not today?" Walt was disappointed.

"David says the ones I have are not good. He wants new samples."

Walt went back to his eating. Between bites he glanced at the pan's bright eyes, watching him. "Okay if I look at the first set?"

"Too late."

"You destroyed them?"

"No. Trudy said if you asked, I must refuse."

Walt's face grew darker. "Does Trudy tell you what to do?"

"Yes. Sometimes I do not obey her." Rupert pursed his lips. "This time David said I should."

Walt's ear was against the ceiling again. He heard the excitement in their voices. He ached to burst in on them, to share their discovery.

"Some of them have flipped back, but the effect is real." It was David talking. "You see that?"

"Yes, yes of course. But most are the wrong way around. They're right-handed when they should be left-handed."

They were talking about polarization. Organic molecules found on asteroids and elsewhere in space twisted transmitted light to the right or left equally, at random, regardless of their type. These they were investigating seemed dominated by a single orientation.

"And vice versa. But it looks as if there really could have been something alive."

She sounded triumphant. "Like nothing that ever lived on Earth—"

Walt pushed away from the ceiling and yanked open his compartment door. He pushed through the corridor—two right angles, one sideways, one up, past the personal hygiene facility to the door of the laboratory.

The dark space was too small for three. Walt stuck his head in. "I have to know what's going on," said Walt. "You don't have to show me any numbers. Just tell me."

David looked up from the eyepiece and glanced at Trudy. Walt thought he looked sheepish.

Trudy looked steadily at Walt, her arms crossed. "It's Sunday, Walt. In a couple of hours you make your—report."

"I was planning too, yes."

"We'd rather not have you making unsupported assertions about what we're doing. Given your record, the only way to be sure of that is not to *tell* you what we're doing."

"That's blunt enough." He turned to David. "It also warrants an official protest."

"When we're certain of our findings, we'll share them with you fully," David said. "In a day or two."

"If we're sure," she added.

Walt sighed. "You know I've been listening to everything you've said?"

"Oh? Then I don't doubt you've gotten it thoroughly confused," she said instantly, and the tilt of her mouth showed him she did know.

He almost lost his temper. "Your condescension is unwarranted. Unless you have deliberately misled me with some written-out fiction you have been playing out for my benefit. And if . . ."

"Damn it, this is childish," said David. "All right, Walt, we'll show you."

"David!" Her surprise was genuine.

He turned to her. "And Walt can do anything he damned well pleases with it. Why not?"

"We've been all through this—"

"And I guess I'm not convinced," said David. "Let's put it to the test. I'm prepared to cancel the mission right now instead of having somebody murder somebody, six weeks or six months down the line."

Trudy stared at him, shocked. Walt kept his silence; he had to remind himself to take a breath.

David said quietly, "Trudy, please go ask Rupert to bring the micrographs down here."

She nodded and leaned toward the door. Her pale eyes met Walt's, and she hesitated. He got out of her way.

Deep in the bottom of the tar pit they had found inclusions of shalelike rock. Sliced thin, magnified ten thousand times, the shale left no doubt of its composition.

"We don't know what they are or where they came from, Walt." David's voice was quiet, intense. "They look a little like stromatolites, those fossil algae mats on Earth, but analogies aren't really helpful. We're not making any hypotheses."

Walt stared at the crisp holographic prints. The microscopic fossil bodies were whole, frozen in death in immense clusters, just as they must have lived.

He looked up at David's sad face and found himself thirsting for answers. He wanted David to tell him that these creatures came from the remains of some ancient planet, blown here on the shock wave of an exploding star, or from some shattered moon of Jupiter, torn to shreds in a grinding cataclysm. Or even that they were sent here. . . .

He wanted answers.

Feverishly he bent to the pages of scripture. In the seventh verse of Genesis he read the words he knew by heart, and they seemed to speak to him afresh: "And God made the firmament and divided the waters which were under the firmament from the waters which were above the firmament. . . . And God called the firmament Heaven."

Muttering, Walt tugged at his whiskers. What were these waters that God had placed above Heaven? Had God created anything to grow in them, as He had in the seas of Earth? Carbonaceous chondrites, the most primitive objects in the solar system, were rich in water.

The logic of it was clear to him. A fire grew in his breast, a fine clear anger. Compared to this single discovery, it hardly mattered if the survey mission continued or not, if David Cohen were disgraced or not, if they despised Walter Norris for bearing witness.

He avoided their eyes as he moved up through the wardroom. Rupert watched him pass, but the others turned away from him to the video monitor; already on, it showed an empty chair.

Walt came onto the flight deck. The windows were unshielded—he averted his eyes from the stars. Momentarily he considered fastening the hatch behind him and decided against it.

He strapped himself loosely into the engineer's couch. The video camera and microphone were aimed, their circuits tuned for broadcast, the switches resting beneath his fingers. "Walter Norris here. Transmission to begin in three minutes." He did not wait for the delayed reply from the Mars relay. He always did this alone. He knew the operation well.

He smoothed the hastily written pages. On them he had penciled an announcement of the discovery of primitive fossil life on asteroid 2013 GA, the text buttressed with such facts and figures as he had gleaned from his hasty examination of the laboratory data. Immediately following was his own explanation of how this remarkable discovery was to be reconciled with the facts of Creation as set forth in Genesis. He studied the words, hummed to himself to relax his throat, silently rehearsed his opening remarks. He was more than usually aware that, below, Trudy and David and Rupert were watching.

Involuntarily his eyes lifted to the windows. The asteroid was invisible, out of sight above the ship. Still he could see the stars. So vast a work of creation, and he, in this ocean of stars, smaller than a microbe. Humility tugged at his heart. Painfully he opened to it.

Walt's eyes fell to the pages he had written. He stared at them a long time. It was time to begin transmitting now; they would be waiting for him.

Finally he pressed the transmit button: "This is Walter Norris. I wish to . . ." He ran out of words. "I just want to ask you all to . . ." Who was he to demand easy answers from God, quick reassurance? In that eternal mind his yearning was acknowledged, so he prayed, but his impatience was less than nothing.

A third time he started. He struggled to swallow the burning lump in his throat. "There will be no report this evening. Please tune in next week—for what promises to be an exciting announcement." Outside the stars turned to rainbows as his eyes filled with tears. "God be with you and bless you all."

THE CONTRIBUTORS

BYRON PREISS, editor, is the author of Bantam's bestseller *Dragonworld*. Considered to be one of the foremost figures in the resurgence of illustrated books in America, Preiss has edited books by Arthur C. Clarke, Fritz Leiber, Philip José Farmer and Frank Herbert for the Masterworks of Science Fiction and Fantasy series. He produced *The Dinosaurs*, a Bantam gift book acclaimed internationally by paleontologists for its accuracy and featured in *Life* magazine in 1981. His record in collaboration with Richard Attenborough, *The Words of Gandhi*, was winner of the 1985 Grammy Award for Best Spoken Word Recording. As the head of a computer design team, Preiss has produced interactive adventures based on *Fahrenheit 451* by Ray Bradbury, *Rendezvous with Rama* by Arthur C. Clarke, *Starman Jones* by Robert A. Heinlein, and *Dragonworld*, which was voted Computer Adventure Game of the Year by *Computer Entertainer*. His monograph on the work of Caldecott Medal-winning illustrators Leo and Diane Dillon was a Hugo Award nominee and was exhibited at the Metropolitan Museum of Art. He holds a B.A. from the University of Pennsylvania and an M.A. from Stanford University.

RUTH ASHBY, the associate editor, was educated at Yale University and the University of Virginia. She has recently completed the script for a computer game based on Robert A. Heinlein's *The Moon is A Harsh Mistress* and intends to be the first editor invited on the space shuttle.

DR. ISAAC ASIMOV's total of published books has passed three hundred volumes. Although his Ph.D. is in chemistry, his popular non-fiction has covered almost every imaginable subject, from quantum physics to the Bible. His is also a winner of the Hugo and Nebula awards for science fiction. Among his novels are the *Foundation* series (winner of a special Hugo for Best Science Fiction Series of all time) and the *Robot* series. He is also the father of the Three Laws of Robotics.

ALAN BEAN began studying drawing and painting in night school twenty-three years ago, while he was still a Navy test pilot. His career as an artist was then set aside temporarily while he served with NASA as an astronaut. He was the Lunar Module Pilot on Apollo 12, becoming the fourth man to set foot on the Moon, in 1969, and commanded the fifty-nine-day Skylab Mission II in 1973. Resuming his art studies in 1974, he had his first exhibition the same year. His work has been shown at the National Air and Space Museum of the Smithsonian Institute and can be seen regularly at the Meredith Long and Company Gallery in Houston, Texas.

DR. GREGORY BENFORD has an established international audience for his articles, short stories, and novels. His novel *Timescape* won the Nebula, British Science Fiction, John W. Campbell, and Australian Ditmar Awards. Dr. Benford, a Woodrow Wilson Fellow, is Professor of Physics at the University of California, Irvine. His nonfiction about science has appeared in *Smithsonian, Natural History*, and *Omni* magazines. He writes entries for the *Encyclopaedia Britannica* on the areas in which he does research, relativistic plasma physics and astrophysics.

RAY BRADBURY has published four hundred short stories and eighteen books, including novels, short stories, poems, and plays. He created the basic scenario for the United States Pavilion at the New York World's Fair in 1964/65, and did similar creative work at Walt Disney's EPCOT in Florida, where he was writer-consultant for Spaceship Earth. His *Windows on the Universe*, a multi-media history of astronomy, is now appearing at the Air and Space Museum in Los Angeles. His latest book is *Death is a Lonely Business*, his first suspense mystery novel.

DR. MICHAEL H. CARR is a geologist with the U.S. Geological Survey in Menlo Park, California. He has worked on a variety of problems in lunar and planetary science, recently focusing on the volcanic and climatic history of Mars and volcanic processes on Io. Among his numerous works on planetary science are *The Surface of Mars* and *The Geology of the Terrestrial Planets*.

DR. CLARK R. CHAPMAN, a Senior Scientist with the Planetary Science Institute and has a particular interest in the surfaces of planets and small bodies. At the Planetary Science Institute, he does research for NASA as leader of the Atmospheres Subgroup of the Galileo Imaging Science Team. He is the president of Commission 15 of the International Astronomical Union and a Past Chairman of the Division of Planetary Sciences of the American Astronomical Society. The most recent of his popularizations of planetary science is *Planets of Rock and Ice*.

ARTHUR C. CLARKE's achievements and honors are both scientific and literary in nature. Chief among them are his fellowship in the Royal Astronomical Society, the Hugo, Nebula, and John W. Campbell Awards, the 1982 Marconi International Fellowship, a Fellowship of King's College, London, and an Oscar nomination (with Stanley Kubrick) for *2001: A Space Odyssey*. In 1979 the president of Sri Lanka nominated him Chancellor of the University of Moratuwa, which is also the site of the Arthur C. Clarke Centre for Modern Technologies. His almost sixty books have sold thirty million copies in twenty languages, and he is credited as the inventor of the concept of the communications satellite.

DR. LAWRENCE COLIN is the Chief of the Space Science Division at NASA's Ames Research Center, located near Mountain View, California. He is also the Project Scientist on the Pioneer Venus Project and the Probe Project Scientist on the Galileo mission to Jupiter to be launched in 1986. He is a co-editor and author of *Venus*.

RICHARD COURTNEY is an illustrator whose work is often identified with that of Maxfield Parrish. He has done considerable work in the publishing field, and his art has been syndicated abroad. He has had several one-man shows in the Midwest.

DR. DALE P. CRUIKSHANK is an astronomer at the University of Hawaii in Honolulu. He conducts a vigorous research program, concentrating on the small bodies of the outer solar system. He helped find the first evidence for methane ice on Pluto, giving early indications that this Planet is smaller than Earth's Moon. He participated in the first measurements of the temperature of Neptune, and has discovered the surface compositions of numerous planetary satellites and asteroids. He is currently specializing in comet studies and observations of the most distant asteroids. His popular writings have appeared in *Sky and Telescope, Scientific American,* and *Astronomy* magazines, and in various books.

BOB EGGLETON was first inspired to draw and paint astronomical subjects by the early space missions and *Star Trek*. He is still in love with all things beyond the skies, and displays his astronomical paintings at science fiction conventions, where they have won many awards. His illustrations also appear on covers of science fiction paperbacks. He lives in Warwick, Rhode Island.

PHILIP JOSÉ FARMER has been to Uranus, and reports that it's a nicer place than New York City to visit but that he would not want to live there. He feels the same about Earth. He is the reputed author of sixty-three books and two children, all of which were accidentally conceived and some of which have gotten good reviews. He plans to retire after dying to an alternate universe which he has designed and built and which is almost paid for.

DR. ANDREW FRAKNOI, the scientific consultant for this book, is the executive officer of the Astronomical Society of the Pacific and a part-time professor of astronomy and physics at San Francisco University. He is the editor of *Mercury* magazine and the author of *Universe in the Classroom*, a resource book for teaching astronomy. He has been co-author of a nationally syndicated newspaper column on astronomy and host of a weekly science talk show on a San Francisco area radio station.

JOHN R. FUDGE is an associate professor of fine arts at the University of Colorado at Denver. His work has been exhibited widely in juried and invitational shows, including the Second Western States/ 38th Corcoran Biennial Exhibition of American Painting.

JAMES GURNEY's illustrations appear on the covers of science fiction and fantasy paperback books. He received a degree in anthropology from the University of California at Berkeley, and later co-authored *The Author's Guide to Sketching*, an instructional book about on-the-spot drawing. His interest in naturalistic portrayals of scenes from myth and history has recently resulted in a series of commissions from the *National Geographic Magazine*.

JOEL HAGEN is a sculptor and painter best known for his realistic models of extraterrestrial life forms, their skulls, and skeletons. He has organized and participated in a number of collaborative projects involving artists, writers, and scientists to explore the possibilities of alien life. He is an active member of the International Association of Astronomical Artists, and uses current information, satellite images, and self-written computer programs as guidelines in his renderings of planetary landscapes. He recently appeared in the PBS documentary *Visions of Other Worlds*.

JOHN HARRIS was born in 1948 in London. A graduate of Exeter College of Art, he divides his time between doing paintings for advertising and book covers, and illustrating books of his own devising. Most recently he has been working on large-scale paintings which, in size and content, come close to his ideal of the frozen cinematic image.

HARRY HARRISON has been an artist, art director, and editor. As a writer, he had a career as the author of numerous true confessions and men's adventures before leaving New York for Mexico in order to write his first novel. He has since written thirty-two novels, and has lived in nearly as many countries. His books have been translated into twenty-one languages. He was founding president of World SF. He received the Nebula Award and the Prix Jules Verne for his novel *Make Room Make Room!*, made into the film *Soylent Green*.

DR. WILLIAM K. HARTMANN is a planetary astronomer at the Planetary Science Institute of Science Applications International in Tucson. He has been a NASA consultant, and has published papers on planetary formation and evolution. He was on the Imaging Team of the 1971 Mariner 9 mission to Mars, which made the first complete photo maps of the red planet with an orbiting spacecraft. He has published two astronomy textbooks and two popular illustrated books on space exploration, *The Grand Tour* and *Out of the Cradle*.

KIKUO HAYASHI, who is a newcomer to science fiction illustration, has been a transportation designer in the auto industry for many years. Persuaded that many of the current science fiction illustrations lack the spirit of scientific imagination, he began to develop a type of SF art that puts more emphasis on the science part of science fiction. Currently, he is co-authoring a science fiction novel.

FRANK HERBERT, a native of Washington state, worked as a newspaper reporter and editor, photographer, news analyst, oenologist, and oyster diver before devoting himself to writing full time in 1970. In 1958, working on a news story about a research station that investigated shifting sand dunes, he first got the idea for *Dune*, winner of the Hugo and Nebula awards and the first book in one of the most popular science fiction series of all time. He is also the author of one non-science fiction novel, *Soul Catcher*. His most recent book is *Eye*.

ISAAC VICTOR KERLOW works in New York City as a designer and animator of visual projects that involve computer graphics technology. He also teaches a course in graphics programming at the School of Visual Arts, and several seminars on computer imaging techniques at the Computer Arts Forum. Mr. Kerlow studied Art and Design in the School of Visual Arts in New York, and obtained his M.S. in Communications Design from Pratt Institute, also in New York. He is a member of the Association for Computing Machinery/Siggraph and the American Institute of Graphic Arts.

ROBERT MCCALL was initially attracted to aviation as a subject by its sound. Following the noises of the Air Force in his paintings led him from aircraft of the 1950s to the space program. Along the way, he has talked his way into most of the vehicles he has painted. His work can be seen in the National Air and Space Museum and the Johnson Space Center, and on a series of eight stamps issued by the U.S. Postal Service. The Air Force has forty-five of his paintings in its collection, and NASA has been collecting them since it was established.

RALPH MCQUARRIE is best known for his work as designer/illustrator on the *Star Wars* trilogy. He started working in film on the animated portions of the CBS News Special Events coverage of the Apollo missions. Other credits include design of spaceships for Steven Spielberg's *Close Encounters of the Third Kind* and *E.T.* Most recent work has involved design for the film *Cocoon*, and book jacket illustrations.

DR. URSULA B. MARVIN is a geologist engaged in research on lunar samples and meteorites at the Smithsonian Astrophysical Observatory. She is also an adjunct member of the Department of Geological Sciences at Harvard. A strong interest in the history of geology led her to write *Continental Drift: The Evolution of a Concept*. Earlier in her career she spent several years exploring for ore deposits with her husband, Thomas C. Marvin, in Brazil and West Africa. She has recently spent three field sessions in Antarctica collecting meteorites and searching for evidence that a comet or asteroid struck the Earth 65 million years ago, bringing a cataclysmic end to the Cretaceous period.

LESLIE MILLER, the designer, is a designer for the Metropolitan Museum of Art and director of The Grenfell Press, a highly regarded publisher of limited editions which has been cited by *The New York Times* for its role in the new wave of publishing as fine art.

DR. DAVID MORRISON, astronomer and planetary scientist, is the Acting Vice Chancellor for Research and Graduate Education at the University of Hawaii. He has held major administrative positions at NASA headquarters in Washington. He received his doctorate in 1969, has published more than one hundred technical papers, and is the author or editor of six books. Dr. Morrison is a member of the imaging science team for the Voyager spacecraft, an Interdisciplinary Scientist on the Galileo Jupiter orbiter and probe, and chairman of the NASA Solar System Exploration Management Council. He has the distinction of having a celestial body named for him: asteroid 2410 Morrison.

PAT ORTEGA has been an artist and illustrator since the age of three. Since 1977 her work has been shown in various science-fiction conventions. Ortega's work has been featured in *Smithsonian, Epic*, and *Omni* magazines, and in Fritz Leiber's *The Ghost Light* and Philip José Farmer's *The Grand Adventure*. She is currently working on science fiction-fantasy children's book stories with co-writer Don Dixon.

PAUL PREUSS began writing novels and articles on science after more than a decade producing documentary and television films. Since 1980 he has published four novels, most recently *Human Error*. Other recent projects include adapting an Arthur C. Clarke short story, "Breaking Strain," as a computer game, and writing and co-producing a television biography of physicist Albert Michelson. He is a frequent contributor to *Science 85* and other national magazines, and regularly reviews books about science for *The San Francisco Chronicle Review*.

MARTA RANDALL, despite having been born in Mexico City, is a fourth-generation Californian with no intention of leaving that state. Since first reaching print in 1972, she has published six novels, the most recent of which is *The Sword of Winter*. A past president of the Science Fiction Writers of America, she lives in Oakland with her husband, Christopher Conley; son, Richard Bergstrasser; new daughter, Caitlin (who is "the most beautiful girl-child ever born"); and an ancient Mazda named Clint.

ROGER RESSMEYER is based in San Francisco and New York. He specializes in location and studio photography combining portraiture, high technology, and special effects. Ressmeyer's work has appeared in *Time, People, Fortune, Newsweek,* and *Science Digest*, among others. His clients include Bantam Books,

AT&T, Apple Computers, CBS, Levi's, NASA, and RCA. A 1975 graduate of Yale University, Ressmeyer is the founder of the Starlight Photo Agency.

BILL SANDERSON's first science fiction drawings were a series of covers for paperback editions of Michael Moorcock's Jerry Cornelius books. More recently he was called upon by Harry Harrison to provide text and glossary illustrations for *West of Eden*. Over the years he has produced several covers for the British science journal *New Scientist*, among other magazines and books.

DR. CHARLES SHEFFIELD is a vice-president of Earth Satellite Corporation, president of the Science Fiction Writers of America, and past president of the American Astronautical Society. He holds B.A. and M.A. degrees in mathematics and a Ph.D. in theoretical physics. His written works include five novels, four short story collections, the best-selling nonfiction volumes *Earthwatch* and *Man on Earth*, and the reference work *Space Careers*.

ROBERT SILVERBERG has been a professional writer since 1953. His work has appeared in *Omni*, *American Heritage*, *Horizon*, and many other publications. Among his best known science fiction books are *The Majipoor Chronicles*, *Dying Inside*, *Tower of Glass*, and *Nightwings*. His non-fiction titles include *Mound Builders of Ancient America*, *The Realm of Prester John*, and *Scientists and Scoundrels: A Book of Scientific Hoaxes*. He is a multi-time winner of the Nebula and Hugo awards for his science fiction.

DR. G. JEFFREY TAYLOR, who wrote the essay about Earth's Moon, is a senior research scientist at the Institute of Meteorites and Department of Geology at the University of New Mexico. He focuses his research on meteorites and lunar samples, helping to decipher the early history of the solar system. Besides contributing more than seventy-five articles to technical journals, he has written two science books for young readers, *A Close Look at the Moon* and *Volcanoes in Our Solar System*. He also co-authored (with R. V. Fodor) a science fiction novel, *Impact*.

DR. JOSEPH VEVERKA teaches astronomy and planetary science at Cornell University, and is a member of the University's Laboratory for Planetary Studies and the director of the Spacecraft Planetary Imaging Facility. His recent research has emphasized studies of the present state and past evolution of satellite surfaces. He is the team leader of NASA's Imaging Systems Science Team. He is also member of the Voyager and Galileo Imaging Science Teams, and previously participated as an Imaging Science Investigator on the Mariner 9 and Viking missions to Mars. In 1979 he was awarded the NASA Medal for Exceptional Scientific Achievement, for his investigations of the moons of Mars.

JACK WILLIAMSON has been writing science fiction since 1928. His newest novel, *Lifeburst*, was published in paperback by Bantam Books. As a professor of English, he helped pioneer science fiction in the classroom, editing a book, *Teaching Science Fiction: Education for Tomorrow*, and publishing a critical study of the early science fiction of H. G. Wells. He is a past president of the Science Fiction Writers of America, and has received their Grand Master Award. His autobiography, *Wonder's Child: My Life in Science Fiction*, was published last year.

ROGER ZELAZNY has been a professional science fiction and fantasy writer for over twenty years, and is best known for his *Amber* series. He has received several Hugo and Nebula awards and holds degrees from Case Western Reserve and Columbia Universities. He is married, has three children, and lives in New Mexico.

FURTHER READING ABOUT THE SOLAR SYSTEM

by
Andrew Fraknoi

1. GOOD GENERAL BOOKS ON THE SOLAR SYSTEM

BEATTY, J., et al., eds. *The New Solar System*, 2nd ed. Sky Publishing and Cambridge University Press, 1982.—Slightly technical survey of the planets and satellites; each chapter by a noted planetary scientist.

BRIGGS, G. and TAYLOR, F. *The Cambridge Photographic Atlas of the Planets*. Cambridge University Press, 1982.—Includes some of the best photographs taken by telescopes on Earth and in spacecraft.

CHAPMAN, C. *Planets of Rock and Ice*. Scribners, 1982.—Eloquent tour of the inner solar system.

MILLER, R. and HARTMANN, W. *The Grand Tour: A Traveler's Guide to the Solar System*. Workman, 1981.—Nice collaboration between an artist and an astronomer.

MOORE, P. and HUNT, G. *Atlas of the Solar System*. Rand McNally, 1983.—Large illustrated atlas; nice reference book.

SAGAN, C. *Cosmos*. 1980, Random House. A superb, highly personal introduction to astronomy by the country's best known astronomer; from the television series of the same name.

SMOLOUCHOWSKI, R. *The Solar System*. Scientific American Library, 1983.—A good, general introduction.

2. SELECTED BOOKS ON SPECIFIC WORLDS

MURRAY, B. and BURGESS, E. *Flight to Mercury.* Columbia University Press, 1977.

DONNE, J. and BURGESS, E. *The Voyage of Mariner 10.* NASA Special Publication 424, 1978.

FIMMEL, R., *et al. Pioneer Venus.* NASA Special Publication 461, 1982.

HUNT, G. and MOORE, P. *The Planet Venus.* Faber and Faber, 1982.

CALDER, N. *The Restless Earth.* Viking Press, 1972.

SHEFFIELD, C. *Earth Watch: A Survey of the World from Space.* Macmillan, 1981.

SHORT, N., *et al. Mission to Earth: Landsat Views the World.* NASA Special Publication 360, 1976.

CADOGAN, P. *The Moon: Our Sister Planet.* Cambridge University Press, 1981.

COOPER, H. *Moon Rocks.* Dial, 1970.

FRENCH, B. *The Moon Book.* Penguin, 1977.

BURGESS, E. *To the Red Planet.* Columbia University Press, 1978.

CARR, M. *The Surface of Mars.* Yale University Press, 1981.

COOPER, H. *The Search for Life on Mars.* Holt, Rinehart and Winston, 1980.

WASHBURN, M. *Mars at Last.* Putnams, 1977.

BURGESS, E. *By Jupiter.* Columbia University Press, 1982.

MORRISON, D. and SAMZ, J. *Voyage to Jupiter.* NASA Special Publication 439, 1980.

WASHBURN, M. *Distant Encounters: The Exploration of Jupiter and Saturn.* Harcourt, Brace, Jovanovich, 1983.

MORRISON, D. *Voyages to Saturn.* NASA Special Publication 451, 1982.

ALEXANDER, A. *The Planet Uranus: A History of Observation, Theory, and Discovery.* Faber and Faber, 1965.

GROSSER, M. *The Discovery of Neptune.* Harvard University Press, 1962.

HOYT, W. *Planets X and Pluto.* University of Arizona Press, 1980.

TOMBAUGH, C. and MOORE, P. *Out of the Darkness: The Planet Pluto.* Stackpole, 1980.

CHAPMAN, R. and BRANDT, J. *The Comet Book.* Jones and Bartlett, 1984.

HUTCHINSON, R. *The Search for Our Beginnings.* Oxford University Press, 1983. (On meteorites.)

3. MAGAZINES FOR KEEPING UP WITH NEW DEVELOPMENTS IN OUR EXPLORATION OF THE SOLAR SYSTEM

Astronomy (published by AstroMedia)
Discover (published by Time-Life)
Mercury (published by the Astronomical Society of the Pacific; see below)
National Geographic Magazine (published by the National Geographic Society)

Planetary Report (published by the Planetary Society; see below)
Science 85 (Published by the American Association for the Advancement of Science)
Science News (published by Science Service)
Scientific American
Sky and Telescope (published by Sky Publishing)

4. ORGANIZATIONS FOR THOSE INTERESTED IN THE SOLAR SYSTEM

The Astronomical Society of the Pacific (1290 24th Ave., San Francisco, CA 94122)

Founded in 1889 on the Pacific Coast of the U.S., the A.S.P. today is an international organization that serves as a bridge between astronomers and the public, and includes among its members professional astronomers, teachers, students, and thousands of people in all walks of life. The Society publishes the non-technical magazine *Mercury,* featuring articles on new developments in astronomy, distributes a monthly sky calendar and star chart for those who want to see the planets for themselves, and offers lectures and workshops around the country. In addition, the A.S.P. issues an annual catalog that includes some of the best images of the universe from large telescopes and spacecraft.

The Planetary Society (P.O. Box 91687, Pasadena, CA 91109)

The Planetary Society was founded by Carl Sagan and Bruce Murray to advance the exploration of the solar system and to educate the public about the results of that exploration. The Society publishes a colorful little magazine called *The Planetary Report,* holds symposia, workshops, and public programs, awards grants for research about the planets and the possibility of extra-terrestrial life, and works in many other ways to expand the public consciousness of the value of planetary research.